LI BO UNKEMPT

Thank you, dear friend, for joining us in this venture, which you are making possible. By so doing, we can both share this book with the world.

@ https://punctumbooks.com/support/

If you're reading the e-book, you can click on the image below to go directly to our donations site. Any amount, no matter the size, is appreciated and will help us to keep our ship of fools afloat. Contributions from dedicated readers will also help us to keep our commons open and to cultivate new work that can't find a welcoming port elsewhere. Our adventure is not possible without your support.

Vive la Open Access.

Fig. 1. Hieronymus Bosch, *Ship of Fools* (1490–1500)

LI BO UNKEMPT. Copyright © 2020 by Kidder Smith and Mike Zhai. This work carries a Creative Commons BY-NC-SA 4.0 International license, which means that you are free to copy and redistribute the material in any medium or format, and you may also remix, transform and build upon the material, as long as you clearly attribute the work to the authors (but not in a way that suggests the authors or punctum books endorses you and your work), you do not use this work for commercial gain in any form whatsoever, and that for any remixing and transformation, you distribute your rebuild under the same license. http://creativecommons.org/licenses/by-nc-sa/4.0/

First published in 2021 by punctum books, Earth, Milky Way.
https://punctumbooks.com

ISBN-13: 978-1-953035-41-7 (print)
ISBN-13: 978-1-953035-42-4 (ePDF)

DOI: 10.21983/P3.0322.1.00

LCCN: 2021933929
Library of Congress Cataloging Data is available from the Library of Congress

Book design: Vincent W.J. van Gerven Oei
Cover image: Painting by Sangchen Tsomo (2013), private collection.

spontaneous acts of scholarly combustion

HIC SVNT MONSTRA

Li Bo
Unkempt

Hir haire vnkembd about hir necke downe flaring.

Ovid, *Metamorphoses*
trans. Arthur Golding (1567)

Text by Kidder Smith
Translations by Kidder Smith and Mike Zhai

p.

Contents

Section I. Li Bo   17

   Chapter 1. Li Bo   19
   Chapter 2. Li Bo   20
   Chapter 3. "There's a Cup of Wine in Front of Us"   21
   Chapter 4. "Spoken Spontaneously"   22
   Chapter 5. "Seeing Off Li Qing on His Return to Huayang River"   23
   Chapter 6. Li Bo (701–762)   24

Section II. Wine   27

   Chapter 7. "Under the Moon"   30
   Chapter 8. "Bring on That Wine"   32
   Chapter 9. "On a Spring Day"   34
   Chapter 10. "Face-to-face with Wine"   35

An Interlude   37

   Chapter 11. "Presented to Chief Administrator Chu of Liyang on the Occasion That This Gentleman Danced Like a Young Child"   38
   Chapter 12. Big Words   42
   Chapter 13. "The Hard Road to Shu"   44

Chapter 14. "Lines of a Short Song"	48
Chapter 15. "A Rhapsody Lamenting Last Remnants of the Spring"	52

Section III. Center of Everything — 55

Chapter 16. Night Music	62
Chapter 17. Commissioner He Zhizhang	66
Chapter 18. Writing Brushes	69
Chapter 19. The Marriage of a Court Woman	70

An Interlude — 73

Chapter 20. In a Boat	74
Chapter 21. A Letter to the Governor	75
Chapter 22. La matière de Li Bo: An Epistemology	77
Chapter 23. "Lines on the Flying Dragon"	85
Chapter 24. The Moister South	88

Section IV. Five Mountains — 91

Chapter 25. Tai, Sacred Mountain of the East	99
Chapter 26. Heng, Sacred Mountain of the South	104
Chapter 27. Hua, Sacred Mountain of the West	109
Chapter 28. "Linked Verse on Changing the Name of Nine Sons Mountain to Nine Flowers Mountain"	113
Chapter 29. Mount Lu	116

An Interlude — 121

Chapter 30. Jade Woman Hotspring	122
Chapter 31. The Grotto-Heaven	126
Chapter 32. Writing on a Baby	132
Chapter 33. "Climbing to the Peak of Great White"	134
Chapter 34. A Horse	137

Section V. Five Daoists — 141

- Chapter 35. The God Laozi — 142
- Chapter 36. A Patriarch — 146
- Chapter 37. A Hermit — 149
- Chapter 38. A Princess — 151
- Chapter 39. A Companion — 155
- Chapter 39. Zhuangzi — 158

An Interlude — 161

- Chapter 40. Climbing Yang Terrace — 162
- Chapter 41. Du Fu — 165
- Chapter 42. Brush Washing Spring — 169
- Chapter 43. Jewel Stairs — 170
- Chapter 44. "Seeing Off Meng Haoran" — 173

Section VI. Violent Death — 175

- Chapter 45. Ci Fei Beheads Two Dragons — 176
- Chapter 46. "Song of the Roving Swordsman" — 179
- Chapter 47. Li Yong (678–747) — 185
- Chapter 48. The Yunnan War — 188
- Chapter 49. "In Imitation of the Ancients" — 195

An Interlude — 197

- Chapter 50. "Tea Called 'Palm of the Immortal,' with a Preface" — 198
- Chapter 51. "Woman on the Silk-washing Rock" — 201
- Chapter 52. "Lotus Picking Song" — 202
- Chapter 53. "For Revenue Manager Lu" — 204
- Chapter 54. Drunk Rock — 206

Section VIIa. The Rebellion, a History — 207

Section VIIb. The Rebellion, the Bright Emperor — 235

Chapter 55. "Distant Parting" — 240
Chapter 56. "The Hard Road to Shu," Reprise — 242
Chapter 57. The Return to Chang'an — 246

Section VIIc. The Rebellion, Li Bo — 249

Chapter 58. Climbing Flower Mountain — 250
Chapter 59. The Wall-eyed Prince — 252
Chapter 60. "In Prison, Submitted to Chief Minister Cui Huan" — 255
Chapter 61. God of Nine Rivers — 256

An Interlude — 259

Chapter 62. "Dreaming of Roaming Tianmu, the Mountain of the Old Lady of Heaven, a Song Left at Parting" — 260
Chapter 63. "Mystery" — 266
Chapter 64. Alchemy — 271
Chapter 65. "Praise on a Painting of the Monk Baozhi" — 280
Chapter 66. Wild Cursive Script — 285

Section VIII. A Banished Immortal — 293

Chapter 67. A Plumper Li Bo of Yore — 294
Chapter 68. "Who Am I?" — 298
Chapter 69. "Given in Parting " — 302

A Postlude — 305

Chapter 70. "3 and 5 and 7 Words" — 306
Chapter 71. Method — 307
Chapter 72. An Apology — 308

Our Gratitude — 309

Afterwords	311
Traktung Yeshe Dorje	312
Maria Dolgenas	315
Bibliographies	317
Primary Chinese Works from before 1100 CE	318
Secondary Works	321
About the Authors	345
Endnotes	349

This book is dedicated to
Il Gran Maestro e il massimo fabbro alchimista del mondo

Li Bo

Chapter 1. Li Bo

Fig. 1. Li Bo in Stroll, by Liang Kai 梁楷 (ca. 1140–ca. 1210)[1]

Chapter 2. Li Bo

We can call him Li Bo. "Bo," as in Bauble. Don't let the wags persuade you to pronounce his name "LIBOR," the London Inter-Bank Offered Rate. (Yes, there are wags in this book.)

Born 701 in China's western borderlands. After teen years in the southwest, spends decades ranging through the central provinces. A thousand poems survive.

A piece of one:

> At dawn I grab a green jade staff,
> set out from Yellow Crane Tower to find immortals in the Five Great Peaks.
> Who cares how long it takes?
> My whole life I've loved to roam these mountains.[2]

手持綠玉杖，朝別黃鶴樓
五嶽尋仙不辭遠，一生好入名山游

Chapter 3. "There's a Cup of Wine in Front of Us"

A zither's playing, greenwood of Dragon's Gate,
a jade flask, good wine as pure as empty space.
Urge on the strings, correct the tuning.
Drinking with you, my friend,
red looks like green, and our faces start to flush.
A Turkic singing girl, her face like a flower,
tends the wine pot, smiling at spring wind,
smiling at spring wind, dancing in her gauze dress.
If you're not drunk yet, how will you ever find your way home?[3]

前有一樽酒行

琴奏龍門之綠桐，玉壺美酒清若空
催弦拂柱與君飲，看朱成碧顏始紅
胡姬貌如花，當墟笑春風
笑春風舞羅衣，君今不醉將安歸

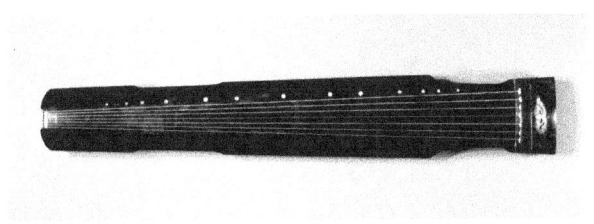

Fig. 2. The *guqin* Lingfeng Shenyun (靈峰神韻) in the Zhongni form.[4]

Chapter 4. "Spoken Spontaneously"

Food comes from the beauty of fields and wilds,
and wine pours down from distant streams.
Rivers flow east, endlessly,
they must know this feeling of goodbye.[5]

口號

食出野田美,酒臨遠水傾
東流若未盡,應見別離情

Chapter 5. "Seeing Off Li Qing on His Return to Huayang River"

Immortal, child of Laozi's household,
your appearance is like bright green spring.
In the spirit grottos where sun and moon secrete themselves,
in cloud and mist, you abandon this worldly world.
You transform heart and mind, nourishing your essence-seed,
hiding in the deep truth of Heaven.
Don't wait a thousand years to return,
when you come back the townscapes here will be all new.[6]

送李青歸華陽川

伯陽儻家子，容色如青春
日月秘靈洞，雲霞辭世人
化心養精魄，隱几寯天真
莫作千年別，歸來城郭新

Chapter 6. Li Bo (701–762)

The outlines of his life are simple. He was born abroad, in an ethnically mixed region of the far west, where Chinese, Uyghurs, Sogdians, and Indians lived together under nominal Chinese rule. Perhaps his first language was Turkic. When he was still small, the Li family moved back to the interior, settling in present-day Sichuan — that's still a rough trek south-west from the Tang capital of Chang'an.

The *Chronology of Li Bo* begins, "According to accounts in his own poetry, Li Bo descended from the ancient General Li Guang."[7] That surname Li is commonplace, but the Tang Emperors claimed descent from the same general, so Li Bo would refer to the royal family as "cousin." There's no family tree for evidence, we rely here on his word as poet.[8]

Li means plumtree, Bo means white, so his name can be read as a chromonym, like Red Skelton's.[9] His public name was Taibo 太白, "Great White."[10] That's also the name of a Chinese mountain, the name of the planet we call Venus, and a perfect translation of the common Turkic name, Appaq.[11]

Li describes his late teen years in Sichuan:

> I once lived in seclusion with the hermit Master East Cliff on the south side of Mount Min.[12] I holed up there several years, never setting foot in town or market. You could count in the thousands the number of rare animals we cared for. When we called, they'd all come eat from our palms, without the slightest starting or suspicion.
>
> The Prefect of Chengdu heard of this and wondered at it. He paid a formal visit to observe us in person, and accordingly awarded us the title "Possessing Dao." But we strongly declined.[13]

He roamed out from Sichuan soon after, never returning. In 726 he made a good marriage, but its circumstances did not turn into poetry — mostly we know him from his poems, so this marriage is mostly invisible to us.[14] And from about age thirty until his death, he roamed again, seeking men of letters, great officials, Daoist masters, mountains, companions, wine, the Emperor.

This roaming (*you* 遊) is not just casual wander or literary flaneurism. Two among its great precursors:

the Daoist sage Zhuangzi 莊子, who

> rode the cloud energies, mounted sun and moon, and roamed beyond the Four Seas,[15]

and the anonymous poet of "Far roaming," from the *Songtexts of Chu*:

> I pace through azure clouds,
> flooding, surging, roaming, ah.[16]

A friend recalls their first meeting a decade later:

> I was originally named Wan, then Dan. When I was still Wan, I ordered my driver to cross the Yangtze — not so great a distance — and find Li Bo. I went first to Mount Tiantai and finally met him when I got back to Guangling. The pupils of his eyes blazed sharply, quivering like a hungry tiger. Sometimes he would dress formally, raffish, elegant, and generous with wine. Since he'd received Daoist ordination in Qi, he might wear the accompanying green silk hood. When young, he'd been a swordsman, and with his own hand run through several people.[17]

Midway through this period, about 742, he made his way to the capital, Chang'an, and was introduced to the court.[18] For a while things went splendidly: the Emperor took a vivid shine to him and "loaned me his horse to ride."[19] Then the honeymoon ended — in slander, perhaps? We don't know how long this took, maybe a year or two. A later biographer saw it like this:

> If you're a dragon, you can be divine among the clouds and rain,
> but you can't be employed by men.
> If you're a phoenix, you can adorn the ruler's court,
> but you can't be tamed by men.[20]

蛟龍能神於雲雨，不能為人用
鳳凰能瑞於王者，不能為人畜

So Li Bo wandered out again, through the central provinces. In 755 rebellion split the realm. He soon found himself in the wrong place, was charged with treason and nearly executed, then released and pardoned. He roamed again, a bit forlorn, until his death in 762 midway up the Yangtze.

Among his thousand poems, here's one that disappeared:

Bright Moon Pond is in Pingwu, Long'an, near Bright Moon Ferry. They say that every night the moon casts shadows here. A poem by Li Bo was once carved into the rock cliff, but over time waters have worn it all away, and now all that remains is a poem by Yuwen Tong of the Song dynasty.[21]

II

Wine

Wine: divine ambrosia, the rocket fuel of immortals, quenching the demon of sobriety. Here's a piece of calligraphy attributed to Li Bo:

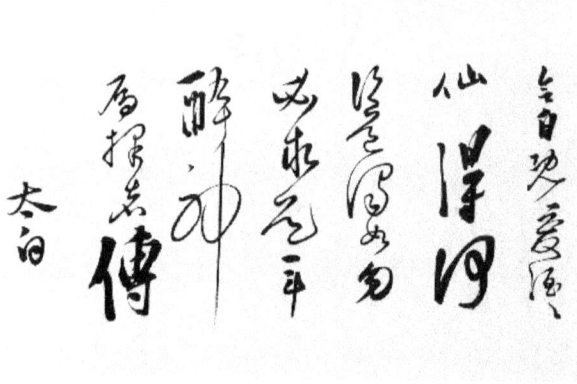

Fig. 3. Calligraphy by Li Bo.[22]

The text:

> I, Li Bo, love wine completely, right now. How to attain the immortality within wine? This Dao always gets muddled. Don't look for it in a ladle! The deity of drunkenness will give transmission to whoever is chosen.
>
> 今白既愛酒，酒仙得何，須道濁如，勿必求道一斗，醉神為擇者傳，太白

Emily Dickinson shows us how this works (I think she must be an American Sufi.)

I taste a liquor never brewed —
From Tankards scooped in Pearl —
Not all the Frankfort Berries
Yield such an Alcohol!

Inebriate of air — am I —
And Debauchee of Dew —
Reeling — thro' endless summer days —
From inns of molten Blue —

When "Landlords" turn the drunken Bee
Out of the Foxglove's door —
When Butterflies — renounce their "drams" —
I shall but drink the more!

Till Seraphs swing their snowy Hats —
And Saints — to windows run —
To see the little Tippler
Leaning against the — Sun!

There is a Li Bo bar in San Francisco Chinatown.[23] And here are four of Li Bo's poems of drinking.

Chapter 7. "Under the Moon"

Under the moon, drinking alone (second of four poems)

Heaven, if you didn't love wine,
the Wine Stars wouldn't be in Heaven.
Earth, if you didn't love wine,
then Earth, you shouldn't have wine springs.
Since Heaven and Earth love wine, right now,
loving wine doesn't embarrass Heaven.
Just hearing this, I'm clearer than a sage,
returning to Dao, I'm as murky as a saint.
Since sage and saint are already drinking, right now,
why seek to become immortal?
Three cups and I penetrate Great Dao,
one full dipper and I join with Perfect Spontaneity.
Just get the pleasure that's in wine,
don't let on about it to the sober.[24]

月下獨酌 其二

天若不愛酒,酒星不在天
地若不愛酒,地應無酒泉
天地既愛酒,愛酒不愧天
已聞清比聖,復道濁如賢
賢聖既已飲,何必求神仙
三杯通大道,一斗合自然
但得酒中趣,勿為醒者傳

The Wine Stars, three stellar gentlemen in our constellation Leo, we will meet them again some pages hence in a Sichuanese bar.[25] They are like a tavern pennant across the sky, so they are sometimes called the Wine Banner (*jiuqi* 酒旗).

Li Bo incarnates these stars. Yes, he has the earth-body that everyone knows, but also, in equal measure, the *po* 魄 or "material-soul" of these stars. Thus this poem, from a century after his death:

> I love Li Bo,
> In this very body he is the Wine Stars' *po*.
> His mouth spews writing all over the Heavens,
> footprints of a human traveler.[26]

> 吾愛李太白，身是酒星魄。口吐天上文，跡作人間客。

More than anyone, Edward Schafer has shown how this works:

> That constellation was his real doppelgänger in the sky. When its brightness or color seemed to change, or when such intruders as comets and novae appeared in it, his own life was profoundly involved.[27]

Where are such stars to be found? Schafer, again:

> So, in the end, it was in the bony planetarium of the skull that the divine asterisms are spread — identical, through a kind of supernatural topology, with the constellations we think we see above our heads. Travel by trance is easily the best method, far superior to either dragon or crane.[28]

Chapter 8. "Bring on That Wine"
for Billie Holiday

> Hey, man, don't you see that River rollin' down from Heaven?
> > It's headin' out to sea, an' it's never comin' back.
> Hey, man, don't you see that mirror in the great hall, grievin' your white hair?
> > Black silk threads in the mornin', snow at night.
> In this life to get what you want, you gotta celebrate,
> > so don't lift some empty golden goblet to the moon.
> For sure we gotta use the stuff we got from God —
> > just drop a thousand pieces of gold, it'll all come roarin' back.
> Stew the chicken, kill the goat, but to be merry
> > you got to drink up all three hundred cups at once.
> Hey Jack, hey there Prez,
> > bring on that wine, don't you stop, man!
> I'll sing a song with you,
> > give me your ear, ok?
> The best music, the finest food, don't do the trick,
> > just vow to be drunk forever an' never sober up.
> All the wise an' worthy of old times got forgotten,
> > only the drunks left us their names.
> When Queen Sheba feasted with King Solomon,
> > the wine cost ten-thousand a barrel, an' everybody frolicked.
> So, boss, how can you say you're short on cash,
> > you have to spend it dry so I can toast you, man.
> Your dappled horse, your fancy furs,
> > just have the kid take 'em out an' trade 'em for good wine.
> Together, sir, we'll melt the sorrows of ten-thousand ages.[29]

將進酒

君不見黃河之水天上來，奔流到海不復回
君不見高堂明鏡悲白髮，朝如青絲暮成雪
人生得意須盡歡，莫使金樽空對月
天生我材必有用，千金散盡還復來
烹羊宰牛且為樂，會須一飲三百杯
岑夫子，丹丘生，將進酒，君莫停
與君歌一曲，請君為我側耳聽
鐘鼓饌玉不足貴，但願長醉不願醒
古來聖賢皆寂寞，惟有飲者留其名
陳王昔時宴平樂，斗酒十千恣歡謔
主人何為言少錢，徑須沽取對君酌
五花馬，千金裘，呼兒將出換美酒
與爾同銷萬古愁

John Thorpe writes:

> Billie Holliday, is anyone catching the set?
>
> > — come
> >   moon's quick's
> >   bright
> >   shine —

Something like the curls of Billie's throat (and the spitball she puts on this word, the whisper with which she lets the other word fall) is open, whether anybody's here to hear it or not, and so much the better if you don't take her as an entertainer.[30]

Chapter 9. "On a Spring Day"

On a spring day I wake from drinking and state my aspirations

Living in this world is like a big dream —
why labor your life away?
So I'll be drunk all day,
and topple over, sleeping in the front hall.

Waking up, glancing round the courtyard,
a single bird sings in the flowers.
Were I to ask the season,
the spring wind would speak in soaring orioles.

The breath goes right out of me.
I pour myself another cup of wine.
I sing in floods, I wait for the bright moon.
When the tune ends, I'll already have forgotten these feelings.

春日醉起言志

處世若大夢，胡為勞其生
所以終日醉，隤然臥前楹
覺來眄庭前，一鳥花間鳴
借問此何時，春風語流鶯
感之欲嘆息，對酒還自傾
浩歌待明月，曲盡已忘情[31]

Chapter 10. "Face-to-face with Wine"

Immortal Redpine nested in Goldflower Mountain,
Divine Anqi swam in Faerie Sea.
These immortals of old took wing,
and where are they now?
This floating life flows quick as lightning,
transforming suddenly to light.
Heaven and Earth never wither, never fall away,
but our beauty moves off, leaving us behind.
Face-to-face with this wine, unwilling to drink,
flush of feeling, whom do I await?[32]

對酒行

松子棲金華，安期入蓬海
此人古之仙，羽化竟何在
浮生速流電，倏忽變光彩
天地無凋換，容顏有遷改
對酒不肯飲，含情欲誰待

An Interlude

Chapter 11. "Presented to Chief Administrator Chu of Liyang on the Occasion That This Gentleman Danced Like a Young Child"

The man behind this poem is Old Laizi 老萊子, Old Master Pigweed, a gentleman of Chu who lived around the time of Confucius (551–479). He must have read in the *Book of Rites* (Liji 禮記) that "As long as your father and mother are still alive, never call yourself 'old,'" because he never did.³³ Here's the first part of his story:

> Old Laizi cared for his parents in a filial manner. Though he'd reached the age of seventy, he would play like a baby, wearing colorful clothing. When he was carrying water into the house, he'd trip on purpose and tumble onto the floor, crying like a little child. Or he'd act like a crow before his parents.³⁴

Or he would "play and dance, imitating a naive and simple child."³⁵ Then they would laugh and forget their age. Here's a stone-carved relief from a mid-second-century CE tomb and a woodblock illustration from the Qing dynasty (1644–1911). (In the stone relief Old Laizi and his parents are in the middle, he on his knees playing with a ball, the two of them in joyous approbation.)

Fig. 4. Stone-carved relief, 2nd c. CE.³⁶

Fig. 5. Qing dynasty-era woodblock print.[37]

Here is Li Bo's poem to the Administrator:

> Presented to Chief Administrator Chu of Liyang on the occasion that this gentleman danced like a young child
>
> May your mother live a hundred thousand years!
> Your respectful service to her is magnificent.
> First by dancing like a young child,
> then by dressing like Old Laizi.
> Because of this you cry like a little boy
> when you topple over drunk, coming home under the moon.
> The human realm lacks this pleasure,
> This pleasure is rarely seen in the world.[38]
>
> 贈歷陽褚司馬時此公為稚子舞
>
> 北堂千萬壽
> 侍奉有光輝
> 先同稚子舞
> 更著老萊衣
> 因為小兒啼
> 醉倒月下歸
> 人間無此樂
> 此樂世中稀

Here's more of Old Laizi's story, after his parents must have died and he and his wife were living as hermits, drinking from brooks and eating wild plants:

> Someone spoke of Old Laizi to the King of Chu. Thereupon the King drove his chariot right to Old Laizi's door. Old Laizi was weaving a basket. The King said, "I wish to trouble you, Sir, with managing the state."
> Old Laizi said, "I give my assent."
> The King left. Old Laizi's wife had been out gathering firewood. When she returned, she said, "Did you consent to it?"
> Old Laizi said, "Yes."

His wife said, "I've heard that someone who can feed you wine and meat can follow that with whip and stick, and someone who can plan your appointment and salary can follow that with the axe of execution. Your wife is not someone who can be controlled by people." Then she threw down her basket and left. Old Laizi also followed, going south of the Yangtze, where they remained. He said, "The feathers and fur of bird and beast can be woven into clothing, and gleaned grains are sufficient for eating."

Old Laizi wrote a book of fifteen fascicles, which spoke of the application of Daoist ideas. No one knows how he ended.[39]

Here she is, having thrown down her firewood.

Fig. 6. Old Laizi and his wife.[40]

Chapter 12. Big Words

Presented to Li Yong

When the peng-bird rises on the wind,
there's only cyclone, ninety thousand miles straight up.
If the wind dies and he falls back down,
he can always rumble back over to the blue Darksea.
My big words seem strange and out of tune,
so everyone laughs coldly at them,
but even Confucius should fear the next generation.
Adults, don't take us lightly![41]

上李邕

大鵬一日同風起
摶搖直上九萬里
假令風歇時下來
猶能簸卻滄溟水
世人見我恆殊調
聞余大言皆冷笑
宣父猶能畏後生
丈夫未可輕年少

Li Bo had a presumptive kinsman named Li Yong 李邕 (678–747), the highest paid prose writer of the age.[42] In 720, when Li Bo was a teenager living in the province we now call Sichuan, Li Yong was posted nearby. Basing himself on some unknown common progenitor, Li Bo called on him and sent in this cheeky poem by way of introduction.

Li Yong was a marveled, moody, brilliant, generous man. *The Old Tang History* says of him,

> Despite his generally good reputation, he was frequently dismissed from office. He would spout disquisitions as he

walked through the streets, unfathomable to those who followed behind. When folks of the Western and Eastern Capitals saw him, they took him for an ancient.[43]

Li Bo's poem mentions "my big words." These refer not just to him but to the mega-word braggadocio of Dongfang Shuo 東方朔 (ca. 160–ca. 93 BCE), wise buffoon to the Martial Emperor of Han, and frequent counterpoint to Li Bo. The Martial Emperor had sent out a call for worthy men to present themselves to the throne. Thousands came forth and were dismissed. Dongfang Shuo sent in this letter:

> [When young, I studied the classics, the military texts and fencing], and by the time I was nineteen I could recite 440,000 words. I am twenty-two, nine feet three inches tall, with eyes like pendant pearls, teeth like ranks of shells, as brave as Meng Ben, nimble as Qingji, scrupulous as Bao Zhu, and loyal as Wei Sheng. Because of this, I am fit to act as a great minister to the Son of Heaven.[44]

The Emperor concluded he was no ordinary man, and kept him on.

The fabulous bird of the first lines comes to us from Zhuangzi, whose own very first words are:

> In the Northern Darksea is a fish called the Kun. I don't know how many thousand miles round its girth is! It transforms into a bird called the Peng. I don't know how many thousand miles long its back is! When it's aroused and takes to flight, it beats the waters for three thousand miles, a swirling cyclone, rising up 90,000 miles.[45]

Chapter 13. "The Hard Road to Shu"

Li Bo wrote for a friend who planned on travelling from the capital of Chang'an to the distant southwest province of Shu.[46]

   Holy shit!
   So murderously high!
      The road to Shu is hard,
   harder than scaling the blue-green open sky.

                How did they do it —
      those ancient kings who opened this land,
   marking out fields, bringing silkworms and fishing nets?

      They walked off into the mist,
      and then it was 48,000 years
   before we smelled the smoke of their wood fires.

      Birds have always had a path
   straight in from Chang'an to Emei Peak,
                but when men began to cut a road,
   earth split open, mountains collapsed, stout warriors had to die
      before iron rods were drilled into the mountainside,
   and wooden planks, raised on scaffolding, were linked
                by ladders straddling the sky.

   Up above,
      six dragons pull the sun through the treetops,
      down below, the river breaks,
   circling back upon itself.
                Even the yellow crane's soaring
                  stops here;
   long-armed apes despair of ever getting to the top.

Snarly gnarly Green Mud Ridge:
>nine switchbacks every hundred steps,
>>wrapping round the cliffs.
Touch the Bear Star,
>pass through Orion,
>>lean back, breathe in the air!
Hold your chest,
>sit down and heave a sigh.

My friend, will you ever make it home again?
I fear you'll never clamber up
>that treacherous, break-neck road.

All you'll see are sad birds
>crying in old trees, males and females
>>winding through the woods,

and you'll hear the cuckoo's call to the night moon
>filling the empty mountain with sorrow.

>The road to Shu is hard,
harder than scaling the blue-green open sky!
When you hear this
>the bloom of your cheeks will wilt and die.

>Peak on peak not a foot below Heaven,
>>dead pines hang headfirst down the sheer walls.
>>Fast rapids, raging falls
>>>crash and clatter,
>>battering cliffs and barreling crags,
ten thousand gullies thunder.

>These are the dangers, oh traveler,
on this long road — why on earth
>would you ever come this way?

Sword Gate Pass,
>spiked and sinister:
>>if one man blocks the way,
>>ten thousand can't get through,
>>>and if that man's a traitor,
>he changes into a wolf.

>>Morning and night,
>>>beware fierce tigers and giant snakes,
>sharpening their teeth to suck your blood,
>mowing you down like fields of hay.

The Brocade City would be lovely,
>if you ever got there,
>but better just go home.
>>>The road to Shu is hard,
harder than scaling the blue-green open sky —
>lean back, look west with a long, last sigh![47]

蜀道難

噫吁嚱
危乎高哉
蜀道之難
難于上青天
蠶叢及魚鳧
開國何茫然
爾來四萬八千歲
不與秦塞通人煙
西當太白有鳥道
可以橫絕峨眉巔
地崩山摧壯士死
然後天梯石棧相鉤連
上有六龍回日之高標
下有沖波逆折之回川
黃鶴之飛尚不得過
猿猱欲度愁攀援

青泥何盤盤
百步九折縈岩巒
捫參歷井仰脅息
以手撫膺坐長嘆
問君西游何時還
畏途巉巖不可攀
但見悲鳥號古木
雄飛雌從遶林間
又聞子規啼夜月
愁空山
蜀道之難
難于上青天
使人聽此凋朱顏
連峰去天不盈尺
枯松倒挂倚絕壁
飛湍瀑流爭喧豗
砯崖轉石萬壑雷
其險也如此
嗟爾遠道之人胡為乎來哉
劍閣崢嶸而崔嵬
一夫當關
萬夫莫開
所守或匪親
化為狼與豺
朝避猛虎
夕避長蛇
磨牙吮血
殺人如麻
錦城雖云樂
不如早還家
蜀道之難
難于上青天
側身西望長咨嗟

Chapter 14. "Lines of a Short Song"

How short, short this bright sun —
our hundred years fill so easily with sorrow.
The vaulted blue-green sky floods on and on,
for ten-thousand eons reality flows on.
The goddess lets down two locks of hair,
already half frost-white.
The Lord of Heaven plays at darts with her
and laughs through a million thousand spaces.
I want to rein in the sun's six dragons,
turn round their chariot, and tether them at world's end.
The Northern Dipper pours fine wine —
I'll persuade each dragon to drink a goblet.
Wealth and honor aren't what we want
to halt the ruination of our brightness.[48]

短歌行

白日何短短，百年苦易滿
蒼穹浩茫茫，萬劫太極長
麻姑垂兩鬢，一半已成霜
天公見玉女，大笑億千場
吾欲攬六龍，回車挂扶桑
北斗酌美酒，勸龍各一觴
富貴非所愿，與人駐顏光

If you have time now for a longer conversation, we'll translate this poem a bit differently. At the fourth line we've said, "for ten-thousand eons, reality flows on." "Reality" is a loose translation of Taiji 太極, the Great Ultimate, that undifferentiated circumstance that is just prior to form — just prior to Yin and Yang.[49] How long can it go on? The Indians measure big time in kalpas, a word that the Chinese, like us, couldn't translate, so they preserved its sound, "kiap-pua" 劫波.[50] It means the life span of a world realm, from when it was created to when it is destroyed and then created once again. In the time of modern physics, this might be some six or seven billion years.[51] So Li Bo actually tells us the Great Ultimate will go on for ten-thousand kalpas.

The goddess in question is Magu 麻姑, whose name means "Hemp Maiden." On one occasion she got a message from her lover Wang, saying, "It's been a long time since you were in the human world. I've just arrived here today, and I'm wondering if you might come and chat awhile with me." She arrived,

> a fine-looking young woman, maybe eighteen or nineteen. Her hair was done up on top of her head, with the remainder falling down to her waist. She said, "Since I've served you, already thrice I've seen the Eastern Sea turn into mulberry groves and planted fields."[52]

And beyond the Eastern Sea lies Fusang 扶桑, "Beside the Mulberries," where the sun starts its circuit, drawn by six dragons through the sky, which in the above translation we've rendered "world's end."

To understand the Lord of Heaven, whose real name is the Eastern King, we'll need recourse again to Dongfang Shuo, that jester to the Han's Martial Emperor. *His Classic of Divine Marvels* (*Shenyijing* 神異經) begins like this:

> Within a mountain in the Eastern Barrens is a great rock room, wherein dwells the Eastern King. He's ten feet tall, with bright white hair, human body, bird face, and tiger tail. He keeps a black bear, who keeps looking around in every direction. He and a Jade Woman are always playing Pitch Pot (*touhu* 投壺 "throw the arrow in the pot"). They get 1,200 tries.
>
> When he gets an arrow to stay in, Heaven suspires for it. When the throw misses and the King can't grab it, Heaven laughs for it.[53]

A commentator explains:

"Suspire" means "sigh." When it says "laugh," it means that flowing fire comes dazzling out from Heaven's mouth. Now, in under-heaven when it doesn't rain but there are lightning flashes, this is Heaven's laughter.[54]

Fig. 7. The Xuanzong Emperor of Ming playing Pitch Pot[55]

In the above translation we portrayed this game as darts, but the arrow game actually goes back to the first millennium BCE. In Tang there was a guy who could always get the arrow in, even with his back turned.[56]

The Northern Dipper is the same constellation that we see in our northern sky. The *Classic of the Precious Ocean of Mysterious Gateways* (*Xuanmen baohai jing* 玄門寶海經) elaborates on its power:

> The stars of the Northern Dipper are the purple seal upon the Great Ultimate, the numinous bed of Mystery Truth. [...] The Yellow Emperor says, "When the cock crows, think of the seven stars of the Northern Dipper, and the heavenly deities will send down the medicine of deathlessness, and seal for you long life without aging."[57]

It doesn't pour just wine: everything comes from it.

Thus a translation of the poem that incorporates the materials from Dongfang Shuo and others:

Lines of a Short Song

How short, short this bright sun —
our hundred years fill so easily with sorrow.
The vaulted azure sky floods on and on,
the ten-thousand kalpa-long Great Ultimate flows on.
Magu lets down two locks of hair —
one half's already frost-white.
The Lord of Heaven sees the Jade Woman
and laughs through a million thousand spaces.
I want to rein in the sun's six dragons,
turn round the chariot, and tether them to Fusang's mulberry tree.
The Northern Dipper pours fine wine —
I'll persuade each dragon to drink a goblet.
Wealth and honor aren't what we want
to halt the ruination of our brightness.

Chapter 15. "A Rhapsody Lamenting Last Remnants of the Spring"

How does Heaven tell the Northern Dipper that it's spring,
oh, and point its handle back to the east again?
These streams roil up, oh, bluest green,
the orchids hang exuberant in all their red fragrance.
I set off to scale the heights,
oh, gazing far as the vastest sea of clouds.
Once my soul's gone out, oh, it's bound to break,
and tears will stream down my cheeks.
So I'll sing to the clear wind and praise the dark blue waves,
the ancient lakes and rivers,
oh, how faint my heart and mind,
oh, floating on the spring wind,

Floating, oh, my thoughts unbound,
recalling days with you, my lord, the dusk unfolding.
Luxuriant foliage crowds the plains, oh, with its fine silk threads,
and I love how the fragrant grasses look like the points of scissors.
I lament that spring dwindles so fast,
and no moment of this regret is ever shallow.
How can the river bends and deep pools,
oh, bear to think their jade-like grasses will soon be gone?
I recall the two women of Xianbei who, forgotten, wandered lost in love,
I sorrow for the two women of Xiang who drowned themselves for it.

Grief without limit, oh, my heart inseparable from all things,
my eyes stopped by this chaos of melancholy.
I am the woman of Wei, longing for her marriage bed,
I am the King of Chu, whose lover turned to mist.

Each time spring returns, oh, the flowers open.
Now the flowers are already spent, oh, and spring has changed.
I sigh because the long river carries off the spring,
I say farewell to the waves vanishing on the Eastern Sea.
Spring does not remain, oh, already the season's lost,
grieving and more grieving, oh, the sound of wind.
I wish I could hang a long rope in blue-green Heaven
to tie up this westward-flying sun.

There seems to be someone, oh, whose feelings are so close to mine,
who travels south and west, in past and present time.
Whenever I see criss-cross of gossamer threads,
I make webs of spring sunlight to keep him here.

Sunk in songs, oh, of lamentation,
pacing, pacing, oh, grieving this parting,
seeing off this soon-distant traveler,
while the wild swans fly slowly out of sight,
drunken, sad, beneath the weeping willow,
only this one thin thread keeping us entwined.

I sigh, gazing after you, my friend,
tears cross my face, and I hate how my own spring has passed.
We cast long shadows in bright moonlight
as I see you off, my friend, to the edge of Earth and Heaven.[58]

惜餘春賦

天之何為令北鬥而知春兮,回指於東方。水蕩漾兮碧色,蘭葳蕤兮紅芳。試登高兮望遠,極雲海之微茫。魂一去兮欲斷,淚流頰兮成行。吟清風而詠滄浪,懷洞庭兮悲瀟湘。何予心之縹緲兮,與春風而飄揚。飄揚兮思無限,念佳期兮莫展。平原萋兮綺色,愛芳草兮如翦。惜餘春之將闌,每為恨兮不淺。漢之曲兮江之潭,把瑤草兮思何堪?想遊女於峴北,愁帝子於湘南。恨無極兮心氳氳,目眇眇兮憂紛紛。披衛情於淇水,結楚夢於陽雲。春每歸兮花開,花已闌兮春改。歎長河之流速,送馳波於東海。春不留兮時已失,老衰颯兮情逾疾。恨不得掛長繩於青天,係此西飛之白日。若有人兮情相親,去南越兮往西秦。見遊絲之橫路,網春暉以留人。沈吟兮哀歌,躑躅兮傷別。送行子之將遠,看征鴻之稍滅。醉愁心於垂楊,隨柔條以糾結。望夫君兮興咨嗟,橫涕淚兮怨春華。遙寄影於明月,送夫君於天涯。

… III

Center of Everything

a. The Great Tang

A century before Li Bo was born, a Turko-Chinese family established a multi-ethnic empire they called the Great Tang (Datang 大唐). It would last three hundred years. During Li Bo's lifetime it looked something like this:

Fig. 8. The territory of the Great Tang in 742.[59]

The Great Tang unified 50,000,000 Chinese speakers and held suzerainty over much of central Asia.[60] Only once before, under the Han (206 BCE–220 CE), had a dynasty demonstrated such dominion, and the Martial Emperor of Han (Han Wudi 漢武帝, rg 140–87) hung over the shoulders of imperial practice.

At the center of everything was Chang'an 長安, "Constant Peace," western capital, fulcrum of the Emperor.[61] An unprecedented concentration of power that radiated across all Asia, and in turn received those foreign energies in its streets and markets, palaces and garrisons.[62] Buddhist temples, a Nestorian Christian church, grape wine, Turkic singing girls, Uyghur money lenders, silk merchants, lavish private gardens, skilled metalsmiths, unemployed soldiers, extravagant poets, one million inhabitants, the largest and most cosmopolitan city in the world. Like this:

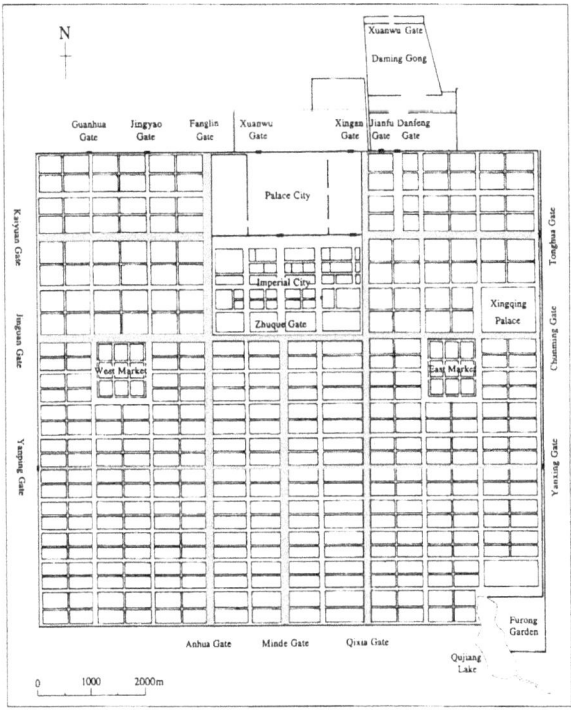

Fig. 9. Map of Chang'an during the Great Tang.[63]

Li Bo glimpsing it:

> As spring colors return to Chang'an,
> they enter Blue Gate Avenue first.
> The new-green poplars don't restrain themselves,
> they turn all topsy-turvy with the wind.[64]

長安春色歸，先入青門道
綠楊不自持，從風欲傾倒

The west wind blows into the streets of Chang'an,
the great avenues of the city spread across the Nine Heavens.[65]

風吹西到長安陌，長安大道橫九天

A piece of moon in Chang'an,
the sound of ten-thousand households shaking out their clothes.
You can always feel the frontier
in the autumn wind that doesn't stop.[66]

長安一片月，萬戶擣衣聲
秋風吹不盡，總是玉關情

So far we've seen the Great Tang in the two dimensions of its physical extent: east–west and north–south. The third dimension is time, but in Chang'an the past is fully present. Especially the Han dynasty: the city has the name and nearly the shape it had then, half a millennium ago.[67] If we are statesmen, we know these Han practices as historical precedent, and they govern our decision making, right now. Language, too: a poem, a compliment, an imperial rescript, these reverberate with 1,500 years of words, both canonical and private — if we are poets, we know these as literary allusion. You could call the whole collection "China" for short.[68] To be well educated is to be child and steward of this realm, and maintain its records.[69]

And then the fourth dimension, space. Here the capital of Great Tang is the node where the Emperor fulfills his most essential function: to bring the blessings of Heaven onto the plane of Earth.[70] The Emperor, then, is divine, and the good ordering of everything on earth — the seasons, cropping, social harmony, human decency — depends on his virtue.[71]

b. The Bright Emperor
For most of Li Bo's life the Great Tang was ruled by a man known as the Bright Emperor (Minghuang 明皇, rg. 712–756).[72] He held more power than anyone within a three-month journey. And more potency. Both these are forms of *yang* 陽, light, sun, the male. The former is denominated in armies, bureaucracies, and agricultural surplus, the latter in awe, splendor, and the control of natural forces.[73] For forty years the Emperor wielded these with almost unimaginable energy and attention. It's not surprising that he had fifty-nine children.[74]

He was also an adroit musician, poet, calligrapher, a student of esoteric Daoism and Indian tantric Buddhism, and thus equally a dévoté of *yin* 陰, darkness, moon, the feminine. In his fifties, he took his son's young wife as lover. Surnamed Yang, she became Yang Guifei 楊貴妃, "Yang the Precious Consort," his world. As his attention faded from empire, his administration lost its head. When rebellion rent the state, the Bright Emperor fled, abandoning the throne. His guard blamed it all on her; the Emperor consented to her strangulation.

Fig. 10. The Bright Emperor[75]   *Fig. 11.* The Precious Consort[76]

c. At Court
A century before Li Bo, in the early years of the dynasty, to write a poem pretty much meant that the names of your father and grandfather and great-grandfather were all already known to the poem's recipients. That is, that you were scion of the Great Fami-

lies that dominated the society of early Tang. These patrilineages constituted a centuries-old self-perpetuating elite, nearly impermeable of entry.[77] They provided the bulk of a national bureaucracy of 10,000 men, half in the capitals and half throughout the realm.[78] Filiality and loyalty were their desiderata, in that order.

As scion, your social relations, your deportment and your learning were all self-consciously based on ancient models, in turn derived from the natural order of things. Confucius and other sages had first discerned these models, and a cumulative cultural tradition had seen to their elaboration. Speaking on their behalf, Peter Bol says, "These cultural forms were real."[79] Education meant mastering them through studied imitation.

Your poetry was similarly model based. Steve Owen says it perfectly:

> In the early seventh century, poetry was primarily a form of stylized social discourse practiced mainly in court circles. [...] The court poetry of the Early Tang rigidly circumscribed the occasions for composition, the topics, the diction, and the structure of poetry. [...] [Its poets were] bound by decorum, committed to aristocratic society and its ambience, held proudly to mannered formality, and disdained the showiness of bold metaphors and stylistic tours de force.[80]

To illustrate, here's a poem by Li Shimin 李世民 (598–649), de facto founding emperor of Tang, who killed his brothers and forced his father into abdication. Known posthumously as Taizong 太宗, the Great Ancestor. Written to Xiao Yu 蕭瑀 (574–648), warrior prince of a former dynasty who had joined the Great Tang and served as Taizong's trusted chancellor.

Presented to Xiao Yu

Only in fierce winds do we know the strong grasses,
only in disorder do we recognize the honest minister.
How does the brave man recognize righteousness?
The wise man must also embrace kindness.[81]

賜蕭瑀

疾風知勁草，板蕩識誠臣
勇夫安識義，智者必懷仁

Li Bo came to the capital around 742. He had no human family of consequence, and his model-work was somewhat lax. He met famous men, officials, the Bright Emperor's sister. And he met the Emperor himself.

What happened then? He wrote marvels. And drank tankards. The Emperor appointed him not as government official (as he may have wished) but to his private Hanlin Academy 翰林, where Li Bo drafted edicts and diplomatic rescripts as well as writing poetry and song lyrics.[82] And after a couple of years he had to leave. Was he indiscreet? (While drinking, about state secrets.) Was he rude? (Making the chief eunuch remove his muddy boots for him.) Was he calumnized? (Malicious gossip due to envy.) Stories like these have been told over and over, the way a painting gets painted over with nearly the same scene, so that you have numerous semi-identical images all atop each other.[83] Or the way when something is very bright, it's hard to keep it in focus along with the ordinary things around it, so we tend instead to see its reflections in those things, to normalize its image.

In the next chapter we'll translate one of these story-sets, and in subsequent chapters offer other vignettes of his life in the capital.

Chapter 16. Night Music

One late spring night the Bright Emperor convened a music party with the Precious Consort in his favorite pavilion. He needed Li Bo to write new lyrics to the old tunes.

Their story is denominated in all the senses: sights, sounds, smells, tastes, body sensations, emotions, where the deities reside.[84] We start with place, a garden in a palace of the imperial city of Chang'an (fig. 9, p. 57).

This city is five to six miles on a side, so its square footage is only slightly less than the twenty arrondissements of Paris. At the top, the north, is the main imperial complex, and nearby along the eastern wall, to the right, are the grounds of the Xingqing Palace 興慶宮, the Palace of Exalted Grace, within which this story takes place. The Bright Emperor had recently moved here to live with his beloved, the Precious Consort.[85] This is what it looks like today:

Fig. 12. The Agarwood Pavilion in Chang'an (upper left)[86]

In the upper left of this photograph is the Agarwood Pavilion (Chenxiangting 沈香亭), the actual site of the music — you can see it more precisely here:

Fig. 13. The Agarwood Pavilion.[87]

Agarwood is intensely aromatic — I would say its closest cousin among mainstream scents is sandal, but it is gorgeously more pungent and complex.[88]

In front of the Pavilion was a garden of tree peonies. Ordinary peonies grow to perhaps a meter tall, and their stems die off each fall. By contrast, a tree peony may grow to three or more meters, and its woody trunk and branches produce blossoms year after year. A picture:

Fig. 14. A peony tree.[89]

This is where our story begins.[90]

> A decade or more previous, during the Kaiyuan period (713–742), His Majesty had first come to prize tree peonies. (They come in four colors: red, purple, light red and true white.) Accordingly he had them transplanted in front of the Agarwood Pavilion, just east of Exalted Grace Pond. The thick flowers were now at the moment of their fullest bloom. On a moonlit night, with the Precious Consort accompanying him in her palanquin, the Emperor ordered select members of the Pear Garden troupe to perform music for sixteen instruments.[91] Li Guinian, the most celebrated vocalist of the time, held the clappers. Directing the musicians, Li prepared to sing.[92]
>
> But His Majesty said, "We're enjoying marveled flowers, and in the presence of the Precious Consort. How can you use old lyrics?" So he had Li Guinian take some gilt paper to the Hanlin Academician Li Bo with orders to come up with three new verses for the Plain and Level modes.[93] Li Bo received the order with delight. He was hung over from a rough night and still half asleep, but he took up his writing brush and composed these verses:

poem #1

Clouds dream up her clothing,
flowers dream her face,
spring winds play on the railing,
dew luxuriant and thick.
Did I see her on the mountaintop
in the forest of jade?
Have we met at the jasper terrace
under the moon?

雲想衣裳花想容，春風拂檻露華濃
若非群玉山頭見，會向瑤台月下逢

poem #2

A sprig of red seduction,
a fragrance congealed in dew.
A night of love at Shaman Mountain
breaking hearts for nothing.
Who's like her in
all the palaces of Han?
Only Flying Swallow,
putting on her rouge.

一枝紅艷露凝香,雲雨巫山枉斷腸
借問漢宮誰得似,可憐飛燕倚新妝

poem #3

Beloved peonies and a beauty who topples kingdoms:
these delight in one another.
The king holds them both
in his smiling gaze.
Releasing spring breezes,
free of care,
she leans on a railing
at the north side of Agarwood Pavilion.[94]

名花傾國兩相歡,長得君王帶笑看
解釋春風無限恨,沈香亭北倚欄干

Li Guinian presented these verses to His Majesty, who had him sing them, accompanied by the strings and winds of the Pear Garden troupe.[95] The Precious Consort drank Liangzhou grape wine from a glass cup decorated with the Seven Treasures, smiling, flush with enjoyment.[96] His Majesty played along on his jade flute, alternating between lead and harmony, then embellishing the music by varying his tempo. When the Precious Consort had finished drinking, she rearranged her embroidered scarves and prostrated repeatedly to His Majesty.[97]

Chapter 17. Commissioner He Zhizhang

A ninth-century story:

> When Li Bo first came up to the capital from Sichuan, he stayed at an inn.
>
> He Zhizhang knew Li Bo's reputation and went to call on him himself. Already struck by Li Bo's bearing, he asked several times to see his writings. Li Bo took out "The hard road to Shu" and showed it to him. Before He Zhizhang had finished, he cried out three or four times, and proclaimed Li Bo a banished immortal. He untied his golden tortoise belt ornament and bought wine with it. They spent several days together getting completely drunk.[98]

Li Bo's poem:

> Drinking wine, recalling He Zhizhang, with a preface
>
> Lord He, tutor to the Crown Prince — as soon as you saw me in the Laozi Temple of Chang'an, you said I was a banished immortal. And so you untied your golden tortoise and used it to buy wine, so that we could enjoy ourselves.
>
> You're dead now. I'm drinking wine, full of sorrow, I recall you and write this poem.
>
> That crazy stranger from Four Bright Mountain,
> that stylish gallant, He Zhizhang.
> As soon as he saw me in Chang'an,
> he called me a banished immortal.
> He used to love the contents of a wine-cup,
> but now he's dust under a pine-tree.
> His golden tortoise, traded for wine —
> tears still wet my kerchief.[99]

對酒憶賀監二首 并序

太子賓客賀公。于長安紫極宮一見余。呼余為謫仙人。
因解金龜換酒為樂。歿後對酒。悵然有懷而作是詩。

四明有狂客，風流賀季真
長安一相見，呼我謫仙人
昔好杯中物，翻為松下塵
金龜換酒處，卻憶淚沾巾

He Zhizhang 賀知章 (659–744) was in his eighties when they met. For fifty years he'd been a champion bureaucrat company man and eccentric drunk.[100] Du Fu, China's great poet and Li Bo's great friend, celebrates He's drinking:

> He sways on his horse like he's on a tipsy ship,
> If he falls into a well blind drunk, he'll just doze there at the bottom.[101]

知章騎馬似乘船，眼花落井水底眠

But He Zhizhang's Daoism was a great secret, so everyone was surprised when he had a dream that he'd "roamed in the house of the Supreme Lord"[102] and suddenly retired to take ordination back home. The Crown Prince himself saw him off from the gates of Chang'an.

Well, he said something important enough about Li Bo that Li Bo rehearses it in both preface and poem. He called him a "banished immortal" (*zhexian* 謫仙). He's the first to do so, and the name stuck.

In ordinary speech this would mean that Li Bo were a divinity, not really a person, but the kind of divinity who'd been punished (banished, degraded, cashiered) to live in the human realm. A halfie. These days we don't much believe in such things—the closest we come is to say that someone's voice is "divine"[103]—but immortality, or the transcendence of earthly strictures, was the heart of Daoist activity. Sometimes meditative practices were the means, sometimes alchemy.[104] Li Bo's practice was wine.[105]

In this poem Li Bo acts as if he hadn't known he was an immortal before He Zhizhang said it. I wonder if this is true.[106]

Chapter 18. Writing Brushes

Li Bo worked in private halls of the imperial palace, drafting proclamations and mandates for the Bright Emperor. In the twelfth lunar month, the period known as "Great Cold,"[107] the brushes froze, and no one could write a word. The Emperor ordered several dozen palace concubines to stand on Li Bo's left and right, each taking an ivory-handled brush and breathing on it. This succeeded, and he was able to write the proclamations.

Li Bo was the recipient of the sovereign's tenderness like this.

> *From the* Tianbao yishi 天寶遺事 *(Lost matters from the Tianbao reign period [742–756])*[108]

Chapter 19. The Marriage of a Court Woman

A bitter ballad

In Chang'an I saw a palace woman taken out to be married, and I felt compelled to write this bitter ballad for her.

At fifteen I entered the royal palace,
a flower smiling in the blush of spring.
A prince chose my jade-white beauty,
we made our bed behind a golden screen.
I coaxed him to the pillow as the moon rose,
we tugged off our clothes in love's spring wind.

Hadn't I heard how Flying Swallow
once stole an Emperor's favor, leaving others endless pain?
Deep sorrow can ruin a woman,
turning thick black hair to tangled frost.
One day I wasn't pleasing,
and now my life means nothing.

I'd pawn my down-lined furs for good wine,
the embroidered dragons have flown from my dancing gowns.
I can't bear to speak this icy pain,
so I'll sing a song for you.
When the strings go silent, my heart breaks,
a pulse of pain throughout the night.[109]

怨歌行

長安見內人出嫁。令余代為怨歌行
十五入漢宮，花顏笑春紅
君王選玉色，侍寢金屏中
荐枕嬌夕月，卷衣戀春風

寧知趙飛燕，奪寵恨無窮
沉憂能傷人，綠鬢成霜蓬
一朝不得意，世事徒為空
鸂鶒換美酒，舞衣罷雕龍
寒苦不忍言，為君奏絲桐
腸斷弦亦絕，悲心夜忡忡

An Interlude

Chapter 20. In a Boat

The *Unified Geography of the Realm* records:

> On moonlit nights Li Bo would travel with Cui Zongzhi from Stone Quarry Jetty to Jinling. While sitting in the boat, he would wear his silk robes from the Imperial Court.[110]

This is not an American soldier ironing his ancient uniform for a VFW Post dinner, nor is it a French country priest vested as Christ's vicar to offer mass, though both of these are indeed acts of magic. Rather it is the way snow falls in the mountains.[111]

Chapter 21. A Letter to the Governor

Around 734 Li Bo wrote the Governor of Jingzhou, seeking patronage. We excerpt a bit of Victor Mair's grand translation of that letter.

> I have heard that, when the empire's chatty scholars gather together, they say to each other, "During one's lifetime, it is not necessary to be a marquis with the income from ten thousand households, if one could hope but once to make the acquaintance of Han, the Governor of Jingzhou." How is it that you have caused men to lionize you to such a degree ? Is it not because you have the spirit of the Duke of Zhou who, in his anxiety not to miss any callers, would interrupt his meals by spitting out his food and his bath by wringing his half-washed hair? The result is that all the elite within the realm rush to you and give you their allegiance. Once having passed the hurdle of gaining your recommendation, their credit increases tenfold. Thus, those gentlemen who are hidden away in retirement like coiled dragons and reclusive phoenixes are all desirous of receiving a good name and establishing their worth with Your Honor.
>
> I pray that your Honor does not pride himself on association with the rich and noble nor scorn the poor and lowly. Then, if among your many guests there would be a Mao Sui, should I but get a chance to show the tip of my head, I shall be that man. I am a commoner from Longxi and have drifted here to Jingzhou. At fifteen, I was fond of swordsmanship and ranged broadly in search of employment with various lords. At thirty, I became an accomplished litterateur and contacted successively a number of high officers. Although I am not quite a six-footer, I am braver than ten thousand men. Princes, dukes, and high ministers admit that I have moral courage and high principles. This, then, has been my

past spiritual biography. How could I venture not to explain it fully to Your Lordship? …

As for my own writings, I have accumulated a large number of scrolls. Although I flatter myself that you will deign to look at them, I fear that these "insect carvings" and trivial exercises will not suit Your Honor's taste…. May you extend your blessings to me in my lowly station, greatly encouraging and rewarding me. It all depends on how Your Lordship views the matter.[112]

白聞天下談士相聚而言曰:「生不用萬戶侯,但願一識韓荊州。」何令人之景慕,一至於此耶!豈不以有周公之風,躬吐握之事,使海內豪俊奔走而歸之,一登龍門,則聲譽十倍,所以龍盤鳳逸之士,皆欲收名定價於君侯。願君侯不以富貴而驕之,寒賤而忽之,則三千賓中有毛遂,使白得穎脫而出,即其人焉。白隴西布衣,流落楚漢。十五好劍術,遍干諸侯;三十成文章,歷抵卿相。雖長不滿七尺,而心雄萬夫。王公大人,許與氣義。此疇曩心跡,安敢不盡於君侯哉?…

至於製作,積成卷軸,則欲塵穢視聽。恐彫蟲小技,不合大人。若賜觀芻蕘,請給紙墨,兼之書人,然後退掃閒軒,繕寫呈上。庶青萍、結綠,長價於薛、卞之門。…幸惟下流,大開獎飾,惟君侯圖之。

AN INTERLUDE

Chapter 22. La matière de Li Bo: An Epistemology

```
JAY These are the hot sheets?
```

Kay pulls a copy of the National Inquirer from the stand and gives the guy a buck.

```
KAY Best damn investigative reporting on
the planet. But hey, go ahead, read the
New York Times if you want. They get lucky
sometimes.
```

— *Men in Black*

Fig. 15. Screenshot from *Men in Black*.[113]

La matière de Bretagne, or the Matter of Britain, is the medieval lore-corpus of Arthur and the others, of Llyr and Lear, Gogmagog, their mythopoeia, the Grail. Information that has been lost from later historians' accounts.[114] In the above scene from *Men in Black,* Agents Jay and Kay are seeking information on an alien landing, data not available to the uptown press. Kay knows where to look: the tabloids. In fact, the *National Inquirer* takes them right to the site, and they work their magic there. (We like the *New York Times* well enough — after all, they keep up with Li Bo.[115] But they have a rather coarse sense of time.)

Like these two Black Men, we find our best leads on Li Bo in the extraterrestrial. Like this story of four celestials who walk into a bar:

> A Daoist ran a wine shop in Chengdu. Four men with fine silk hats and goosefoot staffs used to visit. Each time they'd drink dipper after dipper of wine until they had drunk more than a thousand liters, and they'd always pay their bill. They loved talking about Sun Simiao 孫思邈,[116] King of Medicines, who'd lived a hundred years before.
>
> Someone reported this to the magistrate, who ordered a special investigation. One day when they'd appeared, the magistrate stole over to the wine shop with a few followers. As he watched, the four men came prancing out and bowed twice, talking among themselves. They turned to look at each other, then rose leisurely into the sky, leaving only purple ashes and four staffs by their bar seats. They never appeared again.
>
> At that time the Bright Emperor was fond of Dao, so the magistrate submitted a report on the matter. In response the Emperor issued a proclamation, calling for the late Master Sun, King of Medicines, to be summoned. When the Emperor asked him, Sun replied, "They were Li Bo and the stars of the Wine Constellation, the highest level of immortal. Whenever they come to the human realm, they go everywhere drinking wine. They especially like central Sichuan."[117]

Now, when we pick up any text, we waive our rights to nonfiction. But it's not just that words are unrepentantly mendacious — and who would ever hold that against them? — it's that the *matière de Li Bo* is not fundamentally material. His life is peopled with immortals and with the Queen Mother of the West,[118]

> Clothed in rainbow, trailing a wide belt,
> I go drifting up to Heaven.
> The Queen Mother invites me to her Cloud Terrace,

and the immortal Wei Shuqing and I exchange a formal bow.[119]

> 霓裳曳廣帶，飄拂升天行
> 邀我登雲臺，高揖衛叔卿。

it traffics in the miraculous,

> Early in life I drank the elixir and was freed from worldly attachments,
> I harmonized the energies of body-mind and for the first time attained Dao.[120]

> 早服還丹無世情，琴心三疊道初成。

and culminates in drunken apotheosis, when Li Bo, out in a small boat, is so enamored by the water-moon — what we would call the moon's reflection in the river — that he reaches out to embrace her, he appears to have drowned, and he ascends to the Heavens. Three centuries later, Mei Yaochen 梅堯臣 (1002–60) tells the story:

> Under the Stone Quarry moon, I met Li Bo, the Banished Immortal,
> wrapped in brocade, sitting in a fishing boat at night.
> Drunk, in love with the moon hanging inside the river,
> playing with the moon, he stretched out his hands and fell overboard.
> He couldn't have tumbled into the wet mouth of a river dragon,
> he must have mounted a whale and risen to the azure Heavens.[121]

> 採石月下逢謫仙，夜披錦袍坐釣船
> 醉中愛月江底懸，以手弄月身翻然
> 不應暴落飢蛟涎，便當騎鯨上青天

This world is all swoop and soar:

> Touching Heaven, I pluck the Gourd Star,
> entranced, enraptured, I forget my home.
> I run my hand through the Milky Way
> and get tangled in the Weaving Maiden's loom.[122]

> 捫天摘匏瓜，恍惚不憶歸
> 舉手弄清淺，誤攀織女機。

It flows ever outward and resolves back into itself ceaselessly:

> Wild bamboo split the azure haze,
> a waterfall, in flight, hangs on an emerald peak. [123]

> 野竹分青靄，飛泉挂碧峰。

There is nothing ordinary here, only marvel. And thus it is hardly extraordinary that Li Bo appear in dream to men of the next dynasty:

> The retired official Zhang Zi copied out Li Bo's poems with perfect reverence. Once as he dreamed, Li Bo suddenly descended from the Heavens to discuss poetry with him. Zhang Zi wrote a song to commemorate it, part of which says:

> High Heaven knows I'm always thinking of that man,
> and made him come to the human realm that I could see him in this dream.[124]

> 上天知我憶其人，使向人間夢中見

And it is entirely reasonable that Li Bo might be seen, long after he has joined the moon in water, by people with keen eyes:

> Han Yu used to say that Li Bo attained immortality and left the world. In the early 800s a traveler from Beihai saw Li Bo

and a Daoist priest on a high mountainside, laughing and talking the longest time. Presently they were enveloped by a dark blue mist, and the priest hopped on a red dragon and set off. Li Bo roused himself, took a couple of big strides, and jumped aboard. The two of them rode the dragon off to the east.[125]

What is this Li Bo, then, whose presence creates this world? The Daoist sage Zhuangzi had already described him a thousand years before his birth:

> The great swamps may burn, but they cannot scorch him. The great rivers may freeze, but they cannot chill him. Fierce lightning may shatter the mountains and wind quake the seas, but they cannot alarm him. This kind of man rides cloud energies, mounts the sun and moon, and roams beyond the Four Seas. The transformations of birth and death don't affect him, so how could mere benefit and harm?[126]

In the centuries after Zhuangzi, this presence came to be called a *xian* 仙 or immortal.[127] We've already met four of them in a Sichuanese wine shop. Here are some of their other qualities and actions:

> When on earth, they often live in mountains.
> Riding the elements, they rise and descend at will.
> They roam the whole universe, visible and invisible.
> The female are often more powerful than the male.[128]
> They live an indeterminable length of time, perhaps as long as Heaven-and-Earth.[129]
> They are unharmed by elements of the physical world.
> They cure the ailments of both humans and the natural world.
> They are rare, but hundreds of biographies exist.[130]
> You can become one.[131]

Their physical attributes vary in time and circumstance.[132] Here is how they appeared to the early Ming painter Shang Xi 商喜:

LI BO UNKEMPT

Fig. 16. Four Immortals Saluting the Star-Deity Longevity.¹³³

And to Yan Hui 顏輝 about the year 1300:

Fig. 17. The transmission of the Dao to Lü Dongbin.¹³⁴

So we might say of Li Bo that "his poetry doesn't seem to come from the human realm. Is he, then, fully divine?"¹³⁵ He's not telling. But certainly by normal human standards he seems to be having much too much of a good time, to drink too much, to swagger too joyfully, to delight in his self-presentation.[136] To roam and roam.

And where does Li Bo roam? Someone once asked him. He answered with this poem:

In the mountains, replying to a man of the world

You ask me why I would lodge at Emerald Mountain.
I smile and do not reply, my heart at ease in itself.
Peach blossoms, flowing water, gone out of sight.
There are heavens and earths other than the human.[137]

山中答俗人

問餘何意棲碧山，笑而不答心自閒
桃花流水窅然去，別有天地非人間

By now we can see that this isn't just a nature poem, nor some "state of mind."[138] Concealed in Li Bo's silence are the vibrant, myriad dimensions of the immortals, a grimoire of the world of form, appearance, transformation, and disappearance.[139]

How does the immortal Li Bo abide in the human world? In the 1984 movie *National Lampoon's Bachelor Party* the young heroes set themselves this task: how do you get a living mule through the hotel lobby, up the elevator, and into the room? The solution: disguise it as a mule, in a two-person mule suit from the days of vaudeville.

So too Li Bo, an immortal disguising himself as an immortal.

Fig. 18. Two-person mule suit.[140]

A note on translation:
We've seen how Master Sun, King of Medicines, claims that Li Bo is an immortal, a *xian* 仙. But in English an immortal is someone who never dies. So this translation is *prima facie* incorrect, since a *xian* is like everything else in China, even Heaven and Earth — it arises, it frolics, it dissolves. The common form of the graph, 仙, shows a man 人 standing beside a mountain 山 — it's a pictograph that combines two other pictographs. Apt enough. But the original graph was written 僊, a man 人 beside 䙴, "ascension." So a better translation for immortal might be "ascendant."[141] And the earliest attested usage of xian is as a man at an eighth-century BCE banquet, drunk, rising to dance a bit inappropriately.[142]

Many people in Taoist studies prefer "transcendent," because the *xian* is unbound by worldly concerns. But China's is an utterly immanentist culture — there's no where else to go.

Rob Campany gets around all this in an elegant way, speaking not of deathlessness but of "living as long as Heaven and Earth." And how long is that? And what happens then?

Chapter 23. "Lines on the Flying Dragon"

First, this bit from the *Historical Records* of Sima Qian (ca. 100 BCE):

> The Yellow Emperor extracted copper from Mount Head and with it cast a caldron at the base of Thorn Mountain. As soon as the caldron was completed, a dragon with pendulous chin whiskers descended to greet the Emperor. The Emperor mounted it, and some seventy of his officials and palace ladies mounted after him. Then the dragon ascended. The remaining lesser officials, who had not been able to mount the dragon, grabbed its whiskers, but the whiskers gave way and they fell, dragging down with them the Yellow Emperor's bow.[143]

Then Li Bo:

> Lines on the flying dragon, poem one
>
> The Yellow Emperor cast a caldron at Thorn Mountain,
> distilled the elixir,
> and the elixir became yellow gold.
> He mounted a flying dragon and ascended to the realm of Great Purity.
> But the sadness of clouds like thoughts of the sea bring men to lamentation,
> and the colored faces of the palace women are like flowers
> as they wave their hands like a whirlwind, as they rise into evening's purple glow,
> following the wind, indulging their bodies, boarding the phoenix cart,
> boarding the phoenix cart to go serve the Yellow Emperor.
> Rambling and roaming the blue-green Heaven,
> this unspeakable pleasure.[144]

飛龍引 二首

黃帝鑄鼎于荊山
煉丹砂
丹砂成黃金
騎龍飛上太清家
雲愁海思令人嗟
宮中彩女顏如花
飄然揮手凌紫霞
從風縱體登鸞車
登鸞車,侍軒轅
遨游青天中
其樂不可[145]

Lines on the Flying Dragon, poem two

The waters of Caldron Lake flow leisurely and pure,
when the Yellow Emperor left, his bow and sword remained,
the ancient stories say he left them in this place.
Among the palace women are many flowered faces.
They ride phoenixes through flying smoke, never returning,
mounting dragons, climbing up to Heaven to repair Heaven's Boundary,
repairing Heaven's Boundary, hearing Heaven's speech,
resplendent cloud-river carriages bear the Jade Women,
bear the Jade Women up to the Purple Emperor,
and then the Purple Emperor bestows upon them the moon rabbit elixir of eternal life.
They live longer than Heaven, exhausting the light of sun, moon and stars,
below they see the Queen Mother of the West and her deathless pool.
My eyebrows are already white, like the sound of wind through autumn fog.[146]

其二

鼎湖流水清且閑
軒轅去時有弓劍
古人傳道留其間
後宮嬋娟多花顏
乘鸞飛煙亦不還
騎龍攀天造天關
造天關,聞天語
長雲河車載玉女
載玉女,過紫皇
紫皇乃賜白兔所搗之藥方
後天而老凋三光
下視瑤池見王母
蛾眉蕭颯如秋霜

Chapter 24. The Moister South

From the South, a thousand years before Li Bo, comes this story of the poet Song Yu and his king.

> The King of Chu and Song Yu went roaming in the wetlands of Cloud Dream, where they spied a fine building in the morning clouds. There was an energy in it, a certain *qi* 氣, at every moment endlessly changing. The King asked, "What is this energy?"[147] Song Yu replied, "In the past a former king went roaming in the Gaotang Pavilion. During the day he fell asleep and dreamed he saw a woman. She said, 'I am the fourth daughter of the God of Heaven. My name is Lady Turquoise. I died young and was given the terraces of Shaman Mountain as my fief. I heard that the King has come roaming. I would like to share his pillow and sleeping mat.'"[148]

Elsewhere Song Yu finishes the story:[149]

> The King delighted in her. As she left, she said, "I dwell in the sunny-yang side of Shaman Mountain, at the precipice of High Hill. At dawn I am the morning clouds, at dusk the pouring rain. Morning and morning, evening and evening, below the Terraces of Yang."
>
> At dawn the King looked for her, and it was just as she had said. So he had a temple built there called "Morning Clouds."

They never met again. Here is Li Bo's poem:

Inspiration: poem one of eight

Lady Turquoise, daughter of the God of Heaven,
essence of five colors transforming into morning clouds,
twists her way again into night dreams,
indifferent to the Lord of Chu.

Her brocade quilt wraps the autumn moon,
the silk bed has lost the smell of her sweet lotus.
Who can truly plumb boundless darkness?
— and not just fruitlessly repeat Song Yu's stories.[150]

感興 八首其一

瑤姬天帝女,精彩仕朝云
宛轉入宵夢,無心向楚君
錦衾抱秋月,綺席空蘭芬
茫昧竟誰測,虛傳宋玉文

China's old culture grew in the dry north, the Yellow River plains, among millet fields and tamped earth walls, heartland of Confucius, the *Five Classics,* ideals of government service.

But Song Yu and his king live in the South. Wet-rice culture, paddy fields. The Yangtze and its flooding. Humid days, warm nights, with their unfamiliar plants and fragrances.[151] A moving frontier, aboriginal peoples not fully joined to Empire, shamanic realities.

The North had its anthology of folk songs and ritual hymns, the *Classic of Poetry* (*Shijing* 詩經), stately lines of four words each, one-two, one-two. The South had its own anthology, *The Songtexts of Chu* (*Chuci* 楚辭), long lines and short, wherein we find the story of Song Yu. These poems also tell how a third-century BCE poet–shaman quit himself of the world and journeyed:

I set off at morning from the Ford of Heaven,
At evening I came to the world's western end.
Phoenixes followed me, bearing up my pennants….
Warily I drove along the banks of the Red River,
Then, beckoning the water-dragons to make a bridge for me,
I summoned the God of the West to take me over.[152]

朝發軔於天津兮,夕餘至乎西極。
鳳皇翼其承旗兮,遵赤水而容與。
麾蛟龍使梁津兮,詔西皇使涉予。

And yet the whole thing ends badly. He goes on for three hundred extravagant lines, and then in the last quatrain abruptly collapses.[153]

The *Songtexts* is important to us here for several reasons. First, its poetic expression opened a new form of literary intimacy with the divine, and many hundreds of poets entered thereby. Further, the poems' sensory opulence could never be naturalized as a classic of poetry — they remained always at the edge of gentlemen's culture, facing outwards. They survived because they could pass as literature, and indeed lyric poetry of the Tang is descendant of both northern and southern traditions, a *ménage* that began in the early centuries of the Common Era.[154]

But successful transcendence was always in jeopardy. And most every poet who attempted such a journey was unable to complete it, fell back into the ordinary.[155] Li Bo is nearly unique for being free of this legacy of failure.[156] He has no need for Song Yu's stories, he's already in the soup.[157] Even in his own longing there's never the scent of separation.[158]

IV

Five Mountains

> *My whole life I've loved to roam these great mountains.*
> 一生好入名山游
> — Li Bo

Insofar as this is a book of language, I'd like to begin this section with a look at the Chinese word "mountain," *shan* 山. As you might have guessed, a first-century dictionary points out that it's a pictograph.[159]

If you were a Neolithic plainsman farming north China, you might be put off by mountains' anomalous and anti-agricultural aspect. But because these mountains regulate clouds and rainfall, they still require some kind of skillful propitiation.[160] A century ago, Édouard Chavannes explained it best:

> Mountains, in China, are divinities. They are considered as natural powers that act in conscious manner and that can, by consequence, be made favorable by sacrifice and touched by prayer.[161]

Later, the arch-alchemist Ge Hong 葛洪 (283–343) added his view:

> There's no mountain big or small that does not have its gods and spirits. If the mountain is big, then the god is big. If the mountain is small, then the god is small.[162]

Hence he lists several reasons one might enter a mountain: "to practice Dao, compound medicines, and escape disorder" in the flat-lands.[163] Immortals dwell there, and sometimes a mountain will secrete a sacred text.[164]

But Ge Hong also warns us:

If you don't know the method (*fa* 法, the apotropaic techne) by which to enter a mountain, you will often encounter disaster. Thus the adage,
  Below Mount Hua
  white bones are scattered everywhere.¹⁶⁵

Fig. 19. Mount Hua, Huashan 華山, sacred mountain of the West.¹⁶⁶

Fig. 20. And Mount Heng 橫山, sacred mountain of the North, with a fifth-century CE temple.¹⁶⁷

Fig. 21. "Early Spring," by Guo Xi 郭熙 (ca. 1020–ca. 1090)[168]

Fig. 22. "Lofty Mount Lu," by Shen Zhou 沈周 (1427–1509)[169]

Of course these photographic images postdate Li Bo by a millennium. Even the paintings postdate him several centuries — they are a phenomenon of Song (960–1279) and later dynasties.[170] So for a view contemporaneous with him we must examine these mountains' True Forms (*zhenxing* 真形). Shih-shan Susan Huang explains:

> Broadly speaking, true form can apply to a deity, an icon, a mountain, a purified self, an internal organ, a talisman or a picture. It denotes the original shape something has as part of Dao, the inner, invisible and formless quality of an entity, in contrast to its outer, visible and concrete attributes. With a framework thus established, seeing the true form requires religious discipline and practice.[171]

This diagram is called "The Plan of the True Form of Mount Tai, the Eastern Marchmount," and it indicates the location of its hidden grotto-heavens:

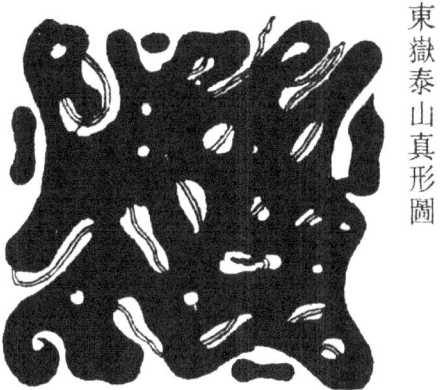

Fig. 23. The Plan of the True Form of Mount Tai, the Eastern Marchmount[172]

How were such diagrams discovered? In one account, the Queen Mother of the West transmitted them to the Martial Emperor of Han in vision.[173] But adept humans can also see them directly. Ge Hong recounts an old instruction and its result:

> "Stay in the rock chamber inside this mountain. Concentrate on the north wall. When you can see that there are characters written on the wall, you will attain Dao."
> Bo He looked at the wall for three years — only then could he see the characters. They had been carved by the Ancients, and they included "The plan of the true form of the five mountains."[174]

Thus:

> If you are destined to accomplish Dao, then enter the mountain and meditate there with sincere concentration. The mountain god himself will then open the mountain, and you will be allowed to see these writings.[175]

How many mountain gods? Each mountain, big or small, has one, says Ge Hong. And every village has a temple to their mountain. And each ruler of China wants to rule them all.[176] Still, already in the first millennium BCE, four Sacred Mountains had been identified,[177] with a dedicated name for their class, *yue* 嶽 or Marchmount.[178] Their role ever since has been to garrison, protect and regulate (*zhen* 鎮) the Empire. Imperial sacrifices were due the Marchmounts, at once worship, domination, and a request for boons.[179] Such ceremony entailed political risk, for the mountain would accept sacrifice only from a worthy ruler.[180] The Martial Emperor of Han went east to ascend Mount Tai in 110 BCE. Certainly the boon he sought was immortality. And to the four mountains of the cardinal directions, he added a necessary fifth, the Center, standing for himself.[181]

The Bright Emperor of Tang succeeded him to Mount Tai in 725. But one man living knew more about all this than he. It was Sima Chengzhen 司馬承禎 (647–735), fourth patriarch of Highest Clarity Daoism — and, it turns out, Li Bo's teacher. Sima explained that the Emperor had been sacrificing to the wrong gods — to lesser gods, not those who controlled the Marchmounts.[182]

> When the Emperor returned from performing the *feng* sacrifice at Mount Tai, he asked Sima Chengzhen, "What gods rule the Five Marchmounts?" […]
>
> He replied, "Right now all the Marchmount temples are dedicated to the gods of their slopes and forests, but these are not the true gods. Within all the Five Marchmounts are grotto-prefectures, and each has a Highest Clarity Perfected One who descends there to administer the office. Mountains and rivers, wind and rain, Yin and Yang, the processes of *qi*-energy — these are what they control. They wear the crowns

and clothing of office, and they're attended by specific numbers of divine immortals [...]."[183]

Thereupon the Emperor proclaimed that there should be a special temple to the Perfected Ones built at each of the Marchmounts.[184]

If Li Bo were a Daoist churchman, we might hear a lot from him about these deities. Instead, he tells us,

I'd shrug if all the Marchmounts fell.[185]

五岳倒為輕

He would rather roam:

Ancient Airs #41

Mornings I play in the Ocean of Purple Sand,
evenings I drape myself in a skirt of cinnabar dusk.
Waving my hand, snapping off a branch
to brush away the western sun,
reclining on a cloud, I roam the farthest borderlands.
My white jade face has already passed through a thousand
 years of frost,
floating floating across the boundless.
Now I prostrate to the Highest Emperor.
He sets me roaming into Great Simplicity,
and pours deathless wine for me in jade cups.
Once I've dined, ten-thousand years go by —
why bother returning to my old home?
I'll go forever, following the distant winds,
and float off carelessly beyond the Heavens.[186]

古風 其四十一

朝弄紫泥海，夕披丹霞裳
揮手折若木，拂此西日光

雲臥游八極，玉顏已千霜
飄飄入無倪，稽首祈上皇
呼我游太素，玉杯賜瓊漿
一餐歷萬歲，何用還故鄉
永隨長風去，天外恣飄揚

Chapter 25. Tai, Sacred Mountain of the East

Roaming Mount Tai (poem 2 of 6)

Clear dawn. I ride a white deer
straight up the mountain to Heaven's Gate.
A gorgeous feathered man stands there,
the pupils of his eyes are square.
I'm clutching at the hanging moss, I start to speak,
when he disappears behind a bank of blue-green cloud.
Something flutters down between these sharp cliffs,
it's a text from him in ancient bird-track script.
I cannot read it.
I sigh three times.
The master I follow has not yet returned.[187]

游泰山六首 其二

清曉騎白鹿，直上天門山
山際逢羽人，方瞳好容顏
捫蘿欲就語，卻掩青雲關
遺我鳥跡書，飄然落岩間
其字乃上古，讀之了不閑
感此三嘆息，從師方未還

Tai 泰. It just means big. The Big Mountain. And so a treatise from the Daoist Canon begins:

> Among the ten-thousand mountains of this world, the Five Marchmounts are the greatest, barring none. Among the Five Marchmounts of this world, Mount Tai is the greatest, barring none.[188]

The Wikipedia describes its ascent, which started two billion years ago:

Taishan now rises abruptly from the vast plain of central Shandong. Geologically, it is a tilted fault-block mountain, higher to the south than north […].

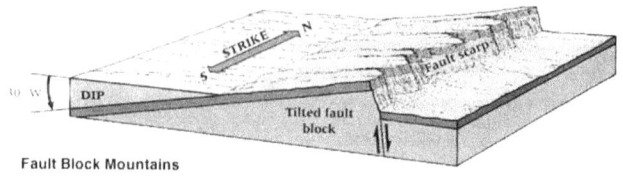

Fig. 24. A tiled fault block.[189]

The gneiss which emerged in the Taishan region is the foundation for all of North China. Six streams flow from the summit, their water renowned for its extremely low mineral content, slight acidity (pH = 6.3) and relatively high oxygen content (6.4 milligrams per liter [mg/l]).[190]

From above, it looks something like this:

Fig. 25. Mount Taishan.[191]

Li Bo visits in 742, seventeen years after the Bright Emperor.[192] He ascends the mountain on a white deer, "that conveyance preferred by the Perfected Ones when they must travel on earth."[193]

Straightaway he debouches from the first thousand-fold stairway into the Gateway to Heaven, its pines covered in hanging lichen.[194] Édouard Chavannes explains:

> By the name "Heaven's Gateway" we designate those passages that appear, when one views them from below, as gateways giving access to Heaven. The most celebrated of these openings is the "Heavenly Gateway of the South," which dominates the last vertiginous flight ofstairs by which one gains access to the plateau of the summit of Taishan.[195]

Fig. 26. The stairway to the Gateway to Heaven, Mount Taishan.[196]

Fig. 27. Hanging lichen (*Usnea filipendula*).[197]

There he meets a lad with the plumage of a bird, that is, an immortal feathered for farthest flight.[198] Like this youth, recovered from a Han dynasty tomb:

Fig. 28. Bronze statue of a boy from a Han Dynasty tomb.[199]

The pupils of his eyes are square. Laozi, too, had square pupils, all the immortals do. It means you're a thousand years old.[200]

The boy gives Li Bo a document in bird-track writing. That's how China became literate, when "the ancient scribe Cangjie 倉頡 looked at the tracks of birds and then knew how to write,"[201] how to represent the world in script. Some suggest that Li Bo's bird-track document was written in the "small seal script" of 220 BCE.[202] Here's an example of that script from Li Bo's kinsman and literary executor, Li Yangbing 李陽冰, the "Document in a Thousand Words" (*Qianzi wen* 千字文).

Fig. 29. "Document in a Thousand Words" (*Qianzi wen* 千字文) by Li Yangbing 李陽冰.[203]

But that script is immysterious — its lineage is entirely human, transmitted between historical teacher and student, it is still practiced today. Much more likely is that Li Bo's text was written in a magical script that can only be read from the inside, wherein Daoist talismans abide:

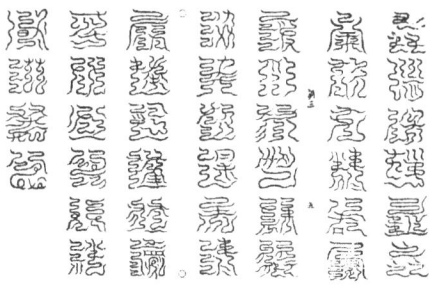

Fig. 30. Daoist talisman.[204]

Chapter 26. Heng, Sacred Mountain of the South

At the river, seeing off the Daoist priestess Chu Sanqing on her way to the sacred mountain of the south

The Daoist priestess of Wu River
ties a lotus flower headscarf.
Her rainbow skirt untouched by rain,
fantastic as the goddess's of ancient dream.
Wearing shoes that shrink distance,
she skims across the waves, raising the finest mist.
Gone to the sacred mountain of the south to seek immortals,
surely she'll see Lady Wei![205]

江上送女道士褚三清游南嶽

吳江女道士，頭戴蓮花巾
霓裳不濕雨，特異陽台神
足下遠游履，凌波生素塵
尋仙向南嶽，應見魏夫人

The sacred mountain of the south, the Southern Marchmount, Hengshan 衡山, in present-day Hunan. Not a solitary mountain peak like the Marchmount of the East but a hundred-mile range of hills, a region numinous long before the fact, later infused with Imperial, Daoist and Buddhist structures, now a tourist destination.

Fig. 31. Mount Heng.[206]

Yes, but who is Lady Wei, and how did she get there?[207] If Li Bo's teacher Sima Chengzhen is the Twelfth Patriarch of Highest Clarity Daoism, Lady Wei is the First.[208] Born Wei Huacun 魏華存 in 252 CE, "from youth she loved the Dao, longing intently to become a divine immortal"[209] and practicing in her father's Celestial Masters (*Tianshi* 天師) lineage. Some thirty years after her legal and social death in 334, she received thirty-one scrolls from the Immortals, which she transmitted in vision to Yang Xi 楊羲 (330–386). These became the root texts of Highest Clarity, and Yang its Second Patriarch and first public voice.[210]

Yang Xi and his successors dwelt south of Nanjing on Mao Mountain, Maoshan 茅山. But by early Tang Lady Wei had manifested robustly in the Southern Marchmount, some 500 miles to the southwest, drawing the same intensity of devotion as the Queen Mother of the West. There, from her Flying Altar (*feiliu tan* 飛流壇), Lady Wei ascended bodily to the Heavens, a deity becoming a yet more subtle form of herself. And it is here that she returns to earth.

The goddess, that site of ascension, and her human disciples emerge together: each creates the other. So just as a holy site can be discovered, it can be lost, through neglect or obscuration.[211] We might expect that in her ascension Lady Wei became purely divine, leaving her body behind. But this assumes her coarse human body were an impediment to that divinity, rather than its instantiation and instrument of manifestation in the earthly realm. She was, after all, already divine. Her ascension, then, is a matter of refinement within a continuity of increasingly subtle modes of existence, yet also a quantum leap to a new function-form in the Heavens — this is a paradoxical universe, both granular and smooth.[212]

And who is Chu Sanqing, now seeking Madame Wei in this south mountain?[213] We can see her now only through this poem — everything else about her has been forgotten for more than a thousand years. Li Bo tells us that she is a Highest Clarity priestess — thus in Lady Wei's tradition of women adepts — and from Wu River, near Soochow. Her name Sanqing 三清 means Three Clarities and refers to the three pure realms of the great Daoist deities.[214] She wears the traditional lotus headscarf of her religious profession.[215] Today she might look more like this:

Fig. 32. A present-day Daoist priestess.[216]

But Li Bo sees in her skirt all the colors of rainbows. That skirt belongs to another god, the Sun, who sang to his consort, a thousand years earlier in the great poetry collection *Songtexts of Chu*:

> Your beauty and music are so enchanting
> that I forget I must leave you and rise into the sky.
> Let the flute sound! Blow the pan-pipes!
> See the priestesses, how skilled and lovely,
> whirling and dipping like birds in flight.
> In my cloud-coat and rainbow-skirt,
> grasping my bow I soar high up in the sky.[217]

More: the "goddess of ancient dream" of line four is the Spirit of Yang Terrace, wetlands consort of the King of Chu, whom we have already met in "The Moister South." Another poem from the same *Songtexts* tells how they met once in dream, but only once.

More: half a millennium later, and inspired by that rhapsody (*fu* 賦) of King and shaman lover, another poet met an ondine by the river's edge. He describes her extravagantly, line after line, in words that Li Bo could not resist:[218]

> She wears embroidered shoes that shrink distance
> and trails a skirt of silken dew,
> exuding the full fragrance of secret orchids.

踐遠遊之文履,曳露綃之輕裾,微幽蘭之芳藹兮

and

> Skimming across the waves with tiny steps,
> her gauze stockings raise the finest mist.

凌波微步,羅襪生塵

But as this poem ends, the deity does not abandon him, nor will the poet turn from her.

In response to these images, and breathing in their fragrance, the great theorist Yan Yu 嚴羽 (1191–1241) asks us to consider who the priestess celebrated in Li Bo's poem might actually be. He concludes, "If you look at the middle four lines, Chu Sanqing must have the same qualities as Yu Xuanji 魚玄機 (844–868)."[219]

And who is Yu Xuanji? Yes, another Daoist priestess of late Tang, but also a courtesan, wild poet, consort of the great boudoir lyricist Wen Tingyun 溫庭筠 (812–870), free roamer.[220] She lived a hundred years after Li Bo, but was, nonetheless, the heroine of his poem.

Chapter 27. Hua, Sacred Mountain of the West

> Song from Cloud Terrace of the Western Mountain, seeing off my friend Cinnabar Hill
>
> Western Mountain, soaring, lofty, you're only great vigor,
> Yellow River, like silk thread flowing from the border of Heaven,
> Yellow River, after ten-thousand miles you brush this mountain and turn,
> you're the hub of a great whirlpool, and the land thunders round you.
> Splendid radiant life-energies, your tangle of five colors,
> only once in a thousand years does a Sage Emperor of such clarity arise.
>
> Once the River Spirit roared, snapped her fingers and split the mountain in two,
> then she spat out flood waves that still shoot as far as the Eastern Sea.
> With her hands she carved out emerald cliffs and cinnabar valleys,
> leaving three great peaks behind the summit that now seem on the verge of collapse.
>
> Once the White Emperor churned the primal life-energy,
> made lotuses from rocks and terraces from clouds.
> These cloud terraces, linked by dark passageways,
> now hide the deathless master Cinnabar Hill.
> Brightstar comes down from Heaven to sweep the floors for him,
> divine Hemp Maiden lightly scratches his back with her talons.

Our Imperial Sovereign governs the economy of Heaven and Earth,
Cinnabar Hill talks Heaven's ways with Heaven's Sovereign.
Coming and going from the palace, his body radiates light,
from fairy islands in the east he returns to this Western Mountain.

Should we receive the jade elixir, we'll drink it with the ancients,
mount two grass dragons, and fly up to Heaven.[221]

西嶽雲台歌送丹丘子

西嶽崢嶸何壯哉，黃河如絲天際來。
黃河萬里觸山動，盤渦轂轉秦地雷。
榮光休氣紛五彩，千年一清聖人在。
巨靈咆哮擘兩山，洪波噴箭射東海。
三峰卻立如欲摧，翠崖丹谷高掌開。
白帝金精運元氣，石作蓮花雲作臺。
雲臺閣道連窈冥，中有不死丹丘生。
明星玉女備洒掃，麻姑搔背指爪輕。
我皇手把天地戶，丹丘談天與天語。
九重出入生光輝，東來蓬萊復西歸。
玉漿儻惠故人飲，騎二茅龍上天飛。

Fig. 33. The western summit of Mount Hua.[222]

Huashan 華山, sacred mountain of the west. To reach the top, men of Tang drove metal spikes into the rock. In their current visage:

Fig. 34. The thousand feet cliff of Mount Hua.[223]

And there is also the river, and its love entanglement with the mountain — not just any river, but the Yellow River (Huanghe 黃河), in whose lower basin Chinese civilization made its birth. It had flowed nearly due south for several hundred miles, but where it meets Huashan, not far from the Tang capital, it abruptly changes course and heads east to the sea. Here, with Chang'an bearing its modern name, Xi'an:

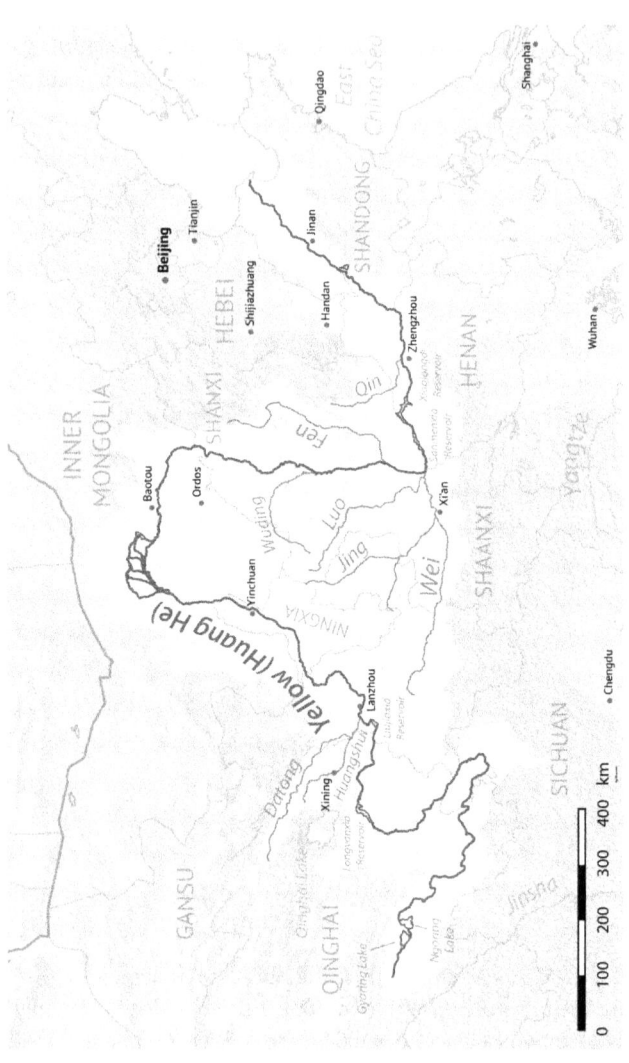

Fig. 35. The Yellow River basin.[224]

Chapter 28. "Linked Verse on Changing the Name of Nine Sons Mountain to Nine Flowers Mountain"

Li Bo's preface to the poem:

> Nine Sons Mountain lies in the southern part of Qingyang County. The mountain is several hundred meters tall, and at its top are nine peaks that look like lotus flowers. I consulted charts to ascertain its name, but found nothing reliable. When the Grand Historian went roaming south, it seems he didn't note it.[225] Its story is absent from the tales of elders and also omitted from the records of noted worthies. Though numinous immortals frequent it, one rarely hears poems or rhapsodies of them. I therefore excised its old name and replaced it in the Registry with the entry "Nine Flowers."
>
> At that time I was seeking Dao along the Yangtze and Huai Rivers and rested in the home of Xiahou Huai.[226] We opened up the shutters and didn't do our hair, just sat looking off at the distant pines and snow. I wrote some linked verse with two or three fellows, one of which I pass on now:

The Very Marvelous splits into yin and yang,
this sacred mountain opens into nine flowers. (Li Bo)
Layered hills retard the morning sun,
cliff tops brightening in the young light. (Gao Ji)
Snow drifts glisten in ravines as dark as yin,
snow gusts fly from a yang-bright ridge. (Wei Quanyu)
All colors shine from the jade-white trees,
hazy, distant, feathered men. (Li Bo)[227]

改九子山為九華山聯句 并序

青陽縣南有九子山。山高數千丈。上有九峰如蓮花。按圖徵名。無所依據。太史公南游。略而不書。事絕古老之口。復闕名賢之紀。雖靈仙往復。而賦詠罕聞。予乃削其舊號。加以九華之目。時訪道江漢。憩于夏侯回之堂。開檐岸幘。坐眺松雪。因與二三子聯句。傳之將來。

妙有分二氣，靈山開九華
層標遏遲日，半壁明朝霞
積雪曜陰壑，飛流噴陽崖
青熒玉樹色，縹緲羽人家

"Feathered men," that is, immortals.

The Very Marvelous, a Marvelous Something (*miaoyou* 妙有) — let's ask Laozi's great commentator Wang Bi 王弼 (226–249) about this:

> One is the number of beginning, thus also the ultimate state of things. When you call it Marvelous Something, you're wanting to speak of Something, but you can't see its shape, so it isn't Something. When you call it Marvelous, you're wanting to speak of Nothing, but things come out from it to be born, so it's not Nothing. Thus you call it Something. This, then, is the Something that is amidst Nothing. It is called "Marvelous Something" or "the Very Marvelous."[228]

A Song dynasty geography reports:

> This mountain is strange and luxuriant. Its tops protrude through the cloud layer, its peaks unusual in appearance. They are nine in number, so it was called Nine Sons Mountain.
>
> At the summit are several acres of pond, and rice paddyfields that can support a thousand people. The ponds hold fish, of which the largest are more than half a meter long. They have large heads and ruddy tails, red fins and crimson

bellies. When people want to see them, they poke a stick in the water, and then the fish jump. Or they throw food into the pond, and when the fish have finished eating, they hide again under water.[229]

Fig. 36. A view of the multiple peaks of Mount Jiuhua.[230]

Fig. 37. Treasure Hall of the Great Hero (*Daxiong baodian* 大雄宝殿) at Mount Jiuhua.[231]

Chapter 29. Mount Lu

A Lu Mountain song that I sent to Empty Boat Lu

I've always been that crazy man taunting Confucius,
"Ah Phoenix, too bad you're too good."
In this dawn I grab a green jade staff, set out from Yellow Crane Tower
to find immortals in the Five Mountains,
who cares how long it takes?
My whole life I've loved these mountains.

Mount Lu! You're more resplendent than anywhere below the Southern Dipper,
Folding Screen Mountain, your nine panels are made of cloud brocade,
and Boyang Lake, bright shadows of black-azure brilliance,
Gold Watchtowers, two great peaks sprouting out before you,
the Silver Stream that hangs off Three Stone Bridges
gazes at the waterfall at Incense Burner Mountain,
a crowd of whirling peaks rising into deep blue sky,
emerald shadows and red morning clouds reflect the rising sun.
However far they fly, birds never get across these heavens.

If you reach the summit, you'll see the border between heaven and earth
and how the vast vast Yangtze flows off with no return.
Yellow clouds ten-thousand miles, the color of driving wind,
white waves at Nine River Junction, mountains of flowing snow.

I love making this Lu Mountain song,
it happened only because of the mountain!

Each time I peer into the Stone Mirror, it purifies my heart
 and mind,
the places ancients walked engulfed now in dark green moss.

This morning I have drunk the elixir. I'm freed from worldly
 feelings,
body-mind in harmony. For the first time I am complete in
 Dao.
In the distance an immortal in the colored clouds,
a lotus in his hand, he's off to pay homage at the Jade Palace.
We'll tryst in the boundless unknown,
and Lu the Rambler and I will meet and roam Great Clarity
 together.[232]

廬山謠寄廬侍御虛舟

影落明湖青黛光，金闕前開二峰長
銀河倒挂三石梁，香爐瀑布遙相望
回崖沓嶂凌蒼蒼
翠影紅霞映朝日，鳥飛不到吳天長
登高壯觀天地間，大江茫茫去不還
黃雲萬里動風色，白波九道流雪山
好為廬山謠，興因廬山發
閑窺石鏡清我心，謝公行處蒼苔沒
早服還丹無世情，琴心三疊道初成
遙見仙人彩云里，手把芙蓉朝玉京
先期汗漫九垓上，愿接廬敖游太清

Li Bo roamed Mount Lu in 758. Visitors had begun coming two
and three centuries earlier, noting that

> its peach and plum trees were already fully grown. […]
> [Soon] tea was planted along its secluded streams. The *Classic of Tea* (*Chajing* 茶經) has recorded the tools necessary for
> this method of cultivation.[233]

Seven hundred years after Li Bo, this is how Mount Lu appeared to the painter Shen Zhou 沈周 (1427–1509):

Fig. 38. Mount Lu, by Shen Zhou 沈周 (1427–1509).[234]

After another seven hundred years it appeared like this to Zhang Daqian 張大千 (Chang Dai-chien, 1899–1983):

Fig. 39. A part of "Panorama of Mount Lu" by Zhang Daqian 張大千 (1981).[235]

At an earlier time Li Bo had said to Mount Lu:

> You and I will meet again — I would not dare foreswear this oath. The cinnabar cliffs and green gorges will reflect this vow in their divinity.[236]

An Interlude

Chapter 30. Jade Woman Hotspring

Written at Jade Woman Hotspring near the walled city of Ying
A Jade Woman riding a chariot cast herself into this spring.[237]

A divine woman died in this remote dark place,
now a river flows from her hotspring.
Beneath the earth yin and yang fuse as burning coal,
this sacred spring opens from their transformation.
A cinnabar fire glistens here,
and white smoke rises through the sand.
Pearls bubble up and over the clear-sky moon,
its white mirror enveloped by empty Heaven.
Life-energy floats in that river, orchid fragrance everywhere,
colors that swell like peach blossoms.
When you know their essence, the ten-thousand things aren't separate —
just as, underground, this river links up the seven Southland lakes.
It heals all sickness,
it restores balance to Dao.
You can clean your robes in its pure waters,
and bless your unbound hair in its steam.
The river spreads through the ancient realm of Chu,
dividing so it may water the fields of ancient kings.
The hotspring should receive a visit from the Bright Emperor,
it doesn't matter that it's rustic and far away!
And you yourself can follow any river to the ocean,
for even tiny brooks will be carried in homage to the sea.[238]

安州應城玉女湯作
神女殁幽境，湯池流大川

陰陽結炎炭，造化開靈泉
地底爍朱火，沙傍歊素煙
沸珠躍晴月，皎鏡函空天
氣浮蘭芳滿，色漲桃花然
精覽萬殊入，潛行七澤連
愈疾功莫尚，變盈道乃全
濯纓掬清泚，晞髮弄潺湲
散下楚王國，分澆宋玉田
可以奉巡幸，奈何隔窮偏
獨隨朝宗水，赴海輸微涓

A fifth-century CE geographer writes:

> There's a hot spring in Hui Marsh. In winter months, while you're still some miles away, you can see white *qi*-energy floating like smoke, shining up and down and shaped like fine silk threads. There's also the form of two shafts of a chariot. It's said that long ago a Jade Woman riding a chariot cast herself into this spring. These days people sometimes see a young woman there, lovely of appearance, idling to and fro.[239]

Today it looks a lot like this:

Fig. 40. The current site of the Huaqing Pool.[240]

This is the Yangtze River basin. This is the ancient kingdom of Chu, the moister South, land of seven lakes, where the King met and lost a shaman lover, and Song Yu recorded it in *The Song-texts of Chu*.

And what is this Jade Woman? And what will happen when you meet her? Well, she could be so many things. In the Daoist text *Zhen'gao* 真誥 she and her many siblings descend bearing texts, splendid young women with yellow skirts, or dressed in green outfits, "like flying birds in their appearance" (*zhuang ru feiniao* 狀如飛鳥).[241] Or they may attend to the needs of the Perfected.

In those milieux we only see her manifestation as a serving girl, or as serving girls by the dozen, sure, she can do that. But actually she is made of light, which is the essence of jade, though not a mineral jade, and her clothing is light as well, but not a light-of-this-world. To tell the truth, she's an immortal herself, in one incarnation the goddess of Mount Tai, in another the Mother of Dao (*daomu* 道母), and so the mother of Laozi.[242]

The Bright Emperor had a fondness for the mountain hotspring of Huaqing 華清, twenty-five kilometers east of the Tang capital, where he first courted his Precious Consort. A later poet tells how:

> As springtime was cold, he bathed her at Huaqing Pool.
> Warm spring waters slid over her smooth plump skin.
> Servant girls helped her from the pool, as she was delicate and frail.
> This was the time she first received the Emperor's grace.[243]

春寒賜浴華清池，溫泉水滑洗凝脂
侍兒扶起嬌無力，始是新承恩澤時

Here's how a twenty-first-century Chinese imagines that scene:

AN INTERLUDE

Fig. 41. A statue of the Precious Consort at the Huaqing Pool complex.[244]

Chapter 31. The Grotto-Heaven

Offered to the Reverend Teacher, the Daoist Priest Gao Rugui on the completion of my ordination and his return to Beihai

Dao is hidden, can't be seen,
its divine writings stored in grotto-heavens.
For forty thousand eons my teacher
transmitted it from one generation to another.
He leaves behind a green bamboo staff,
singing as he goes, walking on purple clouds.
The mind at parting knows not near or far,
held forever in the City of Jade.[245]

奉餞高尊師如貴道士傳道籙畢歸北海

道隱不可見，靈書藏洞天
吾師四萬劫，歷世遞相傳
別杖留青竹，行歌躡紫煙
離心無遠近，長在玉京懸

Li Bo's kinsman Li Yangbing 李陽冰 collected his poems after his death, and wrote a preface to it. Here he speaks of Li Bo's departure from Court around 744:

> The Son of Heaven knew he couldn't keep Li Bo, so he bestowed gold on him and sent him off. Li Bo then went to Kaifeng, where his great-uncle Li Chongyu was Investigative Commissioner. His uncle gave him an introduction to the Daoist Master Gao of Beihai, from whom he requested an ordination register at the Laozi temple of the Purple Polestar in Ji'nan. Li Bo then planned to return to the isles of Penglai, as an immortal who rides on clouds and dwells in deathless Cinnabar Hill.[246]

We know nothing more of Master Gao Rugui,[247] although he figures in another poem of Li Bo on this event.[248] Probably Li underwent an ordination in which he received both a register of protective deities and a talisman, a *lu* 籙 and a *fu* 符. From *The Encyclopedia of Taoism*:

> The *register* records the names and attributes of the divine generals and their soldiers, whom the adept calls upon in visualizations and spells to protect himself, affect healing, and convey petitions to the otherworld. In return, the adept agrees to obey certain precepts. In effect, the adept is entering into a contract with the deities as well as the master who bestows the register.
>
> [Ordination registers may include charts], which consist of images or maps of the cosmos and the names of transcendents, and thereby act as passes for safe conduct to the otherworld.[249]

And:

> Daoist *talismans* are diagrams, conceived as a form of celestial writing, that derive their power from the matching celestial counterpart kept by the deities who bestowed them. […] The most influential Daoist account of the origins of *fu*, found in the *Zhen'gao*, relates them to a primordial form of writing that emerged with the differentiation of the Dao at the birth of the cosmos, still used by the highest gods and available to humans who have received them through proper transmission. The earliest script later became fragmented and simplified into various mortal scripts. The second primordial script, the Cloud-seal Emblems of the Eight Dragons (*balong yunzhuan zhi zhang* 八龍雲篆之章), remained unchanged and is the form used in fu.[250]

Today they still look like this:

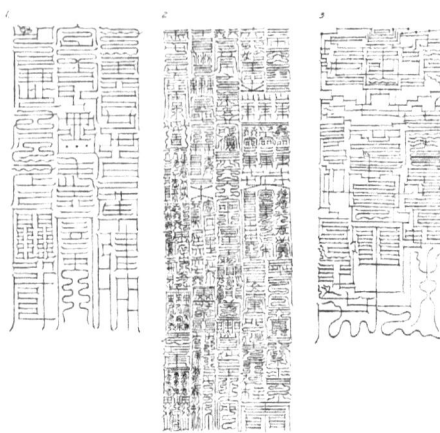

Fig. 42. Daoist talismans.[251]

Perhaps their modern equivalent, now unabashedly commerce-based, look like this:

Fig. 43. A QR code.[252]

Li Bo tells us that "Although Dao is hidden and can't be seen, its divine writings are stored in grotto-heavens (*dongtian* 洞天)." A grotto, and also a heaven, a pure land inside a grotto — what a surprise! For beneath the greatest mountains, hidden from ordinary sight, are great heavens,

> with their own suns, moons and stars, as well as the palaces of divine immortals who control blessings and chastisements

and keep the registers of life and death. This is where the Perfected Ones reside and immortal princes dispose.[253]

The alchemist Ge Hong 葛洪 (283–343) explains:

> [These grotto-heavens] all have true gods within them, and sometimes earth-bound immortals. Numinous mushrooms (*zhi* 芝) and plants grow there. But you can also avoid the great calamities of war in them, not just compound medicines.[254]

There's a grotto-heaven beneath every great mountain, and they connect underground with each other, in an invisible secret network.[255] Later, like many other numinous things, they were systematized, into ten major and thirty-six minor.[256] And like all numinous things, their life-span depended on their relationship with human attention. When that attention began to fade, after Tang, the grotto-heavens faded with it:

> By the early modern period, famous caverns had become synonymous with literary outings, and only artificial caves made within decorative mountain landscapes in urban gardens preserved their memory.[257]

The same Ge Hong explains what it means that Li Bo's teacher leaves a green bamboo staff behind. The story: A certain Fei Changfang meets a thaumaturge who lives in a gourd. His only name is Sire Gourd. Fei serves him properly and is invited into the gourd to receive further teachings. Thereupon:

> Sire Gourd told Fei Changfang, "I will leave on such-and-such a day. Can you go with me?" "I want to go, and I will not go back on my word," Fei replied, "but I wish it were possible to cause my family and loved ones not to realize that I left them [to practice esoteric arts with my teacher]. Is there a way to do this?"

> "Easy," said the Sire. He selected a green bamboo staff and gave it to Fei, with the instructions, "Take this piece of bamboo back home with you. Say that you are ill. Place this staff in the spot where you were lying, and then sneak back here."
>
> Fei did as instructed. After he had left, his family perceived that Fei had died. But his corpse, lying on his bed, was really the bamboo. And so they bewailed and buried him.²⁵⁸

Who, then, is Sire Gourd? He explains himself:

> "I'm an immortal. Fool that I am, I had a post in Heaven, but I was inattentive to my duties, so I was banished, sent back for a while to this human realm."²⁵⁹

Like Li Bo, another banished immortal, though one who recalls his past, present and future.

Li Bo tells us that his teacher treads on purple clouds — more accurately, it's purple smoke. A contemporary of Ge Hong writes of it in his poem cycle, "Roaming in immortality" (*youxian* 遊仙):²⁶⁰

> Red Pine, the immortal, looked down as he roamed on high, driving the wild swan and riding purple smoke.

> 赤松臨上遊,駕鴻乘紫煙

And finally the City of Jade. Ah, it's the dwelling place of the divine Laozi! From the *History of the Wei Dynasty* (*Wei shu* 魏書):

> The wellsprings of Daoism all emerge from Laozi — he said so himself. He was born before Heaven and Earth, manifests in ten-thousand forms. Above, he dwells in the City of Jade, as ancestor to the divine Jade Emperor.²⁶¹

The last line of the poem, "held forever in the City of Jade." "Held," *xuan* 懸, but it actually means "to hang or be suspended," with the feeling of something unresolved, like a law suit that can't be settled. We could say, "He remains forever hovering in the Jade Capital," though in a positive way.

But does Li Bo tell us that he will hang there forever? We've said so, yet that's not actually what *he* says — there is no word "forever" in Chinese, even after the Buddhist invasions, here things can only go on for so long, then they stop, and something else happens. So he says, "He will hang here the longest time." Apologies for our bad translation.

Chapter 32. Writing on a Baby

This is a story of Xu Yunfeng 許雲封 (742–?), virtuoso of the transverse flute or *di* 笛, and also an account of how he got his name. But it begins with the multi-hued brilliance of the poet Wei Yingwu 韋應物 (736–791), born a full generation after Li Bo, holder of the powerful Wei lineage among the aristocratic North China clans, officer in the Bright Emperor's personal guard, and also connoisseur of music, close acquaintance with the members of His Majesty's Pear Garden Troupe.

Now, in the mid-780s, twenty-five years after Li Bo's death, Wei has left capital life for a distant posting to the east. He moors his skiff one frosted autumn night, prepares wine, prepares to write poetry.

> Suddenly he heard the long, mournful sounds of a flute. Wei Yingwu had a penetrating knowledge of music and judged the sound strikingly similar to the sacred music that the Pear Garden flautist Li Mu used to play.[262] When Wei called the player over, he learned that he was Xu Yunfeng, and that Li Mu was his maternal grandfather.
>
> Xu explained: This is my ancestral home, though I haven't been here in many years. At the beginning of the Tianbao period, when I was one month old, the Bright Emperor passed through here on his return from visiting Mount Tai. My grandfather, who was with him, had heard of my birth. Delighting in me, swaddling me, he took me to see the learned Li Bo, so that he could choose a proper name for me. Li Bo had just sat down in a tavern and was loudly calling for wine. The proprietress, He Lan, was over ninety, and she invited Li to drink in an upstairs room. My grandfather ordered wine. Master Li grabbed a brush and wrote drunkenly on my chest:
>
> Who is that man beneath the tree?
> If he doesn't speak, I'll really like him.

If speaking occurs at midday,
the mists will fade and you will realize a treasure.

樹下彼何人
不語真吾好
語若及日中
煙霏謝成寶

My grandfather said, "I requested a name from the scholar, but now I don't understand what you have said."

Li Bo replied, "The name is already in the words. 'The man beneath the tree' is 'wood' 木 and 'child' 子. Wood and child make the graph Li 李. 'Not speaking' is 'no one' and 'words.' 'No one' 莫 and 'words' 言 are Mu 謩. [Together these make Li Mu's name.] 'Like' 好 is 'woman' 女 and 'child' 子. Woman and child together make a maternal grandson. 'If speaking occurs at midday' means 'noon.' 'To speak' 言 and 'noon' 午 are Xu 許 [the grandson's surname]. 'The mists will fade and you will realize a treasure' — this means clouds (*yun* 雲) disperse on the sacred mound (*feng* 封), which is Yunfeng 雲封 [the child's given name]. All this means 'Li Mu's maternal grandson Xu Yunfeng.'"

And so I was named that.[263]

Chapter 33. "Climbing to the Peak of Great White"

> I'm headed west up Great White's peak,
> scrambling to the very top in the evening sun.
> Great White speaks with me,
> opens the Gate of Heaven to me.
> I'll ride off now on cool winds
> and reappear among floating clouds.
> I raise my hand and almost touch the moon,
> going on as if no mountains were there at all.
> Having passed the last peak,
> when would I ever appear here again?[264]

> 登太白峰
>
> 西上太白峰，夕陽窮登攀
> 太白與我語，為我開天關
> 愿乘泠風去，直出浮云間
> 舉手可近月，前行若無山
> 一別武功去，何時復見還

Great White, Taibo 太白, is the name of a mountain near the capital. It's also the name of the planet we call Venus. It's also Li Bo's public name.

That mountain is part of the great east-west chain that protects Chang'an from the south. A millennial home to hermits and refugees, and still that today.[265] Taibo, the tallest peak within the range, 12,000 feet up. The view from there:

AN INTERLUDE

Fig. 44. The view from Mount Taibo.²⁶⁶

The planet Taibo makes war, not love. "Venus is the military. It is also the star of punishment," says the *New Tang History*.²⁶⁷ "When Venus should not yet appear but does appear, throughout the world armies will set forth."²⁶⁸ It is the west, autumn, metal.²⁶⁹

Elsewhere Li Bo writes:

When Venus transits the moon, enemies can be destroyed.

太白入月敵可摧²⁷⁰

All of this is Li Bo, and the great mountain and baleful star merely point in his direction. Thus his contemporary Cui Chengfu (崔成甫 n.d.) writes:

All along I sought Li Bo beyond the Heavens,
but I snagged a drunk immortal in Nanjing.²⁷¹

天外常求太白老，金陵捉得酒仙人

Bo 白, "white," means radiant, effulgent, the brightness of the sun. It also means death, the clothes of mourning.

Tai 太, "extreme, maximum." So Taibo is Maximum White. (This is not an Aryan Nation name.) ²⁷² Here's how Li Bo writes it himself:

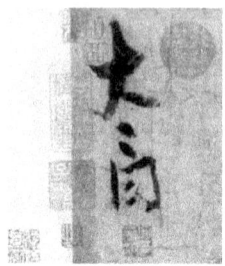

Fig. 45. From Li Bo's calligraphy "Climbing Yang Terrace" (*Shang yangtai tie* 上陽台帖).²⁷³

Lichtenberg sagt, nur wenigen Menschen hätten je reines Weiß gesehen. So verwenden also die Meisten das Wort falsch? Und wei hat er den richtigen Gebrauch gelernt?
— Ludwig Wittgenstein, *Bemerkungen über die Farben* I, 3.

Lichtenberg says that very few people have ever seen pure white. So do most people use the word wrong, then? And how did he learn the correct use?
— Ludwig Wittgenstein, *Remarks on Colour*²⁷⁴

Un soir, un comédien me demanda d'écrire une pièce qui serait jouée par des Noirs. Mais, qu'est-ce que c'est donc un Noir? Et d'abord, c'est de quelle couleur?
— Jean Genet, *Les nègres, clownerie*

One evening, an actor asked me to write a play that would be performed by Blacks. But then, what is a Black? And first of all, of what color?
— Jean Genet, *The Blacks, A Clown Show*²⁷⁵

Chapter 34. A Horse

> Li Bo had a horse named Yellow Mushroom (*huangzhi* 黃芝).
> — From the *Cailan zazhi* 採蘭雜志[276]

That's all the text says. So what's a yellow mushroom? Well, this is not an ordinary fungus — it's a *zhi*-mushroom, we don't have the word for it in English. But "if you ingest it, you may become an immortal."[277] In specific,

> If you take it over long periods, it will lighten your body, so that you do not age, and will extend your years until you are a divine immortal.[278]

Today it looks like this:

Fig. 46. The yellow mushroom.[279]

But perhaps Li Bo's horse got his name from another text, the *Authentic Scripture of the Great Grotto,* which contains this rhymed testimony to the mushroom's prowess:

I drive a team of three dragons,
floating, flying, past everything, up and up,
I breathe the sacred mushroom, in and out,
for eons without decline.[280]

The Bright Emperor, himself a mounted huntsman, had a special love of special horses. His favorite was called "A Whiteness That Illumines the Night" (*Zhaoyebai* 照夜白).

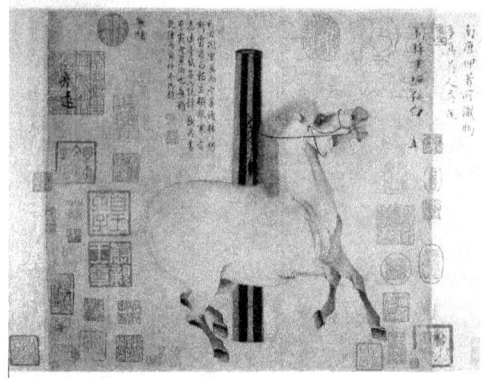

Fig. 47. "A Whiteness That Illumines the Night," by Han Gan (ca. 750).[281]

Since 1977 it has been housed in the Metropolitan Museum.[282]

The Emperor also had a hundred horses trained to dance to music — each fall they'd perform in the Palace of Exalted Grace to celebrate his birthday. Paul Kroll has composed an uncommonly elegant display of their pageant, and translates this ninth-century account:

> It was decreed that the horses be caparisoned with patterned embroidery, haltered with gold and silver, and their manes and forelocks dressed out with assorted pearls and jades. Their tune, which was called "Music for the Upturned Cup," had several tens of choruses, to which they shook their heads

and drummed their tails, moving this way and that in response to the rhythm. Then wood-plank platforms of three tiers were displayed. The horses were driven to the top of these, where they turned and twirled round as if in flight.[283]

Meanwhile, the court ladies were out on the polo-grounds of the West Palace — the sport had recently been introduced from Persia.

Fig. 48. Tang Dynasty-era ceramic sculptures of women polo players.[284]

V

Five Daoists

Chapter 35. The God Laozi

It all started with Laozi 老子 — maybe you know him from when we spelled his name Lao Tzu. Here in Li Bo's poem, he's called Lord Lao (Laojun 老君).[285]

> Paying respects at the temple of Lord Lao
>
> Numinous First Lord! The power
> of your sacred temple awes the spirit.
> Now grasses have grown over the footpath,
> and birds leave deep tracks in the dust.
> Off in the sands, the cinnabar stove's gone out,
> purple smoke no longer hovers over the Pass.
> I'm only sad that a thousand years later
> there's space to spare in this pine and cypress graveyard.[286]

> 謁老君廟
>
> 先君懷聖德，靈廟肅神心
> 草合人蹤斷，塵濃鳥跡深
> 流沙丹灶滅，關路紫煙沉
> 獨傷千載後，空餘松柏林

Laozi, his fabled writing the *Daodejing* 道德經 (Canon of the virtues of Dao) — its lead sentence is devilishly hard to translate, since it's all pun: Dao means "a road, the way, to speak, to lead":

> Dao that can be Dao'ed is not a long-lasting Dao,
> names that can be named are not long-lasting names.[287]

> 道可道非常道，名可名非常名

Right at the start, then, Laozi tells us that his lineage is based in the esoteric, in a nonevident knowledge of how the world works. Even a materialist is forced to accept the inadequacy of language.[288] But others are welcome to go further into his wisdom: wonder-workers, diviners, spirit mediums, life-extenders, herbalists, healers, immortals, martial artists, militarists.[289] Poets, too, in the way their wordful activity exceeds the word. You can even use those teachings as the basis for a theocratic state.[290] The Bright Emperor was fully awed, copying out the text in his own hand for engraving at the Laozi Temple, and later writing his own commentary.

We've just seen the first two sentences of the *Daodejing* (The scripture of Dao's power). These are the next two:

> "Non-Having" names the pregnancy of Heaven and Earth,
> "Having" names the mother of the ten-thousand things.[291]

無名天地之始，有名萬物之母

And so Laozi discerns the Nothing that is rife with all possibility and the Something that gives it birth as all appearance. Before him there wasn't any thing, and afterwards plenty, before him only a (silent) (silence), and after him the whole of everything.[292] So he is a cosmic cervix, twixt Naught and Aught,[293] the two ropes of a swing.[294] And thus in the same breath he is the inventor of language, naming names.

Through much of the twentieth century, by consensus in China and abroad, Laozi did not exist. (This was not a problem for him.[295]) He'd been thought up, it was said, as a stand-in for the otherwise nameless author of the world's second-most translated book, a supposed contemporary of Confucius (551–479).[296] But there are other views. A fourth-century CE devotee gathered some of them:

> His mother felt a great meteor enter her, and became pregnant. Although he received his *qi*-energy from Heaven, because he appeared in a family named Li, he took Li as his surname.

> Some say that Laozi was born before Heaven and Earth. Or that he was endowed with the essence-soul of Heaven, so that he was of the class "numinous and divine."
>
> Some say that his mother carried him seventy-two years before he was born, and that when he was born, he came out of her left armpit. When he was born, he had a white head of hair, so he was called Laozi, "the old child/the ancient master."[297]

But only by the beginning of Tang did someone remember the older stories, and find a better approximated name for him, "Lord Lao (Laojun 老君)." As in *The Scripture in Which the Most High Lord Lao Opens Heaven* (*Taishang Laojun kaitian jing* 太上老君開天徑):

> I have truthfully heard:
> In the space-time before there was Heaven and Earth, incalculably far beyond Great Clarity, inside empty naught, which is a silent absence with no outside, where there is
> naught of Heaven, naught of Earth,
> naught of Yang, naught of Yin,
> naught of sun, naught of moon [...],
> naught of going, naught of coming,
> naught of birthing, naught of dying [...],
> only our Lord Lao, dwelling alone beyond the silent absence of empty mystery, amidst vacant mystery. If you look for him, you won't see him. If you listen for him, you won't hear him. You may call him aught, but you won't see his form. You may call him naught, but the ten-thousand things are born from him [...].
>
> [After vast eons] and then after 10,000 kalpas, and on to a hundred completions, going on yet another 810,000 years, comes the period "Great Beginning." At the time of Great Beginning, Lord Lao descends from vacuous emptiness, and becomes "Master of the Great Beginning,"[298]

which is our world and now. But all these times dwell at one time, which is timelessness, so he's never left home.

Lord Lao, then, is an ancestor one should not miss. The Tang house, equally surnamed Li, recognized him as their progenitor, their First Lord, and offered him imperial rank and title even above their own, sc. Mystery Primal August Emperor (*Xuanyuan huangdi* 玄元皇帝).[299]

Fig. 49. Song dynasty-era stone sculpture of Laozi at the foot of Mount Qingyuan.[300]

Chapter 36. A Patriarch

When Li Bo was in his late twenties, he met the Daoist Master Sima Chengzhen 司馬承禎 (647–735), then in his seventies. Li Bo knew him as his teacher. He recalls:

> Long ago I was in Jingzhou and met Sima of Tiantai. He said that I had the style of an immortal and the bones of Dao, that I could roam the outer edge of the universe with the gods.[301]
>
> 予昔於江陵見天台司馬子微，謂予有仙風道骨，可與神遊八極之表。

Li Bo makes no further mention of Sima anywhere in his works.[302] The following poem, though, expresses something of their relationship. The poem's first words, "Great White," is of course the planet Venus, is a mountain near Chang'an, and also Li Bo's public name.

> Ancient Airs #5
>
> Great White in the sky's deep blue.
> Tiers of forest higher than the stars,
> only a hundred miles below Heaven,
> cut off from the distant world.
> Here a raven-haired old man
> wraps himself in clouds, reclining in pinetree snow.
> He neither smiles nor speaks,
> but lodges deep inside the cliff.
> I've come to meet this Realized Man.
> I prostrate to him and request instruction.
> Radiant, smiling, showing his jade-white teeth,
> he explains the making of the elixir.
> I inscribe his teachings in my bones.
> Then he shoots skyward, his lightning flash already gone.

I look up, but my sight falls short.
The Five Emotions are burning into vastness.
I'll refine the elixir
and forever take leave of this world.[303]

古風 其五

太白何蒼蒼，星辰卜森列
去天三百里，邈爾與世絕
中有綠髮翁，披雲臥松雪
不笑亦不語，冥棲在巖穴
我來逢真人，長跪問寶訣
粲然啟玉齒，授以煉藥說
銘骨傳其語，竦身已電滅
仰望不可及，蒼然五情熱
吾將營丹砂，永與世人別

By all public accounts, Sima Chengzhen is the greatest Daoist of Tang. I don't think it matters how you measure that, though the conventional way to have your biography included in the *Dynastic History* would require four or more items from this polythetic list:

  the right forebears
  skill in essay and poetry
  the Emperor's ear
  a series of high appointments
  administrative acumen
  a wide circle of important friends
  skill in calligraphy, painting and music

Sima Chengzhen had all of these.[304] But he was also successor to the patriarchy of Highest Clarity Daoism. And he was also a great realized master in that tradition. This last is the foundation of it all, while the others are his marvelous skills over apparent phenomena.

The Bright Emperor wrote him poems, gave him titles, composed his epitaph. We've seen how Sima brought Daoist and Imperial cosmologies into alignment on the question of the Marchmounts. And in 724 he conferred initiations on the Emperor, of several kinds. One set seems similar to what Li Bo received — our chapter on grotto-heavens gives details of these, the registers and talismans. Another set included rituals in cosmic parallel to the imperial enthronement rites that had consecrated the Emperor on his ascension to rulership.[305] And it seems that something further happened as well:

> At that time the Bright Emperor held all-under-Heaven, and he deeply loved the methods of Dao. Earnestly he summoned Sima Chengzhen to the Capital, lodging him in the inner palace and showing extreme respect. The Emperor asked him about life extension and transcending this world. Sima took the Emperor aside and spoke privately to him. The Emperor then preserved this secretly, so that no one learned of it.
>
> After that the Bright Emperor ruled the state for more than forty years. Even though An Lushan rebelled and His Majesty withdrew to Shu, he became the Retired Emperor and returned to Chang'an. Only seven years later did he relinquish his life. Truly this is Heaven's calculation, how could he live so long without help from the powers of Dao?[306]

Chapter 37. A Hermit

Sima Chengzhen gave full transmission to only two of his students. One, Li Hanguang, succeeded him as Patriarch of Highest Clarity Daoism.[307] The other is Madame Jiao, recipient of this poem.

> Offered to Madame Jiao, Daoist Master of Mount Song, with a preface
>
> There's a sublime being on Mount Song, the Daoist master Madame Jiao. No one knows where she's from. Some say she was born two centuries ago, though from her appearance you'd guess she's in her fifties or sixties. She practices fetal breathing and abjuring grains,[308] living in a hut on the Lesser Chambers of Mount Song. She moves as if she's flying, ten thousand miles in a flash. People claim she journeys to the Eastern Sea and climbs its Magic Mountains, but actually no one can fathom her travels.
> Inspired by her, I went seeking Dao in the Lesser Chambers, and climbed all thirty-six peaks. Now I spatter about some ink to make this distant offering.

The Twin Chambers are neighbor to the sky,
their thrice-blooming trees hold purple smoke.
Here you dwell, traveler from the Eastern Seas,
perhaps the immortal Hemp Maiden herself.
Dao abides here, unstained by clamor,
your activity dissolves all thoughts.
Sometimes you feast on the heart of osmanthus
or recite scriptures written in moss.
You roam the world's eight corners at your whim
and circuit beyond the sky's nine limits.
Dipping your gourd in the waters of Ying,
you come to Yi River on your dancing crane.

Returning alone to the empty mountain,
you fall asleep caressed by autumn clouds.
The moon dangles dawn's mirror through the vines,
a pine breeze still strums the night's lute.
Your light is concealed within Song Mountain,
your transfigured form resting in a tent of clouds.
As phoenix calls fade into the distance,
your rainbow skirt wafts in the wind,
Just as the Queen Mother of the West
spied Dongfang Shuo in the Emperor's court,
please look after me, banished to this world below.
If only I can receive your sacred scripts,
I vow to carve your teachings in my bones.[309]

贈嵩山焦煉師 并序

嵩丘有神人焦煉師者。不知何許婦人也。又云生于齊梁時。其年貌可稱五六十。常胎息絕谷。居少室廬。游行若飛。倐忽萬里。世或傳其入東海。登蓬萊。竟莫能測其往也。余訪道少室。盡登三十六峰。聞風有寄。洒翰遙贈。

二室凌青天，三花含紫煙
中有蓬海客，宛疑麻姑仙
道在喧莫染，跡高想已綿
時餐金鵝蕊，屢讀青苔篇
八極恣游憩，九垓長周旋
下瓢酌穎水，舞鶴來伊川
還歸空山上，獨拂秋霞眠
蘿月挂朝鏡，松風鳴夜弦
潛光隱嵩岳，煉魄棲雲幄
霓裳何飄搖，鳳吹轉綿邈
愿同西王母，下顧東方朔
紫書儻可傳，銘骨誓相學

Chapter 38. A Princess

Princess Realized-in-Jade (Yuzhen 玉真), dear younger sister to the Bright Emperor and student of Sima Chengzhen.[310] Li Bo writes of her:

> A poem of Princess Realized-In-Jade, the Immortal
>
> The Immortal, Realized-In-Jade —
>   sometimes she's off to Great Flower Peak,
>   at clear dawn she sounds Heaven's drums,
>   she's a sudden whirlwind galloping a pair of dragons,
>   she never stops playing with lightning,
>   she's always moving clouds and never leaves a footprint.
> When she enters the holy peaks of Mount Song,
> Great Echo! The Queen Mother of the West comes out to greet her in response.[311]

玉真仙人詞

玉真之仙人，時往太華峰
清晨鳴天鼓，飈欻騰雙龍
弄電不輟手，行雲本無蹤
幾時入少室，王母應相逢

We also know her in five other ways.

1. *As nun and Daoist priest*
   In February 711, at about age twenty, she and her elder sister Immortal-in-Gold (Jinxian 金仙 [ca. 688–732]) were ordained in a ceremony at the palace.[312] Thereafter each maintained her own abbey within the Imperial City.

   Yet Realized-in-Jade still maintained a somewhat public role.[313] In 735 she represented the throne at her teacher Sima Chengzhen's home base on Mount Wangwu, participating in a multi-day ritual to "harmonize the forces of nature, prevent natural calamities and disasters, prolong the life of the emperor, and guarantee prosperity for the empire."[314] In 744, in her early fifties, she petitioned her brother "to have her royal title revoked, her appanage abolished, and her revenues and manors returned to the throne."[315] He refused, she insisted, he acceded.

2. *As connoisseur of poets*
The princess ran a literary salon at both her abbey and her country estate.[316] She was especially fond of the poet Wang Wei 王維 (699–759), whose Buddhist-related verses of the natural world we still prize today.[317] About 742, when Li Bo came to Chang'an, he was introduced to her, and it is likely she who recommended him to the throne, whence his prominence in the Capital.[318]

3. *As granddaughter of Empress Wu*
That Empress was the most powerful woman in all China's history. Unwilling to rule through her son, she overthrew the Tang and founded her own dynasty, the Zhou 周, in 690. It did not survive her.[319]

From the princess's point of view, that reign was accomplished only by terror: her mother was murdered, her father's life ever uncertain, his allied officials executed in the marketplace. This political style persisted a full decade after the Empress's death in 705 and occasioned a misogynistic backlash. The Princess's ordination protected her from much, but not all, of it — though she was exempt from ordinary marriage,[320] court officials sought to block her abbey and blamed her for the drought of 713.[321]

4. *As recipient of the earliest ordination ceremony for which we have an eyewitness account*
Over ten days and an evening in February 711, she received key ritual texts — "scriptures, commentaries, writs, registers, tallies, talismans, injunctions"[322] — texts that had arisen be-

fore the worlds and been preserved in the heavens, eventually bestowed on certain gods, and only eons later entrusted to a human recipient.[323] These rituals came with oaths of strictest secrecy.[324]

The final day, between 2:00 and 4:00 a.m. on the morning of 20 February 711, Lord Lao, the deified form of Laozi, "descended to the altar and spoke to the Princesses."[325]

5. *As rejected bride of the immortal Zhang Guo*
From the *Old Tang History*, chapter 191:

Zhang Guo 張果. His place of origin is unknown. During the time of Empress Wu he lived in reclusion on Zhongtiao Mountain, coming and going between the Fen and Jin Rivers. At this time people reported that he possessed the secret arts of long life. He himself said that he was several hundred years old. Empress Wu sent an official to summon him, but he pretended to be dead and did not proceed to the Capital […].

[In 733 he accepted the Bright Emperor's invitation to visit the court.] The Emperor first took his seat and warmly asked Zhang about ways of governance and the matters of divine immortals and their elixirs. He also asked about his uncertainties concerning "unfathomable transformation."[326]

The Bright Emperor said to his chief eunuch Gao Lishi, "I've heard that if someone can drink an extract of monkshood[327] without distress, he is a realized Master." When the weather was coldest, he had someone give the monkshood to Zhang. He thereupon drank three goblets, becoming tipsy as if he were drunk. He turned to someone and said, "It's not the best wine." Then he went to sleep. When he awoke, he looked at his teeth in a mirror. They were scorched all black. He ordered the attendants to get him an iron scepter, and he knocked his teeth out, storing them in his sash. Then he took some immortals medicine from his breast, light red, and rubbed down his gums with it. Then he slept again a long time. His teeth all grew back, pure white and gleaming. Only then did the Emperor have full confidence in him.

The Bright Emperor loved divine immortals, and he wanted to ennoble Zhang Guo as a prince, but he hadn't yet said a word about it. Zhang Guo remarked to two officials, "There's a saying, 'To marry to become a prince, that's really dangerous.'" The two men looked at each other, not understanding his words. Then an Imperial Commissioner arrived and announced, "Princess Realized-in-Jade has loved Dao from an early age. His Majesty wishes to bestow her on you in marriage." Zhang Guo gave a great laugh but did not go so far as to accept the command. Only then did the two other men realize the meaning of his previous words. Afterwards he politely declined the offer and returned to the mountains.[328]

Fig. 50. Ren Renfa 任仁發 (1254–1327), "Zhang Guo Meeting with the Bright Emperor,"[329] detail

Chapter 39. A Companion

Song of Cinnabar Hill

Cinnabar Hill — oh, he loves holy immortals!
Mornings he drinks the pure flow of Ying River,
evenings he returns to the purple smoke of Song Mountain summit.
Its thirty-six peaks! The great encircling!

The great encircling — oh, he tracks comets and rainbows.
Mounted on a flying dragon, the wind born from his ears,
he traverses the Yellow River, strides across the Eastern Sea, and goes everywhere like the sky.
I know your roaming heart and mind go on without exhaustion.[330]

元丹丘歌

元丹丘，愛神仙
朝飲穎川之清流
暮還嵩岑之紫煙
三十六峰長周旋
長周旋，躡星虹
身騎飛龍耳生風
橫河跨海與天通
我知爾游心無窮

Yuan Danqiu 元丹丘 (n.d.), a dearest friend, Li Bo's closest companion in Dao. His uncommon surname means "original,"[331] his given name means Cinnabar Hill. "How Cinnabar Hill loves immortals," Li writes. They met in their late twenties, roamed off and on for two decades, studied with the same master,[332] and loved wine. "Young Cinnabar Hill," writes Li in one of his most celebrating poems, "drink up!"³³³ Another time Li Bo writes to him:

> I have been long at Lu River and Mount Huo, and you, dear Cinnabar Hill, roam at Mount Song nearby. We come and go inseparate, in the profound feelings of an old friendship. I get your many letters from retreat, inviting me to go live with you, and joyfully I receive your deep intention. Perhaps I'll drop everything, and take my whole family, and go there and not return. And I write to you, that we may roam together.³³⁴

> 白久在廬霍。元公近游嵩山。故交深情。出處無間。嵩信頻及。許為主人。欣然適會本意。當冀長往不返。欲便舉家就之。兼書共游。因有此贈

So here is one more poem:

> Parting from Cinnabar Hill at Yingyang, on my way to Huai-yang
>
> Master Cinnabar Hill, you and I
> are brothers from different families.
> No ties of office,
> just the plain intimacy of mist at dawn.
> We both chafe in the nets of the world,
> our deep longings remain unfulfilled.
> Pine and cypress stay true through the cold,
> they'd be ashamed to chase springtimes like peach and plum.
> The endless needs of marketplace and court
> will stain and scrape your jade-white face.
> What they take is heavier than mountains,
> what they give is lighter than dust.
> Our souls get gradually overgrown with weeds,
> age and decline join force against us.
> But I have a parting gift in a secret satchel
> that you can use to sustain yourself,
> and we shall feast on the golden elixir

and lodge with Master Hu!
No use to build things here,
a lifetime flashing by in a single day.
Now I leave you, on my way southeast
through endless sorrows.
Our old vows don't shift,
we keep them through all our journeys.
That's all. Goings and comings,
white clouds flying through the Milky Way.[335]

潁陽別元丹丘之淮陽

吾將元夫子,異姓為天倫
本無軒裳契,素以煙霞親
嘗恨迫世網,銘意俱未伸
松柏雖寒苦,羞逐桃李春
悠悠市朝間,玉顏日緇磷
所失重山岳,所得輕埃塵
精魄漸蕪穢,衰老相憑因
我有錦囊訣,可以持君身
當餐黃金藥,去為紫陽賓
萬事難并立,百年猶崇晨
別爾東南去,悠悠多悲辛
前志庶不易,遠途期所遵
已矣歸去來,白雲飛天津

Chapter 39. Zhuangzi

The Daoist sage Zhuangzi 莊子 lived a thousand years before Li Bo. At that time the Central States were still in constant contestation — the First Emperor of Qin would unify them into empire only a century later in 221 BCE. Zhuangzi once wrote:

> Zhuangzi once dreamed he was a butterfly. Flutter flutter, a butterfly. Wasn't he enjoying himself, all as he wished! He didn't know Zhuangzi. Suddenly he awoke, as Zhuangzi as you please. He didn't know if Zhuangzi were dreaming he was a butterfly or if the butterfly were dreaming he was Zhuangzi. Now, there must be some distinction between Zhuangzi and butterfly. This is what is meant by the Transformation of Things.[336]

Li Bo wrote a poem about that, but to understand it we must first go back to the century after Zhuangzi's dream, to this story from the *Historical Records*:

> Shao Ping was Marquis of Dongling under the First Emperor of Qin. When Qin was destroyed, he became a commoner. He was poor, so he grew melons outside the east ward of Chang'an. The melons were lovely, so the people called them "Dongling melons," taking the name from Shao Ping's marquisate.[337]

One final piece of lore, of the mountain islands Penglai 蓬萊, far far to the east in the Eastern Seas, home of immortals and the elixirs of immortality. The First Emperor of Qin sent fruitless expeditions out to bring it all back.[338]

And now Li Bo's poem:

Ancient Airs #8

When Zhuangzi dreams he's a butterfly,
the butterfly *is* Zhuangzi.
But it's never just one body transforming—
the ten-thousand things are doing this all the time.
So know that the streams of Penglai
are always changing back into the Milky Way,
and the man who grows melons at Chang'an's gate
is the former Dongling marquis.
Since wealth and honor are like this,
what are we seeking to accomplish with our convulsive flutter?[339]

古風 其八

莊周夢胡蝶，胡蝶為庄周
一體更變易，萬事良悠悠
乃知蓬萊水，復作清淺流
青門種瓜人，舊日東陵侯
富貴故如此，營營何所求

People are always asking if Zhuangzi turned into a butterfly, or vice versa. But it's never just one body transforming—the ten-thousand things are doing this all the time. That's what is meant by "the transformation of things" (*bianhua* 變化). This transformation is synonymous with the appearancing of all-the-worlds, and Isabelle Robinet has profound and lovely things to say about it.[340]

An Interlude

Chapter 40. Climbing Yang Terrace

The year 744. Li Bo and his young friend Du Fu ascend Yang Terrace, the mountain residence of his late teacher, Sima Chengzhen.[341] At the summit, Li Bo does this calligraphy.[342]

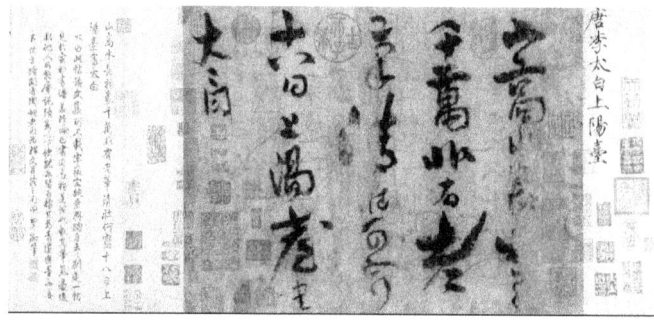

Fig. 51. Li Bo's calligraphy "Climbing Yang Terrace" (*Shang yang-tai tie* 上陽台帖).[343]

His text:

> Tall mountains, long rivers,
> a thousand million images and things.
> Without the brush-stroke of the ancients,
> your lucent vigor will fail you.
>
>> Written by Li Bo, the Great White, on ascending Yang Terrace the eighteenth day of the moon[344]

山高水長，物象千萬
非有老筆，清壯可窮
　十八日上陽台書，太白

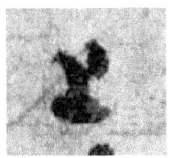

Fig. 52. The character *shang* 上, "ascend," enlarged from the calligraphy.

In 725 the Emperor had requested Sima's presence on Mount Wangwu and built for him the Abbey of Yang Terrace (*Yangtai guan* 陽臺觀).

Sima would live there until his death in 735, aged eighty-nine. At that time his disciples sent this official report to the Bright Emperor:

> On the day of his death, a pair of white cranes circled the altar. A white cloud surged from within the altar, mounting right to Heaven. The Teacher's face appeared to be alive.[345]

The outer Yang Terrace atop Mount Wangwu takes its name from the inner Yang Terrace, the grotto-heaven concealed within that mountain.[346] This grotto-heaven is preeminent among such caverns, the concealment place of Highest Clarity scriptures. *From the Declarations of the Perfected*:

> Lord Pei said, "The Terrace of Yang is the Adjunct Heaven of the Immortals at Mount Wangwu. When they first attain Dao, everyone pays a visit to this Yang Terrace. It's the Palace of the Clear Void."[347]

But Yang Terrace, the terraces of yang, the bright, is also the name of another ancient place, where the King of Chu met his shaman lover. But only for one night.[348]

Li Bo's poem speaks of "a thousand million things and images." "Things" is *wu* 物, and "images" *xiang* 象. "The ten-thousand things" is how you'd say "all the appearances of this world." Regarding *xiang,* Isabelle Robinet writes:

The *xiang* are images that make things apparent; they are part of reality, and inherently contain and manifest the cosmic dimension of things and their structure. This is why the *xiang* are often considered to be the "real forms" (*zhenxing* 真形) of things, or the fundamental substance (*ti* 體) of beings. They are visible but lie before and beyond the world of forms. They allow us to understand the world and to get along in the universe; hence they are guides and models of conduct.[349]

Chapter 41. Du Fu

Who is China's greatest poet? For the last thousand years there have only been two serious contenders, Li Bo and his young admirer Du Fu 杜甫 (712 – 770), with their famously contrastive energies, deep Yin and deep Yang. Here they are together:

1. Li Bo's poem to Du Fu, "Sent to Du Fu from my home below the walls of Sandhill City, by the old kingdoms of Qi and Lu"

   After all, why did I come here,
   to be left high and dry in Sandhill City?
   An ancient tree grows outside the city walls,
   where dusk merges with the sounds of autumn.
   The wine of Lu can't get me drunk,
   the songs of Qi just repeat old sentiments.
   When I think of you, it's like Wen River,
   carrying my message south in its raging flood.[350]

   沙丘城下寄杜甫

   我來竟何事。高臥沙丘城。
   城邊有古樹。日夕連秋聲
   魯酒不可醉。齊歌空復情。
   思君若汶水。浩蕩寄南征

2. From Du Fu's poem to Li Bo, "With Li Bo, looking for Fan the hermit"

   Lord Li, your handsome verse
   is so often like that of Yin Keng.
   We were both pilgrims at Meng Mountain,
   and I cherish you like an older brother.
   We dozed in autumn, drunk under a single quilt,
   we walked in the sun holding hands.[351]

與李十二白同尋范十隱居

李侯有佳句，往往似陰鏗
余亦東蒙客，憐君如弟兄
醉眠秋共被，攜手日同行

3. Li Bo's poem, "For Du Fu, in play"

   I met Du Fu on top of Rice Kernel Mountain.
   It was high noon, and he was wearing a huge rain hat.
   How did you get so skinny since we met?
   "It's because I write such poetry of anguish!"[352]

   戲贈杜甫

   飯顆山頭逢杜甫
   頂戴笠子日卓午
   借問別來太瘦生
   總為從前作詩苦

4. Du Fu's poem, "To Li Bo"

   Autumn now. We're still two tumbleweeds who can't meet up,
   shaming the Great Alchemist because we haven't yet made the elixir.
   Hard drinking, madly singing, letting empty days pass,
   strutting and swaggering, whose hero are we trying to be?[353]

   贈李白

   秋來相顧尚飄蓬
   未就丹砂愧葛洪
   痛飲狂歌空度日
   飛揚跋扈爲誰雄

Both Li Bo and Du Fu are equally an affront to the poetry that preceded them. Both reveal most intimate secrets — Du Fu's are secrets of the vast human realm, while Li Bo's are of the vast… well, I don't know.

So which is China's greatest poet?[354] Chinese littérateurs have argued this a thousand years. Indeed, you could write a history of Chinese poetics based entirely on this contest.[355] So let's set the record straight right now: Li Bo and Du Fu *together* are China's greatest poet. It's a bit like the conundrum of two football players in the 1977 movie *Semi-Tough*:

> Billy Clyde Puckett: There are no 10's.
> Shake Tiller: Janey Woods is a 10.
> Billy Clyde Puckett: No, Janey Woods is a 9. Janey Woods and her sister Patty *together* are a 10.

伯夷：沒有十分女。
叔齊：欸？張麗是個十分女啊。
伯夷：不。張麗和她的妹妹一共為十分女。

Fig. 53. Movie poster for *Semi-Tough*.[356]

For Li Bo that human realm is the theater where the divine puts on its plays, and the human being a perceptual apparatus that somewhat limits the shows that can be presented. He's a tumbling down of luminosity across this space, a shattering of light. He is only here as play.

Mathematicians distinguish between two sizes of infinity, the countable and uncountable. The natural numbers 1, 2, 3… are a countable infinity — they never end, but you can still count them. But between, say, the numbers 4 and 5 there are many, many more numbers than that — you can continue to divide that space forever, and establish more numbers, and between each of those numbers are even more numbers, endlessly. Both Du Fu and Li Bo are infinities, but Li Bo is uncountable — right there between your 4 and your 5 is already everything.

Thus if you want to write good Chinese poetry, you'll be told to imitate Du Fu, never Li Bo.[357] "Indeed," writes Steven Owen, "the originality and variety of Li Bo's work is such that it is very difficult to isolate features that are true for more than a handful of poems."[358] This goes beyond an ability to rhyme "apples" with "Indianapolis," though it is of course related.[359]

> These are the victories of the military lineage.
> They cannot be transmitted in advance.
> — Sun Tzu's *Art of War* (*Sunzi bingfa* 孫子兵法), ch. 1

Chapter 42. Brush Washing Spring

Brush Washing Spring lies outside the Ji'ning customs gate, just a few steps from the Grand Canal.[360] As the water emerges from the earth, it forms a square pool and a round pool. It's said that Li Bo washed his writing brushes here.
— from *The Golden Speculum That Goes by Water* (*Xingshui jinjian* 行水金鑑)[361]

Chapter 43. Jewel Stairs

In 1916 Ezra Pound published *Cathay*,[362] thereby becoming "the inventor of Chinese poetry for our generation" (T.S. Eliot).[363] Many of his translations originate with Li Bo, for example:

> The Jewel Stairs' Grievance
>
> The jewelled steps are already quite white with dew,
> It is so late that the dew soaks my gauze stockings,
> And I let down the crystal curtain
> And watch the moon through the clear autumn.

Pound's original note:

> Jewel stairs, therefore a palace. Grievance, therefore there is something to complain of. Gauze stockings, therefore a court lady, not a servant who complains. Clear autumn, therefore he has no excuse on account of weather. Also she has come early, for the dew has not merely whitened the stairs, but has soaked her stockings. The poem is especially prized because she utters no direct reproach.

> 玉階怨
>
> 玉階生白露
> 夜久侵羅襪
> 卻下水晶簾
> 玲瓏望秋月

Someone else might say:

> Yes, it's that damn fall moon.
> No, he didn't come.

> So how come my good silk stockings
> are all wet?³⁶⁴

Or if you want the sound of the Tang, here is how Li Bo might have said it, in what we now call Middle Chinese.[365] With a translation inspired by such sounds.

> ngjowk keaj jwon
>
> ngjouk keaj sraeng baek lu
> yae kjuw tshim la mjot
> khjak hae sywij tsjeng ljem
> leng luwng mjang tshjuw ngjwot

> Jade steps grief
>
> Jade steps and white dew,
> Long nights of damp shoes,
> Let's let down the shades,
> Ling-long, where's the moon?[366]

A piano reduction of an orchestral piece is a transposition from one musical idiom to another. Essential melody, harmony and rhythm are preserved, but coloration and texture are drastically diminished, and you lose the way the English horn is fighting with the 'cellos.[367] We know how Li Bo's words were pronounced, and in what rough rhythm, but we haven't much been able to reproduce this in any good English. Furthermore, his orchestra has far more sonorities than our own well-tempered keyboard can produce, and instruments that, I fear, we've never even heard. Such as Zhuangzi's bamboo pipes (*lai* 籟), which (like some woodwind families) come in three sizes:

> "You hear the piping of men, but you haven't heard the piping of earth. Or if you've heard the piping of earth, you haven't heard the piping of Heaven!

> "The Great Clod belches out breath and its name is wind. So long as it doesn't come forth, nothing happens. But when it does, then ten thousand hollows begin crying wildly. Can't you hear them, long drawn out? In the mountain forests that lash and sway, there are huge trees a hundred spans around with hollows and openings like noses, like mouths, like ears, like jugs, like cups, like mortars, like rifts, like ruts. They roar like waves, whistle like arrows, screech, gasp, cry, wail, moan, and howl, those in the lead calling out yeee!, those behind calling out yuuu!" […]
>
> "May I ask about the piping of Heaven?"
>
> "Blowing on the ten thousand things in a different way, so that each can be itself — all take what they want for themselves, but who does the sounding?"[368]

Sunlight, becalmed by reflection, refined by indirection, becomes moonlight, coolness penetrating our deepest recesses. Autumn brings Yin's exquisite maturing — the beads of the crystal curtain, the drops of dew on the white stairs, the tears of regret that ripple like arpeggios across black and white keys in a Chopin *Nocturne,* also suffused with seductive lunar melancholy.

AN INTERLUDE

Chapter 44. "Seeing Off Meng Haoran"

Yellow Crane Tower, seeing off Meng Haoran, who is going to Yangzhou

From Yellow Crane Tower my old friend leaves the west
and heads downstream to Yangzhou in the catkin haze of April.
The far reflection of a single sail, blue empty hills and gone,
only the Yangtze flowing on to the edge of Heaven.[369]

黃鶴樓送孟浩然之廣陵

故人西辭黃鶴樓
煙花三月下揚州
孤帆遠影碧空/山盡
唯見長江天際流

Fig. 54. Yellow Crane Tower in 1871.[370]

In modern Wuhan, overlooking the Yangtze from above its steep south banks, "It is said that the immortal Zi'an 子安 landed here on his yellow crane."³⁷¹

The Song dynasty poet Lu You 陸游 (1125–1209) remarks:

> Li Bo climbed this tower to see off Meng Haoran. He wrote:
>
> The glistening of a journeying sail, blue hills and gone,
> You can just see the Yangtze flowing on to the borders of Heaven.
>
> He could still see the mast and sail glistening in the blue hills. If you don't travel by water quite a lot, you don't know these things.³⁷²

It is four hundred miles to Yangzhou, maybe six weeks with the current.

VI

Violent Death

From Li Bo's "Letter to Han Jingzhou":[373]

> When I was fifteen, I loved the art of the sword.[374]

From *The Chronology of Li Bo*:

> He enjoyed swordplay. In his practice of chivalry he killed several men with his own blade.[375]

Chapter 45. Ci Fei Beheads Two Dragons

From the *Huainanzi* 淮南子, chapter 12:

> There was a man from the South named Ci Fei, Ci the Flyer. From the great battlefield of Gansui he'd obtained a treasure sword. When he was halfway across the Yangtze on his way home, the River Lord sent out massive waves, and two dragons wrapped around his boat, seeking his sword. Ci Fei said to the boatman, "In the past when something like this happened, how did you survive?" He replied, "I've never seen it before." At this, Ci Fei closed his eyes and straightaway drew his sword, addressing the dragons, "It's permissible for a warrior to use decorous speech in his requests, but it's not permissible to seize things by force. You river-dwellers of rotting flesh-and-bone, just surrender! How could I have any sympathy for you?" Then he jumped into the river and stabbed the dragons, cutting off their heads. Everyone in the boat survived, and wind and waves subsided. His King ennobled him as Holder of the Gnomon.

Li Bo's poem:

> In praise, as I contemplate a painting of Ci Fei beheading the dragons
>
> Ci Fei beheaded two long dragons —
> you can see it in this old painting.
> Once in the boat, he howled like a tiger,
> roiled the water, and plunged straight into the dragon fight.
> He startled the waves and shook the mountain chains.
> Unsheathing his sword, he drew down thunder and lightning.
> Their scales broke beneath his white blade,
> their blood dyed the dark green river red.

A thousand autumns pass, but when you see this painting, you're face to face with an ancient hero.[376]

觀伙飛斬蛟龍圖贊

伙飛斬長蛟，遺圖畫中見
登舟既虎嘯，激水方龍戰
驚波動連山，拔劍曳雷電
鱗摧白刃下，血染滄江變
感此壯古人，千秋若對面

Here's Ci Fei's twentieth-century legacy:

Fig. 55. Tang Jiyao 唐繼堯.[377]

Tang Jiyao 唐繼堯 (1883–1927), "the last King of Yunnan," was military governor of that far southern province from 1913 to his death in 1927. He named his personal body-guard the Ci Fei Regiment. It was limited to sixty men, all of whom must be six feet tall.

Fig. 56. Members of the Ci Fei Regiment.[378]

Three chapters hence we will translate a Li Bo poem on eighth-century warfare in that same Yunnan.

Chapter 46. "Song of the Roving Swordsman"

The swordsman roams in his rude chin-straps.
A sickle-moon blade hangs, bright as hoarfrost,
from the silver saddle of his white steed.
Forthright as a shooting star,
he kills a man every ten steps,
nothing stops him for a thousand miles.
The deed done, he dusts off his clothes,
and the man and his name both disappear.

On a quiet day he stops by Lord Xinling's for a drink,
unstraps his sword and lays it on his knees,
eats pork roast with Butcher Zhu,
and urges Hou Ying to toast with him.
Three cups, and they're out with an oath —
the Five Peaks will fall before they break it!
Their eyes gone blurry, their ears burning,
their courage flares like white rainbows.

The kingdom is saved by the hurl
of a golden mace, shaking the capital.
For a thousand ages, these warriors
will light up the skies above their great city!
They stand unabashed before the heroes of today —
even in death, a swordsman's bones smell sweet.
Why would you rather hole up in your study,
divining the future until your hair turns white?[379]

俠客行

趙客縵胡纓，吳鉤霜雪明
銀鞍照白馬，颯沓如流星
十步殺一人，千里不留行
事了拂衣去，深藏身與名

閑過信陵飲，脫劍膝前橫
將炙啖朱亥，持觴勸侯嬴
三杯吐然諾，五岳倒為輕
眼花耳熱后，意氣素霓生
救趙揮金槌，邯鄲先震驚
千秋二壯士，烜赫大梁城
縱死俠骨香，不慚世上英
誰能書閣下，白首太玄經

Fig. 57. Screenshot from Akira Kurosawa's *Yojimbo* (1961).[380]

The third century BCE. What we call China is still only a crew of vying states, endemically at war. Lord Xinling, Prince of Wei, generous, curious, daring, ever humble before the wise, whatever their social standing. Thus he obtains the services of Hou Ying, a guard at the city gates yet also a hidden sage, and of Hou Ying's client, Butcher Zhu. But Lord Xinling is also the younger brother of a less talented king, thus always the object of envy, mistrust and calumny.

The neighboring state of Zhao is under siege. Lord Xinling's king dares not send his general and 100,000 troops to its aid. Xinling is honor-bound to Zhao's defense, so Hou Ying tells him: "You will need those 100,000 troops, and to get them, you will need the tiger tally. One half of it is held by the King, the other by his general. If you present the general with the King's half, he will have to accept your command of his troops. Then you can rescue Zhao. The King's favorite concubine owes you her life. She will steal the tally for you."

As Lord Xinling is leaving the capital with the tally, Hou Ying adds: "A general in the field may not always accept the orders of the King. Even after you show him the tally, you may have to kill him. Take Butcher Zhu with you, he can conceal a forty pound mace in his sleeve. Now I will see you off, and then four days later, when you have arrived, I will slit my throat."

And so it is. But afterwards Lord Xinling remains ten years in Zhao, afraid to go home. Only when his King needs his services does he return. Services complete, his life is again in jeopardy. The *Historical Records* tell what happened next.

> So Lord Xinling feigned illness and no longer attended court. He feasted with his retainers long into the night, drinking copiously, and was intimate with many women. For four years he enjoyed wine day and night. In the end he died of it.[381]

Meanwhile Zhuangzi writes of the swordsmen with rude chinstraps, who kill a man every ten steps.

> Chapter 30. Sword Talk[382]
>
> King Wen of Zhao loved swords. Swordsmen crowded through his gate, and he kept three thousand of them as retainers. Day and night they dueled before him, and every year over a hundred were wounded or killed. For three years the King's enthusiasm never flagged, and as his state declined, the feudal lords of other states plotted against him.

In desperation, the crown prince asks Zhuangzi if he can intervene with the King. Zhuangzi agrees.

> "But," said the crown prince, "His Majesty will only meet with swordsmen."

"This is not a problem," said Zhuangzi. "I love swords."

"But the swordsmen His Majesty meets with all have hair like tangled brambles, bristly beards, rude chin-straps on their drooping caps, and short jackets. They glare pop-eyed and speak unpleasantly. The King delights in this. If you insist on wearing a scholar's gown when you see the King, things will definitely go all wrong."

Zhuangzi said, "Then please allow me to prepare the attire of a swordsman."

Three days later the attire was ready, and he went to see the Crown Prince. The Crown Prince then went with him to see the King. The King was waiting with his naked blade drawn. Zhuangzi entered the throne room without haste and regarded the King without bowing.

The King said, "How do you intend to instruct me, now that you've gotten the Crown Prince to open the way for you?"

"I've heard that the King loves swords, so I have a sword to show you."

"What authority does your sword hold?"

"My sword kills a man every ten steps, and nothing stops it for a thousand miles."

The King was greatly pleased and said, "In all the world you have no match!"

Zhuangzi said, "A man with this sword

has no apparent form
but baits you with feigned advantage,
is last to make a move
and first to strike.

The King said, "Please go to your quarters and rest a while. I will give orders to prepare the sport. Then I will summon you."

For seven days the King put his swordsmen to competition. More than sixty were wounded or killed. He chose five or six men to present themselves with their swords outside the throne room. Then he summoned Zhuangzi. He said, "Today let's test how you and these men pay homage to the sword."

Zhuangzi said, "I have long hoped for this."

The King said, "What weapon will you use, a long or short sword?"

He said, "I can manage all of these. But I have three swords. Just tell me which to use. Allow me, though, to discuss them before I try them out for you."

The King said, "Tell me about the three swords."

He said, "I have the sword of the Son of Heaven, the sword of the feudal lords, and the sword of the commoner."

The King said, "What's the sword of the Son of Heaven like?"

He said, "The sword of the Son of Heaven? Its point lies beyond the north frontier, its blade is Mount Tai, its back the central states, its cross-guard the southern states, and its hilt the eastern states. It's wrapped in the barbarian lands, sheathed in the four seasons, wound round by the Eastern Sea, and hangs from the belt of the Holy Mountains. It's ruled by the Five Elements, determined by punishment and virtue, drawn by Yin and Yang, held by spring and summer, and used in fall and winter. When it strikes straight ahead, there is nothing before it. When it strikes upward, there is nothing above. When it strikes down, there is nothing below. When it whirls around, there is nothing on all sides. This sword splits the floating clouds above and severs the ligaments of earth below. If this sword is once used, the feudal lords return to order and all the world submits. This is the sword of the Son of Heaven."

King Wen stood stunned, lost to himself. Then he said, "What is the sword of the feudal lords like?"

Zhuangzi said, "Its point is men of knowledge and bravery, its blade is men of purity and integrity, its back men of wisdom and goodness, its cross-guard men of loyalty and wisdom, its hilt men of valor and daring…."

The Kind said, "What's the sword of the commoner like?"

Zhuangzi said, "The sword of the commoner is used by men with hair like tangled brambles, bristly beards, rude chin-straps on their drooping caps, and short jackets. They glare pop-eyed and speak unpleasantly. When they duel before Your Majesty, their swords chop heads and necks and split open livers and lungs. The men of this sword are no different from fighting cocks — at any moment their lives will be cut off. They are of no use in affairs of state. You, King, hold the seat of the Son of Heaven but love the sword of the commoner. With due respect, you are treating your majesty in a shabby way."

The King then led Zhuangzi up to his throne room. The steward offered food, but the King just paced round and round.

Zhuangzi said, "Please sit quietly and compose your energies. The matter of the sword has been completely played out."

For three months King Wen did not leave the palace. His swordsmen all committed suicide in their quarters.

Chapter 47. Li Yong (678–747)

During the late 740s, when Li Yong 李邕 was 70, he served as prefect of Beihai 北海, in the northeast. At that time court politics were in violent disarray, and wild purges reached nearly to the heir apparent. Li Yong was falsely accused of plotting treason. The *Old History of the Tang* says:

> 747. The new moon of the first month. Li Yong, the prefect of Beihai, and Pei Dunfu, the prefect of Zichuan, were both implicated in the affair of Wang Zeng and Liu Ji. Envoys were sent to execute them on the spot.[383]

Li Bo's *Chronology* states:

> Year 747, the first month. Li Yong, the prefect of Beihai, and Pei Dunfu, the prefect of Zichuan, were executed by flogging with a bamboo staff.[384]

In a nineteenth-century photograph:

Fig. 58. Execution by bamboo staff.[385]

Some ten years later, Li Bo visited Li Yong's ancestral home, which had become a Buddhist temple, and wrote this poem.

> On Xiujing Temple in Jiangxia
> *This temple is Li Yong's former house.*

My kinsman Li Yong's house
is now a temple on the river's southern shore.
No jade tree in the empty courtyard,
holy men sit meditation in the high hall.
Green grass grows in the library,
and white dust covers the zither room.
The peach and plum he planted his whole life
pass into nirvana without attaining spring.[386]

> 題江夏修靜寺
>
> 我家北海宅
> 作寺南江濱
> 空庭無玉樹
> 高殿坐幽人
> 書帶留青草
> 琴堂冪素塵
> 平生種桃李
> 寂滅不成春

"The zither room" refers to Confucius' beloved disciple, Fu Buqi, who could tame men's minds across space, just by plucking his qin 琴 or zither.[387]

VIOLENT DEATH

Fig. 59. Zhou Fang 周昉 (eighth c.), "Tuning the Zither" (*Tiaoqin* 調琴)[388]

Plum tree: in Chinese it is written with the same graph as the surname Li 李.

Nirvana, the extinction of every trace.

Chapter 48. The Yunnan War

Ancient airs #34

Winged call to arms, like falling stars,
tiger tally joined in the garrison town.
With urgent cries they rush to aid the borderlands,
flocks of birds cry through the night.

The white sun shines in the Celestial Palace,
and the Three Bureaus keep government in balance.
Heaven and Earth are unified,
and all is pure and peaceful within the Four Seas.

So why this call to arms?
We're recruiting peasant soldiers in the south,
in June they crossed Lu River
on their expedition to Yunnan.
These fearful farmers aren't real troops,
yet they marched through murderous heat.
With long cries they left their kin,
and the colors drained from the sun and moon.
They wept until their tears became blood,
their hearts broke and they fell silent.
They're hobbled beasts sent to meet fierce tigers,
small fish used as chum to catch fast whales.
Of a thousand who go, not one returns,
thrown into battle, how could they survive?

Better to perfect your virtue
and pacify the barbarians with your awe.[389]

VIOLENT DEATH

古風 其三十四

羽檄如流星,虎符合專城
喧呼救邊急,群鳥皆夜鳴
白日曜紫微,三公運權衡
天地皆得一,澹然四海清
借問此何為,答言楚征兵
渡瀘及五月,將赴云南征
怯卒非戰士,炎方難遠行
長號別嚴親,日月慘光晶
泣盡繼以血,心摧兩無聲
困獸當猛虎,窮魚餌奔鯨
千去不一回,投軀豈全生
如何舞干戚,一使有苗平

Yunnan 雲南, "the place that lies south of the clouds," the farthest reaches of empire. Homeland of the Nanzhao 南詔, who are the ostensible enemy in this poem. These people are not Chinese, maybe Tibeto-Burman, still today they retain some language and custom:[390]

Fig. 60. A present-day Yi woman in traditional dress.[391]

With Tang support, in 737 a local chieftain unified surrounding tribespeople and founded the Nanzhao kingdom. In 750 the military governor of nearby Sichuan attempted to rob Nanzhao envoys on their way to court.

The Nanzhao king retaliated. The *Comprehensive Mirror*, China's magisterial history, reports what happened next:

> The year 751. Summer. On the 29th of May the military governor of Sichuan, with 80,000 troops, attacked the Nanzhao barbarians. He suffered a great defeat south of Lu River. […] The king of Nanzhao announced, "Yunnan does not belong to the Tang."
>
> The military governor attacked again. Sixty thousand of his soldiers died, and he barely escaped with his life. Yang Guozhong concealed the circumstances of the defeat and reported a military victory.[392]

Yang Guozhong, corrupt minister, I'll return to him in a minute.

On this map the main Tang territories are to the right. The kingdom of Nanzhao is rendered in orange. To the north-west is the nascent Tibetan empire, as the great king Trisong Detsen comes to the throne.

Fig. 61. Map of the Nanzhao kingdom, around 879 CE.[393]

And thus the first quatrain of Li Bo's poem:

Winged call to arms, like falling stars,
tiger tally joined in the garrison town.
With urgent cries they rush to aid the borderlands,
flocks of birds cry through the night.

A more literal translation of the first line would be, "Feathered calls to arms, like a meteor." Feathers, for emphasis.[394] On 10 July 1937, Generalissimo Chiang Kaishek used the same phrase as the title of his radio address, seeking to rally all Chinese against the invading Japanese:

Fig. 62. Generalissimo Chiang Kaishek accompanied by the phrase from Li Bo. [395]

A meteor is only bad news: a random disordering in the Heavens, always with an occult message.[396] The *Old Tang History* reports a similar event, seven years prior to the Yunnan war:

On the 4th of April 744 a star as bright as the moon fell in the south-east, landing with great noise. Citizens of the capital spread rumors that officials had been sent out to seize human livers to sacrifice to a star-god called Heaven's Dog. People fed each other's fear, especially in the capital region, so that messengers were dispatched to pacify them.[397]

The second line of the poem reads "the tiger tally was joined in the garrison town." Before a general went on deployment with his troops, he and his ruler would split a tally, each keeping one half. Later, when the general received an order in the field, it would be accompanied by the ruler's half of the tally, and the general could match the two halves, so as to ascertain the order's authenticity. Since ancient times these tallies have often had the shape of a tiger, like this:

Fig. 63. Qin Dynasty-era bronze tiger-shaped tally.[398]

Here, the Chinese general in the outlying garrison receives from the governor general of Sichuan an order to attack, accompanied by the governor's half of the tiger.[399]

We've translated the second quatrain of this poem like this:

The white sun shines in the Celestial Palace,
and the Three Bureaus keep government in balance.
Heaven and Earth are unified,
and all is pure and peaceful within the Four Seas.[400]

The bright white sun is His Majesty. Li Bo's poem states that, because the sun is in the Palace, that is, because the Son of Heaven is ruling in accord with cosmic norms, therefore "Heaven and Earth are unified"—literally, "have attained the One (*deyi* 得一)."[401] But this is all irony—it is Li Bo's best shot at political criticism without becoming executed. The *History* with which we began this chapter concludes by saying that "Yang Guozhong concealed the circumstances of the defeat and reported a military victory to the throne." Yang Guozhong 楊國忠 (died 756) was second cousin to the Precious Consort, Yang Guifei 楊貴妃. No one besides the Bright Emperor seems to have liked him, but perhaps that's because his later activities were the casus belli An Lushan needed to begin his rebellion, five years after this Yunnan war. The military governor of Sichuan was Yang Guozhong's client. Therefore Yang covered up the fiasco. Eventual further mishaps led to the death of 200,000 Chinese troops.

Li Bo can't say this. So instead he asks, with faux naïveté, How can there be disorder, since His Majesty's governance is perfect? And then he tells his poem-story of jungle warfare.[402] (The U.S.A. has also had bad experience in this part of South-East Asia.) And he concludes with a radical suggestion, drawn from the classics. We've translated it as

> Better to perfect your virtue
> and pacify the barbarians with your awe,

but it is more literally, "Better to perform the dance of shield and axe, and pacify the barbarians with your awe." In the story behind this dance, the barbarians are the Miao 苗, some of whom now call themselves Hmong. In ancestral times the Chinese Sage-Kings fought them in the northern heartland, but by Tang they had been driven to the mountains of the deep south, where many still reside.[403] In the following account, the Sage-King in question is Shun, Yu his heir apparent:

> The Miao held fast and would not submit. Yu asked permission to attack them, but Shun said, "My virtue is too thin.

> Military action is contrary to Dao. I cannot manifest a virtue that I myself have not yet accomplished." So he trained for three years, practicing the dance of shield and axe. The Miao tendered their submission.[404]

This account invokes a Dao-ful governance, where the splendor of royal virtue compels all subjects to willing submission. But virtue, *de* 德, also means potency, and the dance of shield and axe is magic, it is intimidating, it is grand display, it is a wisdom that conquers without violence. [405] What of this survived in Tang?[406]

Chapter 49. "In Imitation of the Ancients"

In imitation of the ancients, poem 6 of 12

Solstice. The turning quickens, Heaven and Earth shut down.
Barbarian winds chase the flying mists.
A hundred grasses die under this winter moon,
and the sun's six dragons languish in the barrens of the west.
The war planet rises in the eastern quarter,
a comet drags its ghost filaments of light.
Barbarian chieftains strut like cocks,
far from their native roosts.
Eagles and dogs would be lord and king,
racing to become dragon
and seize the phoenix throne.
The Northern Dipper isn't pouring wine,
the Southern Winnowing Basket is now empty of grain.[407]

擬古 十二首其六

運速天地閉，胡風結飛霜
百草死冬月，六龍頹西荒
太白出東方，彗星揚精光
鴛鴦非越鳥，何為眷南翔
惟昔鷹將犬，今為侯與王
得水成蛟龍，爭池奪鳳凰
北斗不酌酒，南箕空簸揚

An Interlude

Chapter 50. "Tea Called 'Palm of the Immortal,' with a Preface"

I, Li Bo, had heard of Jade Spring Temple with its mountains and clear streams. Stalactite caves are everywhere, and inside them waters from many jade springs blend together. The caves are filled with white bats big as crows — ancient lore calls them "immortal rats." After a thousand years their bodies turn white as snow. They roost hanging by their feet, drinking water from the stalactites — that's perhaps why they live so long.

All along these streams are tea plants, thick as gauze netting, their leaves and branches like emerald jade. The Jade Spring Temple master often picks and drinks this tea himself. He's in his eighties now, his complexion like peaches and plums. This tea is pure, fragrant, smooth and mature. Unlike other teas, it can restore your youth, stop aging, and increase your lifespan.

I traveled to Nanjing to see my nephew, the Buddhist monk Zhongfu. He gave me several dozen packets of this tea, curled and folded into many layers. They were called "tea of the palm of the immortal" because they were shaped like hands. I think they'd just been harvested in the Jade Spring mountains. We hadn't seen each other in ages, so he presented me with this tea and also a poem. He requested my response, which follows. Now later generations of eminent monks and great hermits will know about palm tea because of the Zen disciple Zhongfu and the Blue Lotus Layman Li Bo.

I'd often heard of Jade Spring Mountain,
its caves filled with stalactites.
Immortal Rats like white crows
hang upside down over the clear stream moon.
Tea grows in the central part of the mountain,

where jade springs flow endlessly.
Root and stalk dewy with fragrance —
when you pick and drink it, it will moisten your flesh and bones.
Its green leaves coil thickly,
branches intertwining row after row.
After drying in the sun, the leaves become Immortals' Palms —
they're like the touch of an immortal.
Nobody else has seen this yet,
and who is going to tell them?
My nephew, the Zen adept,
gave me some, and one of his fine poems as well.
By comparison, my own work is so plain
that I'm ashamed, like an ugly woman looking at a famous beauty.
Mornings I sit in great delight and chant his poem,
broadcasting it through all the Heavens.[408]

答族侄僧中孚贈玉泉仙人掌茶 并序

余聞荊州玉泉寺近清溪諸山。山洞往往有乳窟。窟中多玉泉交流。其中有白蝙蝠。大如鴉。按仙經。蝙蝠一名仙鼠。千歲之後。體白如雪。棲則倒懸。蓋飲乳水而長生也。其水邊處處有茗草羅生。枝葉如碧玉。惟玉泉真公常采而飲之。年八十余歲。顏色如桃李。而此茗清香滑熟。異于他者。所以能還童振枯。扶人壽也。余游金陵。見宗僧中孚。示余茶數十片。拳然重疊。其狀如手。號為仙人掌茶。蓋新出乎玉泉之山。曠古未覿。因持之見遺。兼贈詩。要余答之。遂有此作。後之高僧大隱。知仙人掌茶發乎中孚禪子及青蓮居士李白也。

常聞玉泉山，山洞多乳窟
仙鼠如白鴉，倒懸清溪月
茗生此中石，玉泉流不歇
根柯洒芳津，采服潤肌骨
叢老卷綠葉，楚枝相接連

曝成仙人掌,似拍洪崖肩
舉世未見之,其名定誰傳
宗英乃禪伯,投贈有佳篇
清鏡燭無鹽,顧慚西子妍
朝坐有余興,長吟播諸天

When this poem was written in 752, tea was just emerging from the monastery. No one else ever much drank it—it was known only as an obscure specialty beverage in the south, or an awake-drug for meditators, or as a *materium medicum*. A decade later China swam in a tea craze, elite and commoners alike, with tea shops, tea plantations, national distribution systems, and, soon enough, targeted commodity taxes.

By 781 even Tibetans were drinking it:

> The honorable Changlu was dispatched to Tibet. When he was boiling tea in his pavilion, the king [Ch. *zanpu* 贊普, Tib. *bTsanpo* བཙན་པོ་] asked him, "What's this you have?" He replied, "It dispels enervation and relieves thirst, it's called 'tea.'" The King said, "I have some too," and he ordered it brought out. Pointing to each, he said, "This one's from Shouzhou, this from Shuzhou, this from Guzhou, this from Qimen, this from Changming, and this one's from Yonghu."[409]

The nodal moment: in the early 760s Lu Yu 陸羽 (733–804) produced his *Classic of Tea* (*Chajing* 茶經), and at once there was a pedigree and grammar within which a fast-maturing connoisseurship could develop—how to brew, what implements, what waters, the right leaves.[410] And thus the possibilities of ritualized social gatherings for friendship, poetry, exultation, but sober, such that even poet-monks could join. Alcohol, says James Benn, "was faced with a serious rival for the first time in Chinese history."[411]

Chapter 51. "Woman on the Silk-washing Rock"

Woman on the silk-washing rock

You jade-face Ye Stream girl,
azure eyelid makeup, blush red powder.
One pair of gold-clasp shoes,
two feet as white as mist.[412]

浣紗石上女

玉面耶溪女
青娥紅粉妝
一雙金齒屐
兩足白如霜

China's tradition speaks of Four Great Beauties (*sida meinü* 四大美女).[413] The Precious Consort was the last of them. The first was Xi Shi 西施 (fifth century BCE), and she is from this Ye Stream, and she washed silk on this rock. Her lover gave her to the King of Yue, who gave her to the King of Wu, so that her beauty might entrance and thus destroy him.[414] And so it was.

Returning home from Wu, after its demise, Xi Shi drowned herself in the Yangtze River.[415]

Chapter 52. "Lotus Picking Song"

A girl picking lotuses
    by Ruoye Stream
laughs and chats with someone
    hidden among the flowers.
The sunlight on her fresh rouge
    reflects on river bottom,
breezes lift her scented sleeves
    into an open sky.

Who are those rakish youths,
    out riding along the river bank?
In threes and fives
    they flash by the willows.
Dark steeds neigh,
    dashing off through the fallen flowers.
She sees them, hesitates, her heart breaks.[416]

採蓮曲

若耶溪旁采蓮女，笑隔荷花共人語
日照新妝水底明，風飄香袂空中舉
岸上誰家游冶郎，三三五五映垂楊
紫騮嘶入落花去，見此踟躕空斷腸.

Eleven hundred years downstream, arriving in a pine-forest valley in the Tyrol, her song was overheard by Gustav Mahler in his composing hut:

AN INTERLUDE

Fig. 64. Gustav Mahler's composing hut.[417]

But first the poem had to be translated from Chinese into French, from French into German, the German translations adapted by Hans Bethge, the adaptation then re-adapted by Mahler and set to music as the fourth movement of his *Song of the Earth, Das Lied von der Erde.*

Chapter 53. "For Revenue Manager Lu"[418]

Autumn colors know no near or far,
it's all cold mountains once you're out the gate.
White clouds, my familiars, wander
and wait for me within the Cangwu Mountains.
Tell me, Lu Dan's crane,
you're flying west, when are you coming back?[419]

贈盧司戶

秋色無遠近
出門盡寒山
白雲遙相識
待我蒼梧間
借問盧敖鶴
西飛幾歲還

Revenue Manager Lu[420] is Lu Xiang 盧象 (?–763), a Tang aristocrat, unusually skillful administrator but also skilled poet, friend of Wang Wei, linked with Du Fu. During the Rebellion he was captured in the Eastern Capital and served An Lushan's government. With the restoration, he was demoted to Revenue Manager in dismal Yongzhou 永州, the deep south, by the Cangwu Mountains where Sage-King Shun had wandered and died three thousand years before.[421] See the poem "Distant parting," a few chapters hence.

Lu Dan — the same surname, but of an unknown time. From the *Records of Nankang* 南康記 (*Nankang ji*):[422]

> Once there was an official named Lu Dan. When young, he'd mastered the arts of the immortals, and he could unbind himself and fly with the clouds. Each evening he'd mount the sky and return home, and at dawn he'd come back to court. One time he didn't appear at the ruler's morning audience.

He had become a white crane, which circled in the air before the palace, trying to land. The dignitaries of the court threw rocks at it and grabbed a shoe. Lu Dan startled and took his place in the assembly. Everyone was shocked.

Li Bo's poem says, "Tell me, Lu Dan's crane," but he might equally have said, "Tell me, Lu Dan, you crane…."

Chapter 54. Drunk Rock

Drunk Rock is on the banks of Fragrant Springs Creek. Once, when Li Bo roamed here, he circumambulated the rock, shouting drunkenly. Whence its name.

— from *The Record of the Yellow Mountains* (*Huangshan zhi* 黃山志)[423]

VIIA

The Rebellion, a History

The Rebellion of An Lushan

An Lushan, a non-Chinese general commanding the armies of the north-east frontier. In 755 he rebels and soon captures Chang'an. The Bright Emperor flees, his Precious Consort is put to death, his son seizes the throne.

After some years Tang forces reclaim the empire. But it is not the same.

(This may be all you need in order to understand the poems of Li Bo that follow some dozen pages hence. If you don't much care for history, feel free to skip ahead ̂.)

1. The Dictatorship of Li Linfu[424]
The imperial kinsman Li Linfu 李林甫 (d. 752) served as chief minister from 734 until his death eighteen years later. An exceptionally gifted executive, he rationalized the practices of finance, law and trade, without which the Great Tang would have foundered.[425]

As the Bright Emperor's attention turned gradually to private life, he depended increasingly on Li Linfu. But Li served at His Majesty's whim, his position always vulnerable to men just like him. In the mid-740s he devoted his skills to consolidating personal power. For two years his methods remained within the court norms of intrigue, slander and manipulation.

Then the killings began.[426] By decade's end, Li was virtual dictator. Progressively he annihilated not only present talent — administrative, financial and military — but also any possible successors in the next generation. When he died, he left only the mechanisms of authoritarian rule.[427]

The Great Tang depended on ten military governors stationed along the northern frontier. Li Linfu had briefly held such a post — it was a normal career rotation for future chief ministers, and thus no Chinese governor had reason to seek long-term allegiances from his troops. To block others' access to this path, Li arranged that only non-Chinese would be appointed to the frontiers, and that the appointments be made long-term. An Lushan was one of these non-Chinese, and a close client of Li Linfu. When Li died in 752, An's enemies came to power at court. Fearing his own ouster, three years later he rebelled.

2. Cousin to the Precious Consort
Only one man had a base from which to oppose Li Linfu. It was Yang Guozhong 楊國忠 (d 756), second cousin to the Precious Consort Yang Guifei and favored official of the Bright Emperor. On the basis of these relationships, he succeeded Li as chief minister in 752. He had all of Li's jealousies but much less of his administrative acumen.[428]

Yang hated An Lushan. With Li dead, Yang moved increasingly against An, his relatives, his staff. An Lushan reciprocated. And thus the court at Chang'an and the empire's most powerful general were impossibly divided against themselves, and the body politic ruptured.[429]

When An rebelled, he had quick success, immediately capturing the eastern capital Luoyang. But the South held loyal; he could not advance west to Chang'an; and Tang forces nearly severed his supply lines in the north-east. The rebellion might have ended there, but for a single error. The capital could be approached only through the tight defile of Tong Pass 潼關, with 800-meter summits on both its sides. Here Tang forces could easily withstand attack. Yang Guozhong, though, feared the power of the defending general, Geshu Han, almost as much as he feared An Lushan. Against Geshu Han's repeated objections, Yang ordered him to pass through the pass and attack An Lushan's forces on the flat. Geshu Han was defeated, An Lushan moved easily on Chang'an, the Bright Emperor fled with a small entourage in the middle of the night, heading for safety in Yang Guozhong's virtually impregnable home province of Sichuan.[430]

Twenty-five miles west of the capital, his guard mutinies. They blame everything on the Yang family. They kill Yang Guozhong, and they demand that the Emperor put the Precious Consort to death as well. He cannot resist. He gives the order that she be strangled.

3. The Northern Frontier

The Eurasian steppelands extend 6,000 miles from Korea to the Hungarian basin. Generally arid, with extremes of heat and cold — a nomad pastoralism of sheep and horses is the only human activity to which they are well suited. By contrast, China can be defined as a socio-political technology of sedentary agriculture.

Fig. 65. Eurasian steppelands.[431]

Steppe people had long depended on the Chinese for grain, textiles, and metals, as well as the luxury goods used in inter-nomad diplomacy. They generally paid for these with horses. A delicate balance: Successful diplomacy meant trade and peace, failure meant nomad raids — they were born horsemen, no Chinese was a match — or huge and costly Chinese expeditions into unfamiliar landscapes.[432] As nomad ambitions grew in the mid-eighth century, An Lushan and the other governors general north and west were the Tang's one line of defense.[433]

But Tang emperors were of mixed Turkic-Chinese blood. In 626 the Bright Emperor's great-grandfather rode out the gates of Chang'an with six men in order to berate, and dispel, a Turkic force that was threatening the capital. Six years later he had conquered the lot of them and ruled not just as Emperor of Great Tang but also as Heavenly Qaghan over the Turks.[434] This coincidence of rule was not mere military domination, as Jonathan Skaff has deftly shown. Instead it reflected fundamental commonalities between Turkic and Chinese understandings of governance — what Skaff calls "Eastern Eurasian" values and practices.[435] These styles of political relationship were deeply structured in patron-client ties, employing fictive kinship and diplomatic ritual to mark and instantiate political and economic alliances.[436] Such modalities were especially apt to the marches of empire, where neither Chinese nor nomad claimed sole dominance. The vulnerability of the system — and we will see this played out in the Rebellion — is its inscription not in treaty or tradition but in the immediate personal ties of two men. When one dies, or becomes incapacitated, the deal is broken.

Like his great-grandfather, the Bright Emperor was also successful in his frontier policies, orchestrating balances in the steppelands and deterring Tibetan incursions. Twitchett summarizes the situation in 750 like this:

> The defence of the enormously long frontiers was costly both in manpower and in support. But the T'ang court was successful in securing its objectives, and few of the campaigns of Hsüan-tsung's time resulted from an aggressive policy towards China's neighbours or from expansionist ambitions.[437]

When Li Bo served in court, his duties included attention to these matters. It's said that he met with the Bright Emperor, and

> they discussed world affairs. Li Bo drafted "A rescript in reply to the Western Turks," his brush never pausing.[438]

Much soon changed. First, in 751 the Tang's Korean general Gao Xianzhi 高仙芝, whose spectacular campaigns had carried him as far as the Aral and Caspian Seas, was defeated by an army of the Abbasid Caliphate at Talas, on the border of present day

Kazakhstan and Kyrgyzstan. In coming years, the Arabs would continue their way east.

And then the rebellion. The only Tang troops capable of defeating An Lushan were stationed in those western regions. Pulled back to the defense of Chang'an, they left a vacuum that was to be filled by Tibetans and Uyghurs. Chinese control of central Asia was then lost for a thousand years.[439]

4. An Lushan
The *Traces of the Events in An Lushan's life* (*An Lushan shiji* 安祿山事迹) begins:

> An Lushan was a mixed-race barbarian from Yingzhou. When he was young, he was named Yalukshan (Yaluoshan 軋犖山). His mother, from the Asiduk clan, was a Turkic shaman. She was childless, so she prayed to Yalukshan. The deity responded, and she gave birth. That night red light shone all around, and beasts in all directions yowled.

His father was Sogdian — we can tell this from his surname An.[440] His Chinese given name, Lushan, was pronounced Luk-sran in Tang times and is an alternative way of writing Ya-luk-shan. These are both approximations of his original Sogdian name Rokshan — it's an Iranian word meaning "Bright," which we have in English as Roxanne.[441]

Fig. 66. A Sogdian with his hunting owl, Tang ceramic.[442]

His later activities make it difficult to find positive accounts of him in the Chinese sources. Yet even those portray a warrior of unusual girth, strength, vigor and resolution, and his annual reviews speak of "impartiality, honesty and unselfishness."[443] And so he was quickly promoted through the ranks.

And always the possibility of impetuous aggression, as when in 736 he disobeys orders, attacks nomad forces, is badly defeated. By regulation, he should be executed on the spot. When his commanding officer is about to behead him, An retorts, "The barbarians are not yet pacified, yet you can bear to kill a brave officer. Could this be the extent of your strategy?" He is pardoned.[444]

By the 740s he is regularly in Chang'an. His girth has grown to stoutness. In the Selection Examinations of 744, Li Linfu had entertained gross favoritism, but no one dared let on. An Lushan learned of it, spoke candidly to the Emperor. The winning candidate was re-examined by the Emperor and turned out to be illiterate, handing in a blank sheet of paper. Everyone laughed.[445]

Increasingly An is promoted and rewarded. "The Emperor built a mansion for him, elegant and beautiful to the extreme."[446] His eldest son, An Qingzong, is established there as ambassador/hostage, is appointed President of the Court of Imperial Equipage, and is married to a royal princess. "In return An Lushan presents the emperor with slaves, horses, camels, and extraordinary treasures, exotic imports that he was able to procure easily through his ties to the Sogdian and Turkic trading communities."[447]

> In 751 An Lushan requested to become a foster son of the Precious Consort. Thereafter, whenever he entered the Imperial presence, he always prostrated first to her. The Bright Emperor found it strange and asked him about it. He replied, "Your subject is a barbarian. A barbarian puts his mother ahead of his father." His Majesty was greatly pleased and subsequently ordered the Precious Consort's younger siblings to swear brotherhood with him.[448]

I suppose it's An's rough ease that endeared him to the Precious Consort and Bright Emperor, that confidence. He's not your typical Chinese courtier. The Imperial couple seem to genuinely like him — he has the personality of a dynastic founder, but he's not purely hard-edged *yang*, the way Li Linfu is, he can also play *yin*, just like his Imperial sponsors.[449] As in this account:

> It was An Lushan's birthday. His Majesty and the Precious Consort bestowed an abundance of clothes, precious objects, wine and delicacies on him. Three days later, he was called to the inner palace. The Precious Consort had made an enormous set of swaddling clothes for him from fine brocades. She wrapped him in these and had the palace servants carry him about in a gay palanquin.
> His Majesty heard giggling in the inner palace and asked its cause. People said it was the Precious Consort washing her new baby.[450] His Majesty went to have a look. Delighted, he gave the Precious Consort "new-baby washing" money.

He also richly rewarded An Lushan, taking endless pleasure in him.[451]

Later his stoutness grows to obesity, and his eyesight begins to blur.

His stomach hung below his knees, and he weighed 330 catties.[452] When he walked, he'd put his arms around his attendants' shoulders to support his weight — only then could he move about. But when he came before the Bright Emperor, he'd perform the Barbarian Whirlwind dance, quick as the wind.[453]

Li Linfu dies and is replaced by Yang Guozhong, who (of suspicious mind himself) sees only treason in An, and acts to undermine his power, with the natural effect of alienating An, with the natural effect of an escalating alienation of these two men, these twin nexuses of power. So sure of An's treason is Yang Guozhong, that he tells the Bright Emperor to invite him to court in the winter of 754, confident that An will not dare come. But An appears. After that the Bright Emperor will entertain no further doubts about him. But Yang Guozhong treats him with such hostility that when An leaves the capital for home, he travels post-haste by boat and will not disembark until he is in safety three hundred miles to the east.

When An finally rebels, one year later, he claims to have received a secret order from His Majesty to remove Yang Guozhong from power. Yang has maltreated enough other people that a number of Chinese are willing to follow An into revolt. At that point the Bright Emperor seizes An's son at his Chang'an home and executes him. When An learns of this, he massacres the entire surrendering Chinese garrison of Shan Commandery. When he eventually captures the capital, he executes the Emperor's sister and a number of other relatives, sacrificing their bodily organs to his late son.

How did An Lushan understand his rebellion? It's said in the *Histories* that he had planned it for seven or eight years, colluding with his childhood friend Shi Siming 史思明. Perhaps this is true. But I think a better answer lies in the Turkic succession practices within which he lived. Succession was the institutional Achilles heel of Turkic power. The leader's death — or even his weakening — set off a feeding frenzy among sons, relatives and outsiders.[454] This was not foreign to Tang. The de facto founding emperor, Li Shimin, himself part Turk, had come to power in just this way, deposing his father and murdering his brothers.[455]

I expect An understood his move much in these terms. His fictive father, the Bright Emperor, was seventy years old when he rebelled. Yang Guozhong and the Crown Prince were the only other contending forces, and An's power was greater. So An sought to wrest the throne from the diminished Bright Emperor. And in just the same way, the Bright Emperor's own Crown Prince actually *did* usurp the throne while his father was in Sichuan exile.[456]

In turn, when An himself became decrepit two years later, he was killed by his own son. His obesity had become increasingly debilitating, and his eyesight had begun to fail. After the capture of Chang'an, the western capital, he spent most of his time in Luoyang, the eastern capital, in the inner palace. As his physicality deteriorated, so did his mood. In violent agitation, he struck or even killed those who annoyed him. Though he had an heir, he began to favor another son. His heir, fearing his father would disinherit him, conspired to kill him. When the assassin entered his bedroom, An could not find the sword he had hidden under his bed. His son took the throne.

But An's close colleague Shi Siming, co-leader of the revolt, finds this unacceptable. Two years later, in 759, he kills An's son and takes the throne himself. But Shi's own son kills him two years after that. It's the law of the jungle, again and again, nothing aberrant or surprising, and nothing especially moral or immoral.

5. A Historiographic Intermezzo
The activities I've spoken of so far can mostly be accounted for by ordinary human self-interest. That is, they require no more

sophisticated explanatory mode than the simple logic of cause and effect.[457] As such, their story could have been written a thousand years ago. As indeed it was — I've said very little that hadn't been set forth in the histories written soon enough after the events.

Now, though, to different stories. To the Precious Consort and the Bright Emperor. To a different set of realities, not always causal, a court-based world that for two years included Li Bo. If Li Linfu, Yang Guozhong and An Lushan are the playthings of their appetites, the Imperial couple aspires to be the playground of the divine. Yet sometimes they too are its bitches. Those realities are what I really want to know, but they are hidden, mostly in the Bright Emperor. So I will go step by step, starting with the Precious Consort.

6. The Precious Consort

She became Precious Consort when the Bright Emperor took her from her husband, who was his son. She was about twenty, he in his mid-fifties. It is therefore difficult to ascertain much about her, since the usual sober witnesses recoiled in horror from his act, their silence leaving the field to balladeers and pornographers.[458] But it is clear she had extraordinary being, for she found her mate in the most powerful man in the world and kept him young for fifteen years.

In the *Old Tang History* we hear these stories:

> She was proficient at singing and dance, and thoroughly adept at music. She was also unusually good at sizing things up.

And:

> Seven hundred palace workers wove and embroidered for her, and several hundred more did carving and molding. The Prefects of the southern provinces vied to find skilled artisans to create singular objects and exceptional clothing that they could present to her.

Twice she offended the Emperor and was expelled from court, but twice recalled within a day.

As An Lushan's troops were poised to enter Chang'an, the Emperor, Consort and a small entourage fled to Sichuan. Two days out, his guard mutinies. They execute Yang Guozhong, but still they won't desist.

> The Bright Emperor sent his chief eunuch Gao Lishi to make formal inquiry. The guard responded: "The root of this banditry still exists" — this was their way of referring to the Precious Consort. Gao Lishi again petitioned the Emperor, and the Emperor could not prevent it. He gave his command to the Consort, and Gao Lishi went and strangled her at a Buddhist cloister. She was in her thirty-eighth year. She was buried beside the road, to the west of the courier station.
>
> [Three years later when the Retired Emperor passed this place on his return from exile in Sichuan], he had his eunuchs offer oblations to her spirit. He also ordered them to rebury her. But Li Gui, Vice President of the Bureau of Ritual,[459] said, "The officers and men of the Dragon Militant Army executed Yang Guozhong because he betrayed the state and incited rebellion. If you now rebury the late Consort, I fear they will become suspicious and apprehensive. The ritual of reburying cannot be carried out." So the Former Emperor desisted. But secretly he had his eunuchs reinter her some other place.
>
> When the Precious Consort was first buried, her body was wrapped in purple matting. Her skin and flesh had already decayed, but her perfume sachet still remained. A eunuch brought it to the Former Emperor. He looked at it and blanched.[460]

The histories are replete with her extravagance, and that of her beautiful sisters and their kin. But they never once allege that she was cruel, spiteful, stingy, shrewish, vicious, violent, vindictive, high-handed, jealous or manipulative, all the other things that bad Chinese women are always said to be.

7. The Bright Emperor[161]

The future emperor lived his first years under the Terror of his grandmother, the Emperor Wu. (She took the theretofore male title "Emperor" *huangdi* 皇帝 — there is no such animal in Chinese as an Empress.) With extraordinary intelligence and a ruthlessness appropriate to her misogynistic environment, she deposed the future emperor's grandfather and father and founded her own dynasty, the Zhou 周, in 690. The future emperor, his brothers and their parents lived in harsh unpredictability under palace-arrest. When two officials made an unauthorized visit to the deposed emperor, they were executed in the public market. When he was eight, Emperor Wu executed his mother on spurious charges of fortune telling and magic (code words for treason).

Emperor Wu was deposed in 705, when the future emperor was twenty. Over the next eight years he led palace coups against two women who sought to emulate her dynastic ambitions, the Empress Wei and the Taiping Princess, both of whom he ordered to commit suicide. Only in 712 did he ascend the throne.[462]

Yet he ruled with an even hand, not seeking vengeance, welcoming the unflinching advice of his chief ministers. And his warmth was evident to all, especially to his brothers, who were otherwise his competitors. Denis Twitchett comments:

> The princes were an accomplished family, devoted to literature, music and scholarship as well as to the upper-class sports so dear to the T'ang nobility, and shared many of the emperor's tastes. Closest to the emperor was Li Ch'eng-ch'i, who shared his devotion to music and dramatic entertainment and frequently feasted, hunted, played polo or attended cock-fights with him.[463]

And thus Twitchett summarizes the first thirty years of his reign, designated in Chinese as the Kaiyuan period:[464]

> Up to this point the administration had been markedly successful. Reforms had made the empire's government smooth-

er and more efficient than ever before. The regime was prosperous, and it had won a striking series of victories over its foreign enemies. Moreover, this had been accomplished without any purges of the bureaucracy. The aristocrats were firmly in a position of power, while the Confucian scholars in the bureaucracy were carefully kept away from the real seats of power and influence.[465]

As the Kaiyuan period ends in 742, the Bright Emperor's court was the locus of extravagance, ostentation, enrichment, brilliance, plenteousness, of splendor. Everything seemed possible.[466] His Majesty had just connected with the Precious Consort, and so (in Wilhelm Reich's terms) he was getting enough good sex.[467] We have already met his orchestra and dramatic troupe, his painters, his dancing horses, who on command would drink wine from a dish, as in this late Tang gilt-silver jar, in the shape of a northern nomad's leather pouch:

Fig. 67. Tang-era gilt-silver jar.[468]

The Bright Emperor holds these energies in orbit — and also the steppe peoples and bureaucrats and aristocrats — by the power of his majesty, which distracts everyone from their separatism. He overcomes through splendor. Li Bo enters this world, he matches it, he recognizes its reality, he can swim in it, delight in it, and represent it. He can walk away. We have seen his songs for the peony garden night music, his edicts for the Turks, his pleasure in riding His Majesty's horses.

An Lushan first visits now. Like Li Bo, born outside a Chinese-speaking region. Like Li Bo, uncowed by His Majesty, and able to play the fool. To duel with His Majesty. He and the Bright Emperor both loved war, in James Hillman's sense of that phrase.[469] Two high rollers, two men who could found dynasties. Friends — but with a necessary distance between them.[470]

This is also the time of Amoghavajra, greatest of the Indic tantric masters who visited the Bright Emperor's court.[471] He ministered to His Majesty in the mid-740s, giving instructions, bestowing empowerments and perhaps controlling weather.[472] When Rebellion erupted, the Emperor summoned him to Chang'an, where he remained throughout the war.

And especially this is the time of the Emperor's Daoist visions and his efforts to make them the ground for Imperial rule. In 741,

> in the fourth month, the Emperor dreamed that there was a statue of Laozi, the Heavenly Honored One, at the base of the Zhongnan Mountains near the Capital. Men went looking and found it on the banks of Qiao Pool.[473]

Also in 741,

> in the eighth month, a likeness of Lord Laozi appeared vividly in the Kaiyuan Abbey of Lingzhou. A dozen or more Daoist priests could see it for a long time.[474]

And in the fall a courtier met Laozi on the streets of Chang'an. He was told how to find a sacred talisman, which he presented to His Majesty. As a result, the Emperor changed the name of the reign period from Kaiyuan to Tianbao 天寶, "Heavenly Treasure."

Aligning these events with institutional realities, the Emperor established a series of Laozi temples throughout the realm. Each served both to train priests and as a more general force of Daoist education, preparing potential bureaucrats for civil service exams based on Daoist instead of Confucian classics. Laozi, the Imperial ancestor, was recognized as the highest of all possible deities, and his text, the *Daodejing,* the most sacred of all writings in Chinese.[475] This was a new ground of monarchy, explicitly divine, a new politico-religious culture, "an attempt to produce a Taoist form of government unique in Chinese history."[476]

Though some modern historians have dismissed these activities as political exigency, the Bright Emperor did not. He knew the dignity of the divine, and he wrote his own commentary to the *Laozi*. Its Preface is replete with archaic formulae and pomp, so I will translate its opening lines twice, first in paraphrase and then allowing its full formal features to emerge:

> 1. In ancient times Laozi wrote words of mystery, transmitting the true teachings to future generations.
> 2. The primal sage, existent since ancient times, perforce divulged his words of mystery, that he might opportunely convey his genuine lineage and enlighten his descendants.[477]

Here is the Emperor's commentary on the opening lines of chapter 1 of Laozi's text, "The Dao that can be followed is not the constant Dao, names that can be named are not constant names."

> Dao is the marvelous activity of the empty ultimate, names are how one speaks of the nature of things. Activity is only possible with things, thus he says "it can be followed." Names arise in activity, thus he says "they can be named." There is no method for finding right action, and thus action is not constant as a single way. Things are multiple and their names differ, thus they are not constant as a single name. We therefore

force a name on it when we call it Dao, but Dao's constancy has no name.

To practice this, to master this, to enact this, the Emperor needed Li Linfu to care for the details of governance, while he drew down charisma, transforming ordinary splendor into divine grace.[478] As we have seen, in his delegation of authority things went very wrong.

If we are human beings, we want to know how they went wrong. If in addition we are Confucian moralists — and there are a ton of us, in China and elsewhere — we conclude that it was the Emperor's infatuation with Yin, the feminine principle, that secured his downfall.[479] But, as Mark Lewis points out, this is just misogyny coupled with our own self-righteousness.[480]

If we are institutional historians, we might agree with Denis Twitchett that

> unlike some of his successors — and indeed unlike his great predecessor T'ai-tsung — Hsüan-tsung continued his gruelling round of daily audiences, except for periods of state mourning, until 755, when he was already seventy years of age. No emperor, however superhuman, could have kept up the pace of Hsüan-tsung's early years for more than forty years without slowing down.[481]

If we are Protestant, we might say the Bright Emperor neglected governance in favor of sex, entertainment and the occult. But the Emperor never conducted himself frivolously, and I would suggest that the roots of this triad are grounded in love, art and the divine. When psychologists such as Maslow set up hierarchies of needs, these three tend to be on one end of the spectrum, while safety, shelter and food are on another. If you get enough safety and food, they are no longer needs. But the more you get of the other three, the more you want. It's why Maslow calls his high end "self-transcendence" — the larger you become, the more you sense the infinance of possibility.[482]

If we are vulgar Buddhists, we might see the Rebellion as the karmic result of the Emperor's lust for his son's wife. But if we recognize that his deep karma included the obligation to rule, then we could say instead that the Rebellion arose because he didn't fulfill that karmic duty to his subjects. Nonetheless, we don't have ready access to his private religious practices. If he were working intensively with Daoist and Tantric masters, they would have shown him how he could express his passions through active rulership. By this logic, his fault was to stop too soon, in the smaller pleasures of his consort relationship.

If we believe in deities, we might say that the Bright Emperor and his Precious Consort conjured energies they could not control, which demanded payment in blood.

Or we could take a simple materialist view, that he left a power vacuum, and dudes were dudes, and it went badly for everyone.

8. Death

Ryan Flaherty imagines the sixty-thousand untrained peasant soldiers who were sent to defend the Tang from An Lushan's horsemen:

> The blade of the pike is like a scythe, so the peasant feels less alone. With one end of the six-foot pole braced between his feet, the heavy blade swings above him, and he has to be vigilant that some quirk of momentum doesn't drop it on the head of one of the men standing around him. This awareness keeps him preoccupied and distracted from the cold and how his fingers feel like short, useless stubs of twine. I imagine rising above him to look across the field of tightly packed men, pikes eddying like reeds, all facing one way: the exit of the Hulao Pass. Sixty thousand mostly silent men — shifting from foot to foot because of the cold and an almost impenetrable fear that keeps threatening to paralyze them. Listening for it. From the few horses, men yell orders into the wind, and the immense distance dwarfs the tiny radius of their voices in the mass. Every one of them is terribly alone, staring toward

the still-empty pass where reverberating hoof beats are just starting to avalanche down on them.⁴⁸³

The Chinese military historian David Graff tells what happened next: "This untrained rabble was trampled beneath the hooves of An Lushan's veteran cavalry."⁴⁸⁴

We don't know how many people died in the Rebellion.⁴⁸⁵ That's how bad it was. In the contested areas of north China, perhaps one half. That would be some ten million. Combatants are just a fraction of this. When Napoleon said "An army marches on its stomach,"⁴⁸⁶ he meant on someone else's stomach, the stomach of local farmers, who were robbed, raped and killed. And who then met starvation and plague, leading to what the demographers call "excess deaths," that is, a statistically unanticipated mortality due to the heightened vulnerability of individuals and the ecosystem. And then banditry — how else would a man survive, if not by force of arms?⁴⁸⁷ For seven years, armies passed through and through these spaces.⁴⁸⁸

Fig. 68. Tang farmers with their agricultural tools, seventh-century ceramic figures, the Metropolitan Museum of Art.⁴⁸⁹

Du Fu saw this and wrote of it:

The army clerks in Stone Trough

Twilight across Stone Trough Village:
Army clerks are catching people by night.
An old man hops the wall and escapes;
his old wife opens the door.
How horrid the officers' roaring,
how sorrowful the woman's wails.
"Hear now this old woman's story:
I had three sons garrisoned at Ye;
One of them just wrote us saying
the other two have died in battle.
The living live a stolen life,
as for the dead, they're gone forever!
Now there's no one under this roof,
only my suckling baby grandson.
Her mother, who is still alive,
goes about with a tattered skirt.
I'm an old hag, my strength long gone,
but please, take me this night
to join your campaigning in Heyang,
and I may yet cook the morning meal."
The night was long, the words faded,
and I thought I heard a muffled sobbing.
At dawn, I set out on my way
with only the old man to bid me goodbye.

石壕吏

暮投石壕村,有吏夜捉人。老翁逾牆走,老婦出門看。
吏呼一何怒,婦啼一何苦。聽婦前致詞,三男鄴城戍。
一男附書至,二男新戰死。存者且偷生,死者長已矣。
室中更無人,惟有乳下孫。有孫母未去,出入無完裙。
老嫗力雖衰,請從吏夜歸。急應河陽役,猶得備晨炊。
夜久語聲絕,如聞泣幽咽。天明登前途,獨與老翁別。

The Chinese name for the Rebellion is *AnShi zhi luan* 安史之亂, the chaos-ing of An Lushan and Shi Siming. Social order is precious, precarious, expensive, essential. Ninety percent of Tang Chinese were farmers. They depended on absent others for their survival.

9. The Dancing Horses
Paul Kroll translates this account of their demise:

> Subsequently, when His Highness graced Sichuan with his presence, the dancing horses were for their part dispersed to the mortal world. An Lushan, having often witnessed their dancing, coveted them at heart; because of this he had a number of them transported to Fanyang. Subsequently, they were in turn acquired by Tian Chengsi. He knew nothing of them. Confusing them with battle-horses, he installed them in the outer stables. Unexpectedly one day, when the soldiers of his army were enjoying a sacrificial feast and music was struck up, the horses, unable to stop themselves, began to dance. The servants and lackeys considered them bewitched and took brooms in hand to strike them. The horses thought that their dancing must be out of step with the rhythm and, stooping and rearing, nodding and straining, they still vied to repeat their former movements. The stablemaster hurried to report this grotesquerie, and Chengsi ordered that the horses be scourged. The more fiercely this was done, the more precise became the horses' dancing. But the whipping and flogging ever increased, till finally they fell dead in their stalls. On this occasion there were in fact some persons who knew these were the [emperor's] dancing horses, but fearful of Chengsi's wrath, they never ventured to speak.[490]

10. The End of the Han Dynasty
In an early part of this book, when I introduced the staid culture of the court, I stressed its dependency on models from the past. The Sage-Kings of antiquity had discerned the Dao of Heaven and Earth, and instantiated it in their social and literary institu-

tions—that is, in every aspect of high cultural life, public and private. Thus a gentleman's education, comportment, social relationships, his poetry itself, were explicitly based on that ancient wisdom.

The Rebellion made it impossible to sustain this belief. Those cultural forms had failed. And Han dynasty authority faded with them. In *This Culture of Ours,* Peter Bol discusses the "erosion of faith in the possibility of guiding the world by defining correct appearances" and a growing conviction "that the foundation for true ideas about how to act existed independently from culture."[491] Instead of molding oneself in the ancients, one must do as they had done, perceive Dao directly and discover the forms appropriate to current circumstances.[492] The ideology of post-Rebellion literature reflects these shifts as well, with its growing insistence on the writer's singular identity within a private sphere.[493]

Since even before Han times, the Chinese elite had maintained a utopian view of farm life, a commitment to the fiction that every peasant family had equal land holdings. The state thus taxed agriculture on this fantasy of homogeneity, and worked to prevent local elites from accumulating large landed estates. The Rebellion hastened the demise of this thousand-year ideal, as the diminished state abandoned its control of rural life and turned to the commercial taxes that would supply an increasing portion of its income in the coming millennium.

Imperial policy of the early Tang had pursued an overtly multi-ethnic policy,[494] the cultural fruits of which have been richly exposed by Schafer and others. But the Rebellion brought a racist backlash, and Marc Abramson argues that this "was perhaps the crucial point in the formation of an ethnically Han (as opposed to culturally Chinese) identity."[495] That is, the semi-permeable membrane of "Chineseness," which had been primarily constructed from an ability to manipulate the written texts of antiquity, hardened into a race-based criterion.

Finally, the Rebellion created a meritocracy that was to characterize Chinese government until the twentieth century. Lineage, wealth, power, office-holding: for centuries this foursome had been unassailably inseparable. But a military circumstance is wholly pragmatic, and the militarization of north China, which continued for the next two hundred years, past the fall of the Great Tang, couldn't care less for pedigree. By the subsequent Song dynasty (960–1279), the aristocratic Great Families were dead.

For all these reasons, historians have argued that the Rebellion marks the biggest shift in Chinese history between the Qin unification of empire in 221 BCE and China's transformation in the nineteenth, twentieth and twenty-first centuries.[496]

11. How the War Was Won[497]

Meanwhile, in occupied Chang'an, Amoghavajra is doing wrathful mantra. We've seen how the Bright Emperor had called him there at the outbreak of hostilities. He'd been in the northwest with Geshu Han, the general whose forces would soon be forced to leave their strong defensive position east of Chang'an, thus to be disastrously defeated on the plains.

Amoghavajra (Bukong Jin'gang 不空金剛 [704–774]) was Sogdian by birth. He came to China when he was ten.[498] Sent by the Bright Emperor on a diplomatic mission to India and Sri Lanka in 741, he received transmission of the Buddhist tantra that was just emerging in these places, returning in 746 with some five hundred volumes of texts.[499] In 750 he joined service with Geshu Han as preceptor and protector.

Among his eventual disciples were members of the military establishment, the civilian government, the Imperial family, and the two monarchs who succeeded the Bright Emperor, Suzong 肅宗 (rg. 756–62) and Daizong 代宗 (rg. 762–79). With their support he established monasteries training hundreds of monks, a multilingual team that produced seventy translations, and a lineage of East Asian Esoteric Buddhism (Ch. Zhenyan, Jap. Shingon 真言) that persists until today. The modern scholar Geoffrey Goble concludes: "He was easily the most powerful Buddhist cleric in the Tang."[500]

Goble wants to know how this came about. His answer: Amoghavajra's incomparable ability to destroy large numbers of enemies at a distance. He held tantric teachings that were previously unknown to the Great Tang, by which he could "command fierce, lethal deities to kill enemies and rout opposing armies."[501] Though Daoists also possessed military rituals, they were only capable of averting, not of striking. Amoghavajra's primary practice was the fierce deity Acala, Budong 不動, "The immovable wisdom king."[502]

Fig. 69. Statue of Fudou Myouou (Acala), from early 13th century (Kamakura period) Japan [503]

Here is one of his several rites:

> There is also the method for those who wish to cause enemies to perish: obtain rice chaff, recite the spell empowerment and cast [the chaff] into a fire to burn. Also imagine those enemies bound with ropes by the envoy [Acala], led to the southern direction of stifling suffering, vomiting blood, and perishing. Those [enemies] and their ilk will all be unable to recover. Not a single one will survive.[504]

This is how the war was won. Goble explains:

> Though An Lushan met with immediate success, moving rapidly and almost without resistance to within striking distance of the imperial capitals, he was murdered by his son, An Qingxu, with the support of his own commanders. An Qingxu was himself murdered by a trusted associate, Shi Siming (史思明), who was likewise assassinated by his own son, Shi Chaoyi (史朝義), who in turn was abandoned by his own troops and was killed in 763. The invasion and occupation of Chang'an that same year by Tibetan forces was defeated by a gang of rabble. When a force of confederate foreigners organized by Pugu Huai'en invaded the Wei Valley west of Chang'an in 765, their advance was halted by rivers swollen by heavy rain and they were defeated by infighting. The turncoat general Pugu Huai'en slunk off to the northwest where he fell ill and died.[505]

Pulleyblank attributes these matters to luck.[506] But Goble, following the *Old Tang History*,[507] is confident that "these events were attributed [by the Tang elite] to the supernormal intercession of beings commanded by Amoghavajra."[508]

12. Historiography, Again
I realize that, without conscious intent, my method here has been closely allied with the Tang practice of "historical miscellanies" (*zalu* 雜錄), what Manling Luo calls "the piecing together of anecdotes gathered from oral and written sources to create a composite, multifaceted picture of the past, or 'mosaic memory.'"[509] A mosaic implies a whole made up many single pieces. And, indeed, it would be gratifying if there were a single picture emerging from these events, a master narrative, an encompassing theory or historical principle, a totality, that is, a place to stand to know it all. Instead I see only multiple patterns, forming and unforming, without coming anywhere to rest.

We could go further. When the Bright Emperor's grandmother the Emperor Wu was perplexed by reality, her monk-instructor, the Sogdian-Chinese Fazang 法藏 (643–712), told her of Indra's cobweb. It has dewdrops at each interstice, the whole world reflected in each, and each reflecting all the others, ad infinitum, ad nauseam, ad absurdum.[510]

This kind of messes with cause and effect. We've seen how the heuristic of causality explains a lot about An Lushan and Li Linfu, and too we've seen the inadequacies of this mode to account for other realities. Causality is certainly hard on every philosopher: as an empiricist-nihilist, Hume can see the boy's foot kicking and the ball moving, but he can't see anything there he would call "causality."[511] Fazang can't even find anything he would call "a foot" or "a ball." Only shards of light. So he sums up the nature of causality like this: "When Joe Schmo drinks wine, Jane Doe gets drunk" (*Zhang San hejiu, Li Si zui* 張三喝酒，李四醉).[512]

13. *Invocation and Envoi*

Swami Vivekananda, student of the great Ramakrishna, wrote this English-language poem in 1898.

Kali the Mother

The stars are blotted out,
  The clouds are covering clouds,
It is darkness vibrant, sonant.
  In the roaring, whirling wind
Are the souls of a million lunatics
  Just loose from the prison-house,
Wrenching trees by the roots,
  Sweeping all from the path.
The sea has joined the fray,
  And swirls up mountain-waves,
To reach the pitchy sky.
  The flash of lurid light
Reveals on every side
  A thousand, thousand shades
Of Death begrimed and black—

> Scattering plagues and sorrows,
> Dancing mad with joy,
> Come, Mother, come!
> For Terror is Thy name,
> Death is in Thy breath,
> And every shaking step
> Destroys a world for e'er.
> Thou "Time", the All-Destroyer!
> Come, O Mother, come!
> Who dares misery love,
> And hug the form of Death,
> Dance in Destruction's dance,
> To him the Mother comes.[513]

Here is Philip Whalen:

Hymnus Ad Patrem Sinensis

I praise those ancient Chinamen
Who left me a few words,
Usually a pointless joke or a silly question
A line of poetry drunkenly scrawled on the margin of a quick
        splashed picture- bug, leaf,
        caricature of Teacher
    on paper held together now by little more than ink
    & their own strength brushed momentarily over it.

Their world & several others since
Gone to hell in a handbasket, they knew it-
Cheered as it whizzed by-
& conked out among the busted spring rain cherryblossom
    winejars
Happy to have saved us all.[514]

31:viii:58

VIIB

The Rebellion, the Bright Emperor

The Rebellion: The Emperor's Flight to Shu

To Shu, which we call Sichuan, 750 rough miles southwest from the Court. Three hundred years afterward, the magisterial historian Sima Guang 司馬光 (1019–1086) imagines the events of the Emperor's flight and Precious Consort's death. I offer these few excerpts, in Paul Kroll's sympathetic translation, with a few shifts in orthography and nomenclature.[515]

> Abandoning every one of the consorts, princesses, and imperial grandsons who resided outside the palace grounds, they set off before dawn. As His Highness was passing the Supply Depot of the Left, Yang Guozhong requested that it be set afire, saying, "Let it not come under the outlaws' control." His Highness blanched and replied, "If the outlaws, upon their arrival, do not gain it, they will be certain instead to appropriate what they need from the commonfolk. Better to give it them, and let them not oppress my children heavily."
>
> Later that day, as the sun was approaching the midpoint, His Highness had still not eaten. Yang Guozhong offered up some western cakes from the marketplace. Thereupon the commoners vied with each other to offer up their coarse rice, mixed together with wheat and beans. The imperial grandsons vied with each other to eat it, in cupped hands. In a moment it was gone, and they still had not eaten their fill.
>
> By evening, the district Commandant had absconded and the commoners of the district, extricating their own selves, had each one of them taken flight. All of their vessels and utensils for food and drink remained, and the army officers and soldiers confiscated them for themselves. At this time, many of those who were following the Emperor absconded and likewise slipped away. There were no lanterns in the post-station. People pillowed themselves on each other in disarray for slumber, there being no way anymore to discriminate the base from the noble.

The next day they reached the Mawei post-station. The officers and troops were famished and weary, every one of them testy and exasperated. General Chen Xuanli considered the entire disaster to be due to Yang Guozhong and wished to strike him down. [Some soldiers, finding Yang Guozhong speaking with Tibetan envoys, declared that he was plotting revolt with them.] Accordingly, the soldiers pursued and slew him, hacking and butchering his limbs and body. They raised his head on a spear, outside the gate of the post-station.

The soldiers then surrounded the post-station.

His Highness, hearing the clamor and uproar, asked what was taking place outside. His attendants and acolytes answered that Yang Guozhong had rebelled. His Highness took up his staff and put on his sandals, and went out the post-station gate. He consoled and reassured the soldiers, and then commanded them to draw up into ranks; but the soldiers would not respond to him. His Highness had his chief eunuch Gao Lishi question them, and General Chen answered, "Since Yang Guozhong was plotting revolt, the Precious Consort is no longer fit to render service. Let Your Majesty pare away your kindness to her and give the ordinances justly." His Highness said, "We will Ourself dispose it." He passed in through the gate. And he stood, leaning on his staff, his head bowed.

After a time, the Intendant Overseer of the Capital Municipality came forward and spoke, saying: "Now, when the mob is enraged, it is difficult to oppose them. 'Security and peril lie in a notch of the gnomon's shadow.' I would that Your Majesty decide quickly." And he kowtowed till blood flowed. His Highness said, "The Precious Consort has always dwelt deep in the palace. Whereby could she know of Yang Guozhong's plot for revolt?" Said Gao Lishi, "In truth, the Precious Consort is blameless. Yet, with the officers and troops having already slain Yang Guozhong, how can Your Majesty presume even yourself safe from them, if the Precious Consort remains by your side? I would that Your Majesty consider this carefully. If the officers and troops be placated, Your Majesty will be safe." His Highness at last gave the orders for Gao Lishi to lead the Precious Consort to the Buddha Hall, where he put her to death by strangling her.

The corpse, carried on a litter, was deposited in the courtyard of the post-station. General Chen and some others were summoned in to look upon it. They then removed their helmets and loosened their armor; they touched their heads to the ground and implored pardon. His Highness consoled and reassured them, and he commanded them to make known the deed and proclaim it to the soldiers. The General and the others all cried out "Long life!" and, performing a double salutation, exited. Only now did they set in order the companies and files and make plans to move onward.[516]

In this single afternoon, all the tensions of the Emperor's reign are brought to a single point. A Maoist might recognize it as the moment when His Majesty could no longer keep these contradictory forces in motion — that is, the moment when such contradictions became fatally antagonistic.[517] With a few deaths, and drawing up a great deep wrath, the mutinous soldiers undid a structure that had taken fifteen years to build, stripping the Bright Emperor of his consort, his authority and his potency.[518] In the cowardice of his self-preservation, he forgot his Daoist practice and showed himself not much different from the rest of us.

The Emperor entered Shu a month later. His son had already seized the throne, but that news only reached him three weeks after his arrival. Some days later he dispatched his chief ministers to the new Emperor, bearing with them the imperial insignia of office.

Here are three poems by Li Bo. The first two were written well before the Rebellion, but each expresses the qualities of a crucial moment: the Emperor's parting from the Precious Consort, and the rigors of his road to Shu. Li Bo wrote the third poem to celebrate the Former Emperor's return to Chang'an a year and a-half later.

THE REBELLION, THE BRIGHT EMPEROR

Fig. 70. A Tang-era landscape painting entitled "The Bright Emperor's journey to Shu"[519]

Chapter 55. "Distant Parting"

Long before the Great Tang, long before Confucius, even before the idea of a dynasty with patrilineal succession, the Sage-King Yao ceded his throne to Shun, the one true man of virtue that he knew. And gave him his two daughters as well. When Shun died, these two sister-wives grieved on the riverbank by Grotto Lake until their tears turned to blood, spotting the bamboo there ever after. Later Shun ceded that throne to Yu.[520]

There is another account: Shun usurped the throne and imprisoned Yao. And Yu the same with Shun, banishing him into Nine Doubts Mountain.[521]

> Distant parting
>
> Since ancient times
> Yao's two daughters have dwelt
> on the riverbanks of Xiao and Xiang, south of Grotto Lake.
>
> Seawater ten thousand miles straight down —
> who says this parting's not bitter?
>
> Lurid the sun and murky clouds,
> apes cry in the mist,
> ghosts howling in the rain.
>
> If I speak out, how will it help?
> High heaven, I fear, does not reflect my loyalty.
>
> Rumbling thunder, roaring with rage,
> at times like these Yao gave the throne to Shun,
> and Shun to Yu.
> But if the ruler loses his minister,
> a dragon turns into a fish.
> And if power falls to a minister —

THE REBELLION, THE BRIGHT EMPEROR

a rat becomes a tiger.

But others say:
Yao was locked away,
and Shun died in the wilds
of Nine Doubts Mountain,
where any place can be mistaken for any other.

How did the King end in such a lonely grave?
His two wives wept for him among the bamboo emerald clouds.
Following the waves and wind, once gone he did not return.
Gazing toward the pale sycamore mountains, they shook with grief.
Only when the mountains fall and rivers end
will the tears fade from these bamboo leaves.[522]

遠別離

古有皇英之二女,乃在洞庭之南瀟湘之浦
海水直下萬里深,誰人不言此離苦
日慘慘兮雲冥冥,猩猩啼煙兮鬼嘯雨
我縱言之將何補,皇穹竊恐不照余之忠誠
雷憑憑兮欲吼怒,堯舜當之亦禪禹
君失臣兮龍為魚,權歸臣兮鼠變虎
或言,堯幽囚,舜野死
九疑聯綿皆相似,重瞳孤墳竟何是
帝子泣兮綠雲間,隨風波兮去無還
慟哭兮遠望,見蒼梧之深山
蒼梧山崩湘水絕,竹上之淚乃可滅

Chapter 56. "The Hard Road to Shu," Reprise

We have seen this poem before, but now it is the Emperor who is traveling that road.

> Aiyiiieyaw!
> So murderously high!
>   The road to Shu is hard,
> harder than scaling the blue-green open sky.
>
>   How did they do it —
>   those ancient kings who opened this land,
> marking out fields, bringing silkworms and fishing nets?
>
>   They walked off into the mist,
>   and then it was 48,000 years
> before we smelled the smoke of their wood fires.
>
>   Birds have always had a path
> straight in from Chang'an to Emei Peak,
>   but when men began to cut a road,
> earth split open, mountains collapsed, stout warriors had to die
>   before iron rods were drilled into the mountainside,
> and wooden planks, raised on scaffolding, were linked
>   by ladders straddling the sky.
>
> Up above,
>   six dragons pull the sun through the treetops,
>   down below, the river breaks,
> circling back upon itself.
>   Even the yellow crane's soaring
>   stops here;
> long-armed apes despair of ever getting to the top.

Snarly gnarly Green Mud Ridge:
>   nine switchbacks every hundred steps,
>   wrapping around the cliffs.
Touch the Bear Star,
>   pass through Orion,
>   lean back, breathe in the air!
Hold your chest,
>   sit down and heave a sigh.

My friend, when would you be coming back?
I fear you'll never make it up
>   that treacherous, break-neck road.

All you'll see are sad birds
>   crying in old trees, males and females
>   winding through the woods,

and you'll hear the cuckoo's call to the night moon
>   filling the empty mountain with sorrow.

>   The road to Shu is hard,
harder than scaling the blue-green open sky!
When you hear this
>   the bloom of your cheeks will wilt and die.

>   Peak on peak not a foot below Heaven,
>   dead pines hang headfirst down the sheer walls.
>   Fast rapids, raging falls
>   crash and clatter,
>   battering cliffs and barreling crags,
ten thousand gullies thunder.

>   These are the dangers, oh traveler,
on this long road — why on earth
>   would you ever come this way?

Sword Gate Pass,
> spiked and sinister:
> if one man blocks the way,
> ten thousand can't get through,
>> and if that man's a traitor,
> he changes into a wolf.

> Morning and night,
>> beware fierce tigers and giant snakes,
> sharpening their teeth to suck our blood,
> mowing us down like fields of hay.

The Brocade City would be lovely,
> if you ever got there,
> but better to just go home.
>> The road to Shu is hard,
harder than scaling the blue-green open sky —
> lean back, look west with a long, last sigh!⁵²³

蜀道難

噫吁嚱
危乎高哉
蜀道之難
難于上青天
蠶叢及魚鳧
開國何茫然
爾來四萬八千歲
不與秦塞通人煙
西當太白有鳥道
可以橫絕峨眉巔
地崩山摧壯士死
然後天梯石棧相鉤連
上有六龍回日之高標
下有沖波逆折之回川
黃鶴之飛尚不得過
猿猱欲度愁攀援

青泥何盤盤
百步九折縈岩巒
捫參歷井仰脅息
以手撫膺坐長嘆
問君西游何時還
畏途巉巖不可攀
但見悲鳥號古木
雄飛雌從遶林間
又聞子規啼夜月
愁空山
蜀道之難
難于上青天
使人聽此凋朱顏
連峰去天不盈尺
枯松倒挂倚絕壁
飛湍瀑流爭喧豗
砯崖轉石萬壑雷
其險也如此
嗟爾遠道之人胡為乎來哉
劍閣崢嶸而崔嵬
一夫當關
萬夫莫開
所守或匪親
化為狼與豺
朝避猛虎
夕避長蛇
磨牙吮血
殺人如麻
錦城雖云樂
不如早還家
蜀道之難
難于上青天
側身西望長咨嗟

Chapter 57. The Return to Chang'an

The new Emperor recaptured Chang'an in the fall of 757. His father returned there in early winter. To solemnize the event, Li Bo wrote a suite of ten poems in stout and formal language, of which we translate the last. It was an awkward moment, for there seemed to be two Emperors. Li Bo's poem, then, is about reconciling pairs of things. It will require some explanation.

> Ten songs of the Former Emperor on his circuit west to inspect the Southern Capital — number 10 of 10
>
> Through twin passes of the Sword Pavilion, the northern gate to Shu,
> the Former Emperor and his horses return, like villages of clouds.
> In Chang'an the young Emperor relights the Ridgepole Star.
> Hanging in the sky, the pair of sun and moon reflect great yin and yang.[524]

> 上皇西巡南京歌十首 其十
>
> 劍閣重關蜀北門
> 上皇歸馬若雲屯
> 少帝長安開紫極
> 雙懸日月照乾坤

"Former Emperor" is the Bright Emperor's title once his son has usurped the throne. "Former" is literally "Elevated" (*shang* 上) — political necessity sometimes subverts the normal use of words.

The Southern Capital is Li Bo's hometown Chengdu, here sacralized by imperial presence. The "circuit west" is what European monarchs called a royal progress, an inspection tour that marks, claims and recalibrates the territories of the realm.[525]

The Sword Gate Pavilion is a geo-strategic marvel, a mountain pass whose walls are sharp as swords, whose belly is perfectly filled by its fortified pavilion, and whose single opening commands the only entranceway to Shu.[526] It is through this pass that the Former Emperor returned to Chang'an. Because this is a poem about doubling, Li Bo also refers to its twin, a smaller gateway downroad. Today it looks like this:

Fig. 71. Jianmen pass.[527]

Where one man with a halberd
halts ten thousand in their tracks.[528]

一人荷戟,萬夫趦趄

"In Chang'an the young Emperor reopens the Purple Ridgepole," writes Li Bo. That ridgepole is a star, and also a celestial palace, and equally the Emperor: these are three ways of pointing to the same thing. That astral light, the suite of buildings, the Emperor's human body, though, are less things than functions, cosmic activities. But the star comes first: "The ruler builds his palace as its simulacrum (*xiang* 象)," says an ancient commentator.[529] And the Emperor is that star only insofar as he displays his/its majesty. Each earthly brilliance, human or geographical, has its heavenly twin, such that grottos and statesmen and even middling poets are fused with their celestial counterparts.[530] (Li Bo, we know, is Venus.)

The pair of sun and moon, hanging in the sky, reflect great yin and yang. Only instead of yin and yang, Li Bo says Qian 乾 and Kun 坤, the first two hexagrams of the *Yijing* 易經 or *Classic of Change,* which graphs yang and yin as solid and broken lines ☰ ☷. Qian and Kun are also Heaven and Earth, male and female, active and receptive. Here they are sun and moon, and also the Bright Emperor and his son.

This is a classics-based solution to a uniquely awkward political circumstance. For there cannot be such a thing as two Emperors, two One Gods, two suns in a sky — the universe would literally disintegrate, and meaning end. Li Bo, however, celebrates the situation by transforming one sun into a moon, a complementarity. His nonchalance so irritates orthodoxy that a later commentator remarks, "He doesn't know Dao!"[531]

Li Bo holds a cloud satchel of many magic weapons.[532] Here he wields a gate, two emperors, a star, many horses, the sun and moon. This space is not habitable by human beings with human feelings and concerns.

After his return, the once-Bright Emperor lives under palace-arrest for four and a-half years, until his death in 762.

VIIC

The Rebellion, Li Bo

Chapter 58. Climbing Flower Mountain

An Lushan's forces have captured Luoyang, the Eastern Capital. Li Bo climbs Mount Hua, the Sacred Mountain of the West, the "Lotus Flower Mountain."[533] It guards the entrance to Chang'an, the Western Capital, not yet fallen to the rebels.

Ancient Air #17

In the west I climb Flower Mountain.
Far far off I see bright stars,
their pure hands holding lotus blossoms.
With weightless feet they pace Great Purity,
rainbow skirts trailing broad sashes,
billowing as they float higher through the Heavens.
They invite me to climb Cloud Terrace
and salute the immortal Wei Shuqing.
As in a dream, I follow them,
riding a wild goose into the purple dark.
I look down, there's the Luoyang River
swarming with Tartar troops as far as I can see.
Blood flow smears the prairie grasses,
Wolves and jackals wear the robes of office. [534]

古風 其十七

西上蓮花山，迢迢見明星
素手把芙蓉，虛步躡太清
霓裳曳廣帶，飄拂升天行
邀我登雲台，高揖衛叔卿
恍恍與之去，駕鴻凌紫冥
俯視洛陽川，茫茫走胡兵
流血塗野草，豺狼盡冠纓

The story of Wei Shuqing is told in the *Biographies of Holy Immortals* (*Shenxian zhuan* 神仙傳).

> Wei Shuqing was from Zhongshan. He attained immortality by ingesting mica ("cloud mother" *yunmu* 雲母).⁵³⁵ One September day in 109 BCE, the Martial Emperor of Han dwelt at leisure in his upper palace. Suddenly a man, riding a chariot of floating clouds pulled by white deer, landed before the palace. Startled, the Emperor asked him who he was. He said, "I am Wei Shuqing of Zhongshan." The Emperor replied, "If you're from Zhongshan, then aren't you my subject?" Wei did not respond, he just disappeared.⁵³⁶

"With weightless feet they pace the Heaven of Great Purity." That pace is a great magical gait, a retracing of the stars around and through the Dipper, like this:

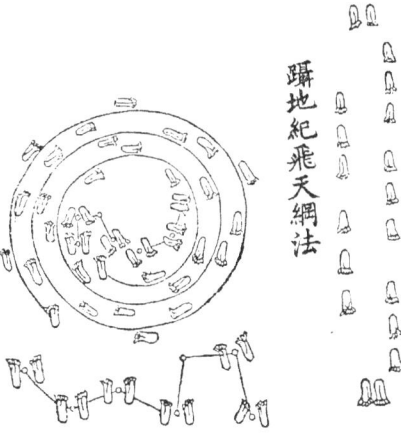

Fig. 72. A diagram showing the inwardly spiraling pattern of Yubu (top) and the dipper pattern of Bugang (bottom).⁵³⁷

Chapter 59. The Wall-eyed Prince

The Prince of Yong 永王 (?–757) was the Bright Emperor's sixteenth son. Intelligent, ugly, strabismic, that is, his eyes misaligned, one pointing straight ahead, the other disconcertingly to the side.

Summer of 756, the Bright Emperor has arrived in Sichuan. On 15 August he appoints four of his sons to manage the realm. The Prince of Yong is given the southern zone, headquartered up the Yangtze, where he has had a base now the last thirty years. Since rebel forces hold the north, tax moneys from the south — already the richest part of China — no longer reach the two capitals but come instead to the Prince, who is thereby able to amass considerable wealth and troops. His assignment is to counterattack the rebels from the south.

On 19 January 757 he sets sail down the Yangtze with his army. Li Bo had been staying at Nine Rivers (Jiujiang 九江), several hundred miles downstream, and the Prince picks him up to adorn his court. At this time Li Bo writes to his friend Jia Zhi 賈至 (728?–772) about his change of fortune.

> A letter to District Defender Jia
>
> For ages I have lived only in the greatest purity, far from the din of public affairs. I am drawn, thin, and fatigued, my abilities slight and my knowledge shallow, insufficient to relieve the calamities of these times. The Central Plains are everywhere deluged, and how could I protect or succor them? But a command from the Prince of Yong is weighty and sublime. He effects a great gathering of elite warriors, and thrice I have received his writs of recruitment. Human concerns are light, but ritual obligation is heavy. Grave times demand urgent action, and it would difficult to decline his request. So I have committed myself to this single course of action, looking ahead now to victory or defeat.[538]

與賈少公書

宿昔惟清勝。白綿疾疲爾,去期恬退,才微識淺,無足濟時。雖中原橫潰,將保以救之?主命崇重,大總元戎,辟書三至,人輕禮重。嚴期迫切,難以固辭,扶力一行,前觀進退。

Only later did Li Bo learn that the Prince was heading downstream not to suppress the An Lushan Rebellion but to secede from the Great Tang, setting up his own dynasty in the south — you may recall that North and South had been distinct kingdoms for the four hundred years that preceded Tang. Word reaches the Emperor, his forces attack the Prince, the Prince has early success, then he is chased downstream, his army collapses, he runs further south, is wounded by an arrow, and a local official captures him and puts him to death.[539]

Li Bo leaves the Prince, I think, somewhat late in the game. He heads back up-stream, and as he is about to reach Nine Rivers, he's arrested, charged with treason, and sentenced to death.

Li's accounts of the Prince affair go through three stages. The letter above is the first, with the appropriately demurring etiquette of a demoiselle. The second stage is described by Arthur Waley in his biography of Li Bo, where he calls Li "a sort of unofficial Poet Laureate" to the Prince's court:

> Meanwhile Li had a thoroughly good time. In a poem called "To the members of the Censorate at Headquarters, at a banquet given by the Fleet," he says that his true talents are in the military line, though they have remained hidden for forty years. At last it has been discovered that concealed at his waist he carries the fabled sword Dragon Pool.[540]

And the third stage, when Li Bo realizes what was up, and speaks of having been press-ganged, nearly, into service with that traitor. Waley quite reasonably translates these poem lines as prose:

The fleet arrived at midnight, and the whole of Nine Rivers became a mass of military banners. I allowed myself to be deceived by false promises and was forced by threats to go on board a transport. But it was in vain that they offered me five hundred pieces of gold. I rejected it as though it had been a mere wreath of smoke and left my post without having accepted my reward.[541]

半夜水軍來,潯陽滿旌旃
空名適自誤,迫脅上樓船
徒賜五百金,棄之若浮煙
辭官不受賞

Chapter 60. "In Prison, Submitted to Chief Minister Cui Huan"

From exile, the Bright Emperor appoints the upright Cui Huan 崔渙 (d. 769) as Chief Minister. From jail, Li Bo sends Cui Huan this poem.

> In prison, submitted to Chief Minister Cui Huan
>
> Barbarian horsemen have captured the Eastern Capital,
> and blood flows across the fields of battle.
> Farms stand abandoned, gates barred against the sun,
> and human life is as fragile as a morning's frost.
> But now a wise minister breathes life into the land,
> once more we can celebrate the health of sea and sky.
> A fabled sage presides at court,
> and officials line up to serve.
> Like stars circling the Pole, they adorn the ruler of the three realms
> and reflect the brilliance of the Two Suns.
> If you think of me under this upturned pot,
> I will wipe away my tears and prostrate to the light of Heaven.[542]

> 獄中上崔相渙
>
> 胡馬渡洛水，血流征戰場
> 千門閉秋景，萬姓危朝霜
> 賢相燮元氣，再欣海縣康
> 台庭有夔龍，列宿粲成行
> 羽翼三元聖，發輝兩太陽
> 應念覆盆下，雪泣拜天光

Chapter 61. God of Nine Rivers

Li Bo spends about half a year in jail. That autumn an Imperial Investigating Censor (*jiancha yushi* 監察御史) reaches the Nine Rivers area. As Censor, he is charged with investigating failures of justice in the realm and reporting these directly to the Emperor, by-passing bureaucratic cronyism. He is especially sensitive to three matters: bureaucratic malfeasance, complaints from people who otherwise lack access to official channels, and the conduct of trials and convictions.

The censor in question is named Song Ruosi 宋若思, and he investigates the circumstances of Li Bo's case. We know what happens next from the title of one of Li's poems:

> Offered to Vice Censor-in-Chief Lord Song, who freed me from jail and took me on staff as his advisor, and who is bringing three thousand southern troops with him to attack Henan, staging now in Nine Rivers[543]
>
> 中丞宋公以吳兵三千赴河南軍次尋陽脫余之囚參謀府因贈之

Li Bo ghost-wrote several documents for Song, including a petition to the Emperor exonerating Li of all crimes.[544] In the writ that follows, Song plans a river crossing with his troops, but the Yangtze is in autumn spate, and he dares not attempt it. He therefore offers a formal ceremony of propitiation to the River God. He will need an accompanying text, so Li Bo writes this for him to declaim at the ceremony:[545]

> A petition of sacrifice to Nine Rivers, written on behalf of Song Ruosi
>
> Humbly I offer meat and wine oblation, and respectfully sacrifice to the Lord of the Numinous Source, the Yangtze

River. You alone, oh God, encompass the primal Yin and Yang, maintaining Heaven and Earth in just balance. You slice through mountains to cut the Three Gorges, open paths so that the Nine Rivers may run. You weave the networks of the southern riverways, and finally reach the Eastern Sea in homage. Animal sacrifice on jade platters accords with ancient rites; the norms of libation should always be upheld.

Now ten thousand chariots stir the dust, and the five preceding Emperors of Great Tang are stained with anguish. Grizzled farmers become white bones, and red blood flows through the royal palace. The cosmic edifice has been turned upside down, and baleful comets have not yet been driven from the sky. All sentient beings rouse their energies to eradicate the primal evil of rebellion. I, Song Ruosi, have established a stout fortress and manifest my vigor everywhere. Following the Heavenly royal command, I have raised a Heavenly army. You, Great River, shine your oceanic colors on its flags and banners as my disciplined troops overawe the countryside.

But now your over-flooding waves gush and surge, their frantic whirling shakes and shocks all men. Only you, oh River God, can make Lord Bo roll up his waves and the sun accept its orders for clear weather, so that our multi-decked warships may proceed across the river and our men and horses be free of every apprehension, so that we may sweep away the monstrous plague from its stronghold in the north and decapitate the vile whales in their capital at Luoyang. Only you, oh River God, can assist us in bringing down succor to the people.

Respectfully proffered with the quintessence of sincerity. May you descend to partake of these offerings of scent and meat.[546]

為宋中丞祭九江文

謹以三牲之奠，敬祭於長源公之靈：惟神包括乾坤，平准天地，劃三峽以中斷，疏九道以爭奔。綱紀南維，朝宗東海,牲玉有禮,祀典無虧。今萬乘蒙塵,五陵慘黷,蒼生悉為白骨,赤血流於紫宮。宇宙倒懸,欃槍未滅,含識結憤,思翦元凶。而況參列雄藩,各當重寄,遵奉王命,大舉天兵。照海色於旌旗,肅軍威於原野。而洪濤譎渤,狂飆振驚。惟神使陽侯卷波,羲和奉命,樓船先濟,士馬無虞。掃妖孽於幽燕,斬鯨鯢於河洛。惟神祐我,降休於民。敬陳精誠,庶垂歆饗。

It is now the autumn of 757. Li Bo is free, he roams the Yangtze region. Then in 758 his sentence is reinstated, though commuted to exile in Yunnan, "South of the Clouds." Then in the general amnesty of 759 he is pardoned once again. But his body is tired, he can travel little, he spends his last three years in the Yangtze basin, dies in late autumn 762.[547]

An Interlude

Chapter 62. "Dreaming of Roaming Tianmu, the Mountain of the Old Lady of Heaven, a Song Left at Parting"

Sailors tell stories of a mountain in the Eastern Sea,
untrustworthy in the mist and swell of waves.
But here in Yue we speak of Tianmu,
you can only see her in that moment between clouds and rainbows.
Heavenly Tianmu's as tall as Heaven, wider than a horizon,
the power of her form surpasses all mountains.
Even mountains 50,000 feet tall collapse
when they're faced with her.

For these reasons I'm about to dream of her in this southeast coastland,
to fly across the moon on Mirror Lake, where Duke Xie once lived.
Lake Moon, illuminate my shadow,
see me off to Sharp Stream,
the sound of its waters ripping ripping, the sobbing of night apes.
Wearing the Duke's shoes, I climb a ladder of blue-green clouds,
mid-way I see the ocean sunrise,
I hear the cock of Heaven crowing in an empty sky.
A thousand cliffs, ten-thousand turns, the path uncertain.
Fascinated by a flower, I lean on a rock, and suddenly it's dark.
The roar of bears and dragon-song overwhelm cliffs and springs,
set the dense forests trembling, shaking loose layers of mountain peaks.
The clouds are full blue-green, close to rain,
smoke rises from the slip-slap waters,

lightning flashes, thunder peals,
they bring these mountains to the edge of collapse.
The rock doors of a subterranean Heaven
burst clamorously open.
Now the sky's both blue-green and black, all washed away, I can't see bottom,
sun and moon shine brightly on the silver-gold terraces.
One after another the Lords of Cloud descend,
wearing rainbows as their clothing, taking the wind for horse.
A tiger strums the zither, and Immortals line up
as a phoenix brings their chariot around.

Suddenly my spirit shakes.
I rise in a flurry, then sigh and sigh.
All I feel now is the present pillow and bed,
I've lost the smoky twilight vision from before.
Worldly pleasures always drain away
like rivers into the Eastern Sea.

So I leave you now, friends, can't say when I'll be back.
I'll graze my white deer between blue-green cliffs,
ready to ride off when I call on the great mountains.
If I had to bend to wealth and power,
my heart would never open.[548]

夢游天姥吟留別

海客談瀛洲，煙濤微茫信難求
越人語天姥，雲霓明滅或可睹
天姥連天向天橫，勢拔五岳掩赤城
天台四萬八千丈，對此欲倒東南傾
我欲因之夢吳越，一夜飛度鏡湖月
湖月照我影，送我至剡溪
謝公宿處今尚在，淥水蕩漾清猿啼
腳著謝公屐，身登青雲梯
半壁見海日，空中聞天雞
千岩萬轉路不定，迷花倚石忽已暝

熊咆龍吟殷岩泉，慄深林兮驚層巔
雲青青兮欲雨，水澹澹兮生煙
列缺霹靂，丘巒崩摧
洞天石扉，訇然中開
青冥浩蕩不見底，日月照耀金銀臺
霓為衣兮風為馬，雲之君兮紛紛而來下
虎鼓瑟兮鸞回車，仙之人兮列如麻
忽魂悸以魄動，恍驚起而長嗟
惟覺時之枕席，失向來之煙霞
世間行樂亦如此，古來萬事東流水
別君去兮何時還
且放白鹿青崖間，須行即騎訪名山
安能摧眉折腰事權貴，使我不得開心顏

The mountain looks like this:

Fig. 73. Mount Tianmu.[549]

This is the moister South — not Chu, with its *Songtexts*,[550] but Yue, its ancient eastern neighbor at the coast, "where sailors tell stories of a mountain in the Eastern Sea."[551]

AN INTERLUDE

Li Bo's poet-hero Duke Xie has been to Tianmu, writing:

At dusk we drop into a hut along Sharp Stream,
morning we climb Tianmu peak.
Tall and taller, it joins with clouds and rainbows.
Once we're home, how will we ever find it again?[552]

暝投剡中宿，明登天姥岑
高高入雲霓，還期那可尋

Duke Xie loved these mountains so much that he invented a shoe to keep his feet level, ascending or descending. His biography in the *Southern Histories* (*Nanshi* 南史) explains:

When he went climbing, he wore wooden clogs. Going up the mountain, he'd remove their front grippers. Going down the mountain, he'd remove their rear grippers.

Li Bo now wears those clogs in his roaming of Tianmu.[553]

And up the *axis mundi* he goes. Up the central channel. Suddenly the underground cavern doors burst open, sun and moon shine at once, and he mounts the wind in the company of tiger and phoenix.

But who is Tianmu, the Old Lady of Heaven, the Holy Beldam? "You can only see her in that moment between clouds and rainbows," says Li Bo, "as tall as Heaven, wider than a horizon."

Her "Tian" means "Heaven," and her "Mu" has the same sound as the word "mother" in ancient Chinese. But that ancient mother-word is written as a pictograph, 母 or 姆, originally a drawing of a woman, emphasizing her breasts,[554] whereas the Mu of this Tianmu is an ideograph: the words "old" and "woman" written side-by-side in a single graph, 姥. It's a neologism not seen in Chinese until around the time of Duke Xie, and after that still strongly associated with the Southeast, its seafaring, and its numinous practices.[555]

So I think this Mu is a non-Chinese word from the native language of Yue — they were an Austronesian kingdom only incorporated into "China" in the later years BCE.[556] It seems to be a term of respect for an older woman, but acknowledging the strong possibility of her mantic powers.[557] And thus Tianmu is the combined Sino-Yue name for a local deity, proprietress of that mountain, of *that* mountain. She does not wander out, does not seek dominion over other deities, does not franchise herself across the Empire.[558] And only in later Tang does organized Daoism move in and establish her as one of its thirty-six lesser Grotto-Heavens.[559]

Who is she? We don't much know. The *Hou Wulu* 後吳錄 says, "In Sharp County there's Mount Tianmu. It's said that climbers hear the sounds of Tianmu, the Old Lady, singing there."[560] And a later text adds that "Glyphs are inscribed on her cliff walls, cut in the shape of the Northern Dipper, who knows how high. Under the spring moon woodcutters hear the clamoring of flutes, drums, pipes, and horns."[561] She's been here longer than China. Li Bo is a late visitor, but she has still bestowed her boons on him.

An old lady? A mountain? A deity? In the thirteenth century Liang Kai 梁楷 paints a man whose body is exactly a mountain. The title given his work is "The Splashed-ink Immortal" (*Pomo xianren* 潑墨仙人), though splashed ink's a technique normally used for landscape painting, not portraits.[562] Like Liang Kai himself, the immortal may be a little drunk. It's not just his shoulder that's hilly, even his head's a mountain.

Fig. 74. The Splashed-Ink Immortal, by Liang Kai.[563]

In a dream we are all people, places and things. We are the dreaming itself. That dreamy diaphaneity is able to contain ordinary realities, though not vice versa — those ordinaries are just a special case within it. But neither reality-category has that much explanatory power.

Five hundred years afterwards, a Japanese monk explains:

> Mountains are constantly walking. Because they're walking, they're constant. Although their walking is faster than the wind, people in the mountains do not know it.[564]

> このゆゑに常安住なり、常運歩なり。山の運歩は其疾如風よりもすみやかなれども、山中人は不覺不知なり。

This walking doesn't stop, Li Bo's walking doesn't stop.

To know that all appearances are diaphaneity. Draw down that tsunami. It will be destroyed. Do it again.

Chapter 63. "Mystery"

Drinking alone at North Mountain, sent to Wei Six

I never heard of ancient hermits
buying a mountain to hide in.
With Dao, all acts are pure,
why worry if people are around?
Now, as I descend this mountain ridge,
all noise subsides, the earth's at ease.
A range of peaks unfolds across my doorway,
a trickle cuts through rock, pulling down countless springs.
The folding screen of cliffs is lost in clouds,
their caverns unfathomably deep.
At dawn and dusk the river shines its true colors,
the woodland air draws tight with evening chill.
That's the moment to pick the Red Persimmon
and cultivate the Mysterious Feminine.
I sit with precious texts and the moon,
brush the frost off my zither.
In the darkness I pour wine
and watch the shadows and empty the cup again.
I miss you, out roaming the world's dusty wind,
why don't you ever laugh at yourself?[565]

北山獨酌寄韋六

巢父將許由，未聞買山隱
道存跡自高，何憚去人近
紛吾下茲嶺，地閑喧亦泯
門橫群岫開，水鑿眾泉引
屏高而在雲，竇深莫能准
川光晝昏凝，林氣夕淒緊
于焉摘朱果，兼得養玄牝
坐月觀寶書，拂霜弄瑤軫

AN INTERLUDE

傾壺事幽酌，顧影還獨盡
念君風塵游，傲爾令自哂

No one can tell us anything about Wei Six. (His number indicates that he's sixth in the birth order of his generation of male cousins within his family lineage.[566]) So we imagine something like this, that he is a kind of uptight friend of Li Bo who wants to do a mountain retreat but never quite gets there, and he thinks he ought to purchase the right property first, with the correct qualities, and only then will he be able to get away from it all.

Li Bo's poem subsumes two background stories. The first:

> The Sage-King Yao invited Xu You to administer all Nine Provinces of his kingdom. Xu You was unwilling to hear of it, [so he fled to the mountains], where he used to wash out his ears in the waters of Ying River.
>
> One day his friend Chao Fu came by, leading a calf that needed water. He saw Xu You washing out his ears and asked him why. Xu You replied, "Yao invited me to administer the Nine Provinces, and I hate the sound of it. That's why I wash my ears."
>
> Chao Fu replied, "You live among high cliffs and deep valleys. Human speech and human ways can't penetrate here. Who can even see you? But in your mind you still go out floating and roaming, seeking to hear of name and fame. You're polluting my calf's mouth!" So he led his calf upstream to give it water there.[567]

The second story comes from the first:

> Zhi Daolin wanted to buy the monk Zhu Fashen a mountain. Zhu Fashen replied, "I never heard of Chao Fu and Xu You buying a mountain to do retreat!"[568]

But Li Bo changes this up. "Where there's Dao, all activities are pure," he says. Roaming this world, only divinity. So you don't need a mountain, but you also don't need solitude, famelessness, non-pollution, red persimmons, anything. And Li Bo himself doesn't even need to bother laughing at his friend. Perhaps he addresses the last line of the poem to Li Bo, "I demand that you sneer at yourself!"

This is a sweet poem. And we could stop right here, were it not for the Mysterious Female. The poem says:

> That's the moment to pick the Red Persimmon
> and nourish the Mysterious Female.

> 于焉摘朱果,兼得養玄牝

I'll let Laozi take care of this for us. In chapter 1 of the Daodejing he speaks of desire and desirelessness, and then adds:

> Together I call them Mystery. More Mysterious than Mystery, the gateway to all marvel.[569]

> 同謂之玄。玄之又玄,衆妙之門。

And then he adds in chapter 6:

> The deity of the valley does not die. She is called the Mysterious Female. The gateway of the Mysterious Female is called the root of Heaven and Earth. Like the soft fabric of everything. Use it and it never wears out.

> 谷神不死,是謂玄牝。玄牝之門,是謂天地根。綿綿若存,用之不勤。

The valley, that is, the vagina. (The is the interpretation of the *Xiang'er* 想爾 commentary to Laozi.) The full-on feminine. From her gateway all Heaven and Earth emerge, that is, all of appearance and non-appearance. Primordially gendered — and indeed, in ordinary usage this Female (*pin* 牝) is always tied to her consort (*mu* 牡).

The sublime Isabelle Robinet goes further, telling us that the Mysterious Female "is a passageway, an entrance situated at the junction of Non-being and Being; it allows Yin and Yang to communicate with each other, and is the place where Yang opens and Yin closes."[570] This is not a unidirectional birth canal but an intermediary moment. And thus itself *in-nate,* that is, unborn.

But sometimes the Mysterious Female is just the Dao. Again, Robinet: "like the Center itself, it has no shape, no direction, and no fixed position."[571]

Indeed mysterious. It is dual, it is singular, it is unmodified.[572] In this logic, we don't get to transcend duality. Nor even sublate it. We're stuck with the shebang — there's no higher or lower view. If you set the yin–yang circle spinning, you can't tell how many of anything there are:

Fig. 75. The yin–yang circle.[573]

Li Bo tells us that he will cultivate the Mysterious Female. If we follow the traditions of Daoist cultivation, this means he will engage particular hygienic practices of diet, pharmacology, sexual yoga, and the breath control techniques we now know as Qigong 氣功.[574] Here the Red Persimmon would represent a parallel, substance-based approach, wherein that fruit is the cinnabar used in the elixir of transcendence.[575]

But Li Bo is doing something more mysterious. He is writing a poem.

Mystery. The first thing she asks us to do is to shut up already, and see what's always already here.[576] Poetry is just the luminous silence that won't shut up. If you look inside that deep valley of poetry's mouth, you'll hear words clambering, rushing to effect the appearancing of Ten Thousand Things. In that diaphanous clamor, Li Bo is only an action verb. He won't stand still long enough to be an immortal, even a banished immortal.[577]

Chapter 64. Alchemy

An outline of making the Great Refined Elixir, for Liu Guandi

the invocation
    Heaven and Earth are a great bellows
    circulating life-force throughout the cosmos.
    Yin and Yang join their tallies,
    and their entwining rouses all life.
    Everything happening of itself, such marvels,
    who could ever know its purpose!
    Woven throughout the four seasons,
    a mesh so fine it has no gap,
    the sun and moon rise and set,
    how could you speak of them separately?

compounding the elixir
    The mercurial maiden rides the river chariot,
    whose shaft and yoke are filled with gold.
    Grasp the pivot, steer the course,
    and forcefully subdue its feathered mount.
    The firebird unfurls in blazing splendor,
    the white tiger guards the true home.
    Boil this to a bitter residue,
    melted and congealed into moist dew.
    It looks like dust on a clear windowpane,
    a dead ash that comes to silence.
    Pound it and cast it in the red vessel,
    seal it through twelve cycles of time.
    Blazing brilliant, it is the Great Refined Elixir,
    inseparable from Dao itself.

the result
    I can reach out and touch the sun,
    the Pure Land is just a stroll away.
    The Lord of Death wipes my name from his files,
    and the Dipper writes it in his Book of Life.

What's holding you back?
Here you are, among the old magicians.
Reputation is only good for power plays,
and success will quickly fall away.
What I seek is immortality,
and you, friend, know that loss trumps gain.
Let's not head for the Bright Emperor's palace
but remember we're the Jade Emperor's guests.
Our phoenix carriage is faster than wind or lightning,
our dragon mount needs neither whip nor quirt.
We'll climb the Nine Heavens in a single bound
and arrive together hand in hand.[578]

草創大還贈柳官迪

天地爲橐籥，周流行太易
造化合元符，交媾騰精魄
自然成妙用，孰知其指的
羅絡四季間，綿微無一隙
日月更出沒，雙光豈雲隻
姹女乘河車，黃金充轅軛
執樞相管轄，摧伏傷羽翮
朱鳥張炎威，白虎守本宅
相煎成苦老，消鑠凝津液
髣髴明窗塵，死灰同至寂
摶冶入赤色，十二周律曆
赫然稱大還，與道本無隔
白日可撫弄，清都在咫尺
北酆落死名，南斗上生籍
抑予是何者，身在方士格
才術信縱橫，世途自輕擲
吾求仙棄俗，君曉損勝益
不向金闕遊，思爲玉皇客
鸞車速風電，龍騎無鞭策
一舉上九天，相攜同所適

Don't worry if the middle section of the poem doesn't make much common sense. It wouldn't have for most of Li Bo's readers, either, it's an alchemist's code, I will explain.

The knowable manifests across a vast continuum of energies, coarse and subtle. At one extreme are the material phenomena of shared daily life, at the other, phenomena so rarified we think of them as divinities or principles or ineffabilities — the angelic, the beautiful. Everything passes along this continuum in both directions. One direction is birth, a coming into being. And then the other direction, a reversal, death, a passing back into the undifferentiated. This functioning is called Dao, and alchemy is a means for mastering it. For though, once having made the trip to birth, most things will travel back only toward death, the alchemist knows how to journey from thick to thin, from coarse to subtle, and to remain on rarefied planes of existence for incalculably long periods of time, until Heaven and Earth themselves pass away. Thus he becomes a *xian* 仙, a word we inadequately translate as "immortal."

An alchemical text provides key markers for negotiating this process. Because the continuum of existence-non-existence has multiple planes, alchemical terms must function such that "Yang" at once names sun, the bright, the heat of alchemical transformation, all active forces of existence, and so on. From the human point of view, this Yang is how our individuated bodies connect to and manifest the primal heat. From the cosmic view, human alchemical practices are how primal Yang embodies its great glory on an ordinary plane. Function, pattern, dynamic: these terms point to the activity that is the nature of this Yang energy, just as quietude, withdrawal, coolth, the moon, point to its inseparable Yin, the dark. But there is only one world, only one something-nothing. And thus the perfected human body is perfectly homologous with the cosmos, reflecting its patterns, energies and geography.

The elixir — a material substance, a subtle energy formation, a patterning of body-mind, all three — is the alchemist's essential tool for his return to Dao. Thus the elixir is called "refined" or "returned" (*huan* 還). This poem describes the process by which such an elixir is compounded. Its terms are rooted in a shifting congeries of experiments that began at least a millennium before the Tang. I will represent this manifold activity using the language of a single text, which emerged as their epitome about the time of Li Bo's birth. This is the *Compact of Three-in-One* (*Cantongqi* 參同契).[579]

Chinese alchemy before the Tang emphasized the compounding of a material-substance elixir. Chinese alchemy after the Tang looked to internal manipulations of coarse and subtle energies within the human body. But this distinction — the division of the physical from the non-physical — obfuscates the alchemical process, which is to overcome bondage to apparent phenomena by making use of apparent phenomena, and thus to become immortal. Because the *Compact of Three-in-One* speaks in multisemic principles, it sustains both practices. As such, it became enormously influential in all later alchemy.

The middle section of Li Bo's poem uses the highly technical language of the *Three-in-One* to describe a compounding of the elixir. The fundamental principle is easy to understand: Mercury (the substance and equally True Yin) and Lead (the substance and equally True Yang) are fused by Fire to create an elixir that restores perfection to the human being.[580] This elixir is called "The Great Return" (*dahuan* 大還).[581] Sometimes that Mercury is represented as the Green Dragon. Its companion is the White Tiger of Lead. Fire is the Vermillion Bird. Here is a seventeenth-century depiction of that triadic process:

AN INTERLUDE

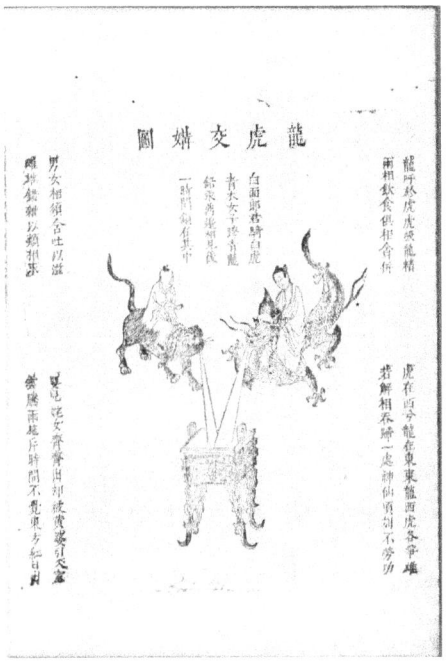

Fig. 76. Copulation of the Dragon and Tiger, from *Direction for Endowment and Vitality* (1615).[582]

Here then is a re-translation of the middle section that returns its language to alchemical terminology:

compounding the elixir
Volatile Mercury mounts Lead and steams off skyward,
so Lead must harness it and return it to the cauldron's waters.
Master this water, the axis of Dao,
and keep Mercury in the fiery pot until its impurities dissolve.
The Vermillion Bird of Fire blazes its bright majesty,
the White Tiger of Lead safeguards the space of transformation.

Reduce and mature the bitter liquid,
evaporate and condense it.
It will look like dust on a clear windowpane,
dead ashes fallen into silence.
Then pound it and mix it, seal it in the red vessel,
regulating the heat through twelve stages of perfection.
Fire-red and splendid, it has become the Great Refined Elixir,
in essence no different from the Dao.

Here's a question I never ask: why did Li Bo write this poem. Was it to get his friend Liu Guandi to make the elixir with him. And what would that mean?

Let's begin with words. As Steve Bokenkamp has shown, Li Bo holds a surprising command of esoteric Daoist language: "He must have achieved a Daoist rank approximate to the Six Dynasties' rank of Disciple of the Three Caverns (*Sandong dizi* 三洞弟子), for he here shows that he was intimately acquainted with the most important scriptures of at least two of the Three Caverns of the Daoist canon."[583]

In this poem, the *Three-in-One* seems to be his primary source of alchemical terminology.[584] Still, that text is not a how-to manual. To physically compound the elixir, you would also need a master, a recipe, ingredients, equipment, time, and a bunch of money. Insofar as Li Bo is a poet, then, is his use of alchemy merely allusive, like his use of the *Songtexts of Chu*? For this to work you no more need substance-material Mercury than you need a substance-material King of Chu.[585]

But let's not slip so quickly into the symbolic.[586] Here are lines from several of his other poems and prefaces:

> I once gathered Mercury at Jianghua and collected Lead at Qingxi. Together Quan Zhaoyi and I have long tended the alchemical fire.[587]

> 嘗彩姹女於江華，收河車於清溪，與天水權昭夷，服勤爐火之業久矣

AN INTERLUDE

Medicinal herbs are hidden in sea and marchmount,
I gather Lead from the banks of blue streams.[588]

 藥物秘海岳，采鉛青溪濱

I spent my whole fortune working the elixir oven.
An ancient face can be made new![589]

 傾家事金鼎，年貌可長新

I still worry that my elixir will be too late
and my ambitions never reach their fullness.
In the mirror, just useless frosty hair,
I'm ashamed before those crane-borne immortals.[590]

 尚恐丹液遲，志愿不及申
 徒霜鏡中發，羞彼鶴上人

This morning I have drunk the elixir.
 I'm freed from worldly feelings,
body-mind in harmony,
 for the first time I am complete in Dao.[591]

 早服還丹無世情，琴心三疊道初成

Ten years ago I left the court, smiling.
When I look in the mirror now, it's all autumn frost.
I put away my sword in a jeweled box,
and refined the elixir with the Queen Mother of the West….
But now I follow neither court nor immortal,
these long despondent years in the human realm.[592]

 十年罷西笑，覽鏡如秋霜
 閉劍琉璃匣，煉丹紫翠房…
 仙宮兩無從，人間久摧藏

On this basis, I will claim that Li Bo is a top-flight alchemist. Nothing in these poems settles into a single, simple mode of reality. His Lead is always transforming, at once substance-physical, psycho-physical, and meta-physical. Always in motion, like the Fire that he and his friend Quan Zhaoyi tend together.[593] He is equally willing to walk away from the whole enterprise, and, he tells us, drink wine with Quan.[594]

What is the elixir? Above all, an activity. An arrangement of space and time, however understood. But only a beginning alchemist seeks to *accomplish* something thereby, to transform a putative ordinary into a sublime. If a Western alchemist works to turn Lead into Gold, Li Bo is turning Gold into Gold. This is not a transitive act, and it is much more enjoyable. Then Lead shows itself as Lead, Gold as Gold, the world as divine, and Li Bo and all beings as immortal. It's a celebration, in his words "the blazing brilliant Returned Elixir, inseparable from Dao."[595]

So his alchemy is a space of pre-ontological pleasure, where Li Bo can touch the sun, and Liu Guandi can come along too, hand in hand, "it's so much more friendly with two."[596] Perhaps this is what "poetry" means.

During the 800s, the last century of Great Tang, three or four Emperors died after ingesting the elixir.[597] Eating material-substance lead and mercury is always a chancy business — but everyone knew this, alchemists, clients, informed public. Steve Bokenkamp translates a ninth-century passage explaining what may be expected:

> On first ingesting cinnabar granules, one's four limbs are without strength and the groin region becomes heavy. Below the navel there is a knotting and pain [...]. One's body often feels like there are insects crawling on it. Sores break out in the mouth. All these are signs that [the elixir] is driving out the various illnesses [that inhabit the body].[598]

So in some circumstances life may be prolonged, in others the physical body may die and the subject be released.[599]

Alchemy was part of the core curriculum during Harvard and Yale's first century.[600]

Chapter 65. "Praise on a Painting of the Monk Baozhi"

The moon in water
totally can't be grasped.
Heart and mind all emptied,
a vast centerless space.
With your bird-claw fingernails, you cut off friends
and walk alone, wrapped in brocade,
a knife sliding through
three dynasties worth of kings.
Your shining painted face
comes and goes nowhere at all.[601]

誌公畫贊

水中之月，了不可取
虛空其心，寥廓無主
錦縿鳥爪，獨行絕侶
刀齊尺量，扇迷陳語
丹青聖容，去住無所

An early Ming witness:

> Today the Monastery of the Numinous Valley has a stone inscription entitled "Praise on a painting of the monk Baozhi." Wu Daozi did the painting, Li Bo the praise, and Yan Zhenqing the calligraphy — these men were called "the three incomparables." The old inscription is already ruined — this is a reinscription, you can no longer see the marvel of the calligraphy.[602]

Wu Daozi 吳道子 (680–ca. 760), greatest painter of the Tang. His "Mountain demon" and his "Eighty-seven divine immortals," their bodies trails of light:

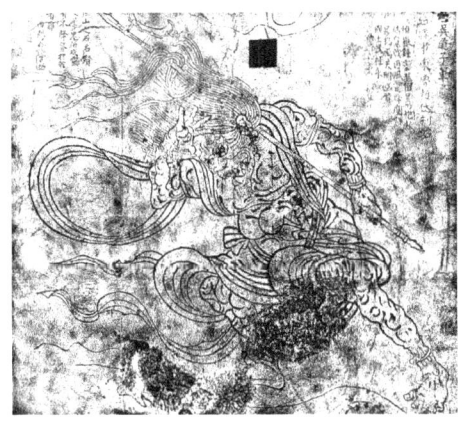

Fig. 77. Mountain Demon, attributed to Wu Daozi.⁶⁰³

Fig. 78. Eighty-seven Celestial People (fragment), by Wu Daozi.⁶⁰⁴

Of his Laozi Temple murals, Du Fu remarks:

> Their dense ranks turn the earth on its axle,
> a wondrous perfection shakes the palace walls.⁶⁰⁵

森羅回地軸,妙絕動宮牆

A ninth-century evaluation of Tang painters couldn't fit him into its ranks, saying merely,

Wu Daozi, by himself. His talents were unleashed by Heaven, he walks alone in this world.⁶⁰⁶

His contemporary Yan Zhenqing 顏真卿 (709–785), greatest of Tang calligraphers. And great too in ways that don't much overlap with Li Bo: a lexicographer, ritualist, patrician (seven of Confucius's disciples share the same surname), moralist, incorruptible public administrator, unshakable loyalist against Rebel imprecations. One thing he and Li Bo do have in common is that they won't be quiet. A dozen times Yan Zhenqing is exiled for his stubborn true speech, and in 783 he's sent to induce the surrender of yet another rebel dynast near the Eastern Capital of Luoyang. He speaks so bluntly that the rebel leader hangs him. He was seventy-six at the time.⁶⁰⁷ Here's a bit of his masterwork, a stone inscription for his great-grandfather:

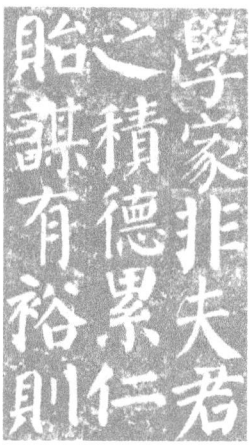

Fig. 79. Stele for Yan Qinli, by Yan Zhenqing.⁶⁰⁸

But who is the monk Baozhi? The *Transmission of the Lamp* (*Jingde chuandenglu* 景德傳燈錄) states:

> As a youth Baozhi became a monk at Daolin Temple, where he practiced Zen meditation. In the late 460s his behavior

suddenly became erratic. He slept here or there, and ate or drank at uncertain times. His hair grew out several inches, and he'd walk about unshod holding his tin-ringed staff, to the end of which he attached a pair of scissors, a bronze mirror, or sometimes a strip or two of cotton cloth. He'd go several days without eating, but with no sign of hunger. Sometimes he would sing songs of a prophetic nature. All the townspeople revered him.

In 488 Emperor Wu of the Qi dynasty declared that Baozhi was bewitching the populace and had him imprisoned in the capital. But at dawn people saw him entering the marketplace. When the matter was investigated, he turned out to be still in jail. The local magistrate reported this, and the Emperor invited Baozhi to visit him in the innreer halls of the Palace. […]

When Emperor Gao of the Liang dynasty ascended the throne, he proclaimed, "Master Baozhi, you leave footprints in the dust of this polluted realm, but your spirit roams in spaces imperceptible and serene. Water and fire can neither drench nor scorch you, snakes and tigers cannot bite or frighten you. When you speak of Buddha's principles, your voice is heard on high. When you discourse on hidden doctrines, you are exalted among the secret immortals. How could you be subject to the emotions and empty phenomena of ordinary people? How could the previous Emperor's decrees be so boorish? From now on you are free to enter the imperial palace at will."[609]

The *Biographies of Eminent Monks* adds:

During the succeeding Chen dynasty there was an imperial bondsman whose whole family served Baozhi devotedly. Once he manifested his True Form (*zhenxing* 真形) to them. In the aureole surrounding him were the marks of a bodhisattva.[610]

That true form is the eleven-headed Avalokiteshvara. Here is Baozhi amidst the process of that revelation:

Fig. 80. Statue of Baozhi, Saiouji, Kyōto.⁶¹¹

You can see three very small worn faces just above his headband.⁶¹²

AN INTERLUDE

Chapter 66. Wild Cursive Script

Huaisu 懷素 (725/737–post-782), great genius of wild cursive calligraphy, here's a glimpse:

Fig. 81. Calligraphy by Huaisu.[613]

It's a portion of a letter. The fourteen graphs say:

> Bitter bamboo-shoots with tea would taste exceptionally great, so I'll go get some straightaway. From Huaisu.

> 苦筍及茗異常佳，乃可徑來。懷素上[614]

Li Bo's poem:

A ballad of cursive script

To the excellent youth Huaisu, "Cherishing Simplicity."
Your cursive script knows no equal in this world,
the Darksea whale flies out from your inkwell,
and a million rabbits are killed to make your brush-tips.

In the autumn months, as the weather cools,
drinkers and poets crowd the hall.
Rolls of paper and fine silk fill their boxes,
and black ink shines on the Xuanzhou inkstones.
You, my Master, lean drunk on your chair,
dispatching a thousand sheets in an instant —
a whirlwind, a galloping storm, the spattering of rain and wind,
falling flowers, flying snow, wilder than any eye sees.
You rise, your brush never stopping —
a line of words as big as the Dipper,
terrible as the voice of god or demon,
traceless as the gait of snake and dragon,
spiraling and shrinking, like startled lightning,
two empires battling for the world.

How many households are there in the seven lake counties?
And every one has a screen covered with your writing.
How many brushmen in by-gone times have found such fame?
And even Zhang Xu will die before reaching this success.
But you, my Master, do not imitate the ancients.
What's most precious is born from Heaven,
so why watch a Persian sword dance to learn to write?[615]

草書歌行

少年上人號懷素，草書天下稱獨步
墨池飛出北溟魚，筆鋒殺盡中山兔
八月九月天氣涼，酒徒詞客滿高堂

箋麻素絹排數廂，宣州石硯墨色光
吾師醉后倚繩床，須臾掃盡數千張
飄風驟雨驚颯颯，落花飛雪何茫茫
起來向壁不停手，一行數字大如斗
恍恍如聞神鬼驚，時時只見龍蛇走
左盤右蹙如驚電，狀同楚漢相攻戰
湖南七郡凡几家，家家屏障書題遍
王逸少，張伯英，古來几許浪得名
張顛老死不足數，我師此義不師古
古來萬事貴天生，何必要公孫大娘渾脫舞

Did Li Bo write this poem? Probably not. He'd been dead some years when Huaisu made a big splash in the capital about the year 768. So most traditional commentators have called it a forgery.[616] But Adele Schlombs, true *connoisseur* of Huaisu, argues that this piece of calligraphy is a forgery too, merely a "freehand copy," not even a tracing or rubbing of Huaisu's work.[617]

Mixed in with real and fake is the secondary artist, an agent emanated from the originating source. Like an Elvis impersonator.[618] Is this mix a dilution?[619] We do the same when we read, though, interposing our own mind between a something and a meaning, making bad copies all the time. Complicit with these fakes, we have offered this piece of calligraphy, this poem, and our translation.[620]

Huaisu, born in poverty, raised in a monastery, devoted above all to the cursive script — this is his early life. Like Li Bo, he seems to have had no significant human teachers. He tells us

> I'd observe how summer clouds formed many strange peaks, and I took them as my master. Summer clouds are constantly transforming in the wind, never with the same configuration. I also happened on cracks in a wall — each one is completely natural to itself.[621]

> 觀夏雲多奇峯，輒嘗師之。夏雲因風變化，乃無常勢，又遇壁折之路，一一自然。

But also, like Li Bo, exceptionally well versed in his artistic traditions.[622]

When Huaisu arrives in post-war Chang'an, his wild swagger is immediately lionized. He brings with him a dizzying "Autobiography" (*Huaisu zishutie* 懷素自叙帖), to wit:

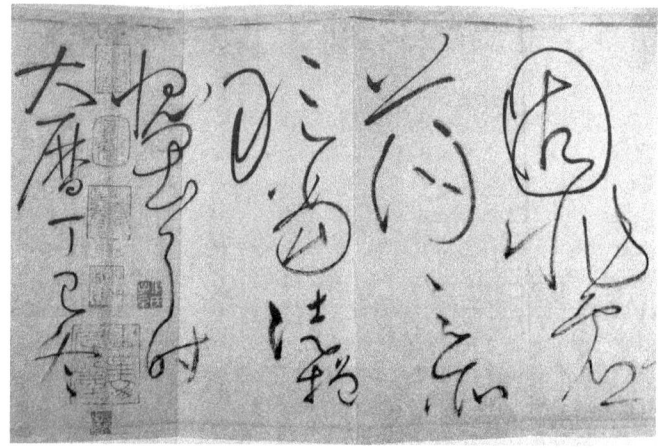

Fig. 82. Facsimile of Huaisu's autobiography (fragment).[623]

The text contains some details of his life, but it's mostly assembled accolades of the famous. Thus it's closer to a CV *cum* reference letters than our sense of autobiography — it's a foot in the door, both stylistically and socially.[624]

Wildness. Not just in calligraphy but in self-presentation, performance. Very drunk, Huaisu executes unprecedented acts of calligraphic marvel. Many times, before many men, an unfettered celebration of great unbridling. Eventually he dies of beriberi.[625]

Schlombs situates these triumphant displays of "wild, dramatic spontaneity" in the socio-intellectual context of Chang'an after the Rebellion.[626] Something had gone terribly wrong, and iconoclasm, a further breaking of symbols, spoke to this directly. She identifies a côterie of new men — mid-level scholar-officials without pedigree or ties to the moribund aristocracy — who adopt Huaisu as a vision of their truer self.[627]

Li Bo has been curated by later Chinese tradition in much the same terms. But these terms are a post-rebellion creation. In his own time Li Bo elicited comments like "This poem would set ghosts and gods to weep,"[628] or "The pupils of his eyes blazed sharply, quivering like a hungry tiger,"[629] or "Even more singular than singular."[630] Post-war the new categories of individual identity, uniqueness and self-expression gradually become available, even necessary, and they scoop him right up.[631] Thus two generations later, poets speak of his "virile élan and untrammeled abandon, his casting off of restraints."[632] So if we approach Li Bo through the last millennium of his Chinese readership, from late Tang onwards, we find him reflected in that mirror.

Here I'll mark some stages through which that curation passes. First, both Li Bo and Huaisu do something unaccountable, something past measure or immeasure, simply overwhelming and mind stopping, like an orgasm. What can you say about that? There's no place to stand and view this from within.

Then, as we've seen, come the names, "untrammeled," "unrestrained," the identification of qualities that surround this ((((energy field)))).[633]

Next the languages of religion enter. For Huaisu, it's Zen 禪 (or, in its Chinese pronunciation, Chan). But that is only in late Tang, a hundred years *post hoc*.[634] And it is an aestheticized religion — "Zen as artistic experience."[635] Eventually Li Bo too is praised in Zen language.[636]

Finally, as Schlombs notes, in the early eleventh century "the image of the *wild monk* was converted into that of a versatile scholar-artist."[637] In the new literatus culture of Song, there's a place for conventions of unconventionality.[638]

This devolution process is yet more striking in the case of Li Bo's close contemporary Mazu 馬祖 (709–788), "Patriarch Ma," co-founder with Huineng 惠能 (638–713) of the Zen style, the only Chinese monk I know who's known by his original family name, "Mr. Ma." Just a few years younger than Li Bo and, like him, growing up in Sichuan. Like him, leaving town and roaming out, then connecting with his own master at the Southern Marchmount, Mt. Heng.[639] His extant speech was collected in the eleventh century as the *Mazu yulu* 馬祖語錄. It consists of two parts — public sermons given before hundreds of monks and lay people, and some thirty private dialogues with students. Mario Poceski has studied these texts intensively and concludes, "I think we have fairly strong grounds to infer that the extant sermons are based on edited transcripts of various talks Mazu gave during his long teaching career."[640] They are also hardly distinguishable from other good Buddhism of the time.

The dialogues are way different. Here Mazu kicks, shouts, beats, indirects, all activities we now associate with the Zen school.[641] Some mild examples:

> What's a Buddha like?
> This very mind, this very Buddha.

>> 大梅問:「如何是佛?」
>> 師云:「即心即佛。」

> Why did Your Reverence say, "This very mind, this very Buddha"?
> To stop the little children crying.
> What's it like when the crying stops?
> Not a mind, not a Buddha.

>> 僧問:「和尚為甚麼說即心即佛?」
>> 師曰:「為止小兒啼。」
>> 問:「啼止時如何?」
>> 師曰:「非心非佛。」

> Please tell me directly the intention of the Patriarch bringing us Zen from the West.
> I'm tired out today and can't answer you. Go ask Zhizang.

>> 僧問:「離四句、絕百非,請師直指西來意。」
>> 師曰:「我今日勞倦,不能為汝說得,問取智藏。」

There is no evidence that anyone taught this way before Mazu.⁶⁴² There is also no evidence that Poceski can find for these stories until 250 years later, in early Song. For this and other good reasons, Poceski considers them recent fabrications, designed to establish the eccentric Zen brand among Song literati eager for iconoclasm.⁶⁴³

I think there are other reasons why we can't find Tang dynasty evidence for these dialogues. They are the most private and personal exchanges imaginable, like the whispering of two lovers. They were never meant to be pawed over, gossiped about, or spread through the realm.⁶⁴⁴

Or to be turned into kōan collections for the instruction of later students. A kōan is a story put by a master to test and entice his student's understanding. The practice evolved from the "question-and-answer" (Ch. *wenda* 問答, Jap. *mondo*) dialogues we see here, and by the eleventh century had become a widely used teaching tool. In 1125 some hundred were collected and printed as the *Blue Cliff Records* (*Biyanlu* 碧巖錄).⁶⁴⁵ Kōan (Chinese *gong'an* 公案) means "a public case." It's what happens when you go to court and your private affairs become the state's possession. Zen Master Dahui 大慧 (1089–1163) burned the printing blocks of the *Blue Cliff Records*.⁶⁴⁶

Huaisu. Li Bo. Mazu. Something unbearable, unhearable, now held under the banner of spontaneity. It's a way of hoping that it never happened.⁶⁴⁷

VIII

A Banished Immortal

Chapter 67. A Plumper Li Bo of Yore

The first we hear about a banished immortal is Dongfang Shuo, some thousand years before Li Bo.⁶⁴⁸ Here's a recent portrait:

Fig. 83. Matsumura Goshun (1752–1811), *Portrait of Tung-Fang Shuo,* ca. 1790. Hanging scroll, ink and light color on paper, Brooklyn Museum.⁶⁴⁹

Dongfang Shuo 東方朔 (ca. 160–ca. 93 BCE), tall, handsome, extroverted, startlingly fast with words, erudite, appallingly honest, connoisseur of braggadocio and wine, a fool of extravagance at the court of the Martial Emperor of Han. By virtue of all these, he became a great favorite of the Emperor.⁶⁵⁰

Once he was given permission to eat in His Majesty's presence. When the meal was over, he stuffed his robe full of the leftover meat and left. His robe was completely soiled.[651]

時詔賜之食於前。飯已,盡懷其餘肉持去,衣盡汙。

And:

Once Dongfang Shuo came to the palace drunk and peed in the upper hall. He was charged with *lèse majesté,* but the Emperor commuted the death penalty and merely reduced him to the rank of commoner.[652]

But he also used these talents to offer frank and caustic remonstrance to the Emperor's profligacy, nepotism and credulity, relying on his wit to turn insolence into audible truth.[653]

Here's how he came to be called a "banished immortal," a role that sustained Li Bo through difficult times. The Queen Mother of the West, extreme goddess among all goddesses, had descended the evening of the Emperor's birthday. Right off, without foreplay, the Emperor wants her peaches of immortality, but she tells him he first needs to control his lust and ambition.

Suddenly a man appeared at the south window, peeking at the immortals. Startled, the Emperor asked, "Who's that?" The Queen Mother replied, "Don't you recognize him? He's your attendant, Dongfang Shuo. He's my neighbor's child. By nature he's very mischievous—three times he came to steal these very peaches [and so was banished] to this stinky, murky realm.

After that the Emperor knew that Dongfang Shuo was no ordinary person.[654]

Shuo and Li Bo share a structural problem: if you're very s*m*a*r*t, and unable to shut up, if you love wine, if you love all appearance, how can you survive the shifting fictions of court life, where every passageway gives way to another, lined with trick mirrors and hidden knives? Shuo succeeded forty years, much longer than Li Bo. Outwardly he played the role of buffoon (*huaji* 滑稽), meaning that he turned his disjunction from court realities into a joke. But he also borrowed another disjunctive device, that of the mountain recluse, and combined it with his own circumstances to create a new, capacious role for himself: he became a "recluse at court" (*chaoyin* 朝隱).[655]

> Merry with drink, and riffing on a local song, Dongfang said, "This dry land is sinking under the waters of the ordinary. I'm going to 'shun the world' at Golden Horses Gate. One can 'shun the world' and 'keep one's body whole' within the palace halls.[656] Why must you dwell amidst deep hills or in a mountain hut?"[657]

Li Bo frequently compared himself to Dongfang Shuo. Here is his "Song of the jade flask."

> Fierce old soldiers beat on their jade flasks, keeping time to the music,
> but in their stout hearts they resent their sunset years.
> Three cups in, they whirl their swords and dance beneath the autumn moon,
> belting out the old songs, weeping tears and snot.
>
> It began when a divine phoenix flew down with a royal invitation.
> Then I called upon the God-Emperor, raised my cup and mounted to the banquet,
> I glorified the ruler, with his nine-fold gated palace and ten-thousand chariots of war,
> I bantered with worthies on the red escalier at the palace's blue-green porte.
> The Heavenly Sovereign received me in audience,
> loaned me one after another of his Flying Dragon horses,
> and then bestowed on me a whip of coral and white jade.

Ordinary people don't recognize Dongfang Shuo
and his great reclusion at Golden Horses Gate — he's a banished immortal!
A true beauty is becoming whether she smiles or frowns,
when an ugly woman imitates her, she just gets uglier.
The King may love his beauty's dimples,
but in the palace jealousy kills.⁶⁵⁸

玉壺吟

烈士擊玉壺，壯心惜暮年
三杯拂劍舞秋月，忽然高詠涕泗漣
鳳凰初下紫泥詔，謁帝稱觴登御筵
揄揚九重萬乘主，謔浪赤墀青瑣賢
朝天數換飛龍馬，敕賜珊瑚白玉鞭
世人不識東方朔，大隱金門是謫仙
西施宜笑復宜顰，醜女效之徒累身
君王雖愛蛾眉好，無奈宮中妒殺人

Chapter 68. "Who Am I?"

In reply to Kāśya, Magistrate of Huzhou, who asked me who I am

I, the Blue Lotus Layman, am a banished immortal,
thirty years I've drunk too much and hidden away my name.
Why, sir, do you need to ask?
In my next life I'll be the Gold Grain Buddha.[659]

答湖州迦葉司馬問白是何人

青蓮居士謫仙人
酒肆藏名三十春
湖州司馬何須問
金粟如來是後身

The name Kāśya tells us that the Magistrate is an ethnic Indian from Central Asia.[660] So he is presumably acquainted with the Gold Grain Buddha. I had to look it up, though, and of course it's somewhat involved. Here's the story, starting with Li Bo's sobriquet.

Blue Lotus Layman is the Buddhist name Li Bo discovered for himself — the lotus flower, always showing pure even while growing in murky waters.[661] Li Bo's line from another poem:

The blue lotus emerging from the muck.[662]

青蓮出塵埃

Layman — a lay devotee or householder (*jushi* 居士), an ordained non-monastic. Well, there's a serious Buddhist supposition that only a monk or nun can attain enlightenment, there's no other way. But Buddha's teaching was there before anyone thought monastically, and so even within the tradition we have the case of Vimalakīrti, a great layman, contemporary of the Buddha, who attained that same realization with no ordination at all.[663] In Chinese, Vimalakīrti is often called Layman Vima (Weimo jushi 維摩居士).[664] In his previous life he was the Tathāgata Golden Grain of our poem,[665] and in Li Bo's own next life, he tells us, he himself is going to be that same Buddha. It's a bit like telling someone, "Right now I'm your ancestor, and in my next life I'll be your progenitor."

The Buddhist layman and the Daoist immortal sit together in a single line of Li Bo's verse, without even a hyphen between them. It would be a shame to think of them antagonistically or syncretically, as if there were two religions squeezing into a single body.[666] But Li Bo also tells us he's a *banished* immortal. And what is that?

We've seen how Dongfang Shuo pulls off the banished immortal role — his offensiveness, wit, practical wisdom. Here is another banished immortal, of a generation or two before Li Bo, to augment the contrast. I'm speaking of Ye Fashan 葉法善 (631–720), great magician and theurgist.[667] An American scholar writes of him:

> He employed ritual powers and spirit-helpers to perform countless amazing rescues, saving ladies and gentlemen, emperors and courtiers, from death, disease, demons, coups, and unprincipled sorcerers. […] His meritorious activities, in faithful service to grateful rulers, served to integrate the cosmos, uniting the world above, the world below, and every corner of the world of men, from imperial court to the most distant frontier.[668]

He served five Emperors, and the Bright Emperor himself wrote his epitaph.[669] At his death, on 12 July 720, "he ascended as immortal in broad daylight."[670]

Ye came with these abilities. He followed no human master, underwent no spiritual training, had no religious affiliation, wrote no texts, trod no path. It's even unlikely he was ever ordained a Daoist priest (*daoshi* 道士). When he was six, he seemed to drown and was gone for three years. On his return, he told his parents that the Azure Lad had given him Cloud Sauce to drink, so he'd stayed away a bit.[671]

So how does an immortal get banished? We know that Dongfang Shuo stole the peaches of immortality. Sire Gourd (in chapter 31, the Grotto-Heaven) tells us that "I was inattentive to my duties, so I was banished, sent back for a while to this human realm." Ye Fashan had been similarly inattentive:

> Once Ye met three deities, all dressed in brocade robes and fancy hats. They said to him, "We're acting on the orders of Laozi, the Great Highest,[672] and we bring you a secret imperial rescript from him. Originally you were an official in the Left Office of Immortals within the Great Ultimate Purple Subtlety.[673] But you were inattentive in copying out the registers of birth and death, so you were banished to the human realm. Make haste to gather merit by serving people. When your merit is complete, you can return to your old position."[674]

And so he spent his entire life in service to others, compelling spirits and demons — this was his sole function, or purpose. In particular, he was apotropaic guardian to the Bright Emperor and his State.[675]

There seem, then, to be two causes for banishment. One is to be naughty, like Dongfang Shuo and Li Bo — it's somehow taken for granted that Li Bo's the kind of being who might offend a celestial bureaucracy. The other is to be inattentive, *buqin* 不勤. The second, though, sheds happy light on the first, for that phrase *buqin* also occurs in chapter 6 of the *Laozi,* but there with the positive meaning of "being without effort and thus inexhaustible."[676] So perhaps banishment is only a term of non-recognition, the name that a scoldy, work-obsessed society reserves for something whose unkempt inexhaustibility lacks all normal explanation.[677] If we remove the stigma of punishment, then each of these immortals is actually a curious visitor to Earth, just a tourist, a style of functioning, certainly not an identity. From the perspective of the divine, banishment is simply a movement from here to here, from a Heaven to an Earth. It's not something that happened once, and is done with, but rather a continuous down-pouring of blessings into the human realm.

This helps us understand why we have no traces of either Ye or Li Bo doing any work to develop their skills. Ye, at least, was born that way, and the Great Highest only sent him here for a bit, presumably because the State needed protection.[678] The *Catholic Encyclopedia* of 1913 defines one division of hagiography as those texts that are "the spontaneous product of circumstances or have been called into being by religious needs of one kind or another."[679] This might also be a Tang definition of Ye Fashan, called here by circumstance, overseen by the Great Highest, and thus a functioning part of the Order of Things[680] — his banishment was just the arrangement through which this could be achieved. Sometimes it's difficult to separate cause and effect.[681]

The earliest account of a banished immortal among the official dynastic histories is in the *Book of the Southern Qi* (*Nanqishu* 南齊書).[682] Like this:

> During the late 480s a man named Cai lived on Cup Mountain in Kuaiji. His given name's unknown. He raised rats there, dozens and dozens of them, and they'd come or go on his command. His speech was variable and mad. He was often called a "banished immortal."[683]

Chapter 69. "Given in Parting"

Given in parting to District Defender Liu of West River

My autumn hair's all thin and short,
I've accomplished nothing.
Laughing, at ease, we pour good Lu wine,
as if you're the ancient tippler Liu Gongrong.
You say I'm Dongfang Shuo,
the planet Jupiter fallen into this human realm.
In commoner's garb we're lords of countless realms,
why should we have to leave the Heavenly Court?
Neither are you, my friend, where you wanted to be,
and you envy the song of geese, vanishing in the sky.
Most people are midges growing in an old wine keg,
how could they know your nature?
You may be a clerk sharpening his quills,
but your heart holds the Red Mountain of the immortals.
I too float like duckweed,
drifting on the waves of these good times.
I have two young concubines
who ride a pair of fine horses.
In spring when East Mountain wine is new,
I'll disappear and leave this phantom fame.[684]

留別西河劉少府

秋發已種種，所為竟無成
閑傾魯壺酒，笑對劉公榮
謂我是方朔，人間落歲星
白衣千萬乘，何事去天庭
君亦不得意，高歌羨鴻冥
世人若醯雞，安可識梅生
雖為刀筆吏，緬懷在赤城
余亦如流萍，隨波樂休明

自有兩少妾，雙騎駿馬行
東山春酒綠，歸隱謝浮名

A New Telling of Tales of This World (*Shishuo xinyu* 世說新語) tells us:

> Liu Gongrong would drink with anyone, noble or debased, without distinction. Someone mocked him for this. He replied, "I have to drink with anyone better than me, so I also have to drink with anyone not as good as me, and I also have to drink with anyone equal to me." So every day he drank with people until he was drunk.[685]

Dongfang Shuo calls his autobiography "The Discourse of Master Nobody."[686] Li Bo has two concubines, but his true consort is Appearance.

A Postlude

Chapter 70. "3 and 5 and 7 Words"

Clear fall wind,
bright fall moon.

Leaves fall, then gather, scatter,
cold crows roost and startle.

When will we see each other again?
This time, this night, I'm feeling bashful.[687]

三五七言

秋風清
秋月明
落葉聚還散
寒鴉棲復驚
相思相見知何日
此時此夜難為情

A POSTLUDE

Chapter 71. Method

> "I only care for Dao, what's that got to do with technique?"
> 臣之所好者道也，進乎技矣。
> — attributed to Cook Ding[688]

At the request of a friend,[689] I thought I'd say a bit about our methods in making this book. In general, we proceed by analogy, by juxtaposition, latency, innuendo, jump cut, dialetheia and flirt.[690] Like a sidewinder, like a Pisces. We like the language of cats and dogs.[691] We also like the Wikipedia and don't consider it infra dig.[692]

By contrast, lawyers are poets who are asked to write in an unequivocally monovalent language, where hermeneuticians can't get their claws in nor rhinos their horns. This is much harder than writing sonnets, and they don't even get to rhyme.[693] So we needn't complain about how much money they earn.

All translations here have been done by us, unless otherwise noted. We tried to avoid the most famous poems, but most of them are spectacularly good, and a number have crept in.[694] When we discover an obscure poem we like, we often find that Paul Kroll has already been there, and done a faultless job with it.

I had a friend in Maine named Al Gardner. He was very fat and a crackerjack martial artist. He told me the difference between ju-jitsu and judō. Both come from the same Japanese word *ju* 柔, meaning "soft," but the former refers to the manifold, largely unarmed arts of medieval Japan, their jitsu (*jutsu* 術) or techniques. Judō, however, was invented in 1882 as a way of life, a physical and moral cultivation, that is, as an attempt to turn these techniques into a dō or Dao, a Way. Al hated it.

So, with apologies to Cook Ding, we have to say we only like technique, we don't actually care that much for Dao.

Chapter 72. An Apology

You, Li Bo, are a great immortal. We are twenty-first-century American rip-off artists. For a moment we've glimpsed 2 or 3% of your shining, which we display here in our bad English. These poets have served you better:

Elling Eide, Paul Kroll, Isabelle Robinet, Edward Schafer

We'd also like to see how these folks would do it:

Tennyson, Mirabai, Gerard Manley Hopkins, Cole Porter, Kalidas[695]

Our Gratitude

First to Zhan Ying 詹鍈 (1916–98), who with his team produced an eight-volume complete collection of Li Bo's writing, *Li Bo quanji xiaozhu huishi jiping* 李白全集校注彙釋集評 (Tianjin 天津: Baihua 百花, 1996). They have gathered all relevant materials and annotated them with unexcelled discernment.

Our gratitude to Paul Kroll is harder to imagine. When I was first reading Li Bo, Paul's writings felt like handholds up the mountain. Only later did I realize that they were the mountain itself. His *Dictionary* defines the literary diction of our next generations. It also asks that we poet up to its aesthetic demands.

Everything in this book comes from elsewhere. I mean this in a very ordinary way. And in an extraordinary way as well. Some benefactors' names appear in the Bibliography, a great cornucopia of wisdom experience that they have made freely available. Other names are strewn through the Endnotes, like gold dust in a carpet. I am probably unaware of my greatest debts.

Sarah Messer worked with us at an early stage of the project. If you find an especially beguiling phrase in a poetic line, it's probably hers. Kid Cooper Levy joined us at the end and added his ferocious, felicitous wit.

Several good friends have read this book in draft, offering encouragement and critique. They include Bobak Bakhtiari, Douglas Penick, B. Love Davis, Sandy Hackney, and Michelle Tupko.

Vincent W.J. van Gerven Oei and Eileen A. Fradenburg Joy of punctum books saw St. Elmo's fire all through the rigging, and worked to bring the ship to harbor.

To all of you, our gratitude.

Afterwords

LI BO UNKEMPT

Afterword
by Traktung Yeshe Dorje

Drinking under the moon by myself for the first time

We three: flowers,
wine jug, and me.

We're drinking by ourselves
without regard.

Hey, hey, bright moon,
I lift my cup to thee.

Three more people: the moon,
my shadow, and me.

Fool moon
couldn't care less for wine.

Silly shadow
just follows me round like a dog.

I'm stuck with you all,
all the way till pleasure turns to spring.

I sing,
my moon wanders along.

I dance,
my shadow staggers along.

Now we're sobering up.
That was some good joy.

Now drinking's done.
Every body goes its own way.

Bound together,
we roam all time without regard.

And some time in some Milky Way
we meet [696]

月下獨酌四首其一

花間一壺酒,獨酌無相親
舉杯邀明月,對影成三人
月既不解飲,影徒隨我身
暫伴月將影,行樂須及春
我歌月徘徊,我舞影零亂
醒時同交歡,醉後各分散
永結無情游,相期邈雲漢

And where-when is that point, Li Bo? Oh, you rascal, you pretend it's somewhen else. If we trust you, you'll take us on a long, entrancing journey through a hundred moons, "Who cares how long it takes, my whole life I've loved this roaming." If we distrust you, you'll take us right now behind the star curtain of the Milky Way and show us our old home. It's up to us, he couldn't care less, but some time in this Milky Way we meet.

Poetry is a belly dancer's veils. Always in spangled motion, always in advertisement for itself. An invitation to knowledge, or a trick of the light. Who wields this veil, a wave or a particle?

If we get Poetry a little tipsy, with flagon on flagon of light, it will disclose the secrets of all three of us: Silence, Words, and You. Of our unkempt three-way love affair. Words claims it was because Silence burbled and destroyed all possibility of meaning. Silence claims it was Words' importunate blandishing, "Look, I got you special bling just for you, excellent stuff like 'pre-ontological' and 'post-apophatic.' I will teach you to say

"Ahh!'" And You, my best beloved? You were there too, and You kept these secrets, until now.⁶⁹⁷

Silence is a tigress in her first heat. You are astride her, or sometimes the lady from Niger inside her. Words is a Russian divorce lawyer who won't shut up.

Silence surrenders itself. Words surrenders parataxis. You surrender your good looks.

It is the way that snow falls in the mountains. Snow is words. It is the natural state describing itself, the first sound, first light. Snow is Li Bo falling down from nowhere.

Up to his eyes in white, he wonders how much bliss we can bear. How much horror. He will haunt us until we answer honestly. He's standing on the earth, the sky keeps falling.

By springtime all the snow is opened and gone.

Li Bo is the only poet I've really envied.

Traktung Yeshe Dorje
White Lotus Farms
Winter solstice, 2020

Afterword
by Maria Dolgenas

Sisters of the dream! Please care for Li Bo in that realm where love and incompletion rule.

Li Bo, display the matrimony, the mother pour, this hopeless joy.

Fig. 84. The moon.[698]

Don't forget to come home.

Bibliographies

Primary Chinese Works from before 1100 CE

Here's a selection of the most important Chinese texts that appear in this book. They're listed in stroke order, with the title in Chinese followed by its English language equivalent. Then comes the author, if known, and approximate date. When there's a useful translation, e.g., by Burton Watson, the entry ends "Trans. Watson" — you'll find the full reference in the Bibliography of Secondary Works under this person's name. All Chinese works are available on line.

太平御覽 Taiping yulan. Imperial reader of the Taiping period. Li Fang 李昉 (925–96) et al.
太平廣記 Taiping guangji. Extensive records from the Taiping period. Li Fang 李昉 (925–96) et al.
水經註 Shuijing zhu. Commentary on the Classic of Rivers. Li Daoyuan 酈道元 (472–527).
文選 Wenxuan. Selections of refined literature. Xiao Tong 蕭統 (501–31). Trans. Knechtges.
史記 Shiji. Historical records. Sima Qian 司馬遷 (145–86 BCE). Trans. Nienhauser.
世說新語 Shishuo xinyu. New account of tales of the world. Liu Yiqing 劉義慶 (403–44). Trans. Mather.
列女傳 Lienüzhuan. Biographies of eminent women. Liu Xiang 劉向 977–6 BCE).
列仙傳 Liexianzhuan. A range of biographies of divine immortals. Second century CE. Trans. Kaltenmark.
竹書紀年 Zhushu jinian. Bamboo annals. Late first millenium BCE. Trans. Nivison.
呂氏春秋 Lüshi chunqiu. The springs and autumns of Mr. Lü. Lü Buwei 呂不韋 (fl. 239 BCE).
尚書 Shangshu. Book of documents. Early first millennium BCE. Trans. Karlgren.
易經 Yijing. The classic of change. Trans. Wilhelm.

抱樸子 Baopuzi. The master who cherishes simplicity. Ge Hong 葛洪 (283–343). Trans. Ware.

神仙傳 Shenxianzhuan. Biographies of divine immortals. Ge Hong 葛洪 (283–343). Trans. Campany.

晉書 Jinshu. History of the Jin. Fang Xuanling 房玄齡 (579–648).

後漢書 Hou Hanshu. History of the Later Han. Fan Ye 范曄 (398–445).

高士傳 Gaoshizhuan. Biographies of eminent scholars. Huangfu Mi 皇甫謐 (215–82).

茶經 Chajing. The classic of tea. Lu Yu 陸羽 (733–804). Trans. Benn.

真誥 Zhengao. Declarations of the perfected. Yang Xi 楊羲 (330–86). Trans. Smith.

淮南子 Huainanzi. Master Huainan (sometime before 139 BCE). Trans. Major.

莊子 Zhuangzi. Ca. 300 BCE. Trans. Graham.

道德經 Daodejing. The classic of the power of the way. Laozi 老子. Fourth century BCE. Trans. Lynn.

資治通鑑 Zizhi tongjian. Comprehensive mirror to aid in governance. Sima Guang 司馬光 (1019–86).

新唐書 Xin Tangshu. New history of the Tang. Ouyang Xiu 歐陽修 (1007–72).

楚辭 Chuci. The songtexts of Chu. Fourth to second centuries BCE. Trans. Hawkes.

說文解字 Shuowen jiezi. Explanations of graphs. Xu Shen 許慎 (fl. 100 CE).

漢武帝內傳 Han Wudi neizhuan. The esoteric biography of the Martial Emperor of Han. Sixth century CE but containing earlier material. Trans. Schipper.

漢書 Hanshu. History of the Han. Ban Gu 班固 (32–92). Trans. Watson.

墨子 Mozi. (470–391 BCE). The Mozi. Trans. Watson.

藝文類聚 Yiwenleiju. Classified collection of literature. Ouyang Xun 歐陽詢 (557–641).

論語 Lunyu. Analects of Confucius/Kongzi 孔子 (551–479). Various.

論衡 Lunhung. Balanced discourse. Wang Chong 王充 (27–100). Trans. Forke.

舊唐書 Jiu Tangshu. Old history of the Tang. Tenth century CE.

Secondary Works

Aceti, Enrica, *Le "Divine" degli anni ruggenti.* Milan: Domus, 1976.

Adshead, S.A.M. *T'ang China: The Rise of the East in World History.* New York: Palgrave Macmillan, 2004.

Ambramson, Marc. *Ethnic Identity in Tang China.* Philadelphia: University of Pennsylvania Press, 2008.

Andersen, Poul. *Taoist Ritual Texts and Traditions with Special Reference to Bugang, the Cosmic Dance.* Ph.D. dissertation, University of Copenhagen, 1991.

Anonymous. "Gonnella, the Court Fool of Ferrara." *The New Monthly Magazine* 16 (1826): 162–67.

Assandri, Friederike. "Mystery and Secrecy in the Contacts of Buddhism and Daoism in Early Medieval China." In *Religious Secrecy as Contact: Secrets as Promoters of Religious Dynamics,* edited by A. Akasoy et al. Leiden: Brill, forthcoming.

Bachelard, Gaston. *The Psychoanalysis of Fire.* Translated by Alan Ross. London: Routledge, 1964.

Barfield, Thomas. *The Perilous Frontier: Nomadic Empires and China.* Cambridge: Basil Blackwell, 1989.

Barrett, Timothy H. *Taoism under the T'ang: Religion & Empire during the Golden Age of Chinese History.* London: Wellsweep, 1996.

Barrie, J.M. *Peter Pan.* New York: Penguin, 1938.

Barros, Carlos. "Hacia un nuevo paradigma historiográfico." *Debates Americanos* 10(2000): 86–96.

Benn, Charles. *China's Golden Age: Everyday Life in the Tang Dynasty.* Oxford: Oxford University Press, 2002.

———. *The Cavern Mystery Transmission: A Taoist Ordination Rite of A.D. 711.* Honolulu: University of Hawai'i Press, 1991.

Benn, James. "One Mountain, Two Traditions: Buddhist and Taoist Claims on Zhongnan Shan in Medieval Times." In *Images, Relics, and Legends: The Formation and Transfor-*

mation of Buddhist Sacred Sites, edited by James Benn. Oakville: Mosaic Press, 2012.

———. *Tea in China: A Religious and Cultural History*. Honolulu: University of Hawai'i Press, 2015.

Berkowitz, Alan. "Account of the Buddhist Thaumaturge Baozhi." In *Buddhism in Practice,* edited by Donald Lopez, 578–85. Princeton University Press, 1995.

Blyth, R.H. *Zen in English Literature and Oriental Classics.* Tokyo: Hokuseidō, 1942.

Bokenkamp, Stephen. *Early Daoist Scriptures.* Berkeley: University of California Press, 1997.

———. "Foreword." In Robert Campany, *To Live as Long as Heaven and Earth: A Translation and Study of Ge Hong's Traditions of Divine Transcendents,* xxi–xxiv. Berkeley: University of California Press, 2002.

———. "Li Bai, Huangshan, and Alchemy." *Tang Studies* 25 (2007): 29–55. DOI: 10.1179/073750307790779513.

———. "Time after Time: Taoist Apocalyptic History and the Founding of the T'ang Dynasty." *Asia Major* 7, no. 1 (1994): 59–88.

Bol, Peter. *"This Culture of Ours": Intellectual Transitions in T'ang and Sung China.* Stanford: Stanford University Press, 1992.

Boltz, William. "The Structure and Interpretation of *Chuang tzǔ*: Two Notes on *Hsiao yao yu*." *Bulletin of the School of Oriental and African Studies* 43, no. 3 (1980): 532–43. DOI: 10.1017/S0041977X00137437.

Boodberg, Peter. "Philological Notes on Chapter One of the Lao Tzu." *Harvard Journal of Asiatic Studies* 20, nos. 3–4 (1957): 598–618. DOI: 10.2307/2718364.

———. "Philology in Translation-Land." In "Cedules from a Berkeley Workshop in Asiatic Philology." In *Selected works of Peter A. Boodberg,* edited by Alvin Cohen, 174–75. Berkeley: University of California Press (1979).

Braudel, Fernand. *Afterthoughts on Material Civilization and Capitalism.* Baltimore: Johns Hopkins University Press, 1977.

Brindley, Erica Fox. *Ancient China and the Yue: Perceptions and Identities on the Southern Frontier.* Cambridge University Press, 2015.

Budick, Sanford, and Wolfgang Iser, eds., *Languages of the Unsayable: The Play of Negativity in Literature and Literary Theory.* Stanford University Press, 1987.

Cahill, Suzanne. "Marriages Made in Heaven." *T'ang Studies* 10–11 (1992–93): 111–22. DOI: 10.1179/073750392787773096.

———. "Night Shining White: Traces of a T'ang Dynasty Horse in Two Media." *T'ang Studies* 4 (1986): 91–94. DOI: 10.1179/tng.1986.1986.4.91.

———. "Practice Makes Perfect: Paths to Transcendence for Women in Medieval China." *Taoist Resources* 2, no. 2 (1990): 23–42.

———. "Sex and the Supernatural in Medieval China: Cantos on the Transcendent Who Presides over the River." *Journal of the American Oriental Society* 105, no. 2 (1985): 197–220. DOI: 10.2307/601701.

Campany, Robert. *Strange Writing: Anomaly Accounts in Early Medieval China.* Albany: SUNY Press, 1996.

———. "The Meanings of Cuisines of Transcendence in Late Classical and Early Medieval China." *T'oung Pao* 91, no. 1 (2005): 1–57. DOI: 10.1163/1568532054905124

———. *To Live as Long as Heaven and Earth: A Translation and Study of Ge Hong's Traditions of Divine Transcendents.* Berkeley: University of California Press, 2002.

Carr, Michael. "Chinese Dragon Names." *Linguistics of the Tibeto-Burman Area* 13, no. 2 (1990): 87–90.

Cassirer, Ernst. *Language and Myth.* New York: Dover, 1946.

Cedzich, Urusla-Angelika. "Corpse Deliverance, Substitute Bodies, Name Change, and Feigned Death: Aspects of Metamorphosis and Immortality in Early Medieval China." *Journal of Chinese Religions* 29, no. 1 (2001): 1–68. DOI: 10.1179/073776901804774578.

Cendrars, Blaise. "The Prose of the Trans-Siberian and of the Little Jeanne of France (An Article Which Blaise Cendrars Wrote for 'Der Sturm,' No. 184-185, Berlin, November 1913)," translated by Roger Kaplan. *The Chicago Review* 24, no. 3 (1972): 3–21. DOI: 10.2307/25294698.

Certeau, Michel de. *The Writing of History.* New York: Columbia University Press, 1988.

Chai, David. *Zhuangzi and the Becoming of Nothingness.* Albany: State University of New York Press, 2019.

Chavannes, Edouard. *Le T'ai chan.* Paris: Leroux, 1910.

Chen, Fan-pen. "Problems of Chinese Historiography as Seen in the Official Records on Yang Kuei-fei." *T'ang Studies* 8–9 (1990–91): 83–96. doi: 10.1179/073750390787970800.

———. "Yang Kuei-fei in Tales from the T'ien-Pao Era: A Chu-kung-tiao Narrative." *Journal of Sung-Yuan Studies* 22 (1990–92): 1–22. https://www.jstor.org/stable/23495588.

Chen Guofu 陳國符. *Daozang yuanliu kao* 道藏源流考 [Investigations into the origin and transmission of the Daoist canon]. Beijing: Zhonghua, 1949.

Chen, Jinhua. *Philosopher, Practitioner, Politician: The Many Lives of Fazang (643–712).* Leiden: Brill, 2007.

Chen, Li. Review of Seymour McNicholas, *Forgery and Impersonation,* in *Journal of Asian Studies* 77, no. 3 (2018): 783–85. DOI: 10.1017/S0021911818000578.

Chesterton, G.K. *Saint Francis of Assisi.* New York: Random House, 1957.

Chiang, Sing-chen Lydia. "Visions of Happiness: Daoist Utopias and Grotto Paradises in Early and Medieval Chinese Tales." *Utopian Studies* 20, no. 1 (2009): 97–120.

Chou Fa-kao (Zhou Fagao 周法高). *A Pronouncing Dictionary of Chinese Characters.* Hong Kong: Hong Kong University Press, 1974.

Chung, Saehyang P. "Hsing-ch'ing Kung: Some New Findings on the Plan of Emperor Hsüan-tsung's Private Palace." *Archives of Asian Art* 44 (1991): 51–67.

Copp, Paul. *The Body Incantatory: Spells and the Ritual Imagination in Medieval Chinese Buddhism.* New York: Columbia University Press, 2014.

Cummings, E.E. *Selected letters of E. E. Cummings*. Edited by George Stade. Ann Arbor: University of Michigan Press, 1972.

Cutter, Robert Joe. *The Brush and the Spur: Chinese Culture and the Cock Fight*. Hong Kong: Chinese University Press, 1989.

Dalia, Albert. *Dream of the Dragon Pool: A Daoist Quest*. New York: Pleasure Boat Studio, 2007.

Davis, Colin. "Etat Présent: Hauntology, Spectres and Phantoms." *French Studies* 59, no. 3 (2005): 373–79. DOI: 10.1093/fs/kni143.

Davis, Richard. "Chaste and Filial Women in Chinese Historical Writings of the Eleventh Century." *Journal of the American Oriental Society* 121, no. 2 (2001): 204–18. DOI: 10.2307/606561.

Deleuze, Gilles. "The Actual and the Virtual." In *Dialogues II*, 148–52. New York: Columbia University Press, 2002.

Derrida, Jacques. *Khôra*. Paris: Galilée, 1993.

deWoskin, Kenneth. *Doctors, Diviners and Magicians: Biographies of Fang-shih*. New York: Columbia University Press, 1983.

Dickens, Mark. "Everything You Always Wanted to Know about Tocharian But Were Afraid to Ask." Archived at https://web.archive.org/web/20060803100222/http://www.oxuscom.com/eyawtkat.htm.

Ding Bangxin 丁邦新. *Minyu Yanjiu ji qi yu Zhoubian Fangyan de Guanxi* 閩語研究及其與周邊方言的關係 [Researches on Min language and its relationship to other dialects]. Hong Kong: Chinese University Press, 2002.

Ding Fang 丁放. "Yuzhen Gongzhu Kaolun" 玉真公主考論 [An examination of the Princess Yuzhen]. *Beijing Daxue Xuebao* 北京大學學報 41, no. 2 (2004): 41–52.

Ditter, Alexei. "The Commerce of Commemorization." *Tang Studies* 32 (2014): 21–46. DOI: 10.1179/0737503414Z.00000000012

Dōgen 道元. *A Primer of Soto Zen: A Translation of Dogen's Shobogenzo Zuimonki.* Honolulu: University of Hawai'i Press, 1979.

———. *Shōbōgenzō* 正法眼藏 (Treasury of the True Dharma Eye), Book 29, "Mountains and Waters Sutra" (*Sansui kyō* 山水經).

Dorn, Ed. *Gunslinger.* Durham: Duke University Press, 1989.

Durand, John D. "The Population Statistics of China, A.D. 2–1953." *Population Studies* 13, no. 3 (1960): 209–56. DOI: 10.1080/00324728.1960.10405043.

Duyvendak, J.J.L. "The Dreams of Emperor Hsüan-tsung." In *India Antiqua,* 102–8. Leiden: Brill, 1947.

Ebrey, Patricia. "T'ang Guides to Verbal Etiquette." *Harvard Journal of Asiatic Studies* 45, no. 2 (1985): 581–613. DOI: 10.2307/2718973.

Edwards, Richard. *The Heart of Ma Yuan: The Search for a Southern Song Aesthetic.* Hong Kong: Hong Kong University Press, 2011.

Eide, Elling. "On Li Po." In *Perspectives on the T'ang,* edited by Arthur Wright, 367–403. (New Haven: Yale University Press, 1973).

———. *Poems by Li Po.* Lexington: Anvil Press, 1984.

Eliot, T.S. Introduction to Ezra Pound, *Selected Poems.* London: Farber, 1928.

Engels, Donald W. *Alexander the Great and the Logistics of the Macedonian Army.* Berkeley: University of California Press, 1978.

Fingarette, Herbert. *Confucius: The Secular as Sacred.* New York: Harper and Row, 1972.

Flaherty, Ryan. "Craquelure." *Conjunctions* 58 (2012): 303–10.

Forke, Alfred. *Lun-heng: Philosophical Essays of Wang Ch'ung.* Leipzig: Harrassowitz, 1907 and 1911.

Foucault, Michel. "Des éspaces autres." *Architecture/Mouvement/Continuité* 5 (1984): 46–49.

Fowler, Sherry. "The Splitting Image of Baozhi at Saiōji and His Cult in Japan." *Oriental Art* 46, no. 4 (2000): 2–10.

Genet, Jean. *Les Nègres, clownerie.* Paris: Gallimard, 1958.

Gesterkamp, Lennert. "The Synthesis of Daoist Sacred Geography: A Textual Study of Du Guangting's *Dongtian fudi yuedu mingshan ji*." *Daoism: Religion, History and Society* 9 (2017): 1–39.

Gill, Sam. "No Place to Stand: Jonathan Z. Smith as Homo Ludens, The Academic Study of Religion Sub Specie Ludi." *Journal of the American Academy of Religion* 66, no. 2 (1998): 283–312. DOI: 10.1093/jaarel/66.2.283

Ginzburg, Carlo. *Jean Fouquet: Ritratto del buffone Gonella*. Modena: F.C. Panini, 1996.

Goble, Geofrey. *Chinese Esoteric Buddhism: Amoghavajra and the Ruling Elite.* Ph.D. dissertation, Indiana University, 2012.

———. *Chinese Esoteric Buddhism: Amoghavajra, the Ruling Elite, and the Emergence of a Tradition.* New York: Columbia University Press, 2019.

Goldin, Paul Rakita. "Reflections on Irrationalism in Chinese Aesthetics." *Monumenta Serica* 44 (1996): 167–89. DOI: 10.1080/02549948.1996.11731290.

Goodenough, Ward. "Introduction" *Transactions of the American Philosophical Society* 86, no. 5, special issue "Prehistoric Settlement of the Pacific" (1996): 1–10.

Graham, Angus C. *Chuang-tzu: The Seven Inner Chapters and Other Writings from the Book "Chuang-tzu."* London: Allen & Unwin, 1981.

———. "The Origins of the Legend of Lao Tan 老聃." In *Studies in Chinese Philosophy and Philosophical Literature*, 111–24. Albany: State University of New York Press, 1990.

Guo Moruo 郭沫若. Li Bai yu Du Fu 李白与杜甫. Beijing: Renmin, 1971.

Hahn, Thomas. "The Standard Taoist Mountain." *Cahiers d'Extrême-Asie* 4 (1988): 145–56.

Hammond, Charles. "Ultimate Truths: Tang Poetry as Magical Discourse." *Journal of Oriental Studies* 29, no. 1 (1991): 19–44.

Harper, Donald. "The *Analects* Jade Candle: A Classic of T'ang Drinking Custom." *T'ang Studies* 4 (1986): 69–93. DOI: 10.1179/tng.1986.1986.4.69.

Hawkes, David, trans. *The Songs of the South: An Anthology of Ancient Chinese Poems by Yuan and Other Poets*. Hammondsworth: Penguin, 1985.
Hayden, Ruth. *Mrs. Delany: Her Life and her Flowers*. London: The British Museum, 1986.
Heine, Steven. "*Mazu yulu* and the Chan Records of Sayings." In *The Zen Canon: Understanding the Classic Texts,* edited by Dale S. Wright, 61–88. Oxford University Press, 2004.
Heller, Natasha. "Why Has the Rhinoceros Come from the West? An Excursus into the Religious, Literary, and Environmental History of the Tang Dynasty." *Journal of the American Oriental Society* 131, no. 3 (2011): 353–70. https://www.jstor.org/stable/41380706.
Herbermann, Charles, et al. *The Catholic Encyclopedia*. New York: The Encyclopedia Press, 1913.
Hillman, James. *A Terrible Love of War*. New York: Penguin, 1988.
Ho Peng Yoke. *The Astronomical Chapter of the Chin Shu*. Paris: Mouton, 1966.
Huang, Shih-shan Susan. *Picturing the True Form: Daoist Visual Culture in Traditional China*. Cambridge: Harvard University Press, 2012.
Hucker, Charles. *A Dictionary of Official Titles in Imperial China*. Stanford: Stanford University Press, 1985.
Hung, William. *Tu Fu, China's Greatest Poet*. Cambridge: Harvard University Press, 1952.
Jia, Jinhua. *Gender, Power, and Talent: The Journey of Daoist Priestesses in Tang China*. New York: Columbia University Press, 2018.
Johnston, Alastair Iain. *Cultural Realism: Strategic Culture and Grand Strategy in Chinese History*. Princeton: Princeton University Press, 1998.
Jones, David. *In Parenthesis*. London: Faber & Faber, 1937.
Jones, Stephen. *Plucking the Winds: Lives of Village Musicians in Old and New China* Leiden: CHIME Foundation, 2004.

———. "Source and Stream: Early Music and Living Traditions in China." *Early Music* 24, no. 3 (1996): 375–88. DOI: 10.1093/earlyj/XXIV.3.375.
Jülch, Thomas. *Der Orden des Sima Chengzhen und des Wang Ziqiao: Untersüchungen zur Geschichte des Shangqing-Daoismus in Tiantai-Bergen.* Munich: Herbert Utz Verlag, 2011.
Jung, Carl. Foreword and appendix to Richard Wilhelm, *The Secret of the Golden Flower.* New York: Harcourt Brace, 1962.
———. *Psychology and Alchemy. The Collected Works of C.G. Jung,* Vol. 12. Princeton University Press, 1968.
Kaltenmark, Max. *Le Lie-sien tchouan: Biographies légendaires des immortels taoïstes de l'antiquité.* Beijing: Université de Paris, Publications du Centre d'études sinologiques de Pékin, 1953.
Karetzky, Patricia. "Imperial Splendor in the Service of the Sacred: The Famen Tea Treasures." *T'ang Studies* 18–19 (2000–2001): 61–85. DOI: 10.1179/073750300787769191
Karlgren, Bernhard. *Grammata Serica Recensa.* Stockholm: The Museum of Far Eastern Antiquities, 1972 [1957].
———."The Book of Documents." *Bulletin of the Museum of Far Eastern Antiquities* 22 (1950): 1–81.
Keightley, David. *The Origins of Chinese Civilization.* Berkeley: University of California Press, 1983.
Kern, Martin. "Announcements from the Mountains." In *Conceiving the Empire: China and Rome Compared,* edited by Fritz-Heiner Mutschler, 331–68. Oxford: Oxford University Press, 2008.
Kirkland, Russell. "From Imperial Tutor to Taoist Priest: Ho Chih-chang at the T'ang Court." *Journal of Asian History* 23, no. 2 (1989): 101–33.
———. "Ssu-ma Ch'eng-chen and the Role of Taoism in the Medieval Chinese Polity." *Journal of Asian History* 31, no. 2 (1997): 105–38.
———. "Tales of Thaumaturgy: T'ang Accounts of the Wonder-Worker Yeh Fa-shan." *Monumenta Serica* 40 (1992): 47–86. https://www.jstor.org/stable/40726940.

———. *Taoists of the High T'ang.* Ph.D. dissertation, Indiana University (1986).

———. "The Last Taoist Grand Master at the T'ang Imperial Court: Li Han-Kuang and T'ang Hsuan-tsung." *T'ang Studies* 4 (1986): 43–67. DOI: 10.1179/tng.1986.1986.4.43.

———. "Three Entries for a T'ang Biographical Dictionary: Wang Hsi-i, Huang Ling-wei, Ho Chih-chang." *T'ang Studies* 10–11 (1992–93): 153–65. DOI: 10.1179/073750392787773041.

Kirkova, Zornica. *Roaming into the Beyond: Representations of Xian Immortality in Early Medieval Chinese Verse.* Leiden/Boston: Brill, 2016.

Kleeman, Terry. "Mountain Deities in China: the Domestication of the Mountain God and the Subjugation of the Margins." *Journal of the American Oriental Society* 114, no. 2 (1994): 226–38.

Knechtges, David. *Wen Xuan, or Selections of Refined Literature.* Princeton: Princeton University Press, 1982–.

Kohn, Livia, ed. *Daoism Handbook.* Leiden: E.J. Brill, 2000.

———. "Daoist Hagiographies: Lord Lao as High God of the Dao." In *God of the Dao: Lord Lao in History and Myth*, 7–36. Ann Arbor: Center for Chinese Studies, University of Michigan, 1998.

———. *Sitting in Oblivion: The Heart of Daoist Meditation* St. Petersburg: Three Pines Press, 2010.

Kroll, Paul. *A Student's Dictionary of Classical and Medieval Chinese.* Revised Edition. Leiden: Brill, 2017.

———. "Between Something and Nothing." *Journal of the American Oriental Society* 127, no. 4 (2007): 403–13.

———. *Dharma Bell and Dhāraṇī Pillar : Li Po's Buddhist Inscriptions.* Kyoto: Italian School of East Asian Studies, 2001.

———. "Divine Songs of the Lady of Purple Tenuity." In *Studies in Early Medieval Chinese Literature*, 149–95. Provo: T'ang Studies Society, 2003.

———. "Four Vignettes from the Court of Tang Xuanzong." *T'ang Studies* 25 (2007): 1–27. DOI: 10.1179/073750307790779496.

———. "Heyue yingling ji and the Attributes of High Tang Poetry." In *Reading Medieval Chinese Poetry: Text, Context, and Culture*, 169–201. Leiden: Brill, 2014.

———. "Lexical Landscapes and Textual Mountains in the High T'ang." *T'oung Pao* 84, no. 1 (1998): 62–101. DOI: 10.1163/1568532982630804.

———. "Li Po's Purple Haze." *Taoist Resources* 7, no. 2 (1997): 21–37.

———. "Li Po's *Rhapsody on the Great P'eng-bird*." *Journal of Chinese Religions* 12 (1984): 1–17. DOI: 10.1179/073776984805308285.

———. "On 'Far Roaming.'" *Journal of the American Oriental Society* 116, no. 4 (1996): 653–69.

———. "Po Chü-i's 'Song of Lasting Regret': A New Translation." *T'ang Studies* 8–9 (1990–91): 97–105. DOI: 10.1179/073750390787970837.

———. "Recalling Xuanzong and Lady Yang: A Selection of Mid- and Late Tang Poems." *T'ang Studies* 35 (2017): 1–19. DOI: 10.1080/07375034.2017.1382435

———. "The Dancing Horses of T'ang." *T'oung Pao* 67. no. 3 (1981): 240–68. DOI: 10.1163/156853281X00100.

———. "The Flight from the Capital and the Death of the Precious Consort." *T'ang Studies* 3 (1985): 25–53.

———. "The Light of Heaven in Medieval Taoist Verse." *Journal of Chinese Religions* 27 (1999): 1–12. DOI: 10.1179/073776999805306795.

———. "The Road to Shu, from Zhang Zai to Li Bo." *Early Medieval China* 10–11 (2004): 227–54.

———. "Verses from on High: The Ascent of T'ai Shan." *T'oung Pao* 69, no. 4 (1983): 223–60. DOI: 10.1163/156853283X00090.

Lagerwey, John. *China: A Religious State.* Hong Kong: Hong Kong University Press, 2010.

———. *Taoist Ritual in Chinese Society and History.* New York: Macmillan, 1987.

Lai, Guolong. "Color and Color Symbolism in Early Chinese Ritual Art: Red and Black and the Formation of the Five

Colors System." In *Color in Ancient and Medieval East Asia*, edited by Mary M. Dusenbury, 25–43. New Haven: Yale University Press, 2015.

Latour, Bruno. *We Have Never Been Modern*. Translated by Catherine Porter. Cambridge: Harvard University Press, 1993.

Levy, Howard. *Biography of An Lu-shan*. Berkeley: University of California Press, 1960.

Lewis, Mark. *China's Cosmopolitan Empire: The Tang Dynasty*. Cambridge: Harvard University Press, 2009.

Li Xueqin 李學勤. *Siku Dacidian* 四庫大辭典, Vol. 2. Changchun: Jilin daxue chubanshe 吉林大學出版社, 1996.

Li, Xiaofan Amy. "Playful You in the Zhuangzi and Six Dynasties Literati Writing." *Journal of the British Association for Chinese Studies* 8, no. 2 (2018): 1–28.

Liscomb, Kathlyn. "Iconic Events Illuminating the Immortality of Li Bai." *Monumenta Serica* 54 (2006): 75–118. DOI: 10.1179.mon.2006.54.1.003.

———. "Li Bai Drinks with the Moon: The Cultural Afterlife of a Poetic Conceit and Related Lore." *Artibus Asiae* 70, no. 2 (2010): 331–86. https://www.jstor.org/stable/41416220.

Liu, Cary Y. et al. *Recarving China's Past: Art, Archaeology, and Architecture of the "Wu Family Shrines."* New Haven: Yale University Press, 2005.

Liu, Jerry C.Y. "Between Classical and Popular: The Book of Tea and the Popularization of Tea-Drinking Culture in the Tang China." *The Journal of Popular Culture* 44, no. 1 (2011): 114–33. DOI: 10.1111/j.1540-5931.2010.00822.x.

Liu Youzhu 劉友竹. "Li Bo yu Yuan Danqiu, Yuzhen Gongzhu Jiaoyou Xinkao 李白與元丹丘,玉真公主交遊新考 [A new examination of Li Bo's relations with Yuan Danqiu and Princess Realized-in-Jade)." *Chengdu daxue xuebao* 成都大學學報 (2002): 18–24.

Lü Huaming 呂華明 et al. *Li Taibo nianpu buzheng* 李太白年譜補正 [Emendations to the chronology of Li Taibo]. Beijing: Zhonghua, 2012.

Luo Jierui 羅傑瑞 (Jerry Norman). *Hanyu Gaikuang* 漢語概況 [Overview of Chinese language]. Published in English as *Chinese* (Cambridge University Press, 1988).

Luo, Manling. "Remembering Kaiyuan and Tianbao: The Construction of Mosaic Memory in Medieval Historical Miscellanies." *T'oung Pao* 97 (2011): 263–300. DOI: 10.1163/156853211X604134.

Luttwak, Edward. *The Grand Strategy of the Roman Empire*. Baltimore: Johns Hopkins University Press, 1976.

Lynn, Richard John. *The Classic of the Way and Virtue: A New Translation of the Tao-te Ching of Laozi*. New York: Columbia University Press, 1999.

Ma, Aliza. "Killer Technique." *Film Comment* (Sept.–Oct. 2015). https://www.filmcomment.com/article/hou-hsiao-hsien-interview/.

MacDonald, George. *Paul Faber, Surgeon*. London, 1879.

Mair, Victor. "Li Po's Letters in Pursuit of Political Patronage." *Harvard Journal of Asiatic Studies* 44, no. 1 (1984): 123–53.

Major, John S. *Heaven and Earth in Early Han Thought: Chapters Three, Four and Five of the Huainanzi*. Albany: SUNY Press: 1993.

Mather, Richard. Shih-shuo Hsin-yü — A New Account of Tales of the World. Minneapolis: University of Minnesota Press, 1976.

Mao Zedong 毛澤東. "Zai yifen jieshao Laozi zhexue shi weiwuzhuyi haishi weixinzhuyi di zhenglun cailiao shang di piyu 在一份介绍老子哲学 是唯物主义还是唯心主义的争论材料上的批语 [A one-minute critical comment to introduce the materials on the struggle as to whether Laozi's philosophy was materialist or idealist]." In *Jianguo Yilai Mao Zedong Wengao*《建国以来毛泽东文稿(第八册)》. (北京：中央文献出版社，1993), vol. 8, p. 632.

———. "On Contradiction." Beijing: Foreign Languages Press, 1967.

Marcus, Greil. *Lipstick Traces*. Harvard University Press, 1989.

McNair, Amy. "Draft Entry for a T'ang Biographical Dictionary: Yen Chen-ch'ing." *T'ang Studies* 10–11 (1992–93): 123–51. DOI: 10.1179/073750392787773050.

McNicholas, Mark. *Forgery and Impersonation in Imperial China: Popular Deceptions and the High Qing State*. Seattle: University of Washington Press, 2016.

McRae, John. *The Sutra of Queen Śrīmālā of the Lion's Roar and The Vimalakīrti Sutra*. Berkeley: Numata Center for Buddhist Translation and Research 2004.

Melville, Herman. *Moby-Dick; or, The Whale*. New York: Harper & Brothers, 1851.

Meyer, Jan de. *Wu Yun's Way: Life and Works of an Eighth-Century Daoist Master*. Leiden: Brill, 2006.

Milne, A.A. *Winnie-the-Pooh*. New York: Dutton, 1926.

Minford, John, and Joseph Lau, eds. *Classical Chinese Literature,* Vol. 1. New York: Columbia University Press: 2000.

Miyakawa, Hisayuki. "An Outline of the Naitō Hypothesis and its Effects on Japanese Studies of China." *The Journal of Asian Studies* 14, no. 4 (1955): 533–52. DOI: 10.2307/2941835.

Miyake, Marc. "Loanwords — Post-Qin, Pre-Modern." In Encyclopedia of Chinese Language and Linguistics, ed. Rint Sybesma, 647–50. Leiden and Boston: Brill, 2017.

Moore, Paul Douglas. *Stories and Poems about the T'ang Poet Li Po*. Ph.D. dissertation, Georgetown University, 1982.

Muscolino, Micah. *The Ecology of War in China: Henan Province, the Yellow River, and Beyond*. New York: Columbia University Press, 2015.

Needham, Joseph, and Lu Gwei-djen. *Science and Civilisation in China, Volume 5: Chemistry and Chemical Technology, Part 2: Spagyrical Discovery and Invention: Magisteries of Gold and Immortality*. Cambridge: Cambridge University Press, 1974.

Needham, Joseph, et al. *Science and Civilisation in China, Vol. 3: Mathematics and the Sciences of the Heavens and the Earth*. Cambridge: Cambridge University Press, 1959.

Newman, William. *Gehennical Fire: The Lives of George Starkey, an American Alchemist in the Scientific Revolution.* Chicago: University of Chicago Press, 1994.

Nienhauser, William H. Review of Stephen Owen, *The End of the Chinese "Middle Ages." Harvard Journal of Asiatic Studies* 58, no. 1 (1998): 287–310.

Nienhauser, William, ed. *The Grand Scribe's Records, Vol. 7: The Memoirs of Pre-Han China.* Bloomington: Indiana University Press, 1994.

Nivison, David. *The Riddle of the Bamboo Annals.* Taipei: Airiti Press, 2009.

Nugent, Christopher. *Manifest in Words, Written on Paper: Producing and Circulating Poetry in Tang Dynasty China.* Cambridge: Harvard University Asia Center, 2011.

Obata, Shigeyoshi. *The Works of Li Po, the Chinese Poet.* New York: Dutton, 1922.

Oster, Jürgen. "Der Körper leicht, das Herz voller Freude." *Taijiquan & Qigong Journal* 3 (2016): 14–21.

Owen, Stephen. *Mi-Lou.* Cambridge: Harvard University Press, 1989.

———. *The End of the Chinese "Middle Ages."* Stanford: Stanford University Press, 1996.

———. *The Great Age of Chinese Poetry: The High T'ang.* Cambridge: Harvard University Press, 1981.

Pan Yihong. *Son of Heaven and Heavenly Qaghan.* Bellingham: Western Washington University Press, 1997.

Pei Fei 裴斐. *Li Bo Ziliao Huibian* 李白資料彙編 [Collated materials on Li Bo]. Beijing: Zhonghua, 1994.

Penny, Benjamin. "Immortality and Transcendence." In *Daoism Handbook,* edited by Livia Kohn, 109–33. Leiden: E.J. Brill, 2000.

Pfister, Rudolf. "Attitudes Towards Laughter and Euphoria in Medieval Chinese Daoist Texts." In *Laughing in Chinese,* edited by Paolo Santangelo, 335–67 (Rome: Aracne, 2012).

Picken, Laurence. *Music from the Tang Court.* 7 Volumes. Cambridge: Cambridge University Press, 1985–.

Poceski, Mario. *The Records of Mazu and the Making of Classical Chan Literature*. Oxford: Oxford University Press, 2015.

Poon, Vincent. "Huaisu's Autobiography." http://www.vincent-poon.com/autobiography-of-huai-su.html.

Porter, Bill. *The Road to Heaven*. Berkeley: Counterpoint Press: 2009.

Pound, Ezra. *Cathay*. London: Elkin Matthews, 1916.

———. *The Pisan Cantos*. New York: New Directions, 1948.

Pregadio, Fabrizio, ed. *The Encyclopedia of Taoism*. London: Routledge, 2008.

———. *The Seal of the Unity of the Three, Vol. 1: A Study and Translation of the Cantong qi, the Source of the Taoist Way of the Golden Elixir*. Mountain View: Golden Elixir Press, 2011.

Protopappas, Frederic Pet. *The Life and Times of Li Po, 701–762 A.D.: An Annotated Translation and Analysis of the Chronology of his Life Taken from his Collected Works*. Ph.D. dissertation, Georgetown University, 1982.

Puett, Michael. "Humans, Spirits, and Sages in Chinese Late Antiquity: Ge Hong's Master Who Embraces Simplicity (Baopuzi)." *Extrême-Orient, Extrême-Occident* 29 (2007): 95–119. DOI: 10.3406/oroc.2007.1087.

Pulleyblank, Edwin. "The An Lu-shan Rebellion and the Origins of Chronic Militarism in Late T'ang China." In *Essays on Tang and Pre-Tang History*, 33–60. Aldershot: Ashgate, 2001.

———. *The Background of the Rebellion of An Lu-shan*. Oxford: Oxford University Press, 1955.

Quine, Willard Van Orman. *Word and Object*. Cambridge: MIT Press, 1960.

Rawson, Jessica. "The Origins of Chinese Mountain Painting: Evidence from Archaeology." *Proceedings of the British Academy* 117 (2001): 1–48. DOI: 10.5871/bacad/9780197262795.003.0001.

Reich, Wilhelm. *The Murder of Christ*. New York: Farrar, Straus and Giroux, 1953.

Richter, Antje, ed. *A History of Chinese Letters and Epistolary Culture*. Leiden: Brill, 2015.

Richter, Antje. *Letters and Epistolary Culture in Early Medieval China.* Seattle: University of Washington Press, 2013.

Riffard, Pierre. *Dictionnaire de l'ésotérisme.* Paris: Payot, 1983.

Robinet, Isabelle. "Le Ta-tung chen-ching: Son authenticité et sa place dans les textes du Shang-ch'ing ching." In *Tantric and Taoist Studies in Honour of R.A. Stein,* Volume 2, edited by Michel Strickmann, 394–433. Brussels: Institut Belge des Hautes Etudes Chinoises, 1983.

———. "Metamorphosis and Deliverance from the Corpse in Taoism." *History of Religions* 19, no. 1 (1979): 37–70. DOI: 10.1086/462835.

———. "Randonnées extatiques des Taoïstes dans les astres." *Monumenta Serica* 32 (1976): 159–273. https://www.jstor.org/stable/40726202.

———. *Taoism: Growth of a Religion.* Translated by Phyllis Brooks. Stanford University Press, 1997.

———. *Taoist Meditation: The Mao-shan Tradition of Great Purity.* Albany: SUNY Press, 1993.

———. "The Taoist Immortal: Jesters of Light and Shadow, Heaven and Earth." *Journal of Chinese Religions* 13 (1985): 87–105.

Robson, James. *The Religious Landscape of the Southern Sacred Peak (Nanyue 南嶽) in Medieval China.* Cambridge: Harvard University East Asia Center, 2009.

Rotours, Robert des. *Le Règne de l'Empereur Hiuan-tsong.* Paris: Collège de France, 1981.

Ruch, Carl. *The World of Classical Myth.* Durham: Carolina Academic Press, 1994.

Ruppli, Mireille, and Sylvie Thorel-Cailleteau. *Mallarmé: la grammaire & le grimoire.* Genève: Droz, 2005.

Schafer, Edward H. "A Trip to the Moon." *Journal of the American Oriental Society* 96, no. 1 (1976): 27–37.

———. "Li Po's Star Power." *Society for the Study of Chinese Religions Bulletin* 6 (1978): 5–15.

———. *Mirages on the Sea of Time: The Taoist poetry of Ts'ao T'ang.* Berkeley: University of California Press, 1985.

———. "Notes on Mica in Medieval China." *T'oung Pao* 43, no. 1 (1955): 265–86. DOI: 10.1163/156853254X00092.

———. *Pacing the Void: T'ang Approaches to the Stars*. Berkeley: University of California Press, 1977.

———. "The Capeline Cantos: Verses on the Divine Loves of Taoist Priestesses." *Asiastische Studien* 32 (1978): 1–33.

———. "The Dance of the Purple Culmen." *T'ang Studies* 5 (1987): 45–68. DOI: 10.1179/tng.1987.1987.5.45.

———. "The Development of Bathing Customs in Ancient and Medieval China and the History of the Floriate Clear Palace." *Journal of the American Oriental Society* 76, no. 2 (1956): 57–82.

———. *The Golden Peaches of Samarkand: A Study of T'ang Exotics*. Berkeley: University of California Press, 1963.

———. "The Jade Woman of Greatest Mystery." *History of Religions* 17 (1978): 387–98.

———. "The Princess Realized in Jade." *T'ang Studies* 3 (1985): 1–24. DOI: 10.1179/tng.1985.1985.3.1.

———. "The Restoration of the Shrine of Wei Hua-ts'un at Lin-ch'uan in the Eighth Century." *Journal of Oriental Studies* 15 (1977): 124–37.

———. "The Scripture of the Opening of Heaven by the Most High Lord Lao." *Taoist Resources* 7, no. 2 (1997): 1–20.

———. "The T'ang Osmanthus." *Schafer Sinological Papers* 38, no. 4 (1989): 1–2.

———. *The Vermilion Bird: T'ang Images of the South*. Berkeley: University of California Press, 1967.

———. "The 'Yeh chung chi.'" *T'oung Pao* 76, no. 4 (1990): 147–207. DOI: 10.1163/156853290X00065.

———. "Wu Yün's 'Cantos on Pacing the Void.'" *Harvard Journal of Asiatic Studies* 41, no. 2 (1981): 377–415. DOI: 10.2307/2719049.

———. "Wu Yün's 吳筠 Stanzas on 'Saunters in Sylphdom' 遊仙詩." *Monumenta Serica* 35 (1981–83): 309–45. https://www.jstor.org/stable/40726512.

Schattschneider, Ellen. "Family Resemblances: Memorial Images and the Face of Kinship." *Japanese Journal of*

Religious Studies 31, no. 1 (2004): 141–62. DOI: 10.18874/jjrs.31.1.2004.141-162.

Schipper, Kristopher. *L'Empéreur Wou des Han dans la légende taoiste: Han wou-ti nei tchouan.* Paris: Ecole Française d'Extrême Orient, 1965.

———. *The Taoist Body.* Berkeley: University of California Press, 1993 [1982].

Schipper, Kristopher, and Franciscus Verellen, eds. *The Taoist Canon.* 3 Volumes. University of Chicago Press, 2004.

Schlombs, Adele. *Huai-su and the Beginnings of Wild Cursive Script in Chinese Calligraphy.* Stuttgart: Franz Steiner, 1998.

Schönberg, Arnold. "Modern Piano Reduction." In *Style and Idea,* 211–13 (New York: Philosophical Library, 1950).

Seidel, Anna. "Imperial Treasures and Taoist Sacraments." In *Tantric and Taoist Studies,* edited by Michel Strickmann, vol. 2, 291–371. Brussels: Institut Belge des Hautes Études Chinoises, 1983.

———. "Taoism, the Unofficial High Religion of China." *Taoist Resources* 7, no. 2 (1997): 39–72.

Shinohara, Koichi. *Spells, Images, and Mandalas: Tracing the Evolution of Esoteric Buddhist Rituals.* New York: Columbia University Press, 2014.

Skaff, Jonathan. *Sui-Tang China and Its Turko-Mongol Neighbors: Culture, Power, and Connections, 580–800.* New York: Oxford University Press, 2012.

Smith, Thomas. *Declarations of the Perfected, Part One: Setting Scripts and Images into Motion.* St. Petersburg: Three Pines Press, 2013.

———.. *Ritual and the Shaping of Narrative: the Legend of the Han Emperor Wu.* Ph.D. dissertation, University of Michigan, 1992.

Snyder, Gary. "Technical Notes & Queries." In *Earth House Hold,* 111–43. New York: New Directions, 1969.

Somers, Robert. "Time, Space, and Structure in the Consolidation of the T'ang Dynasty (A.D. 617–700)." *Journal of Asian Studies* 45, no. 5 (1986): 971–94. DOI: 10.2307/2056605.

Soothill, William. *A Dictionary of Chinese Buddhist Terms.* London: Kegan Paul, 1937.

Soper, Alexander C. "T'ang Ch'ao Ming Hua Lu: Celebrated Painters of the T'ang Dynasty by Chu Ching-hsüan of T'ang." *Artibus Asiae* 21, nos. 3–4 (1958): 204–230. DOI: 10.2307/3248883.

Stanley-Baker, Michael. *Cultivating Body, Cultivating Self.* M.A. thesis, Indiana University, 2006.

Stein, Rolf. *Le monde en petit.* Paris: Champs/Flammarion, 1987.

Steinhart, Nancy Shatzman. *Chinese Imperial City Planning.* Honolulu: University of Hawai'i Press, 1999.

Stimson, Hugh. "The Sound of a Tarng poem: 'Grieving about Greenslope,' by Duh-Fuu." *Journal of the American Oriental Society* 89, no. 1 (1969): 59–67.

Strickmann, Michel. *Notes on Mushroom Cults in Ancient China.* Gent: Rijksuniversiteit, 1966.

———. "On the Alchemy of T'ao Hung-ching." In *Facets of Taoism: Essays in Chinese Religion,* edited by Holmes Welch and Anna Seidel, 123–92 (New Haven: Yale University Press, 1979).

Strickmann, Michel, ed., *Tantric and Taoist Studies in Honour of R.A. Stein.* Volume 2. Brussels: Institut Belge des Hautes Etudes Chinoises, 1983.

Sukhu, Gopal. *The Shaman and the Heresiarch: A New Interpretation of the Li sao.* Albany: SUNY Press, 2012.

Sun Xiaochun and Jacob Kistemaker. *The Chinese Sky during the Han: Constellating Stards and Society.* Leiden: Brill, 1997.

Trungpa, Chögyam. *Glimpses of Space.* Boulder: Vajradhatu Publications, 1999.

Tufte, Edward. *The Visual Display of Quantitative Information.* Cheshire: Graphics Press, 1983.

Twitchett, Denis. *Cambridge History of China, Vol. 3: Sui and T'ang China, 589–906, Part 1.* Cambridge University Press, 1979.

Vaissière, Étienne de la. *Histoire des marchands sogdiens.* Paris: Bibliotèque de l'Institut des Hautes Études Chinoises, 2002.

Translated by James Ward as *Sogdian Traders: A History.* Leiden: Brill, 2005.

Varsano, Paula. *Tracking the Banished Immortal: The Poetry of Li Bo and Its Critical Reception.* Honolulu: University of Hawai'i Press, 2003.

Verellen, Franciscus. "The Beyond Within: Grotto-Heavens in Taoist Ritual and Cosmology." *Cahiers d'Extrême-Asie* 8 (1995): 265–90.

Verlaine, Paul. *Selected Poems.* Translated by Martin Sorrell. Oxford: Oxford University Press, 1999.

Vermander, Benoît. "Qi (Energy) in Chinese," *Ignis* 42, no. 3 (2012): 23–36.

Vervoorn, Aat. "Cultural Strata of Hua Shan, the Holy Peak of the West." *Monumenta Serica* 39 (1990–91): 1–30. https://www.jstor.org/stable/40726900.

———. *Men of the Cliffs and Caves: The Development of the Chinese Eremitic Tradition to the End of the Han Dynasty*. Hong Kong: Hong Kong University Press, 1990.

Waley, Arthur. *The Poetry and Career of Li Po.* London: George Allen and Unwin, 1950.

Wallace, Leslie V. "Betwixt and Between: Depictions of Immortals (*Xian*) in Eastern Han Tomb Reliefs." *Ars Orientalis* 41 (2011): 73–101. https://www.jstor.org/stable/23075960.

Wang, Ao. *Spatial Imaginaries in Mid-Tang China: Geography, Cartography, and Literature.* Amherst: Cambria Press, 2018.

Wang, Zhenping. *Tang China in Multi-Polar Asia: A History of Diplomacy and War.* Honolulu: University of Hawai'i Press, 2013.

Ware, James R. 1966. *Alchemy, Medicine and Religion in the China of A.D. 320: The Nei Pien of Ko Hung.* New York: Dover, 1966.

Warner, Ding Xiang, and Wang Ji. "Mr. Five Dippers of Drunkenville: The Representation of Enlightenment in Wang Ji's Drinking Poems." *Journal of the American Oriental Society* 118 (1998): 347–55.

Watson, Burton. *Courtier and Commoner in Ancient China: Selections from the History of the Former Han.* New York: Columbia University Press, 1977.

———. *Mo-tzu: Basic Writings.* New York: Columbia University Press, 1963.

———. *The Complete Works of Chuang Tzu.* New York: Columbia University Press, 1968.

Weiss, Lucas. "Rectifying the Deep Structures of the Earth: Sima Chengzhen and the Standardization of Daoist Sacred Geography in the Tang." *Journal of Daoist Studies* 5 (2012): 31–60.

Wells, Matthew V. *To Die and Not Decay: Autobiography and the Pursuit of Immortality in Early China.* Ann Arbor: Association for Asian Studies, 2009.

Whalen, Philip. *The Collected Poems of Philip Whalen.* Middletown: Wesleyan University Press, 2007.

Wheatley, Paul. *Pivot of the Four Quarters: A Preliminary Enquiry into the Origins and Character of the Ancient Chinese City.* Chicago: Aldine, 1971.

Wilhelm, Richard. *The I Ching or Book of Changes.* Princeton: Princeton University Press, 1950.

Williams, Nicholas Morrow. "The Pity of Spring: A Southern Topos Reimagined by Wang Bo and Li Bai." In *Southern Identity and Southern Estrangement in Medieval Chinese Poetry,* edited by Ping Wang and Nicholas Morrow Williams, 137–63. Hong Kong: Hong Kong University Press, 2015.

Wittgenstein, Ludwig. *Remarks on Colour.* Oxford: Blackwell, 1977.

Wright, David. "The Northern Frontier." In *A Military History of China,* edited by David Graff, 57–79. Lexington: University of Kentucky Press, 2012.

Wu Hung. *The Wu Liang Shrine.* Stanford: Stanford University Press, 1989.

Xiong, Victor Cunrui. *Sui-Tang Chang'an.* Ann Arbor: University of Michigan Center for Chinese Studies, 2000.

Yang, Shuhui. *Stories to Caution the World: A Ming Dynasty Collection.* Seattle: University of Washington Press, 2005.

Yao, Ping. "Contested Virtue: The Daoist Investiture of Princesses Jinxian and Yuzhen and the Journey of Tang Imperial Daughters." *T'ang Studies* 22 (2004): 1–40. DOI: 10.1179/073750304788913203.

Yates, Robin D.S. "The History of Military Divination in China." EASTM 24 (2005): 15–43. https://www.jstor.org/stable/43151239.

Yi Shitong 伊世同. *Zhongxi Duizhao Hengxing Tubiao* 中西對照恒星圖表 [Tables of the constant stars, east and west]. Beijing, 1981.

Yu Xianhao 郁賢皓. "Li Bai churu Chang'an shiji tansuo 李白初入長安事跡考索 [Investigation of Li Bo's first entry to Chang'an]." In *Li Bo yu Tangdai wenshi kaolun* 李白與唐代文史考論, 16–30. Nanjing: Nanjing shifan daxue chubanshe 南京師範大學出版社, 2007.

———. "Li Bai wannian xingji ji sixiang kaolun 李白晚年行跡及思想考論 [Li Bo's late life wandering and his thought]." In *Li Bai yu Tangdai wenshi kaolun* 李白與唐代文史考論, 114–39. Nanjing: Nanjing shifan daxue chubanshe 南京師範大學出版社, 2007.

———. *Li Bai yu Tangdai wenshi kaolun* 李白與唐代文史考論 [Essays on Li Bo and the literary history of the Tang]. Nanjing: Nanjing shifan daxue chubanshe 南京師範大學出版社, 2007.

———. "'Li Bai yu Tianmu guoji xueshu yanjiu taohui zhuanji' xu 李白與天姥國際學術討會專輯序 [Preface to the edited papers from the International Congress on Li Bo and Mount Tianmu]." In *Li Bai yu Tangdai wenshi kaolun* 李白與唐代文史考論, 712–13. Nanjing: Nanjing shifan daxue chubanshe 南京師範大學出版社: 2007.

———. "Li Bai yu Yuan Danqiu jiaoyou kao 李白與元丹丘交遊考 [Investigations of Li Bo and Yuan Danqui's roaming]." In *Li Bai yu Tangdai wenshi kaolun* 李白與唐代文史考論, 413–33. Nanjing: Nanjing shifan daxue chubanshe 南京師範大學出版社: 2007.

———. "Li Bai yu Yuzhen Gongzhu guocong xintan 李白與玉貞公主過從新探 [New investigations of Li Bo's association with the Princess Realized-in-Jade]." In *Li Bai yu Tangdai wenshi kaolun* 李白與唐代文史考論, 191–202. Nanjing: Nanjing shifan daxue chubanshe 南京師範大學出版社: 2007.

———. *Tianshang zhexianren di mimi—Li Bo kaolun ji* 天上謫仙人的秘密—李白考論集 (Secrets of the heavenly banished immortal—collected investigations of Li Bo). Taipei: Taiwan Commercial Press, 1997.

Zhang, Peter, and Lin Tian. "*Qi* and the Virtual in Daoist and Zen Literature: A Comparison with Western Vitalist Thought." *China Media Research* 14, no. 4 (2018): 99–109.

About the Authors

Kidder Smith was graced to study with Y.K. Kao at Princeton and Peter Boodberg at Berkeley. For some years he taught Chinese history at Bowdoin College, where he also directed the Asian Studies Program. He is senior author of *Sung Dynasty Uses of the I Ching* (Princeton, 1990); *Sun Tzu: The Art of War* (with Denma, Shambhala, 2001); and *Having Once Paused: Poetry of Zen Master Ikkyū* (with Sarah Messer, University of Michigan, 2015). His email is kidder@bowdoin.edu.

Portrait of Kidder Smith by Sangchen Tsomo (private collection)

ABOUT THE AUTHORS

As a boy in Shanghai, Mike Zhai memorized Li Bo's poems in school. Later, at UC Berkeley, he studied modern Chinese poetry under Bei Dao, as well as German literature and music. He holds an MFA in English from Mills College. A lecturer in English at University of Michigan, he founded One Pause Poetry Salon in Ann Arbor in 2016. His poems have been published in Spectrum magazine, and in 2017 he won the Green House Poetry Prize for emerging poets.

Portrait of Mike Zhai by Ilona Sturm (private collection)

Endnotes

Endnotes — A Grimoire

> Je dis qu'existe entre les vieux procédés et le sortilège, que restera la poésie, une parité secrète; je l'énonce ici et peut-être personellement me suis-je complu à le marquer, par des essais, dans une mesure qui a outrepassé l'aptitude à en jouir consentie par mes contemporains.
> — Stéphane Mallarmé, "Magie," *The National Observer*, 28 January 1893.

> I maintain there exists a secret parity between the old methods and sortilege — this remains now as poetry. Stating it thus, I'm privately pleased, perhaps, that my emphases may exceed my contemporaries' capacity for enjoyment.
> — Quoted in *Mallarmé : la grammaire & le grimoire*, by Mireille Ruppli and Sylvie Thorel-Cailleteau (Genève: Droz, 2005), 1.

1 Source: http://www.newworldencyclopedia.org/entry/File:Lipoliangkai.jpg. I wonder if this is Li Bo. Liang Kai isn't telling, and only later on in Song did people insist that it was he.

2 ch12v4p1999. Throughout the present book, a citation of this form indicates chapter 12, volume 4, page 1999 of Zhan Ying's 詹鍈 unexcelled eight-volume collection of Li Bo's writings, *Li Bo quanji jiaozhu huishi jiping* 李白全集校注彙釋集評 (Tianjin 天津: Baihua 百花, 1996).

These lines are from "A Lu Mountain Song Sent to the Imperial Censor, Empty Boat Lu" (*Lushanyao ji Lu Shiyu Xuzhou* 廬山謠寄廬侍御虛舟). For the rest, see Chapter 29.

3 ch3v1p424.

4 Source: http://en.wikipedia.org/wiki/Guqin. Two zithers, the qin 琴 and se 瑟, companionship of plucked silk strings.

You can hear it at Gammaldans, "Teals Descending on the Level Sand (Lo Ka Ping) (1970)," *YouTube,* December 8, 2016, https://www.youtube.com/watch?v=n3eRm7vTrPg.

5   ch13v4p2183.

6   ch15v5p2502.

7   The *Li Taibo nianqian* 李太白年潛 by Xue Zhongyong 薛仲琶 of the Song dynasty. The mid-Qing scholar Wang Qi 王琦 reprints it in his excellent edition of Li Bo's works, *Li Taibo quanji* 李太白全集, where it constitutes Chapter 35. It has been translated by Frederic Pet Protopappas as *The Life and Times of Li Po, 701–762 A.D.: An Annotated Translation and Analysis of the Chronology of His Life Taken from His Collected Works* (Ph.D. diss., Georgetown University, 1982).

For an accounting of Li Bo's life by his kinsman and literary executor, Li Yangbing 李陽冰, see the *Caotang ji* 草堂集 (Grass hut collection), ch1v1p1. It has been translated by Shigeyoshi Obata in his *The Works of Li Po, the Chinese Poet* (New York: Dutton, 1922), 174–82.

8   The *Chronology* also explains his family's presence in the west:

> At the end of the Sui dynasty [early seventh century], his ancestor had some troubles and moved to the Western Regions, hiding out and changing his name. Thus, since the arising of the Great Tang [in 618], the family has been missing from official records. Only in the reign of Empress Wu [684–704] did their descendants return to the interior and make a home in Sichuan.

9   In other circumstance he might have been known as Li the White, or emerged from Ellis Island as Whitey Pflaumer. Cf. Li Hei 李黑, Li the Black, a military officer of the third century CE.

A closer approximation to the Tang pronunciation would be Li Baek. Reconstruction by William Baxter, from Paul Kroll's *Student's Dictionary* (Leiden: Brill, 2017), s.v., though Zhou Fagao 周法高 (*A Pronouncing Dictionary of Chinese Characters* [Hong Kong: Hong Kong University Press, 1974]) would have it more like Pak.

10 At adulthood a gentleman's given name becomes a bit too private for use outside the family, so he takes a cognomen, a *zi* 字, known in English as a courtesy or public name. It is often closely related to his given name. Thus at his majority, Christopher Robin became C.R. Milne.

11 Meaning "perfectly white." See Elling Eide, "On Li Po," in *Perspectives on the T'ang,* ed. Arthur Wright (New Haven: Yale University Press, 1973), 367–403, at 390, for this and other color names of the Li family.

12 Otherwise unknown. This could be a contemporary ceramic sculpture of him, teaching Li:

Fig. 85. Mud man figurines representing two men with a scroll (ca. 1920s). Source: https://www.rubylane.com/item/738907-A248/Vintage-Chinese-Mudmen-Two-Men-w

13 "Letter to Chief Administrator Pei at Anzhou" (*Shang Anzhou Pei Changshi shu* 上安州裴長史書, ch26v7p4025). Pei is

Pei Kuan 裴寬 (679–754), a distinguished official whose biography is in both the old and new Tang Histories.

14 Perhaps to the great-granddaughter of a former prime minister. Later she died.

15 Of the fourth/third century BCE. From chapter 2, "Discourse on Making Things Equal" (*Qiwu lun* 齊物論). Chapter 1 is entitled "Roaming without a Destination" (*Xiaoyao you* 逍遙遊).

16 The Chuci 楚辭, an anthology of poetry from the early third century BCE to the early second century CE. This passage occurs near the end of section 10 in Paul Kroll's marvelously hyperbolic translation. See his "On 'Far Roaming,'" *Journal of the American Oriental Society* 116, no. 4 (1996), 653–69.

On roaming, see Xiaofan Amy Li, "Playful You in the Zhuangzi and Six Dynasties Literati Writing," *Journal of the British Association for Chinese Studies* 8, no. 2 (2018): 1–28.

17 Wei Hao 魏顥 (fl. Kaiyuan period), preface to his *Li Hanlin ji* 李翰林集 (The collected works of the Hanlin scholar Li Bo). In *Li Bo quanji* ch1v1p3.

18 Regarding the date of his arrival, see Yu Xianhao 郁賢皓, "Li Bo Churu Chang'an Shiji Tansuo 李白初入長安事跡考索 [Investigation of Li Bo's first entry to Chang'an]," in *Li Bo yu Tangdai wenshi kaolun* 李白與唐代文史考論 [Essays on Li Bo and the literary history of the Tang] (Nanjing: Nanjing shifan daxue chubanshe 南京師範大學出版社: 2007), 16–30.

19 From Li Bo's "Two Poems Given to My Cousin the Prefect of Nanping, Who's Going Off Wandering" (*Zeng Congdi Nanping Taishou zhi yao, er shou* 贈從弟南平太守之遙二首), ch-10v4p1738.

20 Yang Sui 楊遂, perhaps of the Yuan dynasty. Wang Qi, the Qing dynasty editor mentioned in note 7, also compiled stories

and poems about Li Bo in chapter 36 of his work. This poem comes from anecdote 36, to which Wang appends Yang Sui's "A Record of Li Bo's Old House" (*Li Taibo guzhai ji* 李太白古宅記). Paul Douglas Moore has translated and annotated this material as *Stories and Poems about the T'ang Poet Li Po* (Ph.D. diss. Georgetown University, 1982).

21   Anecdote 44, from the *Sichuan tongzhi* 四川通志 (Sichuan gazetteer).

22   Turns out to be a recent forgery — you can find it all over the web, e.g., http://blog.sina.com.cn/s/blog_98fe1ac1010175ze.html. The Imperial Calligraphy Catalogue of 1120 (*Xuanhe shupu* 宣和书谱) doesn't record it among its half dozen examples of Li Bo's work. Nor is there any mention of it in other historical works, as, for example, owned by so-and-so. Nor do the twenty anecdotes about Li Bo's calligraphy, gathered in Moore's *Stories and Poems about Li Po,* allude to it The colophons by established collectors such as Song Ke 宋克 (1327–87), which I don't show in this excerpt, are also forgeries.

A tippler is drunk on wine, Li Bo is drunk on brightness, brightness is drunk on its own dazzle razzle

The word "wine" occurs in more than two hundred of Li Bo's poems. Some kinds of poetry can only be conducted with wine, otherwise the immortals get very angry.

23   "Li Po Cocktail Lounge," *Atlas Obscura,* https://www.atlasobscura.com/places/li-po-cocktail-lounge/.

24   ch21v6p3272.

25   Well, the Astronomy Bureau of the Qing dynasty (1644–1911) found two more, so now there are five stars in the asterism, see Yi Shitong 伊世同, *Zhongxi Duizhao Hengxing Tubiao* 中西對照恒星圖表 [Tables of the constant stars, east and west] (Beijing: 1981), 121–33.

26   From "Seven Love Poems" (*Qi aishi* 七愛詩) by Pi Rixiu 皮日休 (ca. 834–883), translated in part by Edward Schafer, *Pacing the Void: T'ang Approaches to the Stars* (Berkeley: University of California Press, 1977), 125.

27   Ibid., 124. See his colleague Isabelle Robinet, "Randonnées extatiques des Taoïstes dans les astres," *Monumenta Serica* 32 (1976): 159–273.

28   Ibid., 241. The Wine Stars have been around some time, but the earthly springs were discovered by one Kong Rong 孔融 (153–208), disruptive wit, mordant cynic, jolly soul in the depths of the decaying Han dynasty. Here he sets out wine's three domains:

> The shimmers of the Wine Stars trail through Heaven,
> the district of the Wine Springs is marked out on Earth,
> and the virtues of wine are divulged by men.

> 天垂酒星之燿，地列酒泉之郡，人著旨酒之德

When the Emperor Cao Cao 曹操 (155–220) banned alcohol production due to a grain shortage, Kong wrote him, "Since evil kings are destroyed by lust, why not ban marriage as well?" "Letter to Cao Cao Discussing the Ban on Wine" (*Yu Cao Cao lun jiujin shu* 與曹操論酒禁書). The Emperor couldn't shut him up, so eventually he had him killed.

For further links between wine and wisdom, see Ding Xiang Warner and Wang Ji, "Mr. Five Dippers of Drunkenville: The Representation of Enlightenment in Wang Ji's Drinking Poems," *Journal of the American Oriental Society* 118, no. 3 (1998): 347–55.

29   ch3v1p357.

30   Denver, Colorado, on the eve of his twentieth birthday, January 1965.

31 ch21v6p3315.

32 ch4v2p943. Master Redpine's 赤松子 biography comes first in the *Liexianzhuan* 列仙傳 (Biographies of the immortals, of the second century CE). The text says:

> Master Redpine was lead Rain Maker at the time of the Divine Husbandman .[…] Often he'd visit the Kunlun Mountains and meet the Queen Mother of the West in her chamber. He could move in accordance with wind and rain, up or down.

Of Anqi, that text remarks:

> He sold medicines on the shore of the Eastern Sea. At that time everyone said he was already 1000 years old. The First Emperor of Qin traveled east to see him, and they spoke together for three days and nights.

Later the Emperor sent expeditions to find him again in the Faerie Seas around Penglai Island 蓬萊, but without success. In Highest Clarity Daoism, Anqi is the Perfected One of the Northern Pole (*Beiji zhenren* 北極真人)

33 Section 30, "Record of the Dykes" (*Fangji* 坊記). He must have read it somewhere else, since the Liji didn't exist as such until the Han.

34 Good choice: It's said that when baby crows grow up, they bring food to their mother. See Cheng Gongsui 成公綏 (231–73), "Rhapsody on the Crow" (*Wufu* 烏賦).

This story comes from the *Yiwen leiju* 藝文類聚 (Collection of Literature by Category) of Ouyang Xun 歐陽詢 (557–641), chap. 20, §4, "Filiality" (*Xiao* 孝). The text claims to be quoting the *Biographies of Exemplary Women* (*Lienüzhuan* 列女傳) of Liu Xiang 劉向 (77–76 BCE), but the passage is not found in extant versions of that work, which instead tells the story we translate below, immediately after Li Bo's poem. A compressed version of the *Yiwen leiju* passage can be found in the *Chuxueji* 初學記, *juan* 17, §4, "Filiality" (*Xiao* 孝), 15b–16a.

35   Though Li Bo has obviously heard of Old Laizi's dance, the earliest reference to it I've been able to find is the Yuan dynasty *The Twenty-four Filials* (*Ershsi xiao* 二十四孝) by Guo Juqing 郭居敬, some five or six hundred years later. This line comes from the summation poem attached to his Old Laizi entry.

36   One of a set of engravings from *Illustrated Poems of the Twenty-four Filials* (*Ershisi xiaoti shitu hekan* 二十四孝體視圖和看), illustration by Li Xitong 李系統, printed 1869 by Yishengtang 益生堂. https://3g.china.com/baike_6YCa5L-X5piT5oeC.html.

37   From the Wu Family shrine, Shandong. See Wu Hung, *The Wu Liang Shrine* (Stanford: Stanford University Press, 1989) and Cary Y. Liu et al., *Recarving China's Past: Art, Archaeology, and Architecture of the "Wu Family Shrines"* (New Haven: Yale University Press, 2005). https://en.dpm.org.cn/collections/collections/2009-12-28/1442.html.

38   ch10v4p1747.

39   From the *Biographies of Great Gentlemen* (*Gaoshiji* 高士傳), *juan* 1, of Huangfu Mi 皇甫謐 (215–282). This is a condensation of the story found in the *Biographies of Exemplary Women, juan* 2, "The Worthy and Enlightened" (*Xianming* 賢明).

40   From the *Xinkan Gulienüzhuan* 新刊古列女傳 (*Wenxuanlou congshu* 文選樓叢書 of Ruan Heng 阮亨 [1783–1859]), *juan* 5. https://ctext.org/lie-nv-zhuan/chu-lao-lai-qi/zh.

41   ch9v3p1364.

42 He amassed considerable moneys from the over 800 funerary inscriptions he wrote for men across the empire. Son of the great Li Shan 李善 (630–89), best educated man of his age. On the practice of paid literary performance, particularly for tomb epitaphs, see Alexei Ditter, "The Commerce of Commemoration," *Tang Studies* 32 (2014): 21–46.

43 The *Garden of Literature* biographies (*Wenyuan* 文苑), chap. 190.

44 From his biography in the *Hanshu* 漢書 (History of the Han dynasty), chap. 65. I've stolen many adjectives from Burton Watson's gilded translation of Dongfang's hyperbole (*Courtier and Commoner in Ancient China: Selections from the History of the Former Han* [New York: Columbia University Press, 1977], 79–80). On Dongfang Shuo, see our Section VIII, "A Banished Immortal."

45 "Darksea" is from Bill Boltz's extraordinary article on this passage, "The Structure and Interpretation of *Chuang tzŭ*: Two Notes on *Hsiao yao yu*," *Bulletin of the School of Oriental and African Studies* 43, no. 3 (1980): 532–43). "Girth" is Angus C. Graham's felicitous reading of *da* 大, "large" (*Chuang-tzu: The Seven Inner Chapters and Other Writings from the Book "Chuang-tzu"* [London: Allen & Unwin, 1981], 43).

46 I think the friend must be Wang Yan 王炎, to whom Li Bo addresses his rhapsody (*fu* 賦) on the Sword Gate Pass that is mentioned in this poem, *Jiange fu* 劍閣賦, ch25v7p3905. The rhapsody comes with a subtitle, "Seeing Off My Friend Wang Yan on His Way to Shu." I don't know more of Wang, except that when he died, Li Bo wrote three poems in mourning. See Zhan Ying, ch25v7p3905.

The rhapsody and this poem are very similar, and the rhapsody may have been an early version of, or inspiration for, the poem.

47 ch3v1p290.

"Pull, pull, my fine hearts-alive; pull, my children; pull, my little ones," drawlingly and soothingly sighed Stubb to his crew, some of whom still showed signs of uneasiness. "Why don't you break your backbones, my boys? What is it you stare at? Those chaps in yonder boat? Tut! They are only five more hands come to help us — never mind from where — the more the merrier. Pull, then, do pull; never mind the brimstone — devils are good fellows enough. So, so; there you are now; that's the stroke for a thousand pounds; that's the stroke to sweep the stakes! Hurrah for the gold cup of sperm oil, my heroes! Three cheers, men — all hearts alive! Easy, easy; don't be in a hurry — don't be in a hurry. Why don't you snap your oars, you rascals? Bite something, you dogs! So, so, so, then: — softly, softly! That's it — that's it! long and strong. Give way there, give way! The devil fetch ye, ye ragamuffin rapscallions; ye are all asleep. Stop snoring, ye sleepers, and pull. Pull, will ye? pull, can't ye? pull, won't ye? Why in the name of gudgeons and ginger-cakes don't ye pull? — pull and break something! pull, and start your eyes out! Here!" whipping out the sharp knife from his girdle; "every mother's son of ye draw his knife, and pull with the blade between his teeth. That's it — that's it. Now ye do something; that looks like it, my steel-bits. Start her — start her, my silver-spoons! Start her, marling-spikes!" (*Moby-Dick*, chap. 48)

"Road" translates *dao*, the Way.

48 ch5v2p813.

49 The "Great Appendix" (*Dazhuan* 大傳) to the Classic of Change (*Yijing* 易經) states, "Within Change is the Great Ultimate. It gives birth to the two principles [yin and yang], the two principles give birth to the four images (*xiang* 象), the four images give birth to the eight trigrams," and from that all things arise.

50   Following the reconstruction of Tang phonology by Chou Fa-kao (Zhou Fagao) 周法高, *A Pronouncing Dictionary of Chinese Characters*.

51   Here's a good joke: in the *Vishnu purana* it's said to be 4.32 billion years — see *Wikipedia*, "Kalpa (aeon)," s.v.

52   *The Traditions of Divine Transcendents* (*Shenxian zhuan* 神仙傳). See Robert Campany, *To Live as Long as Heaven and Earth: A Translation and Study of Ge Hong's Traditions of Divine Transcendents* (Berkeley: University of California Press, 2002), 259–70 for the full story, and the back story of her rape. And be sure to see "Miss Hemp" in Edward Schafer, *Mirages on the Sea of Time: The Taoist poetry of Ts'ao T'ang* (Berkeley: University of California Press, 1985), 90–102.

53   Chapter 1, "Classic of the Eastern Barrens" (*Donghuangjing* 東荒經). See Robert Ford Campany, *Strange Writing: Anomaly Accounts in Early Medieval China* (Albany: SUNY Press, 1996), 43–45, where the attribution to Dongfang Shuo is dismissed, but a second-century CE date sustained.

54   Attributed to Zhang Hua 張華 (232–303), but see ibid.

55   Detail of *Ming Xuanzong xingle tu* 明宣宗行樂圖, a six-meter-long hand scroll by Shang Xi 商喜 (active during reign of the Xuanzong Emperor of the Ming dynasty). https://www.shuge.org/ebook/ming-xuan-zong-xing-le-tu-juan/.

56   His name's Xue Shenhuo 薛眘惑, and his feat's recorded in the *Omnibus Record of Court and Commoners* (*Chaoye qianzai* 朝野僉載) attributed to Zhang Zhuo 張鷟 of the Tang.

57   This text is quoted in the opening section of chapter 24 of the *Seven Lots of the Cloud Satchel* (*Yunji qiqian* 雲笈七籤), but I haven't been able to locate it otherwise.

58 ch25v7p3920. If you're a fan of the Songtexts of Chu 楚辭, you'll recognize the shaman's journey through lush and lamentation. For a sensitive treatment of this poem and its generic kin, see Nicholas Morrow Williams, "The Pity of Spring: A Southern Topos Reimagined by Wang Bo and Li Bai," in *Southern Identity and Southern Estrangement in Medieval Chinese Poetry*, eds. Ping Wang and Nicholas Morrow Williams [Hong Kong: Hong Kong University Press, 2015], 137–63).

59 Source: https://www.pinterest.com/pin/529947081121472790/.

60 Over Sogdians and Tocharians (these are Indo-European speakers) as well as over Uyghurs and several other Turkic groups, the Khitan and so on. Not usually the Tibetans. On Tocharians, see Mark Dickens, "Everything You Always Wanted to Know about Tocharian But Were Afraid To Ask," archived at https://web.archive.org/web/20060803100222/http://www.oxuscom.com/eyawtkat.htm.

We might follow Edward Schafer and call this whole thing Chinastan ("The 'Yeh chung chi,'" *T'oung Pao* 76, nos. 4–5 [1990]: 147–207). And then we might designate the Chinese-speaking region, especially the lands north of the Yangtze River, as Tang Central, corresponding to the Chinese term "the central states" (*zhongguo* 中國, the term adopted by Lin Zexu 林則徐 [1785–1850] when he wrote to Queen Victoria in order to represent "China" in relation to the European powers—his draft letter called *Nilun Yingjiliguowang xi* 擬諭英吉利國王檄).

Robert Somers, who follows Edward Luttwak, calls this empire "hegemonic" rather than "territorial," in that Tang Central, the inner zone of power, was surrounded by a series of client tribes "deferring to the power of empire but not entirely under its direct control" ("Time, Space, and Structure in the Consolidation of the T'ang Dynasty (A.D. 617–700)," *Journal of Asian Studies* 45, no. 5 [1986]: 971–94. Luttwak's demonstration is in his *Grand Strategy of the Roman Empire* [Baltimore: Johns Hopkins University Press, 1976].)

61 This constancy stands outside of time. Like the Stanley Brothers, "I Am a Man of Constant Sorrow" (out of Dick Burnett). On the center, see Paul Wheatley, *Pivot of the Four Quarters: A Preliminary Enquiry into the Origins and Character of the Ancient Chinese City* (Chicago: Aldine, 1971). For an account of the intersections of geography, literature, mapping, dreams, and imagination in the immediately following period (roughly 780 to 820), see Ao Wang's aptly entitled *Spatial Imaginaries in Mid-Tang China: Geography, Cartography, and Literature* (Amherst: Cambria Press, 2018).

62 For marveled accounts of city life, its bars and music, clothing, flower crazes, its circadian rhythms, see Charles Benn, *China's Golden Age China's Golden Age: Everyday Life in the Tang Dynasty* (Oxford: Oxford University Press, 2002), chap. 3, "Cities," esp. 47–69, and Edward Schafer, *The Golden Peaches of Samarkand: A Study of T'ang Exotics* (Berkeley: University of California Press, 1963).

63 Source: http://www.sacrificeworldwide.com/images/maps_changan_city.gif This is fractal: as Nancy Steinhart has shown, the layout of the Neolithic house is the same as its compound, which is the same as its town, and the same as that of the Imperial capital. See Nancy Shatzman Steinhart, *Chinese Imperial City Planning* (Honolulu: University of Hawai'i Press, 1999).

64 From "Three Analogies" (*Yuyan san shou* 寓言三首), ch-22v7p3455.

65 From "A Moon Song at Emei Mountain, Seeing Off the Sichuan Monk Tranquility, Who Is Going Up to Chang'an" (*Emeishan yuege song Shu Sengyan ru Zhongjing* 峨眉山月歌送蜀僧晏入中京), ch7v3p1202.

66 From "Ziye's Songs from Wu, Autumn" (*Ziye Wuge* 子夜吳歌), ch6v2p939.

67   And is sited only slightly to the southeast of the former city. Han palace names often stand in for Tang buildings — see Li Bo's poem on the Bright Emperor in Sichuan, which speaks of him living in the Jianzhang Palace 建章, only that's the Han name for it, it's the first of his "Ten Songs of the Former Emperor on His Circuit West to Inspect the Southern Capital" (*Shanghuang xixun Nanjing ge* 上皇西巡南京歌十首, ch7v3p1178).

68   A painter mostly paints another painting — a mountain will look like other mountains painted in the same tradition. Poets are the same way — a mountain will sound like someone else's mountain poem. For the particulars of Chinese mountain poetics, see Paul Kroll, "Lexical Landscapes and Textual Mountains in the High T'ang," *T'oung Pao* 84, no. 1 (1998): 62–101.

69   And so we might notice that everything of Tang is inhabited by… well, we could call them ghosts, or memories, or deities, or history, or poems. Every person, place, and thing we meet has already been spoken of. The memories got here before we did: we can't go anywhere they haven't already been, anywhere they aren't already. And our visit itself becomes another swirling of these patterns — we are not their epigone, but their co-creators. See Colin Davis, "Etat Présent: Hauntology, Spectres and Phantoms," *French Studies* 59, no. 3 (2005): 373–79.

I just said that everything is inhabited by ghosts, but this is not so. There is not some thing being inhabited, there is rather a presencing, there is nothing we might discover behind that presence through exorcistic activity.

It's also misleading that I call this dimension "time," since it implies a sequence of moments. A past and a present, an old and a new. But there was nothing very ancient about it. You knew it the way your body remembers an embarrassing moment from last year. Occasional literary-moral movements to "revive the past" (*fugu* 復古, see Stephen Owen, *The Great Age of Chinese Poetry* [Cambridge: Harvard University Press, 1981], 8–10 et passim) are thus actually presentists in another guise.

This has led some people to claim that time as we know it doesn't exist. But if you lose one dimension, don't you lose them all?

70 His means are ritual, rites that are not strictly Confucian, Daoist nor Buddhist (though all three have a lot to say about it). They entail blood and the ineffable, for during Tang the "state religion continued to involve imperial blood sacrifices to Heaven" (John Lagerwey, *China: A Religious State* [Hong Kong: Hong Kong University Press, 2010], 174). Though rooted in the traditions of ancient monarchs whom Confucius also venerated, this state religion was not the socially-oriented "Confucianism" of the elite, with its ethos of texts and learning, its decorum and public service, about which Peter Bol has written so brilliantly in *"This Culture of Ours": Intellectual Transitions in T'ang and Sung China* (Stanford: Stanford University Press, 1992). Whereas some officials lobbied with the Emperor on behalf of this genteel Confucianism, in the competition with Daoism for Imperial favor, their doctrine "never had a prayer," as John Lagerwey puts it in a celebrated statement from his *Taoist Ritual in Chinese Society and History* (New York: Macmillan, 1987), p 274.

Blood and the ineffable. The blood is offered at the Imperial altars to remove obstructive forces. It's harder to speak of the ineffable, but a Daoist would know that Chang'an is only the center of things on the earth, whereas the true center of everything is the Pole Star, simulacrum of the supreme god Great Singularity (*taiyi* 太一) and the actual source of Imperial authority.

71 There must be a fifth and sixth dimension, but they are only known to immortals. Perhaps they are perfectly interpenetrated with the others. Speaking to the Feminine Principle, Chögyam Trungpa remarked:

> On the quiet, the unborn begins to manufacture a world, an underworld, in mid-air, the bottom of the ocean. It cannot be obstructed nor prevented. If this underground world is very active, the overground world of the established administra-

tion cannot see it. We are talking here about the black market of the mother. That concept is extremely powerful, extremely powerful. It is some kind of invisible atomic bomb that's been manufactured in the basement. ("The Feminine Principle," in *Glimpses of Space* [Boulder: Vajradhatu Publications, 1999], 12–13)

72 He lived from 685 to 762. Often referred to by his posthumous Temple Name, Xuanzong 玄宗 (Mysterious Ancestor) or, more recently, by his given name, Li Longji 李隆基.

73 Control of weather was recently perfected in Beijing, where the summer temperature is never reported to be above 40 degrees Celsius, due to a widespread belief that were it to reach that mark, all state employees would be sent home.

74 Denis Twitchett, *Cambridge History of China, Vol. 3: Sui and T'ang China, 589–906, Part 1* (Cambridge: Cambridge University Press, 1979), 373.

75 Artist unknown. Source: http://commons.wikimedia.org/wiki/File:Tang-xuanzong.jpg.

76 Detail of *Yang Guifei Mounting a Horse,* by Qian Xuan 錢選 (1235–1305 CE). Source: https://en.wikipedia.org/wiki/Yang_Guifei#/media/File:%E4%B8%8A%E9%A9%AC%E5%9B%BE.jpg.

77 Bol, *"This Culture of Ours,"* 33.

78 If you take a paranoid view of the Masons, seeing them as a closed society that controls everything and whose members connect to one another silently across vast distances, then you've got a fair sense of how this works. The bureaucracy's numbers can be measured in various ways. This figure approximates the ranked officials, but their clerks (often hereditary), runners, and so on are many more.

79 Bol, *"This Culture of Ours,"* 77.

80 Owen, *The Great Age of Chinese Poetry*, 3–4. Nearly 50,000 Tang poems survive, assembled in the early eighteenth century as the *Quan Tangshi* 全唐詩 (Complete poems of the Tang).

Perhaps Tang practices of land tenure, water control, taxation, gender relations and religious organization are similarly aligned. A civilization can have only one thought at a time.

81 The last line plays on a much celebrated apothegm of Confucius, which contrasts the leadership styles of the wise (*zhizhe* 知者) and the good (*renzhe* 仁者) (*Analects* 6.23). From *The Complete Poetry of the Tang* (*Quantangshi* 全唐詩).

If we apply modern criteria, forgetting that all cultures are absurd, we might find the early Tang aristocrats to be concrete-sequential, precedent-bound and external-locus-of-control, that is, to be tightly tied to authorities lying outside themselves. (Concrete-sequential, that is, oriented to a linear presentation of empirical information — an aspect of what Anthony F. Gregorc calls "mind styles." External-locus-of-control, that is, dependent on forces that one cannot directly influence — see the work of Julian Rotter and others in personality studies.) But some people find, or make, space within such circumstance. An analogy closer to our own cultural lineage, Mrs Delany (1700–1788), née Mary Granville:

> Her father, Colonel Bernard Granville, was at one time Lieutenant Governor of Hull, and had been member of Parliament for Fowey in Cornwall. His grandfather was Sir Bevil, killed while fighting for Charles II in the Civil War, and Sir Bevil's grandfather was the famous Sir Richard Granville, who died after a heroic encounter between his ship Revenge and the Spanish fleet in the reign of Queen Elizabeth. (Ruth Hayden, *Mrs. Delany: Her Life and Her Flowers.* [London: The British Museum, 1986], 15)

> She was the friend of Handel, corresponded wittily with Swift, was the niece of Lord Lansdowne (poet and patron of Pope), knew Burke, was wooed by John Wesley, entertained and was entertained by Garrick, and saw much of Lord Chesterfield in Ireland. […] King George III and Queen Charlotte were on terms of intimate friendship with her and brought her comfort and happiness in her last years. (ibid., 11–12)
>
> Her father's sister, Lady Stanley, had been a Maid of Honour to Queen Mary; it was intended that Mary should be groomed for a similar position. (ibid., 15)

Married by her loving parents to a gentleman two score years her senior, she wrote:

> I was married with great pomp. Never was woe drest out in gayer colours, and when I was led to the altar, I wished from my soul I had been led, as Iphigenia was, to be sacrificed. (ibid., 24)

But also

> To encourage Mary with her music she was given her own harpsichord, and one day she had the pleasure of hearing it played by Handel. She was immediately struck by the beauty of his playing, and the moment he left the house she sat down to imitate it as best she could. Her uncle, teasing her, asked if she thought she would ever play as well as Handel: "If I did not think I should, I would burn my instrument," she replied. (ibid., 16)

And especially: widowed at 72, she began making "paper-mosaicks," flowers depicted in a cut paper technique she invented. There are perhaps 600 tiny pieces of paper in this collage:

Fig. 86. Source: http://i.telegraph.co.uk/multimedia/archive/01935/flowers1_1935358c.jpg.

82   Denis Twitchett explains:

> The Han-lin Academy was a palace organization directly attached to the emperor himself. It originally comprised a large group of writers, poets, experts in geomancy, diviners, Buddhist and Taoist clergy, artists, painters, calligraphers and even masters of chess, who were at the emperor's disposal in the palace to make his life fuller and more agreeable. In 738 a new section of the Han-lin academy was founded with the establishment of the Academy of Scholars. This new academy, which soon overshadowed the original Han-lin yuan in importance, was a private confidential secretariat dealing with state business and drafting documents for the emperor. (*Cambridge History of China*, 3:450)

83   These overlapping images are collected in Li Bo's *Chronology* (*Nianpu* 年譜) under Tianbao 天寶 year 3 (744 CE), ably translated by Frederic Protopappas in his *The Life and Times of Li Po*, 117–25.

84   But our own currency here is mostly words, with a few images, and the exchange rate isn't that great. And how do you convert tastes into sound?

85   When he was still crown prince, he and his five brothers had lived here too. For his fraternal love, see Paul Kroll, "The

Emperor's Philadelphian Hymn" in his "Four Vignettes from the Court of Tang Xuanzong," *T'ang Studies* 25 (2007): 1–27, at 6ff.

A decade after this story, in 755, rebellion would end his rule and his consort's life. When he returned from exile as Retired Emperor, two years later, he lived here once more, until his death.

86 Source: https://baike.baidu.com/pic/%E5%85%B4%E5%BA%86%E5%AE%AB/1669636/0/d833c895d143ad4b287f9e2584025aafa50f0686?fr=lemma&ct=single#aid=0&pic=d833c895d143ad4b287f9e2584025aafa50f0686.

For detailed maps of the Palace, with its various pavilions, gates, and Dragon Pond, see Victor Cunrui Xiong, *Sui-Tang Chang'an* (Ann Arbor: University of Michigan Center for Chinese Studies, 2000), diagrams 4.5 and 4.6.

For an excellent study of the Palace and its histories, see Saehyang P. Chung, "Hsing-ch'ing Kung: Some New Findings on the Plan of Emperor Hsüan-tsung's Private Palace," *Archives of Asian Art* 44 (1991): 51–67.

87 Source: https://baike.baidu.com/pic/%E6%B2%89%E9%A6%99%E4%BA%AD/876601/0/3bf33a87e950352ab06ef86a5243fbf2b2118b41?fr=lemma&ct=single#aid=0&pic=3bf33a87e950352ab06ef86a5243fbf2b2118b41.

88 In a *parfumerie* today you might find it under the name "oud." Pricey, though. The *Wikipedia* artticle says that "First-grade agarwood is one of the most expensive natural raw materials in the world, with 2010 prices for superior pure material as high as US$100,000/kg." The Deluxe edition of this book might include a scratch-and-sniff, like those perfume ads in *The New Yorker*.

The aquilaria tree is native to South-East Asia. When its otherwise healthy and odorless heartwood is infected by mould, the tree responds by producing the resin agar (Skt. *agaru*), or aloes, thus the term "agarwood." I would like to translate its Chinese name, *chenxiang* 沈香, as "drowning in fragrance," but it is more accurately "sinking fragrance," since the specific gravity of the wood is greater than 1.00, and it sinks in water. For a fine discussion, see Edward Schafer, *The Golden Peaches of Samarkand*, 163–65.

The Pavilion walls were perhaps impregnated with agarwood powder, as were the interior walls of some great Chang'an mansions. See Benn, *China's Golden Age*, 79–80.

89   Source: http://kalemphoto.com/wp-content/uploads/pink-tree-peony.gif.

90   So this is a heterotopia, a special place within a special palace within the special Imperial Palace Complex, within the magic city/siting of Chang'an, within the Great Tang. On heterotopes, see Michel Foucault, "Des espaces autres," in *Architecture/Mouvement/Continuité* 5 (October 1984 [1967]): 46–49.

91   The eponymous Pear Garden was the imperial academy of musical theater and dance, with three hundred students. The Bright Emperor himself oversaw their instruction.

92   With his two brothers, Li Guinian 李龜年 performed widely at private gatherings throughout the two capitals, amassing great wealth. When he sang, "men would put down their wine cups and start to weep (*Taiping guangji* 太平廣記)." Years later, after Rebellion had destroyed his and many other worlds, the poet Du Fu came upon him in the South, "in the season of our falling flowers," and recalled the splendid power of those performances in his poem "Meeting Li Guinian south of the Yangtze" (*Jiangnan feng Li Guinian* 江南逢李龟年).

93   "In ancient music, there were three modes — from high to low they were Plain, Level and Slanted (*qing ping ce* 清平側)." Wang Zhuo 王灼 (1105–81), *Biji manzhi* 碧雞漫志, chap. 5.

94   ch5v2p765. "A beauty who topples kingdoms." Later on it is said, in various ways and in various sources, that the Precious

Consort took offense at the suggestion that she might be such a beauty. See Protopappas, *The Life and Times of Li Po,* pp. 117–25.

95 Well, most all of Li Bo's poems were written to be chanted, intoned, sung. Laurence Picken has found some allied music (*Music from the Tang Court,* 7 vols. [Cambridge: Cambridge University Press, 1985–]), and Stephen Jones has identified some modern descendants (*Plucking the Winds: Lives of Village Musicians in Old and New China* [Leiden: CHIME Foundation, 2004] and "Source and Stream: Early Music and Living Traditions in China," *Early Music* 24, no. 3 [1996]: 375–88).

96 Liangzhou 涼州 is in the corridor linking the Central States with the mixed Turkic regions of the West. Its grape wine was an exotic delicacy. See Schafer, *Peaches,* "Grapes and grape wine," pp. 141ff. The Consort's glass cup is likely of central Asian provenance as well. The Seven Treasures (or Seven Precious Substances, *qibao* 七寶) of Buddhism are, varyingly, gold, silver, crystal, etc.

97 From the *Pine Window Miscellany* (*Songchuang zalu* 松窗雜錄), a Tang dynasty collection of sixteen stories, mostly about the Bright Emperor, attributed to various authors. See Li Xueqin 李學勤, *Siku Dacidian* 四庫大辭典 (Changchun: Jilin daxue chubanshe, 1996), 2:2140. Our text follows the *Chronology of Li Bo,* as emended by the *Taiping guangji.*

For an expanded, colloquial treatment of the story from later times, see Shuhui Yang, *Stories to Caution the World: A Ming Dynasty Collection* (Seattle: University of Washington Press, 2005), Vol. 2, Story 9, 134ff.

98 Meng Qi 孟棨 (875 *jinshi*), from his *Benshishi* 本事詩 (Fundamental stories and poems).

99 ch21v6p3362.

100   He held a series of important posts in the central bureaucracy. "Tutor" is an under-translation: he was one of four high-ranking officials who supervised the daily behavior and political training of the Prince. See Russell Kirkland, "From Imperial Tutor to Taoist Priest: Ho Chih-chang at the T'ang Court," *Journal of Asian History* 23, no. 2 (1989): 101–33.

101   From the longer poem "Eight Who Are immortal while They're Drinking" (*Yinjiu baxian* 飲酒八仙).

102   From his biography in the *New Tang History* (*Xin Tangshu* 新唐書).

103   Or to describe motorcars of the 1930s. See Enrica Aceti, *Le "Divine" degli anni ruggenti* (Milan: Domus, 1976).

104   Should this interest you, we translate one of Li Bo's alchemy poems much later in the book as Chapter 64.

105   This is not entirely true. You don't practice wine, you don't practice meat, you drink and eat.

106   There is also this story:

> When He Zhizhang chanted Li Bo's "Song of the Roosting Crows," he exclaimed, "This poem would set ghosts and gods to weep."

Preserved in various texts, e.g., Fan Chuanzheng 范傳正, *Zeng Zuoshi yi Hanlin xueshi Li Gong xinmubei* 贈左拾遺翰林學士李公新墓碑. The poem in question is *Wuqiqu* 烏栖曲 (ch-3v1p342). Steve Owen explains why this is not a conventional compliment but rather an attempt "to account for something that seemed to transcend the usual limits of literature" (*Golden Age*, 121).

He Zhizhang, of Kuaiji, the old south-east, wet and still redolent with pre-Chinese energies, the ancient state of Yue. His poem on returning there:

> I left home young and come back old.
> My country accent hasn't changed, but my hair's much reduced.
> When children see me, they don't recognize who I am,
> smiling, asking, "Stranger, where're you from?"

少小離家老大回，鄉音無改鬢毛衰
兒童相見不相識，笑問客從何處來

Li Bo wrote his poem to He in 747 when he was visiting He Zhizhang's old dwelling place. (See his other poems on Kuaiji translated later in this book, *Silk Washing Rock,* Chapter 51, and "Mount Tianmu," Chapter 62.) See also his poem bidding He farewell from Chang'an, "Seeing Off He Zhizhang on His Way Home to Yue" (*Song He Binke gui Yue* 送賀賓客歸越, ch-14v5p2394).

He Zhizhang's calligraphy was so admired that we still have bits of it. Here's the word *zheng* 爭, "struggle," from a longer piece:

Fig. 87. Source: http://shufa.guoxuedashi.com/4E89/154363.html.

107 The solar-lunar year is divided into twenty-four two-week segments. "Great Cold" is the last of these, just before the New Year brings on Spring, which arrives in our late January to late February. The text says it occurs in the tenth month, but this

must be incorrect. Probably the graph "two" has been dropped after the graph "ten."

108 Compiled by Wang Renyu 王仁裕 (880–956) during the Five Dynasties period. Quoted by Wang Qi in his chapter 35.

109 ch5v2p696.

110 As recorded in Wang Qi, ch36v3p1642, quoting the *Yitongzhi* 一統志 of the Qing dynasty. On Cui Zongzhi 崔宗之, see Du Fu's poem of the "Eight Who Are Immortals While Drinking" (*Yinzhong baxian* 飲中八仙).

111 Snow is words. It is the natural state describing itself. Snow is words, the first sound, first light. It *is* the natural state, *tout court*. Snow is Li Bo falling down from nowhere, you can't stop the snow, even the Bright Emperor cannot. Even Li Bo cannot.
 By springtime all the snow is opened and gone.

112 ch26v7p4016. Victor Mair, "Li Po's Letters in Pursuit of Political Patronage," *Harvard Journal of Asiatic Studies* 44, no. 1 (1984): 123–53). On the art of letter writing, see Patricia Ebrey, "T'ang Guides to Verbal Etiquette," *Harvard Journal of Asiatic Studies* 45, no. 2 (1985): 581–613). Being immortal doesn't make the tedious vagaries of the human realm go away.

113 Source: http://www.brandchannel.com/home/image.axd?picture=2012%2F5%2Fmen_in_black_weekly_world_news.jpg.

114 From what Carlos Barros calls the common paradigm of contemporary historiography. See his "Hacia un nuevo paradigma historiográfico," *Debates Americanos* 10 (2000): 86–96. Our fondness, then, for the *Old Tang History* (*Jiutangshu* 舊唐書) and its alleged credulity.

115 Shannon Doyne, "Poetry Pairing | 'A Poem of Changgan,'" New York Times, April 10, 2014.

116 He had died some decades earlier, in 682, but he was born a century prior, in 581, or was it 541? He's called the King of Medicines — he recorded more than 7,000 pharmaceutical formulae from earlier periods, and all later medical tradition flows out through him. On his esoteric practices, see Jürgen Oster, "Der Körper leicht, das Herz voller Freude," *Taijiquan & qigong journal* 3 (2016): 14–21.

117 From the *Unofficial History of the Tang* (*Tang Yishi* 唐逸史). For a tender treatment, see Schafer, *Pacing the Void*, 124, and Kathlyn Liscomb, "Iconic Events Illuminating the Immortality of Li Bai," *Monumenta Serica* 54 (2006): 75–118, at 106ff.

118 Xiwangmu 西王母, greatest of all goddesses, but her name better rendered "Royal Mother in the West."

119 "Ancient Airs" (*Gufeng* 古風) #17, ch2v1p104.

120 "A Lu Mountain Song That I Sent to Empty Boat Lu" (*Lushanyao ji Lu Shiyu Xuzhou* 廬山謠寄廬侍御虛舟), ch12v4p1999.

121 Excerpted from the longer "Under Stone Quarry Moon, for Gongfu [Guo Xiangzheng 郭祥正 (1035–1113)]" (*Caishi yuexia zeng Gongfu* 採石月下贈功甫). The *Old Tang History* merely remarks, "Li Bo passed away from excessive drinking. He died at Stone Quarry." Sometimes it takes a while for the truth to come out.

This event may be understood as "deliverance by water" (*shuijie* 水解), a form of the Daoist practice of "deliverance from the corpse" (*shijie* 屍解), in which the adept appears to die but instead is freed from his body and transforms into an immortal. The earliest example I know of water liberation is the account of Qin Gao 琴高 in *The Arranged Biographies of Immortals* (*Liexian zhuan* 列仙傳) attributed to Liu Xiang 劉向 (ca. 77–76

BCE). For a discussion, see section D, "Li Bai's aquatic metamorphosis" of Kathlyn Liscomb, "Li Bai Drinks with the Moon: The Cultural Afterlife of a Poetic Conceit and Related Lore," *Artibus Asiae* 70, no. 2 (2010): 331–86.

And for a most refined discussion of deliverance from the corpse, see Isabelle Robinet, "Metamorphosis and Deliverance from the Corpse in Taoism," *History of Religions* 19, no. 1 (1979): 37–70. Somewhat less satisfying is Urusla-Angelika Cedzich, "Corpse Deliverance, Substitute Bodies, Name Change, and Feigned Death: Aspects of Metamorphosis and Immortality in Early Medieval China," *Journal of Chinese Religions* 29, no. 1 (2001): 1–68.

122 "Roaming Mount Tai" (*You Taishan* 遊泰山), poem 6, ch17v5p2805.

123 "On Seeking the Daoist Master of Mount Daitian and Not Finding Him" (*Fang Daitianshan Daoshi bu yu* 訪戴天山道士不遇), ch21v6p3342.

124 Wang Qi, *Li Taibo quanji,* ch36v3p1650.

125 Wang Qi, *Li Taibo quanji,* ch36v3p1647.

126 Chapter 2, "Discourse on Making Things Equal (*Qiwu lun* 齊物論).

127 Please read Isabelle Robinet, "The Taoist Immortal: Jesters of Light and Shadow, Heaven and Earth," *Journal of Chinese Religions* 13 (1985): 87–105.

128 And see Suzanne Cahill's account in "Practice Makes Perfect: Paths to Transcendence for Women in Medieval China," *Taoist Resources* 2, no. 2 (1990): 23–42.

129 For a distinction between "longevity" and "immortality," see Michael Stanley-Baker, *Cultivating Body, Cultivating Self* (MA thesis, Indiana University, 2006).

130 Like those in the *Arranged Biographies of Immortals* (*Liexianzhuan* 列仙傳). It contains seventy-two short biographies of horse doctors, princes, hermits, mages, and divinities. And the *Biographies of Divines and Immortals* (*Shenxian zhuan* 神仙傳) of Ge Hong 葛洪 (283–343), so beautifully translated by Rob Campany as *To Live as Long as Heaven and Earth*, with nearly a hundred biographies.

131 See, *inter alia,* the work of Li Bo's contemporary Wu Yun 吳筠 (?–778), who tells us how in his essay, "One Can Learn How to Be a Divine Immortal" (*Shenxian kexue lun* 神仙可學論). That he had to write it means that not everyone thought it possible.

For further abilities of the immortal, including the power to transform oneself into other beings or objects, see Benjamin Penny, "Immortality and Transcendence," in *Daoism Handbook,* ed. Livia Kohn (Leiden: E.J. Brill, 2000), 109–33.

132 For an insightful survey of immortal poetry in all genres prior to the Tang, see Zornica Kirkova, *Roaming into the Beyond: Representations of Xian Immortality in Early Medieval Chinese Verse* (Leiden: Brill: 2016).

In loose speech, a *xian* is just a superlative, a genius, an incomparable, the way the proprietary entitling of European monarchs became available to King Oliver and Duke Ellington. Thus we could call Steve Owen a *wenxian* 文仙 for his miraculous work in Chinese literature — were he Irish, his name might be Steve O'Wen, Steve of Literature. Or we could say that "xian" is used to stand for the ec-static transformations of the human realm, its innate magical realism. Think of Michael Jackson dancing.

133 Source: http://commons.wikimedia.org/wiki/File:Shang_XiFour_Immortals_Salute_Longevity.jpg. For an earlier period, see Leslie V. Wallace, "Betwixt and Between: Depictions of Immortals (*Xian*) in Eastern Han Tomb Reliefs," *Ars Orientalis* 41 (2011): 73–101.

134 "Yunfang du Lü Chunyang 雲房渡呂純陽," https://www.pinterest.pt/pin/328199891570636442/.

For a discussion of the relationship of painting and immortality, see Paul Rakita Goldin, "Reflections on Irrationalism in Chinese Aesthetics," *Monumenta Serica* 44 (1996): 167–89.

135 More literally, "Is his apotheosis, then, complete?" (*Qi shenhua suozhi ye* 其神化所至邪). This remark was made of another Sichuanese, Sima Xiangru 司馬相如 (179–17 BCE), the poet to whom Li Bo has been most compared. Attributed to Yang Xiong by Liu Xin 刘歆 of Eastern Han in his *Xijing zaji* 西京雜記 (Miscellaneous records of the western capital). Quoted by Owen, *Great Age*, 111.

No wonder, then, that Li Bo's a bit orthogonal to ordinary human concerns. See, *inter alia,* Owen's astute observation that "he is more convincing when he described an encounter with an immortal or a flight through the heavens than when he described some social occasion at which he was actually present" (ibid., 114), since like most poets he is best with what is actually in front of him.

136 It can get worse. The greatest mid-century translator of Chinese verse, Arthur Waley, concluded that "he appears in his works as boastful, callous, dissipated, irresponsible and untruthful," in other words, as "a drunkard" (*The Poetry and Career of Li Po* [London: George Allen and Unwin, 1950], x.)

137 ch16v5p2623.

138 *Pace* the Chinese readers who like it these two ways — see Zhan Ying, 2624ff.

139   And the Chinese reader will also get a whiff of Peach Blossom Spring (*Taohuayuan* 桃花源), the magic land behind a waterfall, where an ordinary man found immortality — the famous story by Tao Qian 陶潛 (365–427).

140   http://www.dhgate.com/product/getProductImages.do?act=getProductImages&itemcode=213449982&pid=ff80808149a2e9e70149c0574ad407e6.

141   The *Shuowen* 說文 defines *xian* as "to live a long time and then ascend and depart." Zhuangzi (in his chapter "Heaven and Earth" 天地) says, "he lives for a thousand years, and when he gets bored with earth, he departs by rising."

142   Shijing #220, "When the Guests First Go to Their Mats" (*bin zhi chu yan* 賓之初筵). For the word family of *xian,* see Bernard Karlgren, *Grammata Serica Recensa* (Stockholm: The Museum of Far Eastern Antiquities, 1972 [1957]), no. 206: "to rise high; caper about, dan."

143   Chapter 28.

144   ch3v1p372.

145   Douglas Penick writes:

> So the dragon emerges from the cauldron.
> It is clear that there were mountains involved.
> Multitudes of slaves and craftsmen are not mentioned.
> And the dragon emerges.
> The dragon actually, for her part, couldn't care less. It's some kind of dragon dream she's having.
> The Emperor and his court cross over and become weightless and strange.
>
> But lesser people will not allow it.
> It must be real.

They grab at things and obtain precious relics.
Things that fall to earth (die).

146   Purple's not merely imperial, it is celestial, divine, near invisible. See Paul Kroll, "Li Po's Purple Haze," *Taoist Resources* 7, no. 2 (1997): 21–37).

The Queen Mother, her deathless light of sun, moon and stars, this is larger than that. See Paul Kroll, "The Light of Heaven in Medieval Taoist Verse," *Journal of Chinese Religions* 27 (1999): 1–12, esp. 9–11.

147   It's *qi* 氣, *pneuma,* the primal breath. See Peter Zhang and Lin Tian, "*Qi* and the Virtual in Daoist and Zen Literature: A Comparison with Western Vitalist Thought," *China Media Research* 14, no. 4 (2018): 99–109).

148   As preserved in Li Shan's 李善 notes to the *Selection of Refined Writings* (*Wenxuan* 文選). This piece is from Jiang Yan's poem, *Pan Huangmen zhuo wang* 潘黃門悼亡.

149   In the introduction to his "Gaotang Rhapsody" 高唐賦 from *The Songtexts of Chu*.

150   ch22v7p3435. Her five colors are indeed from her father Heaven. Thus the goddess Nü Gua 女媧 "smelted and refined these five colors of stones and used them to patch the grey-blue sky" (as reported by Wang Chong 王充 [27–ca. 100 CE] in his *Critical Essays* (*Lunheng* 論衡), the chapter "Discussing Heaven" (*Tantian* 談天), as translated by Edward Schafer in *Pacing the Void,* 39.)

Verlaine finds mystery in the sweet smell of thyme:

> Que ton vers soit la bonne aventure
> Éparse au vent crispé du matin
> Qui va fleurant la menthe et le thym…
> Et tout le reste est littérature.

> May your verses themselves be that luck,
> scattered in the crisp morning wind
> that smells of mint and thyme…
> And all the rest is just "literature."

We also admire Martin Sorrell's translation of the last word as "LIT-RIT-CHER." See Paul Verlaine, *Selected Poems,* trans. Martin Sorrell (Oxford: Oxford University Press, 1999), 125.

151 Ah, but these aren't just fragrant plants, they are the tools of a shaman vegetalista. See Gopal Sukhu's *The Shaman and the Heresiarch: A New Interpretation of the Li sao* (Albany: SUNY Press, 2012).

152 The poet is Qu Yuan 屈原 and this is his "Encountering Trouble" (*Li sao* 離騷) one of the world's most beautiful poems. David Hawkes, trans., *The Songs of the South: An Anthology of Ancient Chinese Poems by Yuan and Other Poets* (Hammondsworth: Penguin, 1985), 77–78.

153 This is mostly Gopal Sukhu's translation of the ending:

> But as we ascended toward the effulgent festival of the August Ones,
> suddenly I caught sight of my former home below.
> My chariot driver seemed about to weep, and my steeds, looking pensive,
> twisted their necks to look back. They would go no further.
>
> 陟升皇之赫戲兮，忽臨睨夫舊鄉
> 僕伕悲餘馬懷兮，蜷局顧而不行

Sukhu, *The Shaman and the Heresiarch,* 194. Sure, blame it on the horses. Actually, it's just that this vast vastness is uninhabitable for him, his social gravity ever pulling him down and down. So he chooses to descend, resumes daily life in its refusal of the sacred.

And then politics take control: he will drown himself in a material-substance river just to spite his unworthy sovereign, who has been unwilling to recognize his loyal service. And thereby, as Paula Varsano relates, the shaman poet is transformed into a Confucian martyr. See her *Tracking the Banished Immortal: The Poetry of Li Bo and Its Critical Reception* (Honolulu: University of Hawai'i Press, 2003), 166ff.

154   The poem is also a stylistic ancestor of the great tradition of rhapsody (*fu* 賦), obsessive, overwritten, elegant verse of places, objects, emotions. Li Bo wrote eight, one of which we've translated in chapter 15 as "A Rhapsody Lamenting Last Remnants of the Spring." For a wild translation of the best of these, see Paul Kroll, "Li Po's *Rhapsody on the Great P'eng-bird*," *Journal of Chinese Religions* 12 (1984): 1–17.

155   Thus when these men go looking for immortals, especially the female immortal, it usually ends in tears. The sincerity of their longing, which they imagine might draw them closer to the deity, only repels her. There are so many examples of this in the *Songtexts of Chu* and elsewhere! This sadness prevails even over the great Guo Pu 郭璞 of the third/fourth century — Varsano notes that "Guo Pu's shaman/adept/poet and the flirtatious, tantalizing deity never consummate their relationship" (*Tracking the Banished Immortal*, 199–200).

Pretty much the only men who consummate their relationship with an immortal are themselves immortal. Suzanne Cahill has translated a lavish account of a multiple wedding performed by the Queen Mother of the West for a set of Jade Maidens and their male suitors. The ancient hermit-immortal Chaofu 巢父 ("Nest Father") sings to his consort:

Jade flute and rose-gem pistil have been just right for night;
Why not make a single flower open across the dawn?

See Cahill, "Marriages Made in Heaven," *T'ang Studies* 10–11 (1992–93): 111–22, at 116, a study and translation of Du

Guangting's 杜光庭 (850–933) *Biographies of Immortals from the Walled City* (*Yongcheng jixian lu* 墉城集仙錄). I could not say what esoteric practices lie beneath this account.

Oh, but that's not actually how things work, with impermeable roles and singular identities. Cahill has also translated a set of poems from a century or two after Li Bo, where a poet tells of the King of Chu and his lover, or some other person and an immortal, or a regular guy and the breeze, and sometimes they have sex and sometimes we don't know if they have sex, or if the poet is having sex, somewhere else, the whole time, maybe only in his poem. See her "Sex and the Supernatural in Medieval China: Cantos on the Transcendent Who Presides over the River," *Journal of the American Oriental Society* 105, no. 2 (1985): 197–220.

156   One other guy made it out. Paul Kroll tells of it in his study "On 'Far Roaming,'" *Journal of the American Oriental Society* 116, no. 4 (1996): 653–69). Cao Zhi 曹植 (192–232) also made a good connection with the deity, see his "Rhapsody on the Luo River Goddess" (*Luoshen fu* 洛神賦).

157   The Fisherman is a famous poetic trope within the discourse of transcendence. You always hope to meet him, but he's mysterious and hard to find, perhaps an immortal in disguise. However, as Steve Owen points out, Li Bo does not seek the Fisherman, he is he (*Great Age,* 136).

158   "May I too become like the mist that gives itself up into morning" (attributed to Marguerite Porete). Perhaps this is the difference between a poet and an immortal.

159   The *Shuowen Jiezi* 說文解字 (Explaining simple graphs and analyzing compound graphs) of Xu Shen 許慎, ca. 100 CE.

160   If you're an epigraphy fan, check out these earlier forms:
- Xmu ding X 母鼎 (Shang, CHANT 2026) (late second millennium BCE)

- Shanfuyi ding 山父乙鼎 (Western Zhou, CHANT 1561) (early first millennium BCE)
- Zhaodiao shanfu fu 召弔山父簠 (early Springs and Autumns, CHANT 4601) (eighth century BCE)

For the CHinese ANcient Texts Database (CHANT) images, see http://www.chant.org/Default.aspx under the respective identifying number.

See also the Shanghai Museum, "Bamboo Strips Confucian Analects" 上博竹書，孔子詩論 (上海博物馆藏战国楚竹书), Chu, Warring States (fourth century BCE), http://rcc.whu.edu.cn/a/cwhzlyd/jb/2011/0625/243.html.

161 "Les montagnes sont, en Chine, des divinités. Elles sont considérées comme des puissances naturistes qui agissent d'une manière consciente et qui peuvent, par conséquent, être rendues favorables par des sacrifices et touchées par des prières" (Édouard Chavannes, *Le T'ai chan* [Paris: Leroux, 1910]). We might say that the deity comes first. The mountain co-emerges with it.

162 *Baopuzi* 抱樸子 (The Master who embraces simplicity) chap. 17, "Climbing and Fording [Mountains and Streams]" (*Dengshe* 登涉). See Matthew V. Wells, T*o Die and Not Decay: Autobiography and the Pursuit of Immortality in Early China* (Ann Arbor: Association for Asian Studies, 2009).

For a contrastive view, which understands Ge Hong as an arch-humanist, see Michael Puett, "Humans, Spirits, and Sages in Chinese Late Antiquity: Ge Hong's Master Who Embraces Simplicity (Baopuzi)," *Extrême-Orient, Extrême-Occident* 29 (2007): 95–119.

163 *Baopuzi,* chap. 17.

164 Such as the Lingbao *Wupian zhenwen* 靈寶五篇真文 (Perfected script in five tablets), for a glimpse of which see James Robson in the *Encyclopedia of Taoism,* s.v., 1074.

165 *Baopuzi,* chap. 17. For how mountains became less fearsome shortly after this time, see Kroll, "Lexical Landscapes and Textual Mountains in the High T'ang."

166 Source: https://upload.wikimedia.org/wikipedia/commons/d/d9/1_mount_hua_shan_china_2011.jpg.

167 Source: https://upload.wikimedia.org/wikipedia/commons/d/d5/Xuankongsi.jpg.

168 Source: https://upload.wikimedia.org/wikipedia/commons/thumb/8/86/Guo_Xi_-_Early_Spring_(large).jpg/1200px-Guo_Xi_-_Early_Spring_(large).jpg.

169 Source: https://i.pinimg.com/736x/af/f5/ff/aff5f-f60a503263a96e2fbc524bfd122--chinese-landscape-landscape-art.jpg.

170 See Jessica Rawson, "The Origins of Chinese Mountain Painting: Evidence from Archaeology," *Proceedings of the British Academy* 117 (2001): 1–48.

171 Shih-shan Susan Huang, *Picturing the True Form: Daoist Visual Culture in Traditional China* (Cambridge: Harvard University Press, 2012), 135.

172 Source: http://m.doczj.com/doc/3d8e2843be1e650e52ea998a-2.html.
  Such plans of a mountain's True Form predate the Tang. They contain the power of the mountain god, and just carrying them on your body gives perfect protection — you no longer have to visit the mountain to obtain this. "There are no more important Daoist writings than these" (Ge Hong again, the *Baopuzi,* chap. 19).

173 *The Inner Biography of the Martial Emperor of Han* (*Han Wudi neizhuan* 漢武帝內傳), sixth century CE but containing earlier material.

174 The *Shenxian zhuan* 神仙傳 (Biographies of divine immortals). Rob Campany suggests that Bo He 帛和 was a close contemporary of Ge Hong (*To Live as Long as Heaven and Earth*, 136).

175 *Baopuzi*, chap. 19.

176 Thus a major function of regional officials has always been to control all local deities in the imperial name. Paul Kroll writes:

> Jean Levi's work in particular has made clear that the chief conceptual role of state officials in medieval times was as representatives of the state cult, the Confucian tao, centered on the "Son of Heaven" — not as political placemen. We have become so used to speaking of T'ang government functionaries as bureaucrats (with the unavoidable connotations, for us, of the corridors of power, the steps of the Capitol) that we look right past their defining activities as religious emissaries. Like the Taoist priests, they aimed to exert control over the sundry local gods — the gods of the profane — of any region, who were worshipped through "irregular cults" ("Lexical Mountains," 67).

177 Just as, already in Neolithic farming, the fields were laid out north–south–east–west.

178 I think it's worthwhile having a dedicated English name for them, too, and so, following Edward Schafer, I call them Marchmounts, "march" meaning "margins, boundary, frontier." See his *Pacing the Void*, 6. "Over the march of two worlds, that of the imagination, and that of fact, her soul hovered fluttering." George MacDonald, *Paul Faber, Surgeon* (London, 1879).

179 Especially the *feng* 封, an enfeoffment ceremony, described in the *Historical Records* (*Shiji* 史記) of Sima Qian 司馬遷 (d. 86 BCE), chap. 6. See Martin Kern, "Announcements from the Mountains," in *Conceiving the Empire: China and Rome Compared,* ed. Fritz-Heiner Mutschler (Oxford: Oxford University Press, 2008), 331–68.

180 The ruler had first to "wake" the mountain, get its attention, expose himself to those consequences.

181 These are Laozi's fingers.

182 See Lucas Weiss, "Rectifying the Deep Structures of the Earth: Sima Chengzhen and the Standardization of Daoist Sacred Geography in the Tang," *Journal of Daoist Studies* 5 (2012): 31–60.

183 On *qi* as "energies," see Benoît Vermander, "Qi (Energy) in Chinese," *Ignis* 42, no. 3 (2012): 23–36.

184 Combining the accounts in the *Xuxianzhuan* 續仙轉 (Continued biographies of immortals) and the *Old Tang History* (Jiu Tangshu 舊唐書), chap. 192. See Russell Kirkland, *Taoists of the High T'ang* (Ph.D thesis, Indiana University, 1986), 54 and 57.

The Perfected Ones look a lot like imperial bureaucrats, and we may wonder, with Durkheim, if they are just the projection of social realities upon the unseen. But we could also take the inverse view, that society is just a projection of the gods. Or somewhere in between: that the gods are pretty hard to hear, so people mostly hear their own voices. These deities demand someone with the clairaudience of Sima Chengzhen, and the kindness to translate their speech into a local dialect. And so Highest Clarity priests took over the management of mountain spirits for the Emperor. And natural spirits that had become national gods submitted to Highest Clarity Perfected Ones, and its Daoism became state orthodoxy.

The title of Terry Kleeman's article tells what happened next: "Mountain Deities in China: the Domestication of the Mountain God and the Subjugation of the Margins" (*Journal of the American Oriental Society* 114, no. 2 [1994], 226–38). But note that the old gods of "slopes and forest" were still there, and still demanding blood sacrifice. They had been bypassed, not fired — it's very hard to fire a real god.

185 From "Song of the Roving Swordsman" (*Xiake hang* 俠客行), ch3v1p489.

186 "Airs" translates *feng* 風, "wind," but is used here to mean "style." Still, we prefer something like "Ancient Aires." The poem is ch2v1p196.

187 ch17v5p2796.

188 *A History of Mt Tai* (*Daishi* 岱史) by Cha Zhilong 查志隆 (1558 *jinshi*), Schipper #1472.

189 Source: https://en.wikipedia.org/wiki/File:Teton_fault_block.jpg

190 *Wikipedia,* "Taishan," s.v.

191 Source: https://upload.wikimedia.org/wikipedia/commons/8/8d/TaiShan.jpg. For more images, more descriptions and more inscriptions, see Lia Wei (Wei Liya) 魏離雅, *Lithic Impressions II* (Chengdu: Sichuan Fine Arts Institute, 2019.

192 And wrote a suite of six marvel poems on the occasion. We would translate all six, but Paul Kroll has presented them with such vividness and acumen that it would be redundant. We recommend his work to you, the "Verses from on High: the Ascent of T'ai Shan," *T'oung Pao* 69, no. 4 (1983): 223–60.

193   Ibid., 241, as we learn from *The Comprehensive Record of the Anomalous* (*Guangyi ji* 廣異紀). Zhan Ying's *Li Bo quanji* reports that "When a deer is more than a thousand years old, its fur turns white."

Fig. 88. Paul Caponigro, "Running White Deer," Wicklow, Ireland, 1967

194   *Usnea filipendula*, called in Chinese "pine lichen" (*songluo* 松蘿) for its most common place of growth or "woman's lichen" (*nüluo* 女蘿) for its supposed clinging. "Like human hair," it is said.

195   Chavannes, *Le T'ai chan*, 45.

196   Source: https://whc.unesco.org/en/list/437/.

197   Source: https://en.wikipedia.org/wiki/Usnea_filipendula.

198   The Songtexts of Chu explains:

> A plumed man in the cinnabar hills, oh,
> he must be an immortal visiting from his old home of deathlessness.

仍羽人於丹丘,留不死之舊鄉
— "Far Roaming" (*Yuanyou* 遠遊)

The younger they look, the older they are.

199 Source: http://proj1.sinica.edu.tw/~hantomb/c/tomb/objects2/objects/B/351192.jpg, now in the Xi'an Museum. From the Western Han (206 BCE–25 CE).

200 See the various notes in *Li Bo quanji,* quoting the unidentified "writings of the immortals."

201 *Huainanzi* 淮南子, chap. 16, "Discussing Mountains" (*Shuoshan xun* 説山訓).

202 Zhan Ying lists some in his *Li Bo quanji.*

203 Source: https://www.pinterest.com/pin/444308319472764672/.

204 Source: http://wxpic.7399.com/nqvaoZ-toY6GlxJuvYKfWmZlkxaJhpc-bna9ip4yNeK/CYgdSTwqKVioDNoWirkLKhkGimi3t61qWLfI-WIeYSWjJqGoprCn3-Hg7CanJuYoKpogtWAmou8aqiFY3eF-faZ8oqqtatunrnl7xKeCen26gXiop2iZZ5J4q62Slp-scKGmnMo.jpg.

Earlier we saw the "True Form of Mount Tai," which is a Daoist script based in energy patterns (*qi* 氣), not in bird tracks or human writing. By contrast, the examples here resemble, but are not assimilable to, Chinese graphs. See Chapter 31, below, "The Grotto-Heaven," for the history of their revelation.

Bark removed, the trunk shows the traces of burrowing insects:

ENDNOTES

Fig. 89. Photo by the author

Fig. 90. Photo by the author

The Tibetan traditions speak of "dakini script," the writing of playful female wisdom deities, the innate magical quality of the phenomenal world in limitless variety. Only a dakini, or an adept, can read it. A Tibetan folk song:

> Dakinis write one another in their own script.
> The worn road before your house is written in dakini script,
> lines of dirt going and going.
> Birds write dakini script on the sky,
> and bees hum songs written in that language.
> The dakini script of the sky is just the sky,
> it neither goes nor stays.
> The dakini script around your eyes
> wrinkles and crinkles when you smile or frown.

One night in August 1964 at Gary Snyder's house in north Kyoto, Nanao Sakaki sat on the tatami completely covering a piece of paper in squiggly lines. The next night Philip Whalen got very stoned and read the document to the assembled guests.

> As the war ended, Ezra Pound was incarcerated near Pisa, charged with treason. A local mountain became Mount Tai.
>
> from the death cells in sight of Mt. Taishan @ Pisa
> . . .
> and Mt Taishan is as faint as the wraith of my first friend

And he saw the Sage-King Shun there as well:

> > "sunt lumina," said Erigena Scotus
> > as of Shun on Mt Taishan　　　顯
> > in the hall of the forebears
>
> — From the *Pisan Cantos* #74, line 78, and #77, line 51.

205　ch15v5p2495.

206　Source:　https://en.wikipedia.org/wiki/Mount_Heng_(Hunan)#/media/File:HengshanMountains.JPG.

James Robson has written extensively on Mount Heng. See his *The Religious Landscape of the Southern Sacred Peak (Nanyue 南嶽) in Medieval China* (Cambridge: Harvard University East Asia Center, 2009).

207 Robson tells the Tang-end of her story in his ibid., chap. 6, "Lady Wei and the Female Daoists of Nanyue," 184–212.

208 It really depends on how you count. If you skip over Lady Wei, and begin only when Tao Hongjng 陶弘景 (456–536) took the lineage big, Sima is the Fourth.

209 From her biography in chap. 58 of the *Taiping guangji* 太平廣紀 (Extensive records from the Taiping era).

210 These writings explain how one may discover the astral and terrestrial deities of Celestial Masters within the human body. Thus they locate spiritual practice in that private space, rather than in ritual, liturgy and congregation. Similarly, whereas the sexual rites of the Celestial Masters took place between warm human bodies, in Highest Clarity they occur between the yin and yang of a solitary practitioner. Thus when Lady Wei betroths Yang Xi to a Perfected Consort round midnight on the evening of 27 July 365, she tells him:

> Though you are now publicly presented as mates, this only establishes your respective functions, with she the inner and you the outer. You must not recklessly follow the filthy practices of the world by performing with her base deeds of lewdness and impurity. You are to join with the holy consort through the meeting of your effulgent spirits.

Zhen'gao 真誥, "The Declarations of the Perfected," chap. 1. My translation follows that of Stephen Bokenkamp, *Early Daoist Scriptures* (Berkeley: University of California Press, 1997), 177. I am always moved by the precision of hour and date with which Yang kept his records.

211 A generation before Li Bo, Lady Wei's place of apotheosis had required rediscovery. This was accomplished by the Daoist priestess Huang Lingwei 黃靈微 (ca. 640–721) in 693, who sent the recovered relics to Empress Wu. See Russell Kirkland, "Three Entries for a T'ang Biographical Dictionary: Wang Hsi-i, Huang Ling-wei, Ho Chih-chang," *T'ang Studies* 10–11 (1992–93): 153–65, at 156ff.

212 This is about the Planck length. You can't get any smaller than that.

213 Her quest itself, of course, increases the likelihood that others can also meet Lady Wei.

214 Jade-Pure Clarity (*Yuqing* 玉清), Highest Clarity (*Shangqing* 上清) and Great Clarity (*Taiqing* 太清).

215 The *Taiping yulan* 太平御覽, chap. 675, says that the adept of high rank "wears a purple lotus head-scarf" (see *Li Bo quanji*, 2496).

216 Source: https://rossrosen.com/on-becoming-a-daoist-priest/.

217 Dongjun 東君, "Lord of the East," seventh of the "Nine Songs" of Hawkes, trans., *The Songtexts of Chu,* 113, freely revised. Cf. Sukhu, *The Shaman and the Heresiarch,* 206.

218 It's Cao Zhi 曹植 (192–232), son of the warlord Cao Cao and one of China's great poets. It's the "Rhapsody on the spirit of Luo River" (*Luoshen fu* 洛神賦). (You might also like to find the painting by Gu Kaizhi.)

219 The author of *Blue Wave Talks Poetics* (*Canglang shihua* 滄浪詩話), which first argued that the High Tang of Li Bo and Du Fu had set the model for all Chinese poetry. Cited in *Li Bo quanji,* 2497.

220   You can even read about her on *Wikipedia*.

221   ch6v2p1024.

222   Source: https://commons.wikimedia.org/wiki/File:Hua_Shan.jpg.

223   Source: https://upload.wikimedia.org/wikipedia/commons/1/1a/Thousand_feet.JPG

224   Source: https://commons.wikimedia.org/wiki/File:Yellowrivermap.jpg.

225   It's Sima Qian (d. 110 BCE), the greatest of all China's historians. His autobiography (*zixu* 自序) says only:

> When I was twenty, I went roaming south along the Yangtze and Huai Rivers, climbed Kuaiji, sought the cave of Yu, peered at Jiuyi Mountains, and floated down the Yuan and Xiang Rivers (*Shiji* 史記, chapter 130).

226   It's not clear who he is, though Xiao suspects he is a forebear of Prime Minister Xiahou Zi of Xuanzong's reign (847–59) (noted in *Li Bo quanji,* ch23v7p3601).

227   ch23v7p3599. His friends were Gao Qi 高霽 and Wei Quanyu 韋權輿. All we know is that Gao was from the area and Wei had been appointed Prefect there.

228   From his *Laozi zhu* 老子主, commentary on chap. 42. See Richard John Lynn, *The Classic of the Way and Virtue: A New Translation of the Tao-te Ching of Laozi* (New York: Columbia University Press, 1999). Sun Chuo 孫綽 (320–77) elaborates in his "Rhapsody on Mount Tiantai" (*Tiantaishan fu* 天台山賦):

The Great Vacuity enacts the Marvelous Something of Spontaneity. Molten, it makes the rivers and streams, congealed it makes the mountains and hills.

229 "The Record of Jiuhua Mountain" (*Jiuhuashan ji* 九華山紀), preserved in *Taiping yulan,* chap. 469.

230 Source: https://commons.wikimedia.org/wiki/File:Jiuhuashan_Dizang_Dian_view.jpg.

231 Source: https://commons.wikimedia.org/wiki/File:Jiuhuashan_higher_Daxiong_Baodian.jpg.

232 ch12v4p1999.

233 From Mao Deqi 毛德琦 (Qing period), *Lushan zhi* 廬山誌 (A record of Mount Lu), chap. 4 and 7. On Lu Yu's 陸羽 (733–804) *Classic of Tea,* see Chapter 50 "Tea," below.

234 https://commons.wikimedia.org/wiki/File:Lofty_Mt.Lu_by_Shen_Zhou.jpg

235 Source: http://www.hasta-standrews.com/features/2016/10/31/three-thousand-times-infinity-zhang-da-qian-1899–1983. Five feet wide, here they are looking at it:

Fig. 91. Chang and his assistants copy wall paintings

at Yulin Caves, May 1943. Source: https://www.asianart.com/exhibitions/changdaichien/intro.html

236   Wang Qi, ch36v3p1623. From Huang Ying's 黃鶯 *Dushizhu* 杜詩註 (Notes on Du Fu's poetry).

237   Sheng Hongzhi 盛弘之 (of the Liu Song dynasty), *The Record of Chu* (*Jingzhou ji* 荊州記).

238   ch20v6p3080.

239   Sheng Hongzhi, *The Record of Chu*.

240   Source: https://commons.wikimedia.org/wiki/File:Lintong_Xian_China_Huaqing-Pool-21.jpg.

241   The *Zhen'gao*, from the Highest Clarity tradition, *The True Instructions* or *Declarations of the Perfected*. Entry for year 429 CE (*yuanjia liunian* 元嘉六年). So here they are Jade Maidens, their divinity not fully revealed.

242   Or his consort. See, *inter alia*, the third-century CE *Laozi zhong jing* 老子中經 (Central Scripture of Laozi), where she's called Mysterious Radiance of Great Yin (*Taiyin xuanguang* 太陰玄光). Edward Schafer describes her varied magnificence in the "Star Women" section of his *Pacing the Void,* 131–48, and grants her great illumination in "The Jade Woman of Greatest Mystery," *History of Religions* 17 (1978): 387–98.

243   Bo Juyi 白居易 (772–846), "Song of Long-lasting Regret" (*Changhen ge* 長恨歌), one of China's favorite poems, written two generations after the event

244   Source: https://en.wikipedia.org/wiki/Huaqing_Pool#/media/File:%E8%B4%B5%E5%A6%83%E5%87%BA%E6%B5%B4.jpg. Edward Schafer discusses these springs in "The Development of Bathing Customs in Ancient and Medieval Chi-

na and the History of the Floriate Clear Palace," *Journal of the American Oriental Society* 76, no. 2 (1956): 57–82.

245   ch15v5p2445.

246   For Li Yangbing's text, *the Caotang ji* 草堂集, see ch1v1pp1–3. On Tang practices of collecting and circulating texts, see Christopher Nugent, *Manifest in Words, Written on Paper: Producing and Circulating Poetry in Tang Dynasty China* (Cambridge: Harvard University Asia Center, 2011)

247   His dwelling place, Beihai, means Northern Ocean, but it's just an area east of Ji'nan on the way to the Bohai sea. Li Bo's poem tells us his teacher is from the Celestial Masters (*Tianshi* 天師) lineage, but Terry Kleeman points out that "the term Celestial Master had by the Tang been debased to the point that it could be used for any prominent Taoist" (*Encyclopedia of Taoism,* 986), so we've translated it as "Daoist Master." Nonetheless, the 64th generation direct lineage descendant of the Celestial Masters founder lives and practices in Taiwan today.

248   "Seeking the Dao in Anling..." (*Fangdao Anling* 訪道安陵...), ch9v3p1474.

249   *Encyclopedia of Taoism,* "Overview," 41. For Li Bo's delight on receiving this investiture, see Edward Schafer, "Li Po's Star Power," *Society for the Study of Chinese Religions Bulletin* 6 (1978): 5–15.

250   *Encyclopedia of Taoism,* 36, orthography adjusted.
   Steve Bokenkamp (in his Foreword to *To Live as Long and Heaven and Earth,* xi) points us to the following passage in the *Zhen'gao* (Declarations of the Perfected), chap. 1. (See also the translations by Thomas E. Smith, *Declarations of the Perfected, Part One: Setting Scripts and Images into Motion* [St. Petersburg: Three Pines, 2013], 49–50.) It is the evening of the 28th of July,

365 CE. Lady Wang has descended from within the divine enceinte of Purple Subtlety, and Yang Xi prostrates to her and asks:

> "You, a sublime perfect being, have come down into this murky realm in your very body, and yet you have never once written anything in your own hand. Is it because the base and exalted are just too far apart, so that the true forms would not be visible here?" […]
>
> She replies: "It is much as you have said, Mr. Yang. The concealed luminosity, the empty Mystery — there are no paths within them that anyone could follow. Speech emerges from them into empty space — no creature could trace it there. This luminosity and speech careen about, borne on swiftness, transforming, elusive, unfettered. They sink and float, dark and drifting, minnows darting through blazing silence. Tossed into a fordless pond, dragged by billowing winds, they ride an empty boat downstream. This is emptiness within Reality, Being within emptiness, and the formless within Being.
>
> "When we put all this to writing, splattering ink across paper, it pours out in splendid patterns that exceed the visible. Only the brush of Mystery can draw its native brilliance. If you're bound to apparent material substance, then you're covertly corrupting this purity — that's what happens to the forms that are transmitted into this murky realm. When soaring dew takes on bone and flesh and has intercourse with the world below, then the High blemishes the unbridled truth of its song, and the low transgresses its boundaries. It's not something we do, the numinous laws don't allow it."

Li Bo doesn't hold much truck with boundaries and their separation.

251 Source: https://i.pinimg.com/736x/1a/56/7c/1a567c73327c5 5d417e1d28312634fed--salute-font.jpg.
"The rigor Taoists showed in transmitting and inscribing talismans can be seen in how extremely well examples found in

the Dunhuang manuscripts or archeologically excavated accord with those printed in the Ming canon" (*Encyclopedia of Taoism,* "Overview," 38).

These three talismans are from chapter 1 of the "Precious Registers [Corresponding to the Grade] of Disciple of the Three Luminaries of the Great Arcane, a Heavenly Treasure of the Shangqing Dongzhen Division" (*Shangqing dongzhen tianbao dadong sanjing baolu* 上清洞真天寶大洞三景寶籙), see Schipper #1385. They are:

1. The supreme Lord Laozi's talismanic register of the golden tiger (*Taishang Dijun jinhu fulu* 太上帝君金虎符籙),
2. The talisman of the divine tiger (*Taishang shenhu fu* 太上神虎符),
3. Register of the flying paces of the void and permanent stars (*Taishang feibu kongchang lu* 太上飛步空常籙).

252 I have no idea where this random QR comes from, or where it goes. The wags in this book would have it that their silliness is wisdom, too, enticing Li Bo to show more of himself. But they should read the medieval Daoist canon, which, as Rudolf Pfister as shown, concludes that "Laughter is involuntary, even compulsive […], something to avoid, and sometimes an illness symptom" ("Attitudes towards Laughter and Euphoria in Medieval Chinese Daoist Texts," in *Laughing in Chinese,* ed. Paolo Santangelo [Rome: Aracne, 2012], 335–67, at 350.)

253 Modified from Franciscus Verellen's translation of Du Guangting 杜光庭, who is quoting the lost *Jade Scripture of Tortoise Mountain* (*Guishan yujing* 龜山玉經), in Verellen, "The Beyond Within: Grotto-Heavens in Taoist Ritual and Cosmology," *Cahiers d'Extrême-Asie* 8 (1995): 265–90, at 273.

See also Sing-chen Lydia Chiang, "Visions of Happiness: Daoist Utopias and Grotto Paradises in Early and Medieval Chinese Tales," *Utopian Studies* 20, no. 1 (2009): 97–120 and Thomas Hahn, "The Standard Taoist Mountain," *Cahiers d'Extrême-Asie* 4 (1988): 145–56.

254 The *Baopuzi* 抱樸子, chap. 5.

255 See the *Declarations of the Perfected* (*Zhen'gao* 真誥), chapter 11.
Meng Tian 蒙恬 (d. 210 BCE) was a great general of the First Emperor of Qin, and built much of the Great Wall for him. After his Emperor's death, he was arrested and forced to commit suicide. He asks himself, "What crime have I committed against Heaven, that I should be condemned to death?" And he answers, slowly: "My crime is certainly worthy of death. When I built the Great Wall, more than ten-thousand miles from east to west, I was unable to avoid cutting the arteries of Earth, those water-bearing channels below the ground. This is indeed my crime" (*Historical Records* [Shiji 史記], chap. 88).

256 That systematization was the beginning of the end — and certainly the great Tang Daoist Du Guangting 杜光庭 (850–933) had something to do with it. See Lennert Gesterkamp, "The Synthesis of Daoist Sacred Geography: A Textual Study of Du Guangting's *Dongtian fudi yuedu mingshan ji*," *Daoism: Religion, History and Society* 9 (2017): 1–39.

257 Miura Kunio 三甫國夫 in the *Encyclopedia of Taoism*, 372. For an intimate account of their afterlife in Song times onward, see Rolf Stein, *Le monde en petit* (Paris: Champs/Flammarion, 1987).

258 Translation by Robert Campany, *To Live as Long as Heaven and Earth*, 152, modified.

259 The *Biographies of Divine Immortals* (*Shenxian zhuan* 神仙傳), chap. 9, "Sire Gourd."

260 The great geomancer and classical commentator Guo Pu 郭璞 (276–324). Or, with Schafer, we might call his poems "Excursions in Sylphdom." See Schafer's "Wu Yün's 吳錫 Stan-

zas on 'Saunters in Sylphdom' 遊仙詩," *Monumenta Serica* 35 (1981–83): 309–45.

261   *Treatise on Buddhism and Laoism* (*ShiLao zhi* 釋老志).

262   We don't know much of Li Mu, though the Song dynasty poet Si Xi 四錫 celebrates him in the long "Song of Li Mu Playing the Flute" (*Li Mu chuidi ge* 李暮吹笛歌). The sacred songs (*faqu* 法曲) are a musical genre that derived at first from Indic Buddhist and then Daoist musics, blended in the centuries before Tang with Chinese musical practices. It was particularly loved by the Bright Emperor.

263   Wang Qi, *Li Taibo quanji,* ch36v3p1619–20. From the "The Record of Li Mu Playing the Flute" (*Li Mu chuidi ji* 李暮吹笛記) by Yang Juyuan 楊巨源, courtier of a generation after Li Bo's death (789 *jinshi,* still alive in 833). Wang Qi points out the discrepancy of dates: the Bright Emperor visited Mount Tai in 726, but the first year of Tianbao was 742.

In Chinese, such rebus-pictograms are called *mi* 謎, "words hidden within words," that graph itself an ideogram conjoining the words "word" 言 and "astray" 迷. You may recall a crucial *mi* in *The Story of the Stone/Dream of the Red Chamber*. Did your grade-school child ever write "my" under "wear," like this:

wear
 my

264   ch19v6p2964. Parts of the poem are translated in Schafer, *Pacing the Void,* 125.

265   The South Mountains (Nanshan 南山, or Zhongnan Shan 終南山) run some hundred miles below the green lowlands of Chang'an.

James Benn writes of dwellers in this mountain range in "One Mountain, Two Traditions: Buddhist and Taoist Claims on Zhongnan Shan in Medieval Times," in *Images, Relics, and Legends: The Formation and Transformation of Buddhist Sacred Sites* (Oakville: Mosaic Press, 2012). And Bill Porter speaks of the mountain's contemporary hermits in *The Road to Heaven* (Berkeley: Counterpoint Press, 2009). And all along beneath the mountainscape are grotto-heavens (*dongtian* 洞天), linked caverns wherein immortals dwell.

In his penultimate line, Li Bo's line, "Having past the last peak," is more literally "Once I've gone past Wugong Mountain," that's the companion peak to Taibo in the Nanshan range.

266 Source: https://en.wikipedia.org/wiki/Mount_Taibai#/media/File:Taibai-Dadian-Shan-3x.jpg.

267 Chapter 33. Thus *The Secret Canon of Venus* (*Taibo yijing* 太白陰經), the military strategy text by Li Bo's near contemporary Li Quan 李筌. For a discussion, see Robin D.S. Yates, "The History of Military Divination in China," EASTM 24 (2005): 15–43.

268 The *Huainanzi* 淮南子, chap. 3, in John Major, *Heaven and Earth in Early Han Thought: Chapters Three, Four and Five of the Huainanzi* (Albany: SUNY Press, 1993), 76.

269 See the *Historical Records* (*Shiji* 史記) chapter on astronomy, the *Tianguan shu* 天官書, discussed by Sun Xiaochun and Jacob Kistemaker in *The Chinese Sky during the Han: Constellating Stards and Society* (Leiden: Brill, 1997). The Han view is maintained by its successor star texts, such as that found in the *History of the Jin Dynasty* (*Jinshu* 晉書), studied by Ho Peng Yoke in *The Astronomical Chapter of the Chin Shu* (Paris: Mouton: 1966). Much of this information is summarized in the *Kaiyuan Zhanjing* 開元占經 (Divination canon from the Kaiyuan period) of Gautama Siddha et al., completed in 729, in turn summarized by Joseph Needham et al. in *Science and Civilisation in China, Vol. 3: Mathematics and the Sciences of the Heav-*

ens and the Earth (Cambridge: Cambridge University Press, 1959), §19–25, 398ff.

A key text of Highest Clarity Daoism, the *Scripture of the Eight Pure Ladies* (*Basu jing* 八素經, Schipper #426), describes the planet as "the round mirror of the essence of metal" (preserved in chapter 3 of the *Supreme Secret Essentials* [*Wushang biyao* 無上必要, Schipper #1138]). Schafer discusses the section on the planet Mars in *Pacing the Void,* 212, where he writes tellingly of planetary power:

> The planets are conspicuous concentrations of supernatural power; their movements are rapid and irregular, and so tend to inspire a sense of uneasiness and even dread (ibid., 217).

270 "The Barbarians Have No Real Men" (*Hu wuren* 胡無人), ch3v1p476.

271 "Presented to Li Bo" (*Zeng Li Shi'er Bo* 贈李十二白), QuanTangshi 全唐詩, chap. 261. Ahh, but Dongfang Shuo 東方朔 (160–93) is also said to be that Venus. See *Comprehensive Meaning of Mores* (*Fengsu tongyi* 風俗通義), chap. 2, and Section VIII of this book.

272 And thus Laozi says,

> The bright Dao seems dim,
> the smooth Dao seems rough,
> the great white seems sullied.
>
> — chapter 41

273 For the provenance of this piece of calligraphy, see Chapter 40, "Climbing Yang Terrace."

274 Ludwig Wittgenstein, *Remarks on Colour* (Oxford: Blackwell, 1977). Pierre Hadot insists that the structure of its writing is as significant as any ascribed "content."

275 Agnes Martin and Herman Melville have also explored parts of this question. Li Bo uses the word "white" over 500 times in his 1,000 poems.

276 *The Miscellaneous Notes on Picking Orchids.* Author and period unknown—perhaps late Song or Yuan. Preserved in the *Langhuan ji* 瑯嬛記 of Yi Shizhen 伊士珍 of the Yuan Dynasty and gathered in Wang Qi, *Li Taibo quanji*, ch36v3p1620.

277 "From antiquity the *zhi*-mushroom has been regarded as an auspicious plant. Thus it's also called 'the numinous mushroom' (*lingzhi* 靈芝)." See the *Hanyu dazidian* 漢語大字典, poor cousin of the *OED*, *zhi*, s.v.

278 The *Bencao gangmu* 本草綱目, *Compendium of Materia Medica*, summa of all surveys of the Chinese pharmacopeia, completed in 1578 by Li Shizhen 李時珍. The fourth-century *Baopuzi* 抱樸子 notes, "It grows on all the Five Marchmounts, but especially on Mount Qi" (chap. 5). See Michel Strickmann, *Notes on Mushroom Cults in Ancient China* (Gent: Rijksuniversiteit, 1966).

279 Source: https://www.healthline.com/nutrition/reishi-mushroom-benefits.

280 The *Dadong zhenjing* 大洞真经 of Yang Yi 楊羲 (330–86), a foundational text of Highest Clarity Daoism, divulging the techniques of joining Heavenly and bodily deities, the mushroom a preferred entheogen. Schipper #6. See Isabelle Robinet, "Le Ta-tung chen-ching: Son authenticité et sa place dans les textes du Shang-ch'ing ching," in *Tantric and Taoist Studies in Honour of R.A. Stein,* ed. Michel Strickmann (Brussels: Institut Belge des Hautes Etudes Chinoises, 1983), 2:394–433.

281 Source: https://commons.wikimedia.org/wiki/File:Han_Gan_Night-Shining_White.jpg. Painted about 750 by Han Gan 韓幹 (c. 706–83). The horse's name is usually translated as

"Night Shining White." On the painting's political implications, see Suzanne Cahill, "Night Shining White : Traces of a T'ang Dynasty Horse in Two Media," *T'ang Studies* 4 (1986): 91–94.

282 The Sephardic Baghdadi Indian banker Sir Percival David had acquired it in China in the 1930s.

283 Paul Kroll, "The Dancing Horses of T'ang," *T'oung Pao* 67, no. 3 (1981): 240–68. Translated from the *Miscellaneous Records of the Bright Emperor* (*Minghuang zalu* 明皇雜錄) by Kroll, 244–45. Their activity is not entirely new — we have Han ceramics with acrobats standing on horses' backs.

284 Source: http://mongolschinaandthesilkroad.blogspot.com/2015/09/cosmopolitan-metropolis-along-silk-road.html. Tomb figures in Tang three-color glaze (*sancai* 三彩). If you're looking for a game just now, try the Beijing Sunny Time Polo Club, or the Nine Dragons Hill Polo Club in Shanghai.

285 On Laozi's Daoist credentials, see Livia Kohn, "Daoist Hagiographies: Lord Lao as High God of the Dao," in *God of the Dao: Lord Lao in History and Myth,* ed. Livia Kohn (Ann Arbor: Center for Chinese Studies, University of Michigan, 1998), 7–36.

286 ch19v6p2983.

In Li Bo's poem, a human Laozi left home and wandered west — this is the story told in chapter 63 of Sima Qian's *Historical Records* (*Shiji* 史記). The Keeper of the Pass had seen purple haze in the distance, so he knew a sage was on the way. Laozi arrived and somehow agreed to spill the beans; the Keeper recorded them as the *Daodejing.* Then the two of them went off through desert sands. In Li Bo's telling, they have now both died, and the alchemical stove cooking in the cinnabar field of their bellies has gone out.

We've mentioned that our access to Li Bo's poetry is primarily through two sources, the eighteenth-century edition of Wang Qi 王琦 (*Li Taibo quanji* 李太白全集) and the mighty 1996 assemblage of Zhan Ying. Of this poem Wang Qi remarks, "It is definitely by Li Bo" (see his ch21v2p976). Zhan's team, however, cites evidence that, except for three words, it was instead composed by the Bright Emperor, on the occasion of his 749 visit to the Temple of Lord Lao just north of the eastern capital Luoyang: a stele at the temple was inscribed with the poem in the Emperor's distinctive calligraphy. Section VII of our book, "The rebellion," addresses the Emperor's deep devotion to Laozi.

287 For a breathtaking version of this first sentence, and first chapter, see Peter Boodberg, to wit,

Lodehead lodehead-brooking : no forewonted lodehead;
Namecall namecall-brooking : no forewonted namecall.

"Philological Notes on Chapter One of the Lao Tzu," *Harvard Journal of Asiatic Studies* 20, nos. 3–4 (1957): 598–618. His father, commander of the Soviet fleet in Vladivostok:

Fig. 92. Alexey Pavlovich Budberg (1869–1945). Source: https://www.wikidata.org/wiki/Q4097978.

288 During the first decades of the People's Republic of China, all philosophy — all thought — was either materialist (*weiwuzhuyi* 唯物主義) or idealist (*weixinzhuyi* 唯心主義), either Good or Evil. Laozi was a round puzzle piece that was hard to

fit into square holes. See Mao Zedong, "*Zai yifen jieshao Laozi zhexue shi weiwuzhuyi haishi weixinzhuyi di zhenglun cailiao shang di piyu* 在一份介绍老子哲学 是唯物主义还是唯心主义的争论材料上的批语) [A one-minute critical comment to introduce the materials on the struggle as to whether Laozi's philosophy was materialist or idealist]," in《建国以来毛泽东文稿(第八册)》(北京:中央文献出版社, 1993), 632.

289 The category that encompasses the most of these is *fang-shi* 方士, "gentlemen of the formulae." The term is broadly conceived and spills out in all directions. See Kenneth deWoskin, *Doctors, Diviners and Magicians: Biographies of Fang-shih* (New York: Columbia University Press, 1983).

Taijiquan 太極拳 is the most recent martial lineage to claim roots here. The *Daodejing* has several passages on using the military (see chap. 31, 50, and 57), and the *Sun Tzu Art of War* (*Sunzi bingfa* 孫子兵法) mirrors an allied way of working with the dual nature of phenomena.

290 The Celestial Masters 天師, beginning in 142 CE Sichuan under Zhang Daoling 張道陵 (34–156). The eighty-fourth patriarch of this sect now lives in Taiwan. Kristopher Schipper received transmission from him, see his excellent book, *The Taoist Body* (Berkeley: University of California Press, 1993 [1982]).

291 Reading *shi* 始 "inception," as its cognate *tai* 胎 "the pregnant womb."

292 Silence may no longer be at the cutting edge of critical theory, but it remains the cutting edge of reality. (See Sanford Budick and Wolfgang Iser, eds., *Languages of the Unsayable: The Play of Negativity in Literature and Literary Theory* [Stanford: Stanford University Press, 1987].)

293 Naught and aught are the gifts of Peter Boodberg, "Some Philological Notes on the Lao Tzu." Please also enjoy Paul Kroll's presidential address to the American Oriental Society, "Between

Something and Nothing," *Journal of the American Oriental Society* 127, no. 4 (2007): 403–13. We could also say *owt* and *nowt,* derived from Old English *a wiht* and *ne wiht,* meaning "anything" and "nothing" in Yorkshire dialect.

294 People continue to worry this, as if there really were two things. See, *inter alia,* David Chai, *Zhuangzi and the Becoming of Nothingness* (Albany: SUNY Press, 2019).

295 As *Wikipedia* explains, "*Qi* does not exist." *Wikipedia,* "Shiatsu," s.v. Qi, pronounced "kwee," I think.

296 The most parsimonious accounting of this modern myth is Angus Graham's. See his "The Origins of the Legend of Lao Tan 老聃," in his *Studies in Chinese Philosophy and Philosophical Literature* (Albany: SUNY Press, 1990), 111–24.

297 The *Extensive Records from the Taiping Period* (*Taiping guangji* 太平廣記), biography of Laozi, chap. 1 of the section on Divine Immortals (*shenxian* 神仙), quoting, among others, the *Biographies of Divine Immortals* (*Shenxianzhuan* 神仙傳).

298 Schipper #1437. See Edward Schafer, "The Scripture of the Opening of Heaven by the Most High Lord Lao," *Taoist Resources* 7, no. 2 (1997): 1–20.

299 For the Daoist-oriented religious legitimization of rule assumed by Tang Gaozong 唐高宗 at the establishment of Tang, see Stephen Bokenkamp, "Time after Time: Taoist Apocalyptic History and the Founding of the T'ang Dynasty," *Asia Major* 7, no. 1 (1994): 59–88.

In "Taoism, the Unofficial High Religion of China," Anna Seidel writes of the numerous Japanese missions to the Great Tang, each of them seeking the most enduring Chinese principles of governance, calendar, art and religion on which to establish the new nation of Japan. In 753, a Japanese ambassador asked the Bright Emperor if he might take the Buddhist master

Jianzhen 鑒真 home with him. An awkward moment followed, writes Seidel, and instead

> the Emperor suggested that they take a Daoist master whom he esteemed much more highly. The ambassador declined: "Our ruler is not fond of the teachings of the Daoists."

See Seidel, "Taoism, the Unofficial High Religion of China," *Taoist Resources* 7, no. 2 (1997): 39–72, at 57. It seems Japan did not want to bind itself to the family religion of the Chinese state.

300 At Mount Qingyuan 清原, just outside Quanzhou 泉州, the southern coast, from the Song dynasty. Source: https://en.wikipedia.org/wiki/Laozi#/media/File:Laozi_002.jpg.

301 In the rhapsody that follows this account, Sima becomes Zhuangzi's huge, magnificent Great Bird, who soars over all (*Dapeng fu* 大鵬賦, ch25v7p3880). This bird is the *peng* 鵬 — see the opening lines of Zhuangzi, his chapter 1. And please also note William Boltz's remarkable article on it, "The Structure and Interpretation of *Chuang tzŭ*."

302 Apart from recording him in a list of Highest Clarity Patriarchs in his paid eulogy for Hu Ziyang 胡紫陽 ("A Memorial and Stele-inscription for Master Hu Ziyang of Handong" [*Handong Ziyang Xiansheng beiming* 漢東紫陽先生碑銘], *Jiwai shiwen* 集外詩文 v8p4494, see 4500).

303 ch2v1p50.

304 Descended from the Emperors of the Jin 晉 (265–420). Chap. 12 of the 1590 CE *Complete Writings on the Zither* (*Qinshu daquan* 琴書大全) of Jiang Keqian 蔣克謙) discusses his compositions, both musical and literary, on the instrument. In general, see the account by Chen Guofu 陳國符 in his *Daozang Yuanliu Kao* 道藏源流考 [Investigations on the origin and

transmission of the Daoist canon] (Beijing: Zhonghua, 1949), 52ff.

And then there are the private Daoists, scrupulously concealed within appearance.

305 See Anna K. Seidel, "Imperial Treasures and Taoist Sacraments," in *Tantric and Taoist Studies,* ed. Michel Strickmann (Brussels: Institut Belge des Hautes Études Chinoises, 1983), 2:291–371.

On Sima's interpenetration with the political realm, see Russell Kirkland, "Ssu-ma Ch'eng-chen and the Role of Taoism in the Medieval Chinese Polity," *Journal of Asian History* 31, no. 2 (1997): 105–38), and the dissertation of Thomas Jülch, published as *Der Orden des Sima Chengzhen und des Wang Ziqiao: Untersüchungen zur Geschichte des Shangqing-Daoismus in Tiantai-Bergen* (Munich: Herbert Utz Verlag, 2011).

306 *Extensive Records of the Taiping Period* (*Taiping guangji* 太平廣記), chap. 21, "Divine Immortals." The passage has also been translated by Russell Kirkland, *Taoists of the High T'ang* (Ph.D. diss., Indiana University, 1986), 59.

Sima practiced in the Highest Clarity lineage (or, if you prefer, "Supreme Purity" [*Shangqing* 上清]). We can understand it as a church, with priesthood, texts, temples, doctrines, deities. But especially with individual meditative practices of breath and visualization. Yet we can't quite call it "individual," for the personal body consists of numerous gods, the same as you find in the various Heavens outside yourself, and the practices include sitting and forgetting yourself, and forgetting those deities as well — see, for example, Sima's best known work, *Zuowanglun* 坐忘論, translated into English by Livia Kohn as *Sitting in Oblivion: The Heart of Daoist Meditation* (St. Petersburg: Three Pines Press, 2010). I'm ashamed to speak so superficially about something so profound. If this material interests you, please seek out the wondrous writings of Isabelle Robinet.

307   Like his teacher, Li Hanguang 李含光 (683–769) was often sought by the Bright Emperor, but he always had some ailment that prevented his attendance at court. He and Li Bo traveled in overlapping circles, the way they hang out together here in this endnote, but there is no ostensible record of their interactions. On Li Hanguang, see Russell Kirkland, "The last Taoist Grand Master at the T'ang Imperial Court: Li Han-Kuang and T'ang Hsuan-tsung," *T'ang Studies* 4 (1986): 43–67.

308   In fetal breathing (*taixi* 胎息) one breathes like an embryo, that is, through navel and pores, rather than the nose or mouth. Catherine Despeux notes an early mention in the fifth-century biography of Wang Zhen 王真 (of the Later Han dynasty) from the Hou Hanshu 後漢書, chap. 82 (see *Encyclopedia of Taoism,* 953).

Abjuring grains (*juegu* 絕谷 or *bigu* 辟穀) frees the practitioner from the staple foods of China — wheat, millet, rice, what everyone lives on — and replaces them with herbs, dew, breath. Schipper discusses this in the "Immortals" chapter of *The Taoist Body,* 167ff. See also Robert Campany, "The Meanings of Cuisines of Transcendence in Late Classical and Early Medieval China," *T'oung Pao* 91, no. 1 (2005): 1–57.

For more general considerations, see Shawn Arthur, *Early Daoist Dietary Practices: Examining Ways to Health and Longevity* (Lanham: Lexington Books, 2013).

309   ch34v3p1439. On osmanthus, see Edward Schafer, "The T'ang Osmanthus," *Schafer Sinological Papers* 38, no. 4 (1989): 1–2 and *The Vermilion Bird: T'ang Images of the South* (Berkeley: University of California Press, 1967), 196ff.

Li Bo inscribes traces of immortality all through Madame Jiao. The gourd of Ying River belongs to another ancient hermit (Xu You 許油, see Chapter 65, "Mystery"); the Hemp Maiden Magu 麻姑 is often to the Eastern Seas (see Chapter 14, "Lines of a Short Song"); and Mount Song, wherein Madame Jiao conceals herself, itself conceals the chief Grotto-Heaven of the realm (see Chapter 31, "The Grotto-Heaven"). Thus arrayed,

Madame Jiao becomes empowered to hold Li Bo's intention, she as Queen Mother, he as Dongfang Shuo (see Section VIII, "A Banished Immortal").

310   Though she was a princess, no one now remembers when she was born or died. Most likely it was 692 and 762. She was, then, a decade older than Li Bo. Du Guangting 杜光庭 (850–933) writes of her: "Princess Realized-in-Jade loved Dao and took Heavenly Teacher Sima as Her Teacher" (in *Records of the Divine Traces of the Heavenly Altar of Mount Wangwu* [*Tiantan Wangwushan shengji ji* 天壇王屋山聖迹記], chap. 6).

See also Yu Xianhao 郁賢皓, "*Li Bo yu Yuzhen Gongzhu guocong xintan* 李白與玉貞公主過從新探 [New investigations of Li Bo's association with the Princess Realized-in-Jade]," in his *Li Bo yu Tangdai wenshi kaolun* 李白與唐代文史考論, 191–202, and Jinhua Jia, *Gender, Power and Talent: The Journey of Daoist Priestesses in Tang China* (New York: Columbia University Press, 2018).

311   ch7v3p1219. Li Bo's phrase "to sound the drums of Heaven" can mean making thunder. But it also refers to a particular Daoist practice:

> When you tap the two upper and two lower front teeth together, this is called "sounding Heaven's drums…." In order to concentrate your practice so as to summon the most numinous beings, you should sound Heaven's drums. Tap precisely the four center teeth, close the mouth, refrain from speech, and make a long, deep sound.

Zhan Ying (p. 1221) ascribes this text to the "Nine Truly High Most Precious Writings, the Scripture of Divine Brightness" (*Jiuzhen gaoshang baoshu shenmingjing* 九真高上寶書神明經), as quoted in the *Seven Lots from the Bookbag of the Clouds* (*Yunji qiqian* 雲笈七籤), *juan* 31. But I've found no trace of such a text. My edition of the *Yunji qiqian* instead ascribes it to the otherwise unknown *Scripture of the High Preciously Divine Bright-*

ness Protocol (*Gaoshang baoshen mingke jing* 高上寶神明科經). See Kristofer Schipper and Franciscus Verellen, eds., *The Taoist Canon, Vol. 1: Antiquity through the Middle Ages* (Chicago: University of Chicago Press, 2004), 593.

Tooth tapping is described in various parts of the Daoist canon, and one is advised to do it 3, 7, 9, 12, 24, 32, or even 160 times. The text translated above does not specify the number for sounding Heaven's drums. Tapping the front teeth temporarily blocks the nerve channel that conducts conceptual thought, thus facilitating meditative concentration. When the tapping is done for longer periods at approximately ninety times per minute, it also produces the effect of shamanic drumming.

312 Studied extensively by Charles Benn in *The Cavern Mystery Transmission: A Taoist Ordination Rite of A.D. 711* (Honolulu: University of Hawai'i Press, 1991). Two hundred ten Tang princesses are recorded in the *Tang Histories*. Eleven took ordination, she and her sister the second and third. See Ping Yao, "Contested Virtue: The Daoist Investiture of Princesses Jinxian and Yuzhen and the Journey of Tang Imperial Daughters," *T'ang Studies* 22 (2004): 1–40, at 1.

313 After her older sister's death in 732, she was the Bright Emperor's only surviving full sibling. See Edward Schafer, "The Princess Realized in Jade," *T'ang Studies* 3 (1985): 1–24 and "The Capeline Cantos: Verses on the Divine Loves of Taoist Priestesses," *Asiatische Studien* 32 (1978): 1–33.

For a summary of her political role, see Timothy H. Barrett, *Taoism under the T'ang: Religion & Empire during the Golden Age of Chinese History* (London: Wellsweep, 1996), 49ff. See also Liu Youzhu 劉友竹, "*Li Bo yu Yuan Danqiu, Yuzhen Gongzhu jiaoyou xinkao* 李白與元丹丘，玉真公主交遊新考 [A new examination of Li Bo's relations with Yuan Danqiu and Princess Realized-in-Jade]," *Chengdu daxue xuebao* 成都大學學報 2 (2002): 18–24. And Yu Xianhao 郁賢皓, *Tianshang zhexianren di mimi—Li Bo kaolun ji* 天上謫仙人的秘密—李白考論集

[Secrets of the heavenly banished immortal — collected investigations of Li Bo] (Taipei: Taiwan Commercial Press, 1997), 228ff.

314 Benn, *The Cavern Mystery Transmission,* 15. It was for the dedication of Sima's Abbey of Sunlit Terrace (*Yangtai guan* 陽臺觀), which the Bright Emperor had had built for him, and where he was to live until his death in 735. See the *Old Tang History,* chap. 192. We translate Li Bo's poem on the abbey in Chapter 40, "Climbing Yang Terrace."

315 Benn, *The Cavern Mystery Transmission,* 15.

316 Perhaps including music, too. See Ding Fang 丁放, "*Yuzhen Gongzhu kaolun* 玉真公主考論 [An examination of the Princess Yuzhen]," *Beijing daxue xuebao* 北京大學學報 41, no. 2 (2004): 41–52.

317 Benn, *The Cavern Mystery Transmission,* 50 discusses the visits of Wang Wei and also of the poets Zhang Yue 張說 (663–730) and Gao Shi 高適 (ca. 704–65).

318 It's commonly thought that Wu Yun 吳筠 (d. 778) brought Li Bo with him when he was invited to Court in 742, but Jan de Meyer shows it's unlikely that they knew each other. See his *Wu Yun's Way: Life and Works of an Eighth-Century Daoist Master* (Leiden: Brill, 2006). Wu Yun's poetry has been brilliantly translated by Edward Schafer in "Wu Yün's 'Cantos on Pacing the Void,'" *Harvard Journal of Asiatic Studies* 41, no. 2 (1981): 377–415) and "Wu Yün's 吳筠 Stanzas on 'Saunters in Sylphdom' 遊仙詩."

319 On the Empress, see N. Harry Rothschild's aptly entitled *Emperor Wu Zhao and Her Pantheon of Devis, Divinities, and Dynastic Mothers* (New York: Columbia University Press, 2015).

320 Except for Princess Immortal-in-Gold, her other seven elder sisters were all married off politically by the time of her ordination.

321 The politics behind this are studied by Yao, "Contested Virtue."

322 Benn, *The Cavern Mystery Transmission,* 73.

323 See Benn, *The Cavern Mystery Transmission,* 15, for this accounting.

324 Benn, *The Cavern Mystery Transmission,* 2. The ritual consisted of the conferral of certain Lingbao scriptures. For a discussion of Lingbao and its texts, see Isabelle Robinet, *Taoism: Growth of a Religion,* trans. Phyllis Brooks (Stanford: Stanford University Press, 1997), chap. 5, 149–83.

325 Benn, *The Cavern Mystery Transmission,* 120, translating Zhang Wanfu's account of the investiture. The Bright Emperor had three visions of Laozi, who revealed hidden treasures to him and sanctified his rule. See J.J.L. Duyvendak, "The Dreams of Emperor Hsüan-tsung," in *India Antiqua* (Leiden: Brill, 1947), 102–8.

326 *Bianhua bu ce* 變化不測, that is, the transformations of yin and yang, of the universe's natural processes, which have no apparent constancy and thus cannot be known by common means. The *Old Tang History* adds:

> There was a man named Xing Hepu who was skilled at reckoning people's lifespans. The Bright Emperor ordered him to do a reckoning of Zhang, but no one could figure out when he'd been born. There was also a man named Shi Yeguang, who was good at inspecting people for demons. [His biography is found immediately following that of Zhang Guo in the *Old Tang History.*] The Bright Emperor commanded Zhang

to sit close by him and then ordered Shi Yeguang to inspect him. Shi Yeguang said, "Where is Zhang Guo just now?" Shi Yeguang was right across from him, but he still couldn't see him.

327   Aconitum, a potent poison, known also as wolf's bane, for its use in Europe for killing wolves. Employed in China for both medicine and warfare. "The main causes of death are ventricular arrhythmias and asystole, paralysis of the heart or of the respiratory center. The only post-mortem signs are those of asphyxia" (*Wikipedia*, "Aconitum," s.v.).

328   The biography in Ouyang Xiu's 歐陽修 (1007–72) *New Tang History* (*XinTangshu* 新唐書) is virtually the same, despite Ouyang's propensity to purge elements of myth or superstition. (See Richard Davis, "Chaste and Filial Women in Chinese Historical Writings of the Eleventh Century," *Journal of the American Oriental Society* 121, no. 2 [2001]: 204–18].) Ouyang adds Zhang Guo's autobiographical statement: "I was born in the *bingzi* year of Emperor Yao [c. 2100 BCE], where I had the rank of palace attendant."

329   The emperor on his throne, left. Zhang Guo, right. His young attendant, foreground.
   Zhang Guo traveled by white mule, often seated backwards upon it. When he got to his destination, he'd fold up the mule like paper and stick it in his wallet. When he wanted to ride again, he'd take out the mule, spray water on it, and it would return to full size. In this painting the mule seems to have escaped its brocade container and eluded Zhang's young attendant as well.

330   ch6v2p1032. And echoing in Li Bo's ears is this line from Zhuangzi, "Do you know how it is, when heart and mind roam the inexhaustible?" (chap. 25, *Zeyang* 則陽).
   The poem was written in 734, when the two were retreatants at Mount Song, the central Marchmount. One of its clusters has

thirty-six peaks, and from these flows the Ying River of this poem. See Yu Xianhao 郁賢皓, "*Li Bo yu Yuan Danqiu jiaoyou kao* 李白與元丹丘交遊考 [Investigations of Li Bo and Yuan Danqi's roaming]," in *Li Bo yu Tangdai wenshi kaolun* 李白與唐代文史考論 [Essays on Li Bo and the literary history of the Tang].

331   From before there was time. Every Hells Angel receives a pair of Original Jeans at initiation, which he will never wash.

332   Hu Ziyang 胡紫陽 (dates unknown), preceptor to the Bright Emperor, recluse, in the lineage of Sima Chengzhen. See Li Bo's unusual poem about him, "Remembering Our Old Roams, Sent to Yuan Yan, Aide-de-camp at Qiaojun" (*Yijiuyou, ji Qiaojun Yuan Canjun* 憶舊游寄譙郡元參軍), ch12v4p1942, translated and annotated by Paul Kroll, "Heyue Yingling Ji and the Attributes of High Tang Poetry," in *Reading Medieval Chinese Poetry: Text, Context, and Culture,* ed. Paul Kroll (Leiden: Brill, 2014), 169–201. Li Bo also wrote "A Memorial and Stele-inscription for Master Hu Ziyang of Handong [*Handong Ziyang Xiansheng beiming* 漢東紫陽先生碑銘]," *Jiwai shiwen* 集外詩文 v8p4494, 4500).

333   We've translated this piece in the "Wine" section, where it is dedicated to Billie Holiday. Yuan Danqiu is almost unknown, except through Li's poems, a dozen of which are addressed to him. Nothing of him survives in the *Complete Poems* or *Prose of the Tang,* nor in the *Old* or *New Tang History.*
  From the *Songtexts of Chu,* the poem "Far Roaming":

> I went on to see the feathered men of Cinnabar Hill,
> dwelling in their ancient home of deathlessness.

The commentator Wang Yi adds, "At Cinnabar Hill, day and night are always bright."
  Cinnabar, with also the meaning "the elixir of immortality." On the history of cinnabar's magic, see Guolong Lai's essay,

"Color and Color Symbolism in Early Chinese Ritual Art: Red and Black and the Formation of the Five Colors System," which he relates to its generation from apotropaic but also highly toxic substances (in *Color in Ancient and Medieval East Asia,* ed. Mary M. Dusenbury [New Haven: Yale University Press, 2015], 25–43).

334 From "For the Songshan Recluse Cinnabar Hill, with a Preface" (*Ti Songshan yiren Yuan Danqiu shanju, bingxu* 題嵩山逸人元丹丘山居并序), ch23v7p3589.

335 ch13v4p2151.

336 Chapter 2, "The Sorting That Evens Things Out" (*Qiwulun* 齊物論). For an ideal translation, see Graham, *Chuang-tzu.* What if they're both awake at the same time? There can be a Lord Lao, the deified Laozi, but there can never be a Lord Zhuang—the Daoist Protectors won't tolerate it.

337 *Shiji* 史記 of the Grand Historian Sima Qian 司馬遷. This is from chap. 53, "The Hereditary House of Chief Minister Xiao" (*Xiao Xiangguo shijia* 蕭相國世家).

338 On these fabulous isles, see "P'eng-lai" in Schafer's *Mirages on the Sea of Time,* 51–60.

339 ch2v1p62.

340 As natural processing, as an ultimate truth irreducible to either oneness or multiplicity, as the magical powers of adepts to transform physical substances, and as the immortal's mode of emancipation. See, *inter alia,* her magnificent "Metamorphosis and Deliverance from the Corpse in Taoism," *History of Religions* 19, no. 1 (1979): 37–70.

Very different for Ovid. His metamorphoses are unidirectional, motivated and often violent. The epigram to this book: "Hir haire vnkembd about hir necke downe flaring." So far this could be a Li Bo poem. But in this instance Laurel/Daphne is fleeing Apollo. He wants her down-flaring hair, he wants to have sex with her. He is ready to rape. She prays to her mother goddess, who transforms her into a laurel tree. Still Apollo paws at her bark — his lust is not transmuted by her deliverance.

Apollo's brother/alter ego is Dionysius. In Ovid's telling, only one arrow from Eros is needed to resurrect their atavistic unity. (For the terms of their necessary interchangeability, and its roots in Greek matriarchy prior to the Indo-European invasions of 3,000 BCE, see Carl Ruch, *The World of Classical Myth* [Durham: Carolina Academic Press, 1994], chap 5, esp. 103ff.) This is Ovid's idea of a joke. In China such anxieties were far more deeply concealed — the Greco-Roman mythopoeia is a whole different ballgame. Gary Snyder comments: "China cast off mythology, which means its own dreams, with hairy cocks and gaping pudenda, millennia ago" ("Technical Notes & Queries," in *Earth House Hold* [New York: New Directions, 1969], 120).

I grew up in a small town where lived a scruffy drunken biker. He killed himself in a wreck. The funeral home dressed his body and beard, all combed out and neat. He was unrecognizable in that coffin.

Fig.93. Bernini, *Apollo and Daphne* (1622–1625) Source: https:// commons.wikimedia.org/wiki/File:Bernini_(c%C3%B3pia)_-_ Apolo_e_Dafne.jpg

341 On Mount Wuwang, some fifty miles north of the Eastern Capital, a few days walk. The poet Gao Shi 高適 (704–765) was with them too.

342 It's the only piece of writing that everyone today agrees is in Li Bo's own hand. The Imperial Palace Collection held it until the Revolution of 1911, then it vanished. In the 1950s a private collector gave it to Chairman Mao, who himself composes verse in the style of Li Bo. Now in the Palace Museum, Beijing.

343 Source: https://en.wikipedia.org/wiki/Li_Bai#/media/File:Libai_shangyangtai.jpg.

344 *Jiwai shiwen* 集外詩文 v8p4522.

345 The *Old Tang History,* chap. 192. See also the treatment in Russell Kirkland, "Ssu-ma Ch'eng-chen and the Role of Taoism in the Medieval Chinese Polity," *Journal of Asian History* 31, no. 2 (1997): 105–38.

346 As we saw in Chapter 31, such caverns are underground pure lands, linked through subterranean networks of earth-channels across all the Great Tang.

347 *Zhengao* 真誥, chap. 5.

348 See Chapter 24, "The Moister South."

349 *The Encyclopedia of Taoism,* 1086. Elsewhere, in *Taoist Meditation: The Mao-shan Tradition of Great Purity* (Albany: SUNY Press, 1993), she notes that the practices of Highest Clarity Daoism, into which Li Bo was initiated, "are situated halfway between bodily techniques and intellectual contemplation" (49), represented by the world of images.

350 ch21v4p1917.

351 Yin Keng (511–563), master of the five-word line. I'm so unschooled that I'd never heard of him, and so mistook his name Yin Keng 陰鏗 for the phrase *yinjian* 陰鑑, "a mirror made of Yin." This is one of a dozen poems Du Fu sent Li Bo — for some others, see Wang Qi, *Li Taibo quanji,* ch32v31481ff.

352 *Waishi* 外詩, v8p4422.

353 ch1v1p99.

354 See, on one side, William Hung, *Tu Fu, China's Greatest Poet* (Cambridge: Harvard University Press, 1952).

355 This was Paula Varsano's dissertation project, now available as the first part of her scrupulous book on Li Bo, *Tracking the Banished Immortal*. See also Guo Moruo's 郭沫若 unfortunate *Li Bai yu Du Fu* 李白与杜甫 (Beijing: Renmin, 1971).

356 Source: https://www.pinterest.com/pin/269441990177191491/. A film by Michael Ritchie, with Burt Reynolds and Kris Kristofferson. Lotte Lenya plays Ida Rolf, in her last film performance.

357 Famous advice, often proffered. See, *inter alia,* Varsano, *Tracking the Banished Immortal,* 77, 108, *et passim.* And Owen, *Great Age,* 109.

358 Owen, *Great Age,* 128.

359
> And if that's not loving you,
> then all I've got to say, is
>   God didn't make little green apples
>   and it don't rain in Indianapolis
>   in the summertime.
>
> — Burt Bacharach

See Steve George, "Tom Jones little green apples," *YouTube*, March 28, 2017, https://www.youtube.com/watch?v=u9keurl5Teg.

360   Present-day Ji'ning 濟寧, southern Shandong Province, on the way between the rice-rich south and the Eastern and Western capitals.

361   By Chuan Zehong 傳澤洪 of the Qing. From Wang Qi, *Li Taibo quanji,* ch26v3p1638.

362   Ezra Pound, *Cathay* (London: Elkin Matthews, 1916).

363   In the introduction to Pound's *Selected Poems* (London: Farber, 1928). Eighteen poems, out of the notes of the late Ernest Fenollosa. Perhaps best to call them collaborations as much as translations.

364   We could go further in our abbreviations. There's a line in "Climbing Crane Tower" (*Deng guanque lou* 登鸛雀樓) by Li Bo's contemporary Wang Zhihuan 王之渙 that reads in standard translation:

   The Yellow River flows into the sea.

   黃河入海流

A friend translates this as "Lunchtime." She explains, "Yellow is egg is lunch, and flow is time."
   William Shakespeare explains:

   SNOUT: O Bottom, thou art changed! What do I see on thee?
   BOTTOM: What do you see? You see an ass head of your own, do you?
   Exit SNOUT
   Enter QUINCE
   QUINCE: Bless thee, Bottom, bless thee. Thou art translated.
      Bottom's translation is more radical than Quine's.

365   Reconstructions by William Baxter, out of Paul Kroll, *Dictionary*, modified. Reconstructions of medieval Chinese pronunciations were already coming into place a hundred years back. Some fifty years ago, Hugh Stimson had already urged us to deal with its implications for poetics in his "The Sound of a Tarng poem: 'Grieving about Greenslope,' by Duh-Fuu," *Journal of the American Oriental Society* 89, no. 1 (1969): 59–67. This has been accomplished analytically — see for example Elling Eide's "On Li Po." But it has not led to much musical translation.

In the 1950s Peter Boodberg inaugurated an allied sensibility, to tonal patterns in Regulated Verse, leading him to re-write a well-known Wang Wei poem. See "Philology in Translation-Land," from his "Cedules from a Berkeley Workshop in Asiatic Philology," in *Selected Works of Peter A. Boodberg,* ed. Alvin Cohen (Berkeley: University of California Press, 1979), 174–75.

366   And then there is this fragment of another poem attributed to Li Bo, only twelve words survive, as in a dream:

> Jeweled steps detain the bright moon for just one night,
> for three full springs the gilded palaces are filled with falling flowers.
> Propitious snow…

> 玉階一夜留明月，金殿三春滿落花，瑞雪…
> — Zhan Ying, 外集詩文 v8p4513.

367   Schönberg disdained the practice: "A piano reduction comes into being, not like a work of art — from unknown causes — but like a useful object — for known reasons, for a particular purpose" ("Modern Piano Reduction [1923]," in *Style and Idea* [New York: Philosophical Library, 1950], 211.) Perhaps he never heard this collaboration: davidhertzberg, "Bach / Busoni / Dinu Lipatti, 1950: Ich ruf' zu Dir, Herr Jesu Christ (After BWV 639)," *YouTube,* September 22, 2011, https://www.youtube.com/watch?v=gkUZX77vNtc.

368   From chapter 2, rapturously translated by Burton Watson in *The Complete Works of Chuang Tzu* (New York: Columbia University Press, 1968).

369   ch13v4p2204. We've combined the two strongest witnesses of the third line.

370   Source: https://en.wikipedia.org/wiki/Yellow Crane Tower#/media/File:HuangHe_Tower2.jpg.

371   From the sixth-century *History of the Southern Qi,* "Treatise on the Prefectures and Garrisons," part two (*Nanqishu, zhoujunzhi xia* 南齊書,州郡志下). His story is in the *Arranged Accounts of Immortals* (*Liexianzhuan* 列仙傳) from the Eastern Han.

372   Chap. 3 of his *Record of Entering Shu* (*RuShuji* 入蜀記).

373   The letter is entitled *Yu Han Jingzhou shu* 與韓荊州書. Its recipient is Han Chaozong 韓朝宗 (686–750), a modest public servant. The letter was probably written in 734. It has been translated in full by Victor Mair, "Li Po's Letters," 129ff.

374   Riffing on the *Analects* of Confucius, chap. 2: "When I was fifteen, I set my will on study."

375   By "Chronology" I mean two works, the first now nested within the second. The earlier was compiled by Xue Zhongyong 薛仲邕 during the Song dynasty. Xue relied on sources such as the two *Tang Histories,* prefaces to collections of Li Bo's poems, collections of Tang miscellanea, and so on, as well as Li Bo's poems themselves. His work is the *Li Taibo nianqian* 李太白年潛. Wang Qi 王琦 added his notes in 1759, supplementing and sometimes correcting Xue's remarks. His work is the *Li Taibo nianpu* 李太白年譜. Their combined text offers a year-by-year account of Li's activities, including surmises about which poems were written in which year. It constitutes *juan* 35 of Wang's *Li*

Taibo quanji 李太白全集. The present entry is from Kaiyuan 8, v3p1576. As mentioned in the notes to our chapter 6, above, this juan has been translated in its entirety by Frederic Protopappas, entitled *The Life and Times of Li Po*. That *Chronology* is best read within another, more recent *Chronology,* the *Li Taibo nianpu buzheng* 李太白年譜補正 [Emendations to the Chronology of Li Taibo] by Lü Huaming 呂華明 and others (Zhonghua shuju, 2012), which incorporates five other chronologies of Li Bo.

376 c28v8p4214. Compared to the Chinese language, English is impoverished when it comes to dragon words. Just look at Michael Carr, "Chinese Dragon Names," *Linguistics of the Tibeto-Burman Area* 13, no. 2 (1990): 87–90, which lists a ton. Here Li Bo speaks of *jiao* 蛟 and *long* 龍. It would be pleasing to distinguish these as "kraken" and "dragon," but the two word-systems don't pair up.

377 Source: https://commons.wikimedia.org/wiki/File:Tang_Jiyao_9.jpg.

378 Source: https://commons.wikimedia.org/wiki/File:%E9%9B%B2%E5%8D%97%E9%83%BD%E7%9D%A3%E5%BA%9C%E4%BD%BD%E9%A3%9B%E8%BB%8D.jpg.

379 ch3v1p489.

380 Source: https://www.moma.org/calendar/events/4272. This is *Yojimbo,* made in Japan, with apologies to veterans of the Kang Ri 抗日 campaigns.

The chivalric mode, the *wuxia* 武俠. Its ancestors are the independent, honor-driven warriors of the pre-Imperial period, its descendants the knights-errant of contemporary film and fiction. They cannot bear injustice, especially the suffering of the vulnerable. As such, they roam outside both law and custom, both state and family. But they are loyal past death to anyone who will see their true virtue. See the *Historical records,* chap.

86 (The Assassins, *Cike liezhuan* 刺客列傳) and the novels of Jin Yong 金庸.

You can find a gorgeous and materially correct variation of all this, set during the Great Tang, in *The Assassin* (*Cike Nie Yinniang* 刺客聶隱娘), Hou Hsiao-hsien/Hou Xiaoxian's 侯孝賢 2015 film. Hou states: "In the Tang Dynasty, a prominent poet named Li Bai wrote some verses about an assassin. This is the earliest example I know of wuxia literature" (Aliza Ma, "Killer Technique," *Film Comment*, Sept.–Oct. 2015, https://www.film-comment.com/article/hou-hsiao-hsien-interview/).

This is Tennyson:

The great brand
Made lightnings in the splendor of the moon,
And flashing round and round, and whirled in an arch,
Shot like a streamer of the northern morn,
Seen where the moving isles of winter shock
By night, with noises of the northern sea,
So flashed and fell the brand Excalibur.

Idylls of the King—Sir Belvidere throws the dying Arthur's sword Excalibur into the sea.

381 *Shiji* 史記, chap. 77. But please read the full account there, which is the Grand Historian at his best. You can find a hurried translation at http://classical-chinese.blogspot.com/2008/02/shiji-77-biography-of-prince-of-wei.html or a better one in William Nienhauser, ed., *The Grand Scribe's Records, Vol. 7: The Memoirs of Pre-Han China* (Bloomington: Indiana University Press, 1994).

382 Does anyone think this is by Zhuangzi? Angus Graham (in *Chuang-tzu*) argues that this chapter, and its neighboring chapters 28–31, are not "Daoist" but come from the school of Yang Zhu 楊朱 (ca. 350 BCE), as they attend particularly to concerns of "keeping the body intact" and questions of "what are my true interests" (ibid., 221).

383 *Basic Annals* 9, 833.

384 Wang Qi, *Li Taibo nianpu,* chap. 35. This style of punishment dates from the immediate pre-Tang period.

All states seek to monopolize the power to give death. The traditional Chinese state also sought to control those powers that give life, to trees and grasses, poultry, the clouds and rain. In the 1960s Communist Party block-workers kept track of the menstrual cycles of all women in their jurisdictions.

385 Source: https://www.dailymail.co.uk/news/article-2202574/Missionary-photos-early-1900s-life-China-years-imperial-rule.html.

386 ch23v7p3597.

387 He's known both as Mi Ziqian and Fu Buqi 宓子賤/宓不齊. See the *Lüshi Chunqiu* 呂氏春秋, chap. 108, *Jubei* 具備.

388 Source: https://commons.wikimedia.org/wiki/File:唐周昉调琴啜茗图.jpg.

389 ch2v1p162.

390 You can visit their ancient capital at Dali 大理 — many Chinese tourists will be there, too.

391 Source: https://en.wikipedia.org/wiki/Yi_people#/media/File:Yi_woman_in_traditional_dressing.jpg. The woman pictured here is Yi 彝 — the Nanzhao may have been Bai 白.

392 The Comprehensive Mirror as an Aid in Governance (*Zizhi tongjian* 資治通鑑) of Sima Guang 司馬光 (1019–86), *Tang ji* 唐記, §32.

393 Source: https://en.wikipedia.org/wiki/Yi_people#/media/File:Nanzhao.png.

394   Short for "flying feather call to arms." A millennium previous, a general inserted a feather in his letter of emergency recruitment, the phrase stuck. See the *Historical Records* (*Shiji* 史記), the biography of Han Xin 韓信, chap. 93, and Pei Yin's 裴駰 comments.

395   Source: http://s2.sinaimg.cn/orignal/46f178fenc423decd19e1. The photo's title is "Lushan Flying Feather Call-to-Arms" (*Lushan yanshuo feiyao guomin kangzhan tongfengqi* 廬山演說飛羽檄國民抗戰同風起). The caption reads:

> If warfare breaks out, then it makes no difference if you're north or south, young or old, no matter who you are, everyone has the responsibility to hold our ground and resist, everyone must resolve to give their whole heart.

396   For a discussion, see Schafer, *Pacing the Void,* 89ff.

397   Chap. 9.6a. "Heaven's Dog" migrates to Japan, where it takes up the role of *tengu,* long-nosed monster/protector:

Fig. 94. Source: https://commons.wikimedia.org/wiki/File:Karasu-Tengu-Statue.jpg.

398   Source: https://commons.wikimedia.org/wiki/File:%E6%9D%9C%E8%99%8E%E7%AC%A6.jpg.

399   The hero of the Roving Swordsman poem we translated in two chapters previous got his girlfriend to steal the king's half of the tally, so that he could deceive a general with a false order. (As you may recall, the general didn't fall for it, so they had to kill him anyway, but that tally got them in the door.)

400   The Celestial Palace is more literally a Purple Subtlety, *Ziwei* 紫微. But there's a bit more to it. *Zi,* purple, the magic color of the Emperor— these days you can see its approximation on the walls of the Imperial City, Beijing. But we imagine it more like this:

Fig. 95. The color purple.

More fundamentally, though, Zi is luminosity emerging from darkness. In his Dictionary, Paul Kroll writes that it's "associated emblematically with the depths of heaven, astral divinities, celestial phenomena, spectral visitations, cosmic totality and wholeness."

Wei is another beautiful word. It means hidden, slight, profound, subtle, that is, hard to find. It thus names that luminous limn between nothingness and somethingness, the circumstance in which shadowy *qi*-energies start assembling on their way to becoming the poetry of apparent phenomena. In Daoist lingo, between Naught and Aught, *wu* 無 and *you* 有. There's a divine host of possibilities hidden in that between, unknown to either extreme. In Taoist studies, wei is often translated "tenuity," for its subtlety. But I think it's more rugged than that.

The Emperor's palace is this Ziwei, but only in reflection. The real Ziwei is in the sky. It's the fifteen stars that surround and protect the Pole Star at the very center of Heaven. Thus Ziwei stands as well for that center, that star, and that star is also the Deity of Heaven, that ultimacy. And only in this sense is Ziwei also the physical abode of the earthly Son of Heaven, His Majesty. It's a kind of *enceinte* (in Schafer's words, *Pacing the Void,* 47 *et passim*), and see Paul Kroll, "Divine Songs of the Lady of Purple Tenuity," *Studies in Early Medieval Chinese Literature* (2003): 149–95, at 157. Here's how it looks — you can see the fifteen stars arcing around the Palace, with the Northern Dipper (*beidou* 北斗) at the bottom.

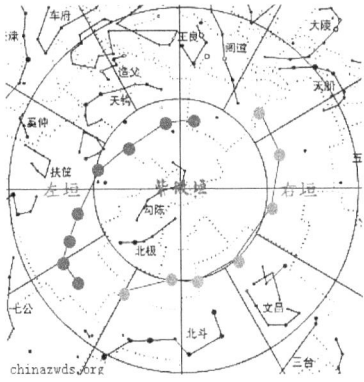

Fig. 96. The fifteen stars protecting the Pole Star.

A Han dynasty scholar explains how this works:

> The Deity of Heaven resides in Heaven the same way a ruler dwells on earth. The ruler dwells within a double barrier, and so it's appropriate that the Deity of Heaven should be inside a secret, hidden place. The ruler dwells within the buildings of his palace, and so Heaven also has its Great Subtle Purple Palace. (Wang Chong 王充, *Lunheng* 論衡, chap. 23 *Leixu* 雷

虛." Our thanks to Schafer for identifying this passage, *Pacing the Void*, 47.)

This Deity of Heaven is Taiyi 太一, the Great Singularity, Grand Monad, the ruler of everything. (Even if you don't know Chinese, you can read these two graphs: the first is a person with hands spread wide, the second is the numeral one.) In Highest Clarity Daoism, Taiyi resides in the head and also represents one's immortal identity or true self (*zhenwu* 真吾).

401 "Attain the One" is Laozi's phrase. See chap. 39 of his *Daodejing*.

402 See also his poem *Zhanchengnan* 戰城南 (*Jiwai shiwen* 集外詩文, v8p4449), which describes similar circumstances. Arthur Waley has translated it as "Fighting south of the ramparts" in *The Poetry and Career of Li Po*, 35.

403 This is the story of Chinese civilization on the move, the southward extension of a socio-logos of farming technology in every direction that geography would allow. A Chinese friend of mine had a Miao fabric posted on her office door. She said to me, "Don't you like this Chinese art?"

404 From the *Taiping yulan* 太平御覽 (part six of the *Huangwang* 皇王 section), also found in the *Yiwen leiju* 藝文類聚, chap. 11. This account of earliest times survives only in Tang-era collectania, but a number of pre-Imperial texts (the *Lüshi chunqiu* 呂氏春秋, the *Yantielun* 鹽鐵論, the *Hanfeizi* 韓非子, etc.) contain varyingly sanitized versions.

405 We have no direct knowledge of "the dance of shield and axe," but I imagine it as something like the Maori posture-dance, the haka, which you may have seen in the movie *Whale Rider*.

406 There are further ways to inscribe military disaster. This one is by Charles Minard (1781–1870), showing Napoleon's Rus-

sian catastrophe. An army of 480,000 went out, 10,000 came home. The width of the orange band shows their outflow, the black their return.

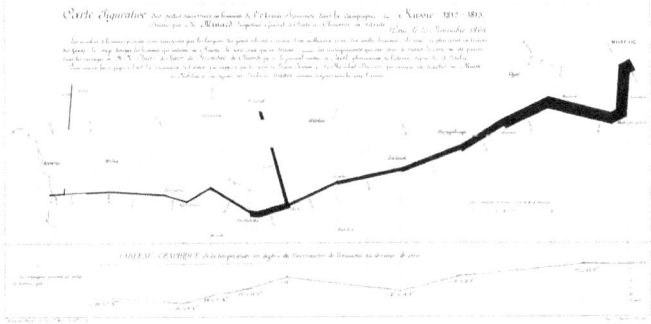

Fig. 97. Charles Minard's 1869 chart showing the number of men in Napoleon's 1812 Russian campaign army, their movements, as well as the temperature they encountered on the return path. Source: https://commons.wikimedia.org/wiki/File:Minard.png.

Edward Tufte, great genius of information design, points out that

> *Six* variables are plotted: the size of the army, its location on a two-dimensional surface, direction of the army's movement, and temperature on various dates during the retreat from Moscow. It may well be the best statistical graphic ever drawn. (*The Visual Display of Quantitative Information* [Cheshire: Graphics Press, 1983], 40)

Tufte's inquiry into what makes it so good: ibid., chap. 9 "Aesthetics and Technique in Data Graphical Design," 176ff.)

Étienne-Jules Marey: "It defies the pen of the historian in its brutal eloquence." (French scientist, physiologist and chronophotographer [1830–1904], as quoted in *Wikipedia,* "Minard," s.v.)

407   ch22v7p3414. Perhaps written in early 756, as the Rebellion sweeps over the Great Tang.

408   ch17v5p2729.

409   From the *Tangguoshibu* 唐國史補, chap. 3, story 100. I owe knowledge of this account, and all my knowledge of tea in China, to James Benn, *Tea in China: A Religious and Cultural History* (Honolulu: University of Hawai'i Press, 2015), where this story appears on page 46.

This king must be Trisong Detsen (r. 755–797), who had sent 200,000 troops into Chang'an in 763 and is said to have invited Padma Sambhava to Tibet to introduce the tantric teachings. Changlu ("Dzyanglu" in the Tang pronunciation) is unlikely to be Chinese, but I can't track him down.

410   Lu Yu, literatus, raised as a monk, devout Buddhist layman, proselytizer for tea, soon after his death apotheosized as the Patron Deity of Tea (*chashen* 茶神).

411   Benn, *Tea in China,* 42. For an affectionate telling of the far more elaborate wine parties, with board games, extensive drinking rules (including penalties for the infractors thereof), poetry competition, and untoward revelry, with its attendant material culture, see Donald Harper, "The *Analects* Jade Candle: A Classic of T'ang Drinking Custom," *T'ang Studies* 4 (1986): 69–93.

For another archeologically based account, this time of the Emperor's tea service utensils, see Patricia Karetzky, "Imperial Splendor in the Service of the Sacred: The Famen Tea Treasures," *T'ang Studies* 18–19 (2000–2001): 61–85.

For a problematization of using the categories "elite" and "popular" in Lu Yu's tea cult, see Jerry C.Y. Liu, "Between Classical and Popular: The Book of Tea and the Popularization of Tea-Drinking Culture in the Tang China," *The Journal of Popular Culture* 44, no. 1 (2011): 114–33.

412   ch25v7p3739.

ENDNOTES

413 The category is not so innocent: three of the women brought down a kingdom, dying in the process. China is afraid of vagina.

414 Li Bo's "Song of Roosting Crows" tells of her time with the King of Wu (*Wuqiqu* 烏栖曲, ch3v1p342). Arthur Waley translates it on page 48 of his *Poetry and Career of Li Po*. See also Li Bo's suite of songs on the beauties of Yue, *Yuenüci* 越女詞 (ch24v7p3733).

415 Following the account in *Mozi* 墨子, chap. 1.5, *Qinshi* 親士. It is often rumored that Li Bo was kicked out of the Bright Emperor's court because a poem of his compared the Precious Consort to Xi Shi.

416 ch4v2p571. Or do their hearts break? Or does Li Bo ask, "Why does this break my heart?"

417 Source: https://commons.wikimedia.org/wiki/File:Steinbach_Gustav_Mahler_Komponierh%C3%A4uschen_3.jpg.

418 For Ludwig Kärnbach.

419 ch19v4p1735.

420 For his title, "Revenue Manager," see Charles Hucker, *A Dictionary of Official Titles in Imperial China* (Stanford: Stanford University Press, 1985), #5643.

421 Now in southern Hunan, but the same latitude as Guilin 桂林, by the confluence of the Xiang and Xiao Rivers, where Shun's two wives had mourned his death.

422 Of Deng Deming 鄧德明 (fifth century), as preserved in the *Commentary on the Water Classic* (*Shuijing Zhu* 水經註) of

Li Daoyuan 酈道元 (466 or 472–527), the hydro-geography of China's river systems, chap. 37.

423   From Wang Qi, ch36v3p1641. The text is now incorporated in the *Huangshan zhi dingben* 黄山志定本 by Min Linci 閔麟嗣 of the Qing. Fragrant Springs lies in today's He Prefecture 和縣, Anhui Province, not far from the Yellow Mountains range.

424   For a fine summary, and this apt phrase, see Edwin Pulleyblank, *The Background of the Rebellion of An Lu-shan* (Oxford: Oxford University Press, 1955).

425   The view from Cambridgeshire:
   Twitchett: Li brought a "tidy and precise approach to problems of administration." *Cambridge History of China,* 3:415.
   And Pulleyblank, "He possessed qualities that were much rarer among the Chinese of those days than a knowledge of obscure expression or the ability to compose in the balanced style. He had a passion for order and system" (*The Background of the Rebellion of An Lu-shan,* 55).
   In another circumstance he would have made the trains run on time.

426   In Chapter 47 of this book, we've seen how Li Linfu had Li Bo's kinsman Li Yong beaten to death on an empty charge of treason.

427   His death, then, was "the real close of the brilliant epoch of Hsüan-tsung." See Pulleyblank, *The Background of the Rebellion of An Lu-shan,* 102–3.

428   On his way to power Yang had served as military governor in his homeland, the present-day Sichuan province. As we saw in Li Bo's poem on the Yunnan war, Chapter 48, it was Yang who sanctioned the disastrous southern campaign of 752 that resulted in 80,000 Chinese deaths.

429 Twitchett, *Cambridge History of China,* 3:449.

430 I have called this an error on Yang Guozhong's part. But it was not a random error or an accident. Theorists of accidents like H.W. Heinrich speak of a domino effect, where each factor leads to the next in necessary sequence. Here, instead, we have a congeries of contradictory tendencies, whose qualities are already built into a configuration of politics. If the disaster had not been triggered at Tong Pass, it would have found another means of expression.

431 Map by David Wright from "The Northern Frontier" (in David Graff, ed., *A Military History of China* [Lexington: University of Kentucky Press, 2012], 59).

432 See David Wright's very useful account. See also Wang Zhenping, *Tang China in Multi-Polar Asia: A History of Diplomacy and War* (Honolulu: University of Hawai'i Press, 2013).

433 For half of history, parts or all of China have been ruled by nomad conquerors. (Khubilai Khan is just the most famous of these.) See Thomas Barfield, *The Perilous Frontier: Nomadic Empires and China* (Cambridge: Basil Blackwell, 1989).

434 Turkic for khan of khans, king of kings. Thereupon thousands of leading Turkic families moved to Chang'an and assumed roles in government administration. See Wright, "The Northern Frontier," 68.

And for these strategic reasons alone, Chang'an, capital of the world's most powerful state, was located a hundred miles up a dry and agriculturally insufficient valley in China's northwest, where food must be imported from the richer South.

435 Jonathan Skaff, *Sui-Tang China and Its Turko-Mongol Neighbors: Culture, Power, and Connections, 580–800* (New York: Oxford University Press, 2012).

436 What Max Weber calls patrimonialism or patrimonial-bureaucratic government. See ibid., 276, who notes that these ideals "had sufficient legitimacy in the Tang Empire to be incorporated into the dynasty's eight canonical categories of loyalty" (ibid., 100).

437 Twitchett, *Cambridge History of China,* 3:443. And see S.A.M. Adshead, *T'ang China: The Rise of the East in World History* (New York: Palgrave Macmillan, 2004), which argues that at this moment the Great Tang held hegemony in Eurasia.

Students of foreign policy and war argue about the relationship between *Realpolitik* and native cultural styles. In *Cultural Realism: Strategic Culture and Grand Strategy in Chinese History,* Alastair Iain Johnston establishes their inextricability, with a case study of Ming dynasty relations with the steppe (Princeton: Princeton University Press, 1998).

438 *Xuanhe shu [hua] pu* 宣和書/畫譜, the catalogue of Song imperial archives of painting and calligraphy, quoted in Wang Qi ch36v3p1653.

439 And it was the steppeland Manchus who got it back for them, as the multi-ethnic Qing dynasty (1644–1911).

440 Pulleyblank has clarified this in his chap. 2, "The Origins of An Lu-shan." Sogdiana, an Indo-European-language speaking kingdom centered on Bactria and Samarkand. On the Sogdians, see Étienne de la Vaissière, *Histoire des marchands sogdiens* (Paris: Bibliotèque de l'institut des hautes études chinoises, 2002), translated by James Ward as *Sogdian Traders: A History* (Leiden: Brill, 2005).

441 Which is the name of Alexander the Great's third wife, princess of Bactria. See Pulleyblank, *The Background of the Rebellion of An Lu-shan* ,15.

442 Source http://www.sothebys.com/fr/auctions/ecatalogue/2015/important-chinese-art-n09393/lot.258.html. At Sotheby's estimated between $180.000–250.000.

443 See his biography in the *Old Tang History*, which has been translated by Howard Levy as *Biography of An Lu-shan* (Berkeley: University of California Press, 1960).

444 *Zizhitongjian kaoyi* 資治通鑑考異, for year Kaiyuan 24, month 4, translated by Pulleyblank, *The Background of the Rebellion of An Lu-shan,* 22. See also 116n67.

445 See Pulleyblank, *The Background of the Rebellion of An Lu-shan,* 84 and 162n15.

446 *JiuTangshu,* chap. 200.

447 Pulleyblank, *The Background of the Rebellion of An Lushan,* 56.

448 *JiuTangshu,* chap. 200.

449 "In Hook's his dark nature there was a touch of the feminine, as in all the great pirates, and it sometimes gave him intuitions." (J.M. Barrie, *Peter Pan* [New York: Penguin, 1938], chap. 8, "The Mermaid's Lagoon")

450 A pun. The phrase is "to wash good fortune into the baby," but "good fortune" is written with the same "lu" as An Lushan's name.

451 *Zizhi tongjian* 資治通鑑, chap. 216.

452 How much is that? Well, by the usual conversion, it's only 170 pounds avoirdupois. I'm a skinny white guy, and I weigh that much — there must be some error in the record. "Catty

(*kati*)" is a Malay word (like "Mandarin") that found its way into early Sino-European pidgeon.

453 *JiuTangshu,* chap. 200. Perhaps he suffered from diabetes, which might have then affected his eyesight.

454 And thus it's said the Mongol siege of Vienna failed only when Ögedei, the Great Khan, died in 1241, and the hordes were recalled to determine his successor.

455 "Even Li Shimin's rise to power through fratricide had more in common with the succession practices of the steppe than with those of Chinese tradition" — this is Mark Lewis, *China's Cosmopolitan Empire: The Tang Dynasty* (Cambridge: Harvard University Press, 2009), 150, drawing on Barfield, *The Perilous Frontier,* 139–44, and Pan Yihong, *Son of Heaven and Heavenly Qaghan* (Bellingham: Western Washington University Press, 1997), 181.

Thus a parallel overstatement from the great Japanese Sinologist Naitō Kōnan, in its summary by Hisayuki Miyakawa:

> On his throne the Emperor was a representative of the aristocracy — the imperial position was its organ. He was, as it were, the common property of his aristocratic family and relatives. They could enthrone him, depose him, or murder him. ("An Outline of the Naitō Hypothesis and Its Effects on Japanese Studies of China," *The Journal of Asian Studies* 14, no. 4 [1955]: 533–52)

456 So perhaps this is why the Bright Emperor didn't suspect him of disloyalty. An Lushan was completely loyal as long as power was properly wielded.

457 There were no particular economic causes to the Rebellion. Thus a Marxian analysis would resemble *The Eighteenth Brumaire of Louis Napoleon* rather than *A Contribution to the Critique of Political Economy.*

458 An example of the first is one of China's most famous poems, Bo Juyi's 白居易 "Song of Long-lasting Regret" (*Changhen'ge* 長恨歌). Regretfully, I would suggest that the poem reduces their relationship to a love story, with a bit of aestheticized religion thrown in at the end. A good translation is Paul Kroll, "Po Chü-i's 'Song of Lasting Regret': A New Translation," *T'ang Studies* 8–9 (1990–91): 97–105.

An example of the second is "Tales from the Tianbao Era in All Keys and Modes" (*Tianbao yishi zhugongdiao* 天寶遺事諸宮調), a chantefable that Chen Fan-pen believes to have been performed primarily in expensive brothels. See her "Yang kuei-fei in Tales from the T'ien-Pao Era: A Chu-kung-tiao Narrative," *Journal of Sung-Yuan Studies* 22 (1990–92): 1–22.

Paul Kroll has collected other, more nuanced poems in "Recalling Xuanzong and Lady Yang: A Selection of Mid- and Late Tang Poems," *T'ang Studies* 35 (2017): 1–19.

The historians' silence: see Fan-pen Chen, "Problems of Chinese Historiography as Seen in the Official Records on Yang Kuei-fei," *T'ang Studies* 8–9 (1990–91): 83–96.

The historians' silence: knowing the power of words, they could not bear to name the event. For this power of naming, see Ernst Cassirer, *Language and Myth* (New York: Dover, 1946 [1925]). Or the silence of Margaret Meade's Trobriand Islanders when they were asked about incest and rape.

459 If we properly understand Herbert Fingarette's discussion of Confucius, a better translation would be "The Bureau of Ritual Magic." See his *Confucius: The Secular as Sacred* (New York: Harper and Row, 1972).

460 *Jiu Tangshu,* ch 51. Certeau would claim that history begins with separation — of the present from the past, the living from the dead — an alienation that the historian must overcome through rhetoric. But these people are not dead — you can ask them about each other, the way the Bright Emperor offers oblations to the Precious Consort after her death. In Li Bo's poetry as well, past and present share a single ontology. See Michel de

Certeau, *The Writing of History* (New York: Columbia University Press, 1988).

461 Once more we have problems with our sources. Denis Twitchett explains how our knowledge of the Emperor derives from a single text, the *State History* (*Guoshi* 國史) of Liu Fang 柳芳 of the year 760, and why that account is unreliable:

> Liu Fang was writing under singularly difficult political conditions. He was working at the command of the new emperor Su-tsung, who had deposed Hsüan-tsung by a flagrant act of usurpation, and needed to present the last years of his father's reign as a period of misgovernment in order to provide some moral justification for his act. Meanwhile, however, Hsüan-tsung himself was still alive, and many of the leading figures of his latter years were still active and in positions of power. […]
> The resulting account of Hsüan-tsung's reign is thus a patchy one. It is well documented and generally favourable until about 741, but comparatively slender and extremely critical in tone for the last years of the reign.

The other contemporary records were lost in the fires of Chang'an. And thus the *Old* and *New Tang Histories* and the *Comprehensive Mirror* are similarly dependent on Liu Fang. (Twitchett, *Cambridge History of China,* 3:463.)

462 Twitchett:

> He was still only twenty-eight years old, and the three years of vicious political intrigue and constant struggle which he had experienced since he led the coup against the empress Wei form a prologue indivisible from the political history of his reign and had a lasting effect upon his conduct of the empire's affairs. (Ibid., 3:345)

463 Ibid., 3:373. For Li Bo's poem on cockfights, see Robert Joe Cutter, *The Brush and the Spur: Chinese Culture and the Cock Fight* (Hong Kong: Chinese University Press, 1989), 65ff.

464 Chinese dates are not assigned against a specific reference point, such as the Hegira of Mohammed. Rather, they are points within a period within a specific emperor's reign. Thus the Bright Emperor called his first period Kaiyuan 開元, "Opening the primal," and Kaiyuan 1 marks our year 713.

465 Twitchett, *Cambridge History of China,* 3:421.

466 A poet's image may be apt here: "We are extending constantly, expanding like a flood or an earthquake. There is a sense of spreading, shaking the earth, and creating more and more cracks in it." Chögyam Trungpa, *Journey without Goal* (Boston: Shambhala, 2000), 80.

467 See Wilhelm Reich, most conveniently *The Murder of Christ* (New York: Farrar, Straus and Giroux, 1953).

468 Source: https://en.wikipedia.org/wiki/Tang_dynasty#/media/File:Gilt_silver_jar_with_pattern_of_dancing_horses.jpg.

469 James Hillman's *Terrible Love of War* begins:

> One sentence in one scene from one film, Patton, sums up what this book tries to understand. The general walks the field after a battle. Churned earth, burnt tanks, dead men. He takes up a dying officer, kisses him, surveys the havoc, and says, "I love it. God help me I do love it so. I love it more than my life."

And: "The whole bloody business reveals a god, therewith placing war among the authentic phenomena of religion. And that is why it is so terrible, so loved, and so hard to understand" (*A

Terrible Love of War [New York: Penguin, 1988], 83). The French *guerre* (and its Romance language cognates) derives from the Germanic word we have in English as "war," because of the confusion around Latin's *bello/bella*.

470   Only deeply similar beings can deeply wound each other. When NASA brought rocks back from the moon, they sequestered them against the risk of bacteriological hazards. But the possibility of such infection requires millennia of prior intimacy.

471   The first was Śubhākarasiṃha (*Shanwuwei* 善無畏 [637–735]), the second Vajrabodhi (*Jin'gangzhi* 金剛智 [671–741]), with whom Amoghavajra apprenticed in his teens.

472   For these and other details, see Geofrey Goble, *Chinese Esoteric Buddhism: Amoghavajra and the Ruling Elite* (Ph.D. diss., Indiana University, 2012), 62–63. On page 124 he translates a story from chapter 8 of the *Taiping guangji* 太平廣記 telling of Amoghavajra's rain making abilities, which apparently drowned a few people across town:

> In the courtyard of the temple, he hastily constructed five or six plaster dragons, then sprinkled them with water and scolded them in a barbarian language (*huyan* 胡言). After a long time he dismissed them and laughed. In a little while there was a cessation of rain.

473   *Cefu yuangui* 冊府元龜, chap. 53.

474   Ibid.

475   The text was several times carved in stone. For an informed instrumentalist sketch of these developments, see Barrett, *Taoism under the T'ang*, 54–73.

476 Ibid., 59. For the music, costumes and gestures, see Edward Schafer, "The Dance of the Purple Culmen," *T'ang Studies* 5 (1987): 45–68.

477 "Preface to the Bright Emperor's Commentary on the Laozi" (*Tang Xuanzong yuzhu Daodejing xu* 唐玄宗御註道德經序).

478 Charisma, in Weber's sense of an authority deriving from the divine.

479 See, *inter alia,* Lin Lu-tche, *Le règne de l'empereur Hiuan-tsong,* trans. Robert des Rotours (Paris: Collège de France, 1981), 240:

> Comme l'empereur Hiuan-tsong était depuis longtemps au pouvoir, petit à petit il s'abandonna à des désires extravagants and négligea les affairs gouvernmentales.

> The Emperor, having been so long in power, bit by bit abandoned himself to extravagant desires and neglected government affairs.

480 Lewis, *China's Cosmopolitan Empire,* 40.

481 *Cambridge History,* 413.

482 See Abraham Maslow's 1943 article, "A Theory of Human Motivation," variously reprinted.

483 Ryan Flaherty, "Craquelure," *Conjunctions* 58 (2012): 303–10. You might also read David Jones, *In Parenthesis* (London: Faber & Faber, 1937).

484 David Graff, *Medieval Chinese Warfare 300–900,* quoted in Flaherty, "Craquelure," 304.

485 See John D. Durand, "The Population Statistics of China, A.D. 2–1953," *Population Studies* 13, no. 3 (1960): 209–56.

486 *The Oxford Dictionary of Phrase and Fable* attributes the saying to both him and Frederick the Great. Already in the late first millennium BCE, Sunzi's *Art of War* recommends living off the land. For the best study of this question in the early periods, see Donald W. Engels, *Alexander the Great and the Logistics of the Macedonian Army* (Berkeley: University of California Press, 1978).

487 I wish I could write of their daily life with the intimacy and warmth of Braudel. The human faces within the market, the simultaneity of small and large scales, the smells. "I may have taken too much pleasure in these details," is his faux-confession in *Afterthoughts on Material Civilization and Capitalism* (Baltimore: Johns Hopkins University Press, 1977), 20. The subtitle of volume one, omitted in the English-language edition, is "The possible and the impossible: men face to face with their daily life" (ibid., 6). Our own book would be very different had it been written in French.

488 When we eat red meat, as I do almost every day, we participate in this killing.

489 Source: https://www.metmuseum.org/art/collection/search/56153; https://www.metmuseum.org/art/collection/search/56152; https://www.metmuseum.org/art/collection/search/56154.

490 Kroll, "The Dancing Horses," 102–3. Natasha Heller tells us of the elephants and rhinoceros that the Bright Emperor had received in tribute. An Lushan captured them, and he

> was certain that the animals would bow to him as the new emperor, thus demonstrating that all under heaven would recognize his rule. However, the elephants failed to kneel

when they were brought in, sending him into a fury. He ordered all the animals to be thrown in a pit, where they were stabbed and set afire. ("Why Has the Rhinoceros Come from the West? An Excursus into the Religious, Literary, and Environmental History of the Tang Dynasty," *Journal of the American Oriental Society* 131.3 [2011], 353–70, at 359–60)

491 Peter Bol, *This Culture of Ours* (Stanford: Stanford University Press, 1992), 3.

492 And thus

> Knowing what was good and doing good were matters not of knowing the right forms to imitate but of having the right ideas in mind. This effort, which made ideas more real than culture and which required that each man think for himself and write in a style true to his understanding, undermined the goal of a shared, normative culture to serve as the basis for civil order. As long as the excitement of breaking with convention and several hundred years of cumulative tradition lasted, only a few worried about the consequences of doing away with universal cultural models, for the new ideas about learning promised to enable all shih [the literate elite] to transformed themselves into self-conscious, morally independent men of intellectual integrity. (Ibid., 109)

493 For an excellent introduction, see Stephen Owen, *The End of the Chinese "Middle Ages"* (Stanford: Stanford University Press, 1996), to be read in conjunction with the review by William H. Nienhauser in the *Harvard Journal of Asiatic Studies* 58, no. 1 (1998): 287–310.

494 Marc Ambramson, *Ethnic Identity in Tang China* (Philadelphia: University of Pennsylvania Press, 2008), 144–48.

495 Ibid., ix.

496 The first to note this was the Japanese Sinologist Naitō Kōnan, a good century ago. See the convenient summary of his ideas in Miyakawa, "An Outline of the Naitō Hypothesis and its Effects on Japanese Studies of China."

497 This section is entirely in the debt of Geoffrey Goble and his revealing dissertation, *Chinese Esoteric Buddhism*, now a book of this name published by Columbia University Press.

498 Discounting rumors of an Indian father, Goble demonstrates his likely Sogdian parentage — his mother was surnamed Kang 康, suggesting she was from Samarkand. On the presence of that city in the Tang imagination, see Schafer, *The Golden Peaches of Samarkand*.

499 This is also the time of Padma Sambhava's visit to the Tibet of King Trisong Detsen (r. 755–797), as we saw in Chapter 50, "Tea."

500 Goble, *Chinese Esoteric Buddhism*, 132. For an account of how Amoghavajra not only commands but becomes the deity, see Koichi Shinohara, *Spells, Images, and Mandalas: Tracing the Evolution of Esoteric Buddhist Rituals* (New York: Columbia University Press, 2014). Paul Copp discusses Amoghavajra's transformation of *dhāranī* from incantory spells into corporal modes of power (see *The Body Incantatory: Spells and the Ritual Imagination in Medieval Chinese Buddhism* [New York: Columbia University Press, 2014), esp. chap. 2].

501 Ibid.

502 In the traditional description:

His face is expressive of extreme wrath, wrinkle-browed, left eye squinted or looking askance, lower teeth biting down the upper lip. He has the physique of a corpulent child. He bears a straight sword in his right hand, and a lariat or noose in his left. He is engulfed in flame, and seated on a huge rock base. (*Wikipedia*, "Acala," s.v.)

503   Source   https://commons.wikimedia.org/wiki/File:%E4%B8%8D%E5%8B%95%E6%98%8E%E7%8E%8B%E5%9D%90%E5%83%8F-Fud%C5%8D_My%C5%8D%C5%8D_MET_DP356182.jpg.

504   Goble, *Chinese Esoteric Buddhism,* 158 quoting the Trisamaye II (T 21.1200).

505   Ibid, 160.

506   See Edwin G. Pulleyblank "The An Lu-shan Rebellion and the Origins of Chronic Militarism in Late T'ang China," in *Essays on Tang and Pre-Tang History* (Aldershot: Ashgate, 2001), 33–60.

507   *Old Tang History,* chap. 68, citing the *Sutra of Humane Kings* (*Renwang jing* 仁王經).

508   Goble, *Chinese Esoteric Buddhism,* 160.

509   Manling Luo, "Remembering Kaiyuan and Tianbao: The Construction of Mosaic Memory in Medieval Historical Miscellanies," *T'oung Pao* 97 (2011): 263–300.

510   Or an infinite netting with diamonds at every knot, reflecting every other knot. Like this:

Fig. 98. Yayoi Kusama's *Infinity Room* in the Hirschhorn Museum.

On Fazang, see Jinhua Chen, *Philosopher, Practitioner, Politician: The Many Lives of Fazang (643–712)* (Leiden: Brill, 2007).

511 See the brief account in the *Routledge Encyclopedia of Philosophy*, summarizing the argument of *A Treatise of Human Nature*, 1.3.14. It all comes down to how you hold time. Hume might appreciate Ed Dorn's point in *Gunslinger* (Durham: Duke University Press, 1989 [1968]), 11, the Madame speaking,

> and this Texan insisted he was
> payin for my girl's time
> and he could use it any way he
> saw fit
> as long as he was payin like
> and I had to explain
> a technical point to that Shareholder namely,
> that he was payin for
> her *ass*, which is not time!

512 OK, what he actually said was *shishi wuai* 事事無礙, "mutually interpenetrating non-obstruction," because appearances aren't in conflict — his song about Joe Schmo came later. This circumvents Hume's demands that the two events of cause and effect be proximate in space. A modern philosopher explains it this way: "According to Hume, if I throw a rock, and at that moment someone's window in China breaks, I would not conclude that my rock broke a window on the other side of the world" (http://www.iep.utm.edu/hume/#SH3b). Hmmm.

513

Fig. 99. Kali Puja at Roy Chowdhury House at Barasat. Source: https://en.wikipedia.org/wiki/Kali_Puja#/media/File:Kali_Fatakeshto_Arnab_Dutta_2010.JPG.

514 Philip Whalen, *The Collected Poems of Philip Whalen* (Middletown: Wesleyan University Press, 2007), 105–6.

515 Paul Kroll, "The Flight from the Capital and the Death of the Precious Consort," *T'ang Studies* 3 (1985): 25–53.

516 The title of Sima Guang's work, the first universal history of China in 1300 years, is *The Comprehensive Mirror to Aid in Governance* (*Zizhi tongjian* 資治通鑑). This excerpt is from chapter 218. Among other things, Sima's history is a status-based argument for an Emperorship responsive to the remonstrances of scholar-officials like himself. One bête-noire is the magical maneuvers of rulers like the Bright Emperor. The Mawei executions are, then, a moment for Sima Guang to voice own his views through the words of a Tang official, who spoke thus:

> "That An Lushan embraced and laid up dire intentions was assuredly not a matter of only a single day. And yet, when there were those who came directly to the palace pylons to report of his schemes, Your Majesty time and again punished them, thus bringing it about that he has been able to carry out his treacherous revolt to the fullest degree and resulting in Your Majesty' s exodus and flight. Presumably it was in regard to situations of just this sort that the Former Kings made an effort to draw out and call upon the loyal and the well-born, so as to broaden their own insight and perception. But those vassals who have resided at court have regarded such utterances as ineffable, only ingratiating themselves through flattery and blandishments. Owing to this, Your Majesty has not in any instance been able to be cognizant of affairs outside the gates and pylons of the palace. Even your subjects in the weedy countryside have recognized certainly that this day was coming for a long time."
>
> His Highness said, "This is due to Our dim-sightedness, and Our regrets have nowhere else to extend," and, with a consoling injunction, sent him away.

Sima Guang's model Emperor is a Yes Man.

517 See Mao Zedong, "On Contradiction" (Beijing: Foreign Languages Press, 1967 [1937]), 18: "Man's knowledge of matter is knowledge of its forms of motion, because there is nothing in this world except matter in motion and this motion must assume certain forms."

518 In Japanese Zen, the kōan student hopes to meet a similar moment, when his whole life-identity may be shattered like crystal skeet by a single blow of the master's stick, Bright Emptiness.

519 Close eleventh-century copy of an eighth-century composition. https://archive.shine.cn/sunday/now-and-then/Emperor-Xuanzongs-Journey-to-Shu/shdaily.shtml

520 See *The Book of Documents* (*Shangshu* 尚書).

521 The *Bamboo Annals* (*Zhushu ji'nian* 竹書紀年).

522 ch3v1p267. Like the late quartets, this poem is among the most analyzed in the literature. Editor Zhan Ying has collected some two dozen of these discussions, 273–81.

523 ch3v1p290. See Paul Kroll, "The Road to Shu, from Zhang Zai to Li Bo," *Early Medieval China* 10–11 (2004): 227–54.
  The opening line, "Aiyiiieyaw!", is in Sichuan dialect, a startlement, a surprise, only sound, the first emergence of poetry before its surrender to words. It's how appearance shows its lingerie to itself, in light, sound, touch. Then Li Bo weaves these into a human language. But that language isn't oriented to nouns and pronouns, such as "Li Bo" or "you" and "I."

524 ch7v3p1178.

525 Recorded as early as *The Book of Documents* (*Shangshu* 尚書) of the first millennium BCE. For these practices in the preceding Shang dynasty, see David Keightley, "The Late Shang State," where the king "displayed his power in frequent travel, hunting and inspecting along the pathways of his realm […] moving through a landscape pregnant with symbolic meaning, giving and receiving power at each holy place," in Keightley, *The Origins of Chinese Civilization* (Berkeley: University of California Press,1983), 552, as quoted in James Robson, *Religious Landscapes,* 32.

526 It was first secured in the third century by the great magus-strategist Zhuge Liang 諸葛亮 (181–234).

527 Source: https://commons.wikimedia.org/wiki/File:Jianmenguan.JPG.

528 In 280 of the Common Era the official Zhang Zai 張載 (no dates) visited his father in Shu and wrote this as an inscription, the *Jian'ge ming* 劍閣銘.

529 Li Shan 李善, his annotation to Pan Yue's 潘岳 poem, "Rhapsody on the Western Excursion" (*Xizheng fu* 西征賦) in the Wenxuan.

530 Schafer, *Pacing the Void,* 120, man and star inseparable, "the one regarded as fused with the other."

531 Zhan Ying, quoting Yang Qixian 楊齊賢 (of the Song), 1196.

532 I stole that phrase from the great eleventh-century compendium of Daoist texts, the *Yunji qiqian* 雲笈七籤 (Seven lots from the bookbag of the clouds) by Zhang Junfang 張君房, who in turn got it from the lore.

533 Another poem on Mount Hua can be found in the "Five Mountains" section of this book.

534 ch2v1p104.

535 See Edward Schafer, "Notes on Mica in Medieval China," *T'oung Pao* 43, no. 1 (1955): 265–86.

536 Chapter 8. For a longer story, see Campany, *To Live as Long as Heaven and Earth,* 271–72.

537 Source: https://artofninzuwu.com/2014/12/26/the-paces-of-yu-the-shamans-steps-and-ame-no-ukihashi/. Associated from the beginning with the sage-emperor Yu 禹. For a summary, see Schafer, *Pacing the Void,* 238–42. See also Poul Andersen, *Taoist Ritual Texts and Traditions with Special Reference to Bugang, the Cosmic Dance* (Ph.D. diss., University of Copenhagen, 1991). Li Bo says more literally that they "voidly pace" (*xubu* 虛步), but this must also be *xubu,* the pacing out of the void.

Douglas Penick writes: "Mushroom cloud burgeons. I see Li Bo on the shore, only making out what it is at the last possible moment."

538 ch26v7p4002. For an account of letters' literary, material, and social contexts, see Antje Richter, *Letters and Epistolary Culture in Early Medieval China* (Seattle: University of Washington Press, 2013) and also her *A History of Chinese Letters and Epistolary Culture* (Leiden: Brill, 2015).

539 That official is Huangfu Shen 皇甫侁. The *New Tang History,* chap. 82, recounts:

> Before the Prince had been captured, his father, the Retired Emperor, had proclaimed, "I degrade him to commoner status, with his sentence of banishment commuted to confinement within the palace." When the Prince had been killed, Huangfu Shen hastily sent the Prince's wife to the Retired

Emperor in Sichuan. The Retired Emperor grieved the longest time.

The Prince's older brother, the new Emperor Suzong, had raised the Prince himself, after his mother had died. He never publicly denounced his crime. He said to his followers, "How could it be that Huangfu Shen seized my younger brother and killed him instead of sending him to Sichuan?" After that he never appointed Huangfu to another post.

540 Waley, *The Poetry and Career of Li Po,* 79 and 80. The poem is *Zai shuijun yan zeng mufu zhushiyu* 在水軍宴贈幕府諸侍御, ch9v3p1601. The Dragon Pool Sword (*longyuan jian* 龍淵劍) was made by Ou Yezi 歐冶子 and Gan Jiang 干將 for the King of Chu more than a thousand years earlier. Looking at its blade is like seeing dragons swimming in a pool.

Albert Dalia has written a historical novel of Li Bo, this sword, and the Yangtze River, starring a blond ghost and a monkey who is usually drunk and functions as ghost hunter. It's *Dream of the Dragon Pool: A Daoist Quest* (New York: Pleasure Boat Studio, 2007).

541 Waley, *The Poetry and Career of Li Po,* 79–80, from the poem "After Having Escaped the Rebellion, by Heaven's Grace Going to Yelang, Remembering Our Old Roaming, Offered to Censor Wei Liangzai of Jiangxia" (*Jingluanli hou, tianen liu Yelang, yijiusyou shuhuai zeng Jiangxia Weitaishou liangzai* 經亂離後，天恩流夜郎，憶舊游書懷贈江夏韋太守良宰), ch10v4p1666.

542 ch10v4p1638.

543 ch10v4p1646.

544 "A Petition of Self-recommendation Written for Censor Song" (*Wei Song Zhongcheng zijian biao* 為宋中丞自薦表, ch26v7p3966), see Waley, *The Poetry and Career of Li Po,* 84–85.

545   On this power of language, see Charles Hammond, "Ultimate Truths: Tang Poetry as Magical Discourse," *Journal of Oriental Studies* 29, no. 1 (1991): 19–44.

546   ch30v8p4393. For a willingness to acknowledge the Yellow River as a living being, still in the 1930s and '40s, see Micah Muscolino, *The Ecology of War: Henan Province, the Yellow River, and Beyond* (New York: Columbia University Press, 2015). Muscolino explains, "The Yellow River was no passive object" (23).

547   For these years, see Guo Moruo, *Li Bai yu Du Fu* 李白與杜甫, 126ff. and Yu Xianhao, "*Li Bo wannian xingji ji sixiang kaolun* 李白晚年行跡及思想考論" in his *Li Bo yu Tangdai wenshi kaolun* 李白與唐代文史考論, 114–39. See also Waley, *The Poetry and Career of Li Po,* 85–97.

548   ch13v4p2101. This poem has always attracted a lot of attention. Yu Xianhao 郁賢皓 reports on a 1999 international conference devoted to it in "'Li Bai yu Tianmu guoji xueshu yanjiu taohui zhuanji' xu 李白與天姥國際學術討會專輯序," in his *Li Bai yu Tangdai wenshi kaolun* 李白與唐代文史考論 [Essays on Li Bo and the literary history of the Tang] (Nanjing: Nanjing shifan daxue chubanshe 南京師範大學出版社: 2007), 712–13. See also the pioneering essay of Elling Eide, "On Li Po," in *Perspectives on the T'ang,* ed. Arthur Wright (New Haven: Yale University Press, 1973), 367–403.

549   Source: https://commons.wikimedia.org/wiki/File:Fuding_-_Dianxia_Zhen_-_P1220446.JPG

550   But that text's "Nine Songs" (*Jiuge* 九歌) and other plaints are present throughout this poem.

551   That mountain is the Continent of Ying, Yingzhou 瀛洲, east by some 700,000 *li*. As Dongfang Shuo, describes it, the Queen Mother of the West has just spoken to the Martial

Emperor of Han about Yingzhou, and the Emperor finally realizes that Dongfang Shuo has actually been there — that he is no ordinary person. The Emperor then invites Shuo into his private chambers to hear more. *The Record of the Ten Continents* (*Shizhou ji* 十洲記) transcribes their conversation:

> Yingzhou is in the middle of the Eastern Sea. Its land is four thousand li square. It's across from Yue, 700,000 *li* to the west. On its upper reach grow divine mushrooms and the plants of immortality. There's also a jade rock, over ten-thousand feet tall. From it emerges a spring with water like sweet-flavored wine, named Jade Sweet Spring. If you drink it, you get drunk after only several pints. It confers long life. There are many immortals on this continent, and their customs are similar to the people of Wu. Its mountains and rivers are like those of the Central States.

Rob Campany, who has studied these matters extensively, supposes that the *Records of the Ten Continents* "consists of a core of Han-era material around which later accretions formed; the text as we have it was probably formed around 300 C.E." He suspects that at an earlier point the text had been part of *The Esoteric Biography of Emperor Wu of the Han* (*Han Wudi neizhuan* 漢武帝內轉). See his *Strange Writing*, 53.

552　The Duke is Xie Lingyun 謝靈運 (385–433). From his much longer "Climbing Mount Linhai" (*Deng Linhaiqiao* 登臨海嶠). Once before Li Bo had also headed out to Sharp Stream, but it was already Tianmu that he was hoping to reach on some future day:

> As we part, I turn toward Tianmu,
> I'll brush off her rocks and sleep on the autumn frost.

辭君向天姥，拂石臥秋霜

From "Parting from Chu Yong on My Way to Sharp Stream" (*Bie Chu Yong zhi Yanzhong* 別儲邕之剡中), ch13v4p2177.

553 Elling Eide hears the sound of these shoes in Li Bo's line "Wearing Duke Xie's Clogs" 腳著謝公屐, in Tang pronunciation something like "kjak djak zia kung giok," "On Li Po," 375.

554 A picture of woman emphasizing her breasts. Attested from ca. 1000 BCE. Karlgren, *Grammata Serica Recensa,* no. 947.

555 The earliest known use is by his grandfather, the great calligrapher Wang Xizhi 王羲之 (303–61), he's trying to buy a goose from an Old Woman (*mu* 姥). See his biography in the *Jin History* 晉書, chap. 15. Wang lived just north of the mountain, and he's the one who gave Mirror Lake its name.

For associations of Mu with the Southeast, see, *inter alia:*

1. "In the south, on New Year's Eve, before they launch their boats, they kill a chicken and do divination with its bones, according to the old ways. If the prognostication is auspicious, they offer the meat to the Deity of the Boats, calling on the Primal Old Man and the Primal Old Woman (*mengmu* 孟姥)." From Duan Gonglu 段公路 (of the Tang), the *Beihulu* 北戶錄 (Record of the northern peoples), chapter on chicken bone divination (*Jigu bu* 雞骨卜).
2. When the Bright Emperor of Jin (rg. 323–26) is setting out on a perilous military expedition, he suddenly encounters an Old Woman (*mu* 姥) selling food at a shop along the road. He asks for her blessing. "She is not an ordinary person," he concludes. From *A New Telling of Tales of the World* (*Shishuo xinyu* 世說新語), chap. 27 "Cunning Tricks" (*Jiajue* 假譎).
3. In his account of the Sui ruler Wendi 文帝, Sima Guang says that the Crown Prince often had an Old Woman Master do divination for him (Kaihuang 開皇 year 20, 600 CE). The commentator Hu Sanxing 胡三省 (fl. 1250s) explains that "An Old Woman Master (*shimu* 師姥) is a woman shaman.

Mu is what you call an old woman — I can't explain it more than that."

556 "Speakers of Austronesian languages appear to have originated in the province of Fujian in China and the nearby island of Taiwan" (Ward Goodenough, "Introduction" *Transactions of the American Philosophical Society* 86, no. 5, special issue "Prehistoric Settlement of the Pacific" [1996]: 1–10, at 3), but by the first millennium BCE they occupied much of the lower Yangtze basin. Han, Tang and later dynasties pushed them further south, though they took their name with them — Yue or Yuet — landing now in what we call Vietnam, or "Yuet-nan (Yuet-South)." A number of Yue cultural practices, "such as tooth extraction, pile building, and cliff burial, continued until relatively recent times in places such as Taiwan" (*Wikipedia*, "Yue (State)," s.v.). See Erica Fox Brindley, *Ancient China and the Yue: Perceptions and Identities on the Southern Frontier* (Cambridge: Cambridge University Press, 2015).

Luo Jierui 羅傑瑞 (Jerry Norman) finds this Mu in Fujian and Taiwan dialects still today. See his *Hanyu gaikuang* 漢語概況 [Overview of Chinese language] (published in English as *Chinese* [Cambridge: Cambridge University Press, 1988]), as quoted in Ding Bangxin 丁邦新, *Minyu yanjiu ji qi yu zhoubian fangyan de guanxi* 閩語研究及其與周邊方言的關係 [Researches on Min language and its relationship to other dialects] (Hong Kong: Chinese University Press, 2002), 24.

Marc Miyake addresses the question of how foreign words enter the Chinese language in his "Loanwords — Post-Qin, Pre-Modern," in *Encyclopedia of Chinese Language and Linguistics*, ed. Rint Sybesma (Leiden and Boston: Brill, 2017), 647–50, though he only analyzes influences from the west and north.

The regime-changing beauty Xi Shi is from Yue.

557 Though when it enters standard Chinese in the immediate pre-Tang period, it loses its attendant magic prowess and retains only the meaning of a female elder or, more generally, the mother of an adult male. See Gunabadra (394–468), *Pronuncia-*

tion and Meaning in All the Sutras (*Yiqieijing yinyi* 一切經音義), who defines mu simply as "a woman elder," and the *Yuanbao jing* 元包經 (The classic of the primordial bundle, modeled on Yang Xiong's 楊雄 *Taixuan jing* 太玄經) of Wei Yuansong 魏元嵩 (fl. 560–580), which pairs her with *gong* 公, a male elder.

558   And thus she avoids incorporation into the Heavenly *Mother*, also pronounced Tianmu 天母. That name usually indicates the pan-Empire Queen Mother of the West (Xiwangmu 西王母), but the Heavenly Mother also appears in several Daoist scriptures under the name Purple Aura Heavenly Mother, Ziguang Tianmu 紫光天母. When she's bathing naked, "nine lotus blossoms unfold, from which [the nine stars of the Northern Dipper] are born." See the The true and unsurpassed Lingbao scripture from the *Jade-Clear Heaven on the Spontaneous Origin of the Northern Dipper* (*Yuqing wushang lingbao ziran beidou bensheng zhenjing* 玉清無上靈寶自然北斗本生真經, Schipper #45).

559   Du Guangting 杜光庭 (850–933) in his *Record of Grottoheavens, Sacred Lands, Mountain Sluices and Notable Mountains* (*Dongtian fudi yuedu mingshanji* 洞天福地嶽瀆名山紀), but the list sometimes confuses her with the nearby "Mountain of Heaven's Eyes," also pronounced *Tianmu* 天目.

560   The *The Later Record of Wu* (*Hou Wulu* 後卿) is the anonymous continuation of the "Geography Treatise" of Zhang Bo's 張勃 (first century BCE) *Wulu*.

561   From the *Gazetteer of All the States* (*Junguozhi* 郡國志), as quoted in the eleventh-century Imperial Survey of the Taiping Period (*Taiping yulan* 太平御覽), chap. 47. The *Junguozhi* is the geographical section of *The Book of Later Han* (*HouHan shu* 後漢書), though originally compiled separately as the *Continuation of the Book of Han* (*Xu Hanshu* 續漢書) by Sima Biao 司馬彪 (ca. 246–306). Except for this Gazetteer, Sima's work is lost. But the passage quoted here is not part of the current *Book of*

Later Han and is likely stray lore that made its way into the *Taiping yulan* somewhere along the way.

562   As Fabrizio Pregadio and others have noted. See his remarks in the *Encyclopedia of Taoism,* 76.

563   Source: https://commons.wikimedia.org/wiki/File:Immortal_in_Splashed_Ink.jpg.

564   The incomparable Dōgen 道元 (1200–1253), whom we may call the founder of Japanese Sōtō Zen, from his *Treasury of the True Dharma Eye* (*Shōbōgenzō* 正法眼藏), Book 29, "Mountains and Waters Sutra" (*Sansui kyō* 山水經).

565   ch12v4p1977.

566   Thus the title of one of Du Fu's poems to Li Bo refers to him as "Li Twelve Bo." This family business is a serious matter. Li Bo addressed poems to at least twenty of his father's kin — "Almost all of them were officials, and some held high rank" (Waley, *The Poetry and Career of Li Po,* 7).

567   Huangfu Mi 皇甫謐 (215–82), *Biographies of Eminent Men* (*Gaoshi zhuan* 高士傳).

568   *A New Account of Tales of the World* (*Shishuo xinyu* 世說新語), chap. 25 "Taunting and Teasing" (*Paitiao* 排調).

569   In one early gloss, this Mystery is only said to be a color, "black tinged with red" (Mao's comments on the *Classic of Odes* [*Shijing* 詩經], #154 "The Odes of Bin Mountain" [*Binfeng* 豳風], "The Seventh Month" [*Qiyue* 七月]). ("Darkness" is a good translation of *xuan,* except that it has a ready antonym, light.) See also Friederike Assandri, "Mystery and Secrecy in the Contacts of Buddhism and Daoism in Early Medieval China," in *Religious Secrecy as Contact: Secrets as Promoters of Religious Dynamics,* eds. A. Akasoy et al. (Leiden: Brill, forthcoming).

570 As quoted in the *Encyclopedia of Taoism,* 1139.

571 Ibid. A rending of space-time reality, surrendered to a something shining through. She looks a lot like the *khōra* χώρα, "location, place," which for Plato is the interval between being and non-being, where the Forms/Ideas are held and through which they pass. See Jacques Derrida, *Khôra* (Paris: Galilée, 1993). Sanford Budick calls it "a place of passage, a threshold" (Budick & Iser, *Languages of the Unsayable,* xv).

At some point we may stumble into the ragged borderlands of language, where our grammar starts to sputter and our nouns miss their prey. Thus the joyful ejaculations of Estlin Cummings at age six:

> FATHER DEAR. BE, YOUR FATHER-GOOD AND GOOD,
> HE IS GOOD NOW, IT IS NOT GOOD TO SEE IT RAIN,
> FATHER DEAR IS, IT, DEAR, NO FATHER DEAR,
> LOVE, YOU DEAR,
> ESTLIN.

From E.E. Cummings, *Selected Letters of E.E. cummings* (Ann Arbor: University of Michigan Press, 1972), 3.

572 Can't even attribute perseity to it. Now, synecdoche is a trope in which part stands for whole, or whole for part. "I saw three sails," where "sail" stands for "boat." "Schenectady pulls it out in the third period," where "Schenectady" stands for the Patriots, the city's high-school ice-hockey team. This tautology sings love songs to itself.

573 Nanzen 南泉 cut the cat in two. Dōgen's 道元 response was, "Yes, you can cut the cat in two, but can you cut it in one?" (*A Primer of Soto Zen: A Translation of Dogen's Shobogenzo Zuimoki* [Honolulu: University of Hawai'i Press, 1979], 37.) You can see why this lineage sets the Advaitists to quailing.

574 This is the view of the influential Heshang Gong 河上公 (Riverbank Master) commentary of the first century CE.

575 Li Bo calls it the Red Fruit. In late imperial and modern Warrior novels, the Red Fruit (*zhuguo* 朱果) is one of the Treasures of Earth, a magic substance of great power, which ripens once every hundred years. I haven't been able to trace this tradition back earlier, nor determine when it began.

576 Always already. See *Wikipedia,* "Always already," s.v. It seems that Laozi said only one sentence, but we've only been able to hear the first half of it.

577 An American poet writes:

> Sometimes I think "I'll give up words." But then She comes, again, and I remember the day appearance became a bedroom and I became a bride.
> Sometimes I decide "Enough of words! No more." But then She whispers in my ear in the language of sunlight and longing — She entices, cajoles, seduces syntax, grammatical structure, illogical pronouns. She sighs "Silence is an ocean but Love! Love is a river flowing out …. in bright language. Silence is a deep but Love is a flood plain, a tumbling waterfall. Come on, my love, enter me with your love words!" and …. I do!! (TYD, https://www.facebook.com/groups/tsogyelgarsangha)

"The possibility of liberated desire finds its recourse in words" (adapted from Stephen Owen, *Mi-Lou* [Cambridge: Harvard University Press, 1989], 156), a post-apophatic hum.

578 ch9v3p1529.

579 Or the *Compact of Three-in-One according to the Classic of Change* (*Zhouyi cantongqi* 周易參同契). I owe my fledgling understanding of this text entirely to the extraordinary labors of

Fabrizio Pregadio and his annotated translation, *The Seal of the Unity of the Three, Vol. 1: A Study and Translation of the Cantong qi, the Source of the Taoist Way of the Golden Elixir* (Mountain View: Golden Elixir Press, 2011). Pregadio has traced its affiliations with multiple ancestors dating from the Han onward and explicated a ton of esoteric doctrine.

580 In Kristopher Schipper's words, "In Chinese physics, these minerals and metals are the products of the interaction of cosmic energies and time and thus constitute the quintessence of our planet" (*The Taoist Body,* 175).

581 Schipper, again: It is "a means to accomplish in a few days the cosmic process of returning to the True. This implies making a fabulous voyage in time, inasmuch as the same process would require millions of years in the macrocosm" (ibid., 178).

582 Source: https://www.academia.edu/5892149/Jouissance_of_Death_Han_sarcophagi_from_Sichuan_and_the_Art_of_Physiological_Alchemy.

583 Bokenkamp gives examples of Li Bo's citation of "arcane names" from the Highest Clarity and Lingbao traditions ("Li Bai, Huangshan, and Alchemy," *Tang Studies* 25 [2007]: 29–55, at 40)

584 Many terms, like White Tiger, are of course endemic to alchemical speech. However, Li Bo's exultation on completing the work, "Fire-red and splendid, it has become the Great Refined Elixir" (*heran cheng dahuan* 赫然稱大還), is a direct quotation from the *Three-in-One.*
    I'll go through the middle section of Li Bo's poem line by line to explore the similarities and differences of the two texts. First our poetic translation, accompanied by the Chinese text and a literal translation. Then the related passage in the *Cantongqi,* with commentary by Pregadio or me.

Line 1

>Our translation: Heat Mercury until it steams off skyward
>姹女乘河車
>Literally: The Lovely Maid mounts the River Chariot

Cantongqi #68:

> The Lovely Maid of the River
> is numinous and supremely divine.
> When she finds Fire, she flies away.
>
> 河上姹女，靈而最神，得火則飛

Pregadio comments:

> The Lovely Maid of the River is True Mercury.... Aroused by fire, she escapes and flies away (205).

The Lovely Maid — Edward Schafer calls her "the Mercurial Maid" and lovingly exposes her seething history in his "Two Taoist Bagatelles," *Society for the Study of Chinese Religions Bulletin* 9 (1981): 1–18.

Line 2

> then harness it with Lead and return it to the cauldron's waters.
> 黃金充轅軛
> its shafts and yoke are filled with yellow gold.

Cantongqi #68:

> If you want to control her,
> the Yellow Sprout is the root.
>
> 將欲制之，黃芽為根

The Yellow Sprout (*huangya* 黃芽) appears in this line as Yellow Gold (*huangjin* 黃金). But jin means both "gold" and "metal," so the Sprout here stands for the metal Lead. Pregadio: "Only the Yellow Sprout, which is True Lead, can hold her. When they meet, they join and generate the Elixir" (Pregadio, *The Seal of the Unity of the Three,* 205).

Line 3

    Master this water, the axis of Dao
        執樞相管轄
    Hold to the pivot and manage the lynch-pin

Cantongqi #22:

    Water is the axis of the Dao;
    its number is 1.
    At the beginning of Yin and Yang,
    Mystery holds the Yellow Sprout.
    It is the ruler of the five metals,
    the River Chariot of the northern direction.

        水者道樞，其數名一。陰陽之始，玄含黃芽。五金之主，北方河車。

Water is Mystery, Dao. It is prior to yin and yang. Water is also the axis of Dao, the pivot on which all activity hinges. Water is also the first of the Five Agents (here called the five metals), which constitute all natural processes. It thus precedes, permeates, envelopes and supports the whole of alchemical transformations.

line 4

    and keep Mercury in the fiery pot until its impurities dissolve
        摧伏傷羽翮
    painfully strip away its wing feathers

Cantongqi #78:

It enters the boiling pot on its head,
its feathers ripped off.

顛倒就湯獲兮，摧折傷毛羽

The volatility of Mercury must be brought under control.

line 5
    The Vermillion Bird of Fire blazes its bright majesty,
        朱鳥張炎威
    The Vermillion Bird displays its bright majesty,

Cantongqi #78:

    A blazing fire is made below....
    The Vermillion Sparrow soars into play,
    flying upwards in the hues of its five colors.

    炎火張設下，朱雀翱翔戲兮，飛揚色五彩

line 6
    the White Tiger of Lead safeguards the space of transformation
        白虎守本宅
    The White Tiger preserves the fundamental home

Cantongqi #78:

    The White Tiger leads the song ahead,
    the green liquid joins after.

    白虎唱導前兮，蒼液和于後

Pregadio comments:

    This section gives another poetical description of the compounding of the Elixir. Lead (the White Tiger, True Yang) first liquefies, so that Mercury (the "green liquid" [Green Dragon], True Yin) can join it and become one with it. […] The Vermilion Sparrow (Fire, Yang) spreads its wings and soars into the air. (ibid., 217)

lines 7 & 8
Reduce and mature the bitter liquid,
evaporate and condense it.
相煎成苦老，消鑠凝津液
Decoct it until it's bitter and mature,
melt and congeal its vital fluids

Cantongqi #78:

Ceaselessly gurgling and burling,
coalescing continuously, one after the other

暴勇不休止，接連重疊累兮

The two passages are related, but there is no lexical overlap between them.

lines 9 & 10
It will look like dust on a clear windowpane,
dead ashes fallen into silence.

髣髴明窗塵，死灰同至寂

It will look like dust on a clear windowpane,
dead ashes fallen into silence.

Cantongqi #39:

Its form looks like ashes or soil,
its shape is like dust on a luminous window.

形體爲灰土，狀若明窗塵

Pregadio comments:

> [The elements inside the vessel] undergo transmutation, taking at first a liquid form and then a solid form, similar to ashes or dust. The compound obtained […] serves as the basis for making the Elixir [which is described next] (ibid., 174).

lines 11 & 12
Then pound it and mix it, seal it in the red vessel,
regulating the heat through twelve stages of perfection.
　擣治入赤色，十二周律曆
Then pound it and mix it, seal it in the red [vessel],
regulating the heat through twelve times.

Cantongqi #40:

> Pound it and mix it,
> and let it enter the Red-colored Gates.
> Seal the joints firmly,
> striving to make them as tight as you can….
> Watch over it with heed and caution,
> inspect it attentively and regulate the amount of warmth.
> It will rotate through twelve nodes,
> and when the nodes are complete, it will again need your attention.
>
> 　擣治并合之，持入赤色門
> 　固塞其際會，務令致完堅…
> 　候視加謹慎，審察調寒溫
> 　周旋十二節，節盡更須親

Pregadio comments:

The description of the refining of the True Lead and True Mercury that had begun in the previous section continues here. The compound obtained in the first part of the method is placed in a tripod and is heated in a furnace. The vessel, this time, should be hermetically closed, as even the slightest leakage of Breath (*qi*) would prevent the Elixir from being compounded. The intensity of heat is regulated according to the system of the "fire times" (*huohou*), which subdivides each heating cycle into twelve stages (ibid., 175).

lines 13 & 14
Fire-red and splendid, it has become Great Refined Elixir,
in essence no different from the Dao.
  赫然稱大還,與道本無隔

The second line is Li Bo's own. But the first appears verbatim in Cantongqi #40. I think this is a direct quotation from that text — my rudimentary search through the Daoist Canon turns up nothing quite like it, except in later responses to the Three-in-One like the *Taishang riyue hunyuan jing* 太上日月混元經 (The supreme scripture of the sun and moon and their origin in chaos, Schipper #656; perhaps late Tang/extant in mid-eleventh century).

585 Perhaps, then, we are better readers of this poem if we know nothing of alchemy. Then the poem makes an impression, like the impression of wind on water.

586 With apologies to Carl Jung and his studies of European alchemy, *Psychology and Alchemy,* Collected Works of C.G. Jung, Volume 12 (Princeton: Princeton University Press, 1968). See also his foreword and appendix to *The Secret of the Golden Flower,* Richard Wilhelm's translation of the *Taiyi jinhua zongzhi* 太乙金華宗旨 (New York: Harcourt Brace, 1962 [1929]).

587 From the preface to a collection of poems "At Nanjing with Assembled Worthies Seeing off Quan Zhaoyi" (*Jinling yu zhuxian song Quan Shiyi Zhaoyi* 金陵與諸賢送權十一昭夷序), ch27v8p4068. See also Li Bo's exuberant praise for the well-known alchemist Sun Taichong 孫太沖, whose Great Refined Elixir was favorably received by the Bright Emperor in 744. Paul

Kroll discusses the background in his *Dharma Bell and Dhāraṇī Pillar: Li Po's Buddhist Inscriptions* (Kyoto: Italian School of East Asian Studies, 2001), 66n154. The text in question is Li Bo's "Inscription on the 'Foding cunsheng' Dharani Pillar at Congming Temple" (*Chongmingsi fodingzunsheng tuoluoni chuangsong* 崇明寺佛頂尊勝陀羅尼幢頌), ch29v8p4237.

588 From "Ancient Airs #4" (*Gufeng* 古風), ch2v1p44. Compare

> I took the Lead-gathering traveler by the hand,
> we washed beside the stream, tying lotus leaves together to make a shelter.

> 提攜采鉛客，結荷水邊沐

From "Lodging at Shrimp Lake" (*Su Xiahu* 宿鰕湖), ch20v6p3146.

589 From the poem "In the Sikong Uplands, Avoiding War, Speaking My Heart" (*Bidi Sikongyuan yanhuai* 避地司空原言懷), ch22v7p3484.

590 From "Ancient Airs #4" (*Gufeng* 古風), ch2v1p44.

591 From "A Lu Mountain Song That I sent to Empty Boat Lu" (*Lushan yao ji Lu Shiyu Xuzhou* 廬山謠寄廬侍御虛舟), ch12v4p1999.

592 From "Left with the Officials at Caonan as They Leave for Jiangnan" (*Liubie Caonan qunguan zhi Jiangnan* 留別曹南群官之江南), ch13v4p2115.

593 Fire is transformation.

> We are going to study a problem that no one has managed to approach objectively, one in which the initial charm of the

object is so strong that it still has the power to warp the minds of the clearest thinkers and to keep bringing them back to the poetic fold in which dreams replace thought and poems conceal theorems. (Gaston Bachelard, *The Psychoanalysis of Fire*, trans. Alan Ross [London: Routledge, 1964], 1)

594 See "Drinking Alone at Pure Brook, on a Riverside Rock, Sent to Quan Zhaoyi" (*Duyue qingxijiang shishang ji Quan Zhaoyi* 獨酌清溪江石上寄權昭夷), ch12v4p1989.

595 My translation here uses the word "elixir," but Li Bo's poem never mentions the word *dan* 丹, the most common name for the elixir. Instead he refers to it as the Great Returned, *dahuan* 大還, or, more accurately, the Great Returning. Even this gerundive form is a concession to the illusion of imperfection. Laozi, too, "Reversion is the movement of Dao" (*fan zhe dao zhi dong* 反者道之動, chap. 40).

596 A.A. Milne, *Winnie-the-Pooh* (New York: Dutton, 1926), chap. 9, "In Which Piglet Is Entirely Surrounded by Water."

In her fourth water, the "Devotion of Ecstasy," St. Theresa cannot be kept on the ground. See also Edward Schafer, "A Trip to the Moon," *Journal of the American Oriental Society* 96, no. 1 (1976): 27–37:

> The real problem in investigating travel in outer space during the T'ang dynasty is to determine what or where outer space was. The Taoists, especially the masters and adepts of the celebrated school of Mao-shan, dominated large areas of thought and even of public life during this period, and for them outer space was indistinguishable from inner space. To put it another way, they made no significant distinction between interstellar and intercellular space. (ibid., 27)

597 See Barrett, *Taoism under the T'ang*, 83, 87, 91 *et passim*.

598   "The discussions of the assembled transcendents on the Return Elixir," in Bokenkamp, "Li Bai, Huangshan, and Alchemy," 53.

599   On the biochemical aspects of elixir poisoning, see Joseph Needham and Lu Gwei-djen, *Science and Civilization in China, Vol. 5: Chemistry and Chemical Technology, Part 2, Spagyrical Discovery and Invention: Magisteries of Gold and Immortality* (Cambridge: Cambridge University Press, 1974). For a view that questions whether any alchemical deaths can be called "accidental," see Michel Strickmann, "On the Alchemy of T'ao Hung-ching," in *Facets of Taoism: Essays in Chinese Religion*, eds. Holmes Welch and Anna Seidel (New Haven: Yale University Press, 1979), 123–92.

600   See William Newman, *Gehennical Fire: The Life of George Starkey, an American Alchemist in the Scientific Revolution* (Chicago: University of Chicago Press, 1994), chap. 2 "Arcan Maiora," esp. 38–42. Starkey (1628–65) devised an alchemical cure for plague, though he eventually died of the disease.

601   ch28v8p4206.

602   Scholar-bureaucrat Yang Shiqi 楊士奇 (1364–1444), as quoted by Wang Qi, ch28v3p1331.

603   Source: https://commons.wikimedia.org/wiki/File:Attributed_to_Wu_Daozi._Flying_Demon._Rubbing_of_a_stone_engraving_in_the_Northern_Yue_Temple_in_Quyang,_Hebei_Province._97,5_cm_high..jpg. An even poorer copy survives today at Baozhi's tomb in Yangzhou — see Alan Berkowitz, "Account of the Buddhist Thaumaturge Baozhi," in *Buddhism in Practice*, ed. Donald Lopez (Princeton: Princeton University Press, 1995), 578–85, at 580.

604   Source: https://en.wikipedia.org/wiki/Wu_Daozi#/media/File:EightySevenCelestials3.jpg. Perhaps this is his draft of a

wall fresco, "Eighty-seven Divine Immortals" (*Bashiqi shenxian juan* 八十七神仙眷).

605 From his poem "Visiting the Laozi Temple North of Luoyang on a Winter Day" (*Dongri Luochengbei ye Xuanyuan Huangdi miao* 冬日洛城北謁玄元皇帝廟), *QuanTang shi* 全唐詩, ch. 224, as quoted in *Celebrated Painters of the Tang* (*Tangchao minghualu* 唐朝名畫錄) of Zhu Jingxuan 朱景玄 (ca. 840). Translation by Alexander C. Soper in his "T'ang Ch'ao Ming Hua Lu: Celebrated Painters of the T'ang Dynasty by Chu Ching-hsüan of T'ang," *Artibus Asiae* 21, nos. 3–4 (1958): 204–30, at 207.

606 Soper, "T'ang Ch'ao Ming Hua Lu," 208. The evaluation mentions one also-ran, but "all other 124 painters of Tang" are placed below him.

It is said of Wu that "When he lowers his brush onto the paper, divinity is present" (*xiabia youshen* 下筆有神). For a discussion, see Richard Edwards, *The Heart of Ma Yuan: The Search for a Southern Song Aesthetic* (Hong Kong: Hong Kong University Press, 2011), 177.

607 See Amy McNair's loving account, "Draft Entry for a T'ang Biographical Dictionary: Yen Chen-ch'ing," *T'ang Studies* 10–11 (1992–93): 123–51. Oh, and Yan also has an intense sweetness for the Han buffoon-sage Dongfang Shuo, writing out an encomium for his portrait at Shuo's shrine in 754 (ibid., 131). And an epitaph for Sima Chengzhen's successor Li Hanguang 李含光 (ibid., 136, where she notes rumors of Yan's fondness for elixirs and the self-disappearing corpse).

608 Source: https://commons.wikimedia.org/wiki/Yan_Zhenqing#/media/File:Yan_Qinli_Stele.jpg. Small sample of the Yan Qinli bei 顏勤禮碑 — stele of Yan Qinli, 780 CE, currently in the Forrest of Stelae, Xi'an.

609 Chapter 27.

610 Chapter 11. Baozhi, then, lived under the Qi, Liang, and Chen dynasties, and Li Bo's poem puns on these — the scissors that cut things to the same height (*qi* 齊) stand for the Qi dynasty, etc. I've compressed this into "cuts through three dynasties of kings."

611 Source: https://b-log-b-log.blog.ss-blog.jp/2016-10-10.

612 It is said that he used his thumbnail to open his skull. For an alternative account, see the *Tiantai* 天台 polemical treatise of the Song, *Fozu Tongji* 佛祖統紀 (*Chronicle of Buddhas and Patriarchs*), T49n2035p366. For a discussion, see Sherry Fowler, "The Splitting Image of Baozhi at Saiōji and His Cult in Japan," *Oriental Art* 46, no. 4 (2000): 2–10, and Ellen Schattschneider, "Family Resemblances: Memorial Images and the Face of Kinship," *Japanese Journal of Religious Studies* 31, no. 1 (2004): 141–62.

613 Source: http://commons.wikimedia.org/wiki/File:%E6%80%80%E7%B4%A0_%E8%8B%A6%E7%AC%8B%E5%B8%96.jpg. This one is now called "The Silk Writing 'Bitter Bamboo-shoots'" (*Kusun tie* 苦筍帖), presently in the Shanghai Museum.

614 Adele Schlombs, to whom I owe most of my knowledge of Huaisu, provides the transcription into modern *kaishu* 楷書 script. See her *Huai-su and the Beginnings of Wild Cursive Script in Chinese Calligraphy* (Stuttgart: Franz Steiner, 1998), 126.

615 ch7v3p1237. Zhang Xu 張旭 (675–750), a contemporary pioneer of the wild cursive style, is said to have improved his calligraphy by watching Lady Gongsun (Gongsun daniang 公孫大娘) perform her sword dance, inspired by Persian or Turkestani styles. See Du Fu's poem and preface, "Observing a Disciple of Lady Gongsun Perform the Sword Dance" (*Guan Gongsun daniang dizi wu jianqi hang* 關公孫大娘弟子舞劍器行).

616 For evidence and argumentation, see Zhan Ying's discussion in ch7v3p1237.

617 As she explains,

> If the brushwork is examined, there is a strange contradiction between the compositional abbreviations on the one hand, and the hesitant execution on the other. The edgy wavering elliptical line in the character *nai* 乃, the diminished momentum of the circular stroke of the character *sun* 筍, or the abrupt contrast between the connecting line and the second stroke in the character *ji* 及, are incompatible with the vigorous performance to be seen in the "Introducing Myself," the *Shiyu tie* 食魚帖, and the *Lügong tie* 綠卄帖, where each stroke is executed with the artist's full energy (Schlombs, *Huai-su and the Beginnings of Wild Cursive Script in Chinese Calligraphy*, 127).

It would be difficult, I think, to trace this world of forgery in Tang times. However, Mark McNicholas has done a swell job with early Qing, when bureaucratic procedures were still not fully clarified, that is, regularized, that is, inoculated against imposture. As a reviewer points out, his book describes a little-known world "where a great variety of counterfeits were in demand and supply, including imperial edicts, tax receipts, arrest warrants, and official seals." See Mark McNichols, *Forgery and Impersonation in Imperial China: Popular Deceptions and the High Qing State* (Seattle: University of Washington Press, 2016), reviewed by Li Chen in the *Journal of Asian Studies* 77, no. 3 (2018): 783–85.

618 I don't mean to get technical, but sometimes it's hard to keep things straight. In the comedy *The Guru* (2002), an Indian charlatan teaches fake tantric sex to a gullible American audience. But the teachings are the actual teachings, and they work, even in a shoddy knock-off. Lettriste Isidore Isou looked like Elvis Presley, and "his field of action may have been high art,

[but] physically, instinctively he was a hound dog" (Greil Marcus, *Lipstick Traces: A Secret History of the Twentieth Century* [Cambridge: Harvard University Press, 1989], 249).

Fig. 100. Isidore Isou in 1951, a bit before the fact. Source: https://en.wikipedia.org/wiki/Isidore_Isou#/media/File:Isidore_Isou,_1951.jpg.

619   In the sociology of religion we could speak of Jesus's power to effect large numbers of people, two thousand years after his death.

620   It's hard to make confident authentication when you're working only from reproductions or a translation. Plus you need an eye like Schlombs's. Still, the poem seems extra hyperbolic to me, like Li Bo in a hurry. Our translation tones it a bit, to comply with our imagined poetic standards.

621   Lu Yu 陸羽, author of the *Classic of Tea,* also wrote the *Biography of the Monk Huaisu* (*Seng Huaisu Zhuan* 僧懷素傳). Here he quotes Huaisu, in the preface to this work.

622   "He was in all respects historical-minded," and "his knowledge of past styles was essential to his calligraphy" (Schlombs, *Huai-su and the Beginnings of Wild Cursive Script in Chinese Calligraphy,* 31). An early source mentions that he

would bury his used brushes, "calling this a brushtomb (*bizhong* 筆塚)" (ibid., 14).

623   Photo by the publisher. In the Palace Museum, Taipei. Ah, but apparently this, and other surviving versions of the text, are Northern Song or later copies. See Vincent Poon, "Huaisu's Autobiography," http://www.vincentpoon.com/autobiography-of huai-su.html.

624   A modern scholar, Guo Moruo 郭沫若 (1892–1978), takes Li Bo's poem as genuine, arguing that it was written in the fall of 759, when Li Bo was visiting Huaisu's hometown of Lingling 零陵 in present-day Hunan. But a key argument against the authenticity of Li Bo's poem is its absence in this autobiography, where such praise is the norm and substance, and the power of Li Bo's name the very currency of Huaisu's self-presentation. Su Shi 蘇軾 (1037–1101) was the first to point this out. See Zhan Ying, ch7v3p1238-39.

625   Schlombs, *Huai-su and the Beginnings of Wild Cursive Script in Chinese Calligraphy*, 29.

626   Ibid., 1.

627   Ibid., 21.

628   He Zhizhang 賀知章 speaking. See our Chapter 17, above.

629   Wei Hao 魏顥 (fl. Kaiyuan period), preface to *Li Hanlin ji* 李翰林集 (The collected works of the Hanlin scholar Li Bo).

630   *Qi zhi you qi* 奇之又奇, Yin Fan 殷璠, in the preface to his 753 CE anthology *Finest Souls of River and Alp* (*Heyue yingling ji* 河嶽英靈集), apt translations by Paul Kroll, "The Road to Shu, from Zhang Zai to Li Bo," *Early Medieval China* 10–11 (2004): 227–54, at 227.

631 You may have already noticed that Li Bo has no shortage of individualities but no discernible identity. The following generations — let's say the 780s to the 820s — saw a new concept of friendship, based on a necessary sense of identity. See Anna Shields, *One Who Knows Me: Friendship and Literary Culture in Mid-Tang China* (Cambridge: Harvard University Asia Center, 2015).

632 Varsano, *Tracking the Banished Immortal,* quoting Yuan Zhen 元稹 (779–831), 39. Literally thousands of poems and essays survive from late Song on, attempting to come to terms with Li Bo. They have been collected in three volumes and 1,208 pages by Pei Fei 裴斐 as *Li Bo ziliao huibian* 李白資料彙編 [Collated materials on Li Bo] (Beijing: Zhonghua, 1994).

633 For a good collection, see Varsano, *Tracking the Banished Immortal,* 35ff.

634 Schlombs quotes Sikong Tu 司空圖 (837–908) on Huaisu's supposed Zennist "instant enlightenment" (*dunwu* 頓悟), on *Huai-su and the Beginnings of Wild Cursive Script in Chinese Calligraphy,* 10. But Huaisu himself, though a Buddhist monk, never spoke of Zen.

635 Yu-kung Kao 高友工, private communication, Princeton, NJ, 1966.

636 As Varsano has shown. See especially her treatments of Yan Yu 嚴羽 (1195–1264), *Tracking the Banished Immortal,* 59–70 *et passim.*

637 Schlombs, *Huai-su and the Beginnings of Wild Cursive Script in Chinese Calligraphy,* 2.

638 And Li Bo can recede into a literary past, as a gesture of freedom made within regulation human culture. Max Weber speaks of this process as "the routinization of charisma" — how

successors seek to maintain the divine power/grace of a lost progenitor.

639 In present-day Hunan. Li Bo met Sima Chengzhen about two hundred miles north in Jiangling 江陵, Hubei.

640 Mario Poceski, *The Records of Mazu and the Making of Classical Chan Literature* (Oxford: Oxford University Press, 2015), 154.

641 See Steven Heine, "*Mazu yulu* and the Chan Records," in *The Zen Canon: Understanding the Classic Texts,* ed. Dale S. Wright (Oxford University Press, 2004), 61–88.

642 Poceski writes: "Indeed, I have not been able to find a single piece of evidence to show that during the Tang periods there was any awareness of the existence of such a thing as the encounter dialogue model, let alone that it was the Chan School's main medium of religious instruction or practice, as is often assumed" (*The Records of Mazu and the Making of Classical Chan Literature,* 156).

643 Like *Seventeen* magazine bad girls in black lipstick. The argument is most clearly made on ibid., 157–58.

644 A devout Buddhist might say that the two centuries of silence are the work of the *dharmapālas*, the dharma protectors, who oversee the safety of the teachings.

645 This is the earliest example I know of the work of art in an age of mechanical reproduction.

646 An ethical question: if someone steals private information and broadcasts it, does it become public information? Or are we committing the same act of theft and desecration each time we look? Receipt of stolen goods — accessory after the fact. There is no statute of limitations for this crime.

Of course the true Zen student is going to steal the teachings anywhere she can get them, without regard to propriety or property rights. But you won't find her talking about it later in a bar.

647 The necessary endpoint of that thinking is this:

> A huge number of Chan stories or exchanges, included in texts such as *Jingde chuandenglu* and *Biyanlu,* can be viewed as little more than nonessential ramblings, a peculiar type of religious 'gibberish. Basically, we are confronted with countless examples of mass-produced textual materials that tend to be highly formulaic, numbingly repetitive, and ostensibly pointless. One of the things that keeps amazing me is how otherwise intelligent or sincere people can take this sort of stuff seriously, although the history of religion is filled with blind spots of that sort. (Poceski, *The Records of Mazu and the Making of Classical Chan Literature,* 171)

Thus Mazu, "Patriarch Horse," meets the same end as the dancing horses of the Bright Emperor. Mistaken identity can compel us to murder.

The feminine (*yin* 陰) is more adept at staying hidden (*yin* 隱) from the rapacious entification of being known. Schafer gives this account:

> In A.D. 334 the purified being who had been known during her career on earth as Wei Hua-ts'un 魏華存 divested herself of her mortal remains to become, for all time, the spiritual mistress of the sacred mountain whose numen presides over the southern marches of China. Thirty years later she revealed the secret scriptures whose ineffable prototypes exist only in the Heaven of Highest Clarity (*shang ch'ing* 上清) to a young man named Yang Hsi 陽羲.

These became the foundation of Highest Clarity Daoism, over which Sima Chengzhen presided during Li Bo's early lifetime. It was characteristic of this Daoism, Schafer continues, that it appealed most of all to unique individuals, men and women who had both native talent and adequate strength of will to undergo long and arduous periods of scriptural studies and physical disciplines. Such rare persons might enjoy the ultimate reward of elevation among the Realized Persons (*chen jen* 真人) in the sky palaces of Highest Clarity. [...] But none of them was worshipped or propitiated in the temples of China as were the great nature gods of the state religion; in a sense they were too exalted for this. [...] These sublime beings engaged only in master-pupil relationships with gifted mortals whose physical bodies might ultimately be transformed into new, purified and immortal entities like their own—beyond ordinary human conception, even if they might occasionally reveal themselves in the masks and costumes of human beings.

It follows that the attempt to trace the icon of the Lady Wei in the surviving literature of the T'ang period is not, in the ordinary sense, the exploration of evidence for the survival of a public cult. It is the search for the persistence of a faded image, or perhaps a glorified one, in whatever sources may prove useful, including poetry and belles-lettres generally. It is as if one might search fragmentary texts for evidence of the honour and esteem in which Mary the mother of Jesus was held centuries after her death, not as a woman, nor as a goddess, the focus of a cult, but as a former human being who has achieved a higher kind of existence. ("The Restoration of the Shrine of Wei Hua-ts'un at Lin-ch'uan in the Eighth Century," *Journal of Oriental Studies* 15 [1977]: 124–37, at 124)

There's nothing much wrong with the sacred masculine, it's just such a poor approximation of reality.

648   "Some thousand years" implies time, the passage of time implies continuity and history. Is there a history of immortality?

> Gibt es eine 'Naturgeschichte der Farben', und wieweit ist sie analog einer Naturgeschichte der Pflantzen? Ist diese nicht zeitlich, jene unzeitlich?
>
> Is there such a thing as a 'natural history of colours' and to what extent is it analogous to a natural history of plants? Isn't the latter temporal, the former non-temporal? (Ludwig Wittgenstein, *Remarks on Colour* (Oxford: Blackwell, 1977), Section III, no. 8.

I once asked a topologist friend if he had any interest in the history of mathematics. "Oh," he said, "like 'In the eleventh century, the number Nine was slightly smaller than it is today.'"

649 Source: https://www.brooklynmuseum.org/opencollection/objects/106265. Matsumura Goshun (1752–1811), *Portrait of Tung-Fang Shuo,* ca. 1790, hanging scroll, ink and light color on paper, Brooklyn Museum.

650 For a summary of materials on Dongfang Shuo, see Aat Vervoorn, *Men of the Cliffs and Caves: The Development of the Chinese Eremitic Tradition to the End of the Han Dynasty* (Hong Kong: Hong Kong University Press, 1990), chap. 4, "Eremitism at Court."

651 The *Historical Records* (*Shiji* 史記), chap. 126 — in this case by Chu Shaosun 褚少孫 (ca. 105–ca. 30 BCE), not Sima Qian.

652 The *Book of Han* (*Hanshu* 漢書), chap. 65, the biography of Dongfang Shuo. But his quick wit soon got him back his post.

653 Opposing the Emperor's plan to build a huge hunting preserve, enable a corrupt relative, and seek immortality from charlatans (the *Shiji*). See his autobiography, "Discourse of Master Nobody" (*Feiyou xiansheng lun* 非有先生論), translated by Burton Watson as "An Essay by Elder Nobody" in *Courtier and Commoner in Ancient China,* 96–105, with its praise for benevo-

lence and righteousness (*renyi* 仁義), prudence and frugality, etc. A kind of Heyoka, then, in the Lakota tradition, contrarian, buffoon, inscrutable.

654   *The Inner Biography of Han Wudi* (*Hanwudi neizhuan* 漢武帝內轉), chap. 6. This story first circulated some hundred years after his death. See Thomas Smith, *Ritual and the Shaping of Narrative: The Legend of the Han Emperor Wu* (Ph.D. diss., University of Michigan, 1992), 526, and Kristopher Schipper, *L'Empéreur Wou des Han dans la légende taoiste: Han wou-ti nei tchouan* (Paris: Ecole française d'extrême orient, 1965).

655   The *Hanshu*.

656   Daoist practices of seclusion and longevity.

657   The *Shiji* again.

658   ch6v2p1002. Shuo makes several other cameo appearances in Li's poetry — early on we translated "Big words" and "Lines of a short song." And in the introduction to Section IV, "Five Mountains," there's a poem whose first line reads

Mornings I play in the Ocean of Purple Sand.

朝弄紫泥海

What are the purple sands where Li Bo plays? Another story of Shuo's mischievous youth explains it — he was three years old at the time:

> Dongfang Shuo returned only after several months, and so his mother flogged him with a bamboo staff. Later he went away again, this time returning only after a full year. When his mother suddenly saw him, and she cried out in alarm, "You've only just come back now, after a full year! How can you be any consolation to me?"

He replied, "Your son went to the Ocean of Purple Sands. It has purple water in which to dye your clothes. I also went to Yuyuan, the pool where the sun sets, to wash away my faults. I left in the morning and returned at noon. Why are you talking about 'a full year'?"

From the *Dongmingji* 洞冥記 (A record of penetrating the mysteries), chap. 1, purportedly of Eastern Han, but, as Campany shows, likely to be much later (*Strange Writing*, 95).

Fig. 101. Pietro Gonnella, jester to the Este family, Dukes of Ferrara. Portrait by Jean Fouquet (1420–81) Source: https://commons.wikimedia.org/wiki/File:Jean_Fouquet-_Portrait_of_the_Ferrara_Court_Jester_Gonella.JPG

He could appear as anyone, lout, courtier, ecclesiastical messenger. Threw his lord into the river to cure his ague. You can read a nineteenth-century version of his story as "Gonnella, the court fool of Ferrara," *The New Monthly Magazine* 16 (1826): 162–67. Carlo Ginzburg sees Christ in his folded arms. See his *Jean Fouquet: Ritratto del buffone Gonella* (Modena: F.C. Panini, 1996), 7.

659 ch16v5p2631.

660 For the name Kāśya, see William Soothill, *A Dictionary of Chinese Buddhist Terms,* s.v. He was posted to Huzhou, the Taihu area near Soochow. We call him "Magistrate," but Hucker would prefer "Chief Administrator" and Kroll "Administrator Equestrian."

661 See his Tea poem, Chapter 50, where he also calls himself by this name. That lotus doesn't seem to grow in China, it's a translation of the Sanskrit *utpala* (*youbuluo* 優鉢羅), the blue lotus, to the shape of whose leaves the Buddha's eyes are likened. See Soothill, *A Dictionary of Chinese Buddhist Terms,* s.v. Not to be confused with Hergé, *Tintin: le lotus bleu* (Paris: Casterman, 1936).

662 From the poem "Accompanying My Young Relative…" (*Pei zushu dangtuzai you Huachengsi sheng Gong Qingfengting* 陪族叔當涂宰游化城寺升公清風亭), ch18v6p2935.

663 In the sutra that bears his name, he debates an assembly of bodhisattvas on the topic of non-duality, that great intimacy within Buddhism. They do poorly, so Vimalakīrti asks Mañjuśrī, the bodhisattva of wisdom, *his* view.

> Vimalakīrti asked Mañjuśrī, "How does the bodhisattva enter the Dharma gate of non-duality?"
> Mañjuśrī said, "As I understand it, it is to be without words and without explanation with regard to all the dharmas — without manifestation, without consciousness, and transcending all questions and answers. This is to enter the Dharma gate of non-duality."
> Mañjuśrī then asked Vimalakīrti, "We have each made our own explanations. Sir, you should explain how the bodhisattva enters the Dharma gate of nonduality." At this point Vimalakīrti was silent, saying nothing. (Translated by John McRae in *The Sutra of Queen Śrīmālā of the Lion's Roar and*

The Vimalakīrti Sutra [Berkeley: Numata Center for Buddhist Translation and Research 2004], 148.)

A Daoist recognizes this silence, and the sutra was translated into Chinese six times. Its insouciance was particularly valued by the Chan 禪 tradition, which we know as Zen from its Japanese incarnation. In the ninth-century Vimalakīrti looked like this, as he silently manifests to Mañjuśrī:

Fig. 102. From the caves at Dunhuang. Source: https://en.wikipedia.org/wiki/Vimalakirti#/media/File:Vimalakirti_debating_Manjusri,_Tang_Dynasty.jpg.

664   And Li Bo's contemporary, the sublime poet Wang Wei 王維, takes this "Weimo" as his sobriquet. The true hero of the tradition, known to us as Layman Pang 龐居士 (740–808), is born four decades after Li Bo.

665   Tathāgata, "come like that, gone like that," the word the Buddha used instead of "I."

666 Among Li Bo's many lovely Buddhist poems, see his trip to a Buddhist monastery with his Daoist buddy Cinnabar Hill, "Made While Discussing Mystery with Cinnabar Hill at Fangchengsi" (*Yu Yuan Danqiu Fangchengsi tan xuan zuo* 與元丹丘方城寺談玄作), ch21v6p3251. And see especially Paul Kroll's book on Li Bo's inscription for a Buddhist monastery, *Dharma Bell and Dhāraṇī Pillar*.

667 Theurgy, from *theos*, "god," and *ergos*, "work." "Theurgy is a type of magic. It consists of a set of magical practices performed to evoke beneficent spirits in order to see them or know them or in order to influence them, for instance by forcing them to animate a statue, to inhabit a human being (such as a medium), or to disclose mysteries" (Pierre Riffard, *Dictionnaire de l'ésotérisme* [Paris: Payot, 1983], 340).

668 Russell Kirkland, in the *Encyclopedia of Taoism,* 1154. But see especially his "Tales of Thaumaturgy: T'ang Accounts of the Wonder-worker Yeh Fa-shan," *Monumenta Serica* 40 (1992): 47–86.

669 "To the best of my knowledge, such homage for an individual outside the imperial family was wholly unparalleled" (Kirkland, *Taoists of the High T'ang,* 127). Earlier, in 717, the Emperor had commissioned Li Yong (see Chapter 12) to compose epitaphs for his father and grandfather.

670 Ibid.

671 That Azure Lad (Qingtong 青童) is no casual youth. He's partner of the Queen Mother of the West, and his Cloud Sauce (*yunjiang* 雲漿) the wine of immortals (see *Han Wudi neizhuan* 漢武帝內轉).

672 Taishang 太上, i.e., Taishang Laojun 太上老君, the deified Laozi, supreme god of the Daoist heavens.

673 On this Celestial Palace, see Chapter 48 on the Yunnan war.

674 Jiang Fang's 蔣防 *Record of Illusory Play, of the Late Tang* (*Huanxi zhi* 幻戲志). From Tokyo University Rare Books collection, http://shanben.ioc.u-tokyo.ac.jp/main_p?nu=C6215000&order=ti_no&no=00723.

675 The Bright Emperor writes of him: "When disloyal ministers entertain schemes, evil and rebellion have never failed to ensue. When these matters were made clear to Ye Fashan, he sallied forth to extend his subtle assistance" (Kirkland, *Taoists of the High T'ang*, 130, modified).

676 These two meanings are mirrored in the English pair, "lax" and "relax." The prefix "re" here has an intensifying force.

677 This immortality goes against the biologic of birth-and-death and thus, a fortiori, against its correlatives in the socio-logic of praise-and-blame.

678 This sounds a bit like the Hindu notion of avatar, but I leave this matter for those with greater understanding.

679 Charles Herbermann et al., *The Catholic Encyclopedia* (New York: The Encyclopedia Press, 1913), 7:106.

680 As Kirkland suggests in the concluding section of his dissertation chapter. After all, no one needs magic in the magic realms, it isn't even discernable there.

681 Thomas Jülch goes further:

> Der Begriff ‚zhexian' 謫仙 – hier mit ‚Unsterblicher in der Menschenwelt' übersetzt – bedeutet wörtlich ‚degradierter Unsterblicher'. Der Begriff bezeichnet eine Person, die bereits Unsterblichkeit erlangt hat, und sich, nur um den

gewöhnlichen Menschen erscheinen zu können, auf eine menschliche Inkarnation einläßt. Da die menschliche Gestalt nicht das wahre Wesen eines vollendeten Unsterblichen abbilden kann, spricht man von einem Unsterblichen, der sich in soteriologischer Absicht selbst zu menschlichem Dasein ‚degradiert' hat. (*Der Orden des Sima Chengzhen und des Wang Ziqiao*, 17n80)

The term "zhexian" 謫仙 — here translated as "an immortal in the human world" — literally means "degraded immortal." The term indicates a person who has already achieved immortality but who takes on a human incarnation to be able to appear to ordinary people. Since a human form cannot represent the true essence of a perfected immortal, one speaks of an immortal who, in a soteriological sense, has "degraded" himself to human existence.

Here the banished immortal is something like a bodhisattva.

682 By Xiao Zixian 萧子显 (489–537).

683 Within the biography of Du Jingchan 杜京產 in the section "Biographies of eminent recluses" (*Gaoyizhuan* 高逸傳). In epidemiology a "vector" is the agent that carries and transmits an infectious pathogen into another living organism, as rats carrying plague-infested fleas.

The eponymous heroine of Gilbert and Sullivan's *Iolanthe* is an immortal fairy, banished from fairyland for a different kind of negligence: she falls in love with a mortal. If the ensuing satire of government, law, society and manners had been performed before the Bright Emperor, everyone involved would have been put to painful death. *Wikipedia* concludes:

> The confrontation between the fairies and the peers [buffoonish members of the House of Lords] is a version of one of Gilbert's favorite themes: a tranquil civilization of women is

disrupted by a male-dominated world through the discovery of mortal love." (*Wikipedia,* "Iolanthe," s.v.)

684 ch13v4p2146.

685 *Shishuo xin yu,* "Dissipation" (*Ren dan* 任誕).

686 *Feiyou xiansheng lun* 非有先生論.

687 ch23v7p3642.

688 *Zhuangzi,* chap. 3, "Essentials of nourishing life" (*Yangsheng zhu* 養生主). The Lord has asked his cook where he gets his cutting skills, and this is the response.

689 OK, it's an imaginary friend.

690 So our demonstrations tend to be discontinuous, layered, pragmatic, ardent and shy. See Sam Gill, "No Place to Stand: Jonathan Z. Smith as Homo Ludens, The Academic Study of Religion Sub Specie Ludi," *Journal of the American Academy of Religion* 66, no. 2 (1998): 283–312. J.Z. Smith:

Fig. 103. Source: http://www.wideawakeminds.com/2009/12/ glimpse-into-great-mind-jonathan-z.html

691 Marianne Moore's praise for the Americanisms of William Carlos Williams.

692 "I like legends, dialects, mistakes of language, detective novels, the flesh of girls, the sun, the Eiffel Tower, the Apache, *les bons nègres*" (Blaise Cendrars, "The Prose of the Trans-Siberian and of the Little Jeanne of France (An Article Which Blaise Cendrars Wrote for 'Der Sturm,' No. 184-185, Berlin, November 1913)," trans. Roger Kaplan, *The Chicago Review* 24, no. 3 [1972]: 3–21, at 3). "Many people have tried to make this essay less unreasonable" (Bruno Latour, *Nous n'avons jamais été modernes,* translated by Catherine Porter as *We Have Never Been Modern* [Cambridge: Harvard University Press, 1993], ix).

693 I'm wrong about this. Pennsylvania Supreme Court Justice J. Michael Eakin often handed down his verdicts in verse. Responding to a drunken equestrian charged with driving under the influence, he wrote

> A horse is a horse, of course, of course,
> but the Vehicle Code does not divorce
> its application from, perforce,
> a steed, as my colleagues said.
>
> "It's not vague," I'll say until I'm hoarse,
> and whether a car, a truck or horse,
> this law applies with equal force.

See *Wikipedia,* "Michael Eakin," s.v.

694 About a dozen of these poems have been translated by Elling Eide in his wonderful *Poems by Li Po* (privately published by the Anvil Press in Lexington, Kentucky, 1984). We take this overlap as a compliment from him on our good sense of things, but in only one case — the prose encomium to the monk Baozhi — did we first came upon the material through his book. A selection of twenty of Eide's translations has been included in

John Minford and Joseph Lau, eds., *Classical Chinese Literature,* vol.1 (New York: Columbia University Press: 2000), 723–42.

695 R.H. Blyth would add Spencer. Fair enough. *Zen in English Literature and Oriental Classics* (Tokyo: Hokuseidō, 1942), 47.

Li Bo's peer group: Hafiz, Ikkyū, Picasso, Kṛṣṇa, the Pseudo-Dionysius. As divinity, Li Bo has no antithesis. But as human, his opposite is the Hungerkünstler.

696 ch21v6p3267. I'm currently in discussions with Elysium Space to have this poem sent into a two-year sun-synchronous decaying orbit via SpaceX in the late spring of 2022. See also rocketlabusa.com.

697 Now we've opened the box, and we want to hear if Schrödinger's cat is alive or dead. But is the cat alive or dead only after Schrödinger has told his friend Wigner?

698 Photo by author.

www.ingramcontent.com/pod-product-compliance
Lightning Source LLC
Chambersburg PA
CBHW071807230426
43670CB00013B/2386